GERMANY

TOP SIGHTS, AUTHENTIC EXPERIENCES

Benedict Walker, Kerry Christiani, Marc Di Duca,
Catherine Le Nevez, Leonid Ragozin and
Andrea Schulte-Peevers

Contents

Welcome to Germany

There's something undeniably artistic in the way Germany's scenery unfolds – the corrugated, dune-fringed coasts of the north, and the moody forests, romantic river valleys and vast vineyards of the centre, all topped by the off-the-charts splendour of the Alps.

You'll encounter history in towns where streets were laid well before Columbus set sail, and in castles set high above rows of half-timbered houses whose flower boxes billow with crimson geraniums.

Germany's great cities – Berlin, Munich and Cologne among them – come in more flavours than a jar of jelly beans. Get ready to be wowed by the full spectrum of cultural colour and flair, from high art and opera to saucy cabaret and a nocturnal universe at the cutting edge of cool.

Few countries have impacted the world as much as Germany. it gave us the Hanseatic League, the Reformation and yes, Hitler and the Holocaust, but also aspirin, the automobile, computer, sticky tape, streetcars and LGBTIQ+ rights. It gave rise to the minds of Einstein, Goethe and Marx, the energy of Luther and the artistry of Beethoven and the Brothers Grimm. Reminders of this rich heritage are everywhere.

Just as rich is the range of hearty cuisine, which you'll soon discover is much more than (but includes) sausages, pretzels, pork knuckle and schnitzel. It's all washed down with massive mugs of cold, frothy beer, the latter being Germany's sixth essential food group. Beyond the clichés awaits a cornucopia of regional and seasonal palate-teasers.

Willkommen in Deutschland!

> *get ready to be wowed by the full spectrum of cultural colour and flair*

Neues Rathaus (p107), Munich

North Sea

Bremerhaven

H

NETHERLANDS

Oldenburg

Bremen

GERMANY

Hano

AMSTERDAM

Osnabrück

Hildesheim

Rotterdam

Münster

English Channel (La Manche)

G

Calais

Düsseldorf

Kassel

Antwerp

BRUSSELS

Bonn

BELGIUM

Koblenz

Frankfurt-am-M

Moselle

Mainz

Darmstadt

LUXEMBOURG

W

LUXEMBOURG

Neckar

Saarbrücken

Stuttgart

PARIS

FRANCE

Strasbourg

Ulm

Lindau

VADUZ

LIECH

BERN

SWITZERLAND

0 200 km
0 100 miles

Vineyards, Moselle Valley (p241)
TRAVEL INK/GETTY IMAGES ©

Plan Your Trip
Germany's Top 12

CANADASTOCK/SHUTTERSTOCK ©

Berlin

The freedom to be yourself

Berlin (p35) is a city for 'seekers'. If you're a connoisseur of the cutting edge, a purveyor of history or just love a good time, this gritty, glamourous, world-class city will win your affections. Its inspiring museums, including the Holocaust and Wall Memorials, tell a complex, tragic tale. But Berlin's focus is here and now – dining runs the gamut, art is as open as your mind can handle and the party doesn't stop until Monday comes. Left: Berlin skyline; Right: Holocaust Memorial (p56)

Potsdam

Prussian palaces and pristine parks

Your camera will love Potsdam's (p85) palaces, parks, architecture and Cold War sites. Just across the Glienicke 'spy bridge' from Berlin, the state capital of Brandenburg was catapulted to prominence by King Frederick the Great. His Sanssouci palace is the crown of this Unesco-recognised cultural tapestry that synthesises 18th-century artistic trends in one stupendous masterpiece. Prepare to be dazzled.

Top: Schloss Sanssouci (p88); Bottom: Bildergalerie (p90), Park Sanssouci

S.BORISOV/SHUTTERSTOCK ©

Munich

Learn why Bavarians boast the most

Bavaria's capital (p97) packs plenty of refreshing surprises under its frequently bright-blue skies. Here, folklore and age-old traditions exist side by side with sleek BMWs, designer boutiques and high-powered industry. The city's museums showcase everything from artistic masterpieces to technological treasures and Oktoberfest history, while its nightlife, locals might say, is second only to Berlin. Frauenkirche (left; p107) and Neues Rathaus (right; p107) in Marienplatz (p106)

3

Schloss Neuschwanstein

The inspiration for Disney's fairy-tale castle

Commissioned by Bavaria's most famous monarch, loopy Ludwig II, Germany's favourite castle (p132) pcomes straight from a fairy-tale storybook. Inside, its fanciful chambers reflect Ludwig's obsession with the mythical past and his favoured composer, Wagner. One of Europe's most visited sites, the castle is said to be the inspiration for Walt Disney's iconic emblem. Today, it continues to inspire tourist masses to make the pilgrimage along the Romantic Road, which culminates at its gates. Schloss Neuschwanstein (at left; p132) and Schloss Hohenschwangau (at right; p134)

Heidelberg

Germany's oldest university town

The 19th-century romantics found beauty and spiritual inspiration in Heidelberg (p139) and so, in his way, did Mark Twain, who was beguiled by the ruins of the hillside castle. Generations of students have attended lectures, sung lustily with beer steins in hand, carved their names into tavern tables and, occasionally, been sent to the student jail. Heidelberg today is a place where age-old traditions endure alongside world-class research, innovative cultural events and a sometimes-raucous nightlife scene. View of Schloss Heidelberg (p144) from the Karl-Theodor-Brücke (p134)

The Black Forest

Silence...what a wonderful thing

Mist, snow or shine, the deep, dark Black Forest (p151) is just
beautiful. If it's nature you seek, this sylvan slice of southwestern
Germany is the place to linger. Every valley reveals new surprises:
half-timbered villages, thunderous waterfalls and cuckoo clocks
the size of houses. Inhale the Alpine air, drive roller-coaster roads
to middle-of-nowhere lakes, have your gateau, walk it off on a gorgeous wooded trail, then hide away in a heavy-lidded farmhouse.

6

Dresden

A phoenix from the ashes of war

The apocalypse came on a cold February night in 1945. Hours of carpet-bombing reduced Germany's 'Florence on the Elbe' (p173) to a smouldering pile of bricks and 25,000 people died. Dresden's comeback is nothing short of miraculous. Painstakingly reconstructed architectural marvels, stunning art collections and a tiara of villas and palaces justify the city's place in the pantheon of European cultural capitals. Frauenkirche (p176)

7

Nuremburg

Toys, trains and castle walls

Nuremberg (p187) may conjure visions of Nazi rallies and grisly war trials, but there's so much more to this energetic city, capital of the state of Franconia. Germany's first railway trundled from here to neighbouring Fürth, leaving a trail of choo-choo heritage. And Germany's toy capital has heaps of things for kids to enjoy. When you're done with sightseeing, the local beer is as dark as the coffee and best employed to chase down Nuremberg's delicious finger-sized bratwurst.

LENA SERDITOVA/500PX ©

Rothenburg ob der Tauber

Moonlit strolls along cobbled lanes

With its jumble of neatly restored half-timbered houses, Rothenburg ob der Tauber (p199) lays on the medieval cuteness with a trowel (as the deluges of day trippers demonstrate). The trick is to experience this historic wonderland at its most magical: early or late in the day, when the last coaches have hit the road and you can soak up the romance all by yourself on gentle strolls along moonlit cobbled lanes. Left: Restored medieval buildings, Rothenburg ob der Tauber (p199); Right: A traditional cuckoo clock

Cologne

The most magnificent medieval cathedral

At unexpected moments you see it: Cologne's cathedral, the city's twin-towered icon, looming over an urban vista and the Rhine. And why shouldn't it? This testament to faith and conviction was started in 1248 and consecrated six centuries later. You can feel the passage of time as you sit in its stained-glass-lit and artwork-filled interior. Climb a tower for unrivalled views of this city-by-the-Rhine (p211).

Top: Kölner Dom ceiling; Above left: Kölner Dom by night; Above right: Kölner Dom entrance

ANGELO BUFALINO/500PX ©

YURY DMITRIENKO/SHUTTERSTOCK ©

IAIN MASTERTON/GETTY IMAGES ©

10

Romantic Rhine Valley

Riverside villages, vineyards and forests

As the mighty Rhine (p225) flows from Rüdesheim to Koblenz, the landscape's unique face-off between rock and water creates a magical mix of the wild (churning whirlpools, dramatic cliffs), the agricultural (near-vertical vineyards), the medieval (hilltop castles, half-timbered hamlets) and the modern (in the 19th-century sense: barges, ferries, passenger steamers and trains). From every riverside village, trails take you through vineyards and forests. Boppard (p234), Rhine Valley

The Moselle Valley

Wine, glorious wine!

A tributary of the Rhine, the Moselle (p241) zigzags lazily for 350km from Koblenz to northern France by way of Luxembourg. It's one of Europe's all-star waterways, hemmed in by ancient villages and miles of vineyards. Many of these cling courageously to vertiginous slopes from which a new generation of winemakers coax elegant, full-bodied rieslings to remember. It was the Romans who introduced grapes to this area; their legacy survives in Trier.

Plan Your Trip
Need to Know

When to Go

Warm to hot summers, mild winters
Warm to hot summers, cold winters
Mild summers, cold winters
Cold climate

Hamburg
GO May–Sep

Berlin
GO May, Jun,
Sep & Oct

Frankfurt
GO May–Sep

Munich
GO Apr, May,
Sep & Oct

Freiburg
GO Apr–Oct

High Season (Jul & Aug)

o Busy roads and long queues

o Room rates at a premium

o Festivals for everything from music to wine and sailing to samba

Shoulder Season (Apr–Jun, Sep–Oct)

o Fewer crowds and often bargain room rates, especially in Berlin

o Blooming flowers in spring; radiant foliage in autumn

o Temperate weather ideal for outdoor pursuits

Low Season (Nov-Mar)

o No queues but shorter hours and some sights close

o Theatre, concert and opera season in full swing

o Ski resorts busiest in January and February

Currency
Euro (€)

Language
German

Visas
Generally not required for tourist stays up to 90 days (or at all for EU nationals); some nationalities need a Schengen Visa (p302).

Money
ATMs widely available in cities and towns, rarely in villages. Cash is king almost everywhere; credit cards are not widely accepted.

Mobile Phones
Mobile phones operate on GSM900/1800. If you have a European or Australian phone, save money by slipping in a German SIM card.

Time
Central European Time (GMT/UTC plus one hour)

Daily Costs

Budget: Less than €100

- Hostel, camping or private room: €15–30

- Transport day pass: €6–8

- Cheap meal: up to €8

Midrange: €100–200

- Private apartment or double room: €60–100

- Three-course dinner at nice restaurant: €30–40

- Three beers in a pub: €9

Top End: More than €200

- Chic loft apartment or top-end hotel: from €150

- Lunch and dinner at top-rated restaurant: €100

- Concert or opera tickets: €50–150

Useful Websites

Lonely Planet (www.lonelyplanet.com/germany) Hotel bookings, traveller forum and more

German National Tourist Office (www.germany.travel)

Facts About Germany (www.tatsachen-ueber-deutschland.de/en) Reference tool on all aspects of German society

Deutsche Welle (www.dw.com) National public broadcaster

Exchange Rates

Australia	A$1	€0.63
Canada	C$1	€0.66
Japan	¥100	€0.78
New Zealand	NZ$1	€0.60
UK	UK£1	€1.11
US	US$1	€0.88

For current exchange rates see www.xe.com.

Opening Hours

The following may vary seasonally and by location:

Banks 9am to 4pm Monday to Friday, usually extended on Tuesday and Thursday, some open Saturday

Bars 6pm to 1am

Cafes 8am to 8pm

Clubs 11pm to early morning hours

Post offices 9am to 6pm Monday to Friday, 9am to 1pm Saturday

Restaurants 11am to 11pm (food service often stops at 9pm in rural areas)

Major stores and supermarkets 9.30am to 8pm Monday to Saturday (shorter hours outside city centres)

Arriving in Germany

Tegel Airport (p303) TXL express bus to Alexanderplatz (40 minutes) and bus X9 for CityWest, €2.80; taxi €25.

Schönefeld Airport (p303) Airport-Express trains (RB14 or RE7) to central Berlin twice hourly (30 minutes), and S9 trains every 20 minutes for Friedrichshain and Prenzlauer Berg, €3.40; taxi to city centre €45 to €50.

Munich Airport (p303) S1 and S8 trains to city centre (40 minutes), €10.80; Lufthansa Airport Bus (every 20 minutes, 40 minutes), €10.50; taxi about €60.

Getting Around

Train Deutsche Bahn operates an excellent, extensive network of high-speed trains and regular regional services.

Car Autobahn routes are fast, safe and fun. Ubiquitous car rentals give you freedom to explore rural areas. Drive on the right.

Bus Some excellent-value deals available on key routes.

Air Domestic air travel is expensive and impractical outside long distance routes.

For more on **getting around**, see p306

Plan Your Trip
Hot Spots for...

Castles & Palaces

Over centuries, Germany has collected castles and palaces like some collect stamps – the feudal system divided the country into fiefdoms until its 1871 unification.

1989STUDIO/SHUTTERSTOCK ©

Füssen
Southern climax of the Romantic Road, nestled at the foot of the alps in the domain of castles.

Schloss Neuschwanstein
Germany's most famous mountaintop castle (p132).

Potsdam
Berlin's most popular day-trip is the former seat of Prussian royalty.

Schloss & Park Sanssouci
Frederick the Great's palace (p88) and gardens.

Heidelberg
Germany's first university town, the inspiration for great writers and intellectuals.

Schloss Heidelberg
This robust ruin (pictured; p144) is illuminated at night.

Enchanting Villages

There's no simpler pleasure than a stroll around a village laced with time-worn lanes, peppered with ancient churches and anchored by a fountain-studded square.

DAVID /500PX ©

Rothenburg ob der Tauber
Hands down one of Germany's most charming medieval villages...and don't it know it.

Stadtmauer
Walk the city walls (p206) for an immersive experience.

The Romantic Rhine Valley
Postcard-pretty villages dot the banks of the magnificent Rhine river, Germany's arterial waterway.

Bacharach
Climb the church tower (pictured; p232) for great views.

Moselle Valley
One of Germany's earliest settled regions, the valley is dotted with postcard pretty villages and towns.

Trier
Features the gorgeous Hauptmarkt (p257).

Churches & Cathedrals

Germany's places of worship are also great architectural monuments, often filled with priceless treasures reflecting artistic acumen through the ages.

MIKHAIL MARKOVSKIY/SHUTTERSTOCK ©

Cologne
Founded by the Romans in 38 BC, Cologne grew into a bustling centre for trade.

Kölner Dom
This cathedral (p215) is seen as one of the finest.

The Black Forest
Freiburg's medieval Altstadt is a storybook tableau of gabled townhouses, cobblestone lanes and plazas.

Freiburg
The minster (p154) cuts an impressive figure.

Munich
Bavaria's richest city has a wealth of fine architecture, including churches galore.

Asamkirche
This late-baroque church (pictured; p106) is epic.

Great Outdoors

Germany is an all-seasons outdoor playground – if you want to relax in nature, ride bikes, cruise rivers, swim, ski or sunbake, your possibilities are endless.

ANDREY_POPOV/SHUTTERSTOCK ©

The Black Forest
As dark and delicious as the famous gateau, the forest gets its name from the canopy of evergreens.

Triberg
Home of Germany's largest waterfall (pictured; p170).

The Romantic Rhine Valley
The Rhine is at its most beautiful in this fertile valley with snaking, sweeping bends.

Koblenz
Experience the Rhine by boat (p238).

Moselle Valley
This valley is not just paradise for fine wine lovers, but is a gentle riverside playground of fields and forests.

Bernkastel-Kues
Easy riding along this disused railway (p254)

Plan Your Trip
Essential Germany

Activities

Rain or shine, Germany's great outdoors are accessible and spectacular, and traversed by thousands of kilometres of groomed trails, bicycle paths, ski runs and waterways. It's largely a land-locked nation, so you won't be coming for the beaches. Whether you're hiking in dark forests ripe for a Brothers Grimm fairy tale, diving into a gem-coloured Alpine lake, cycling along mighty rivers and lake shores, or schussing down slopes backed by mountains of myth while admiring ancient castles in the distance, Germany's natural beauty and diversity is bound to impress.

Shopping

Germany has the whole shebang – modish streetwear in Berlin; organic and farmers markets brimming with the bounty of land and sea; artsy independent boutiques; retro GDR design stores, family-run craft workshops; stationery stores and book-sellers, and high-street chains. Traditional gifts are timeless – who can resist bringing home a cuckoo clock, ceramic stein or a natty pair of Lederhosen? And then there's the beer...and the cheese...and the wine... and the bakeries, bratwurst...BMWs even... consumerism is big in Deutschland, while the price tags are refreshingly not.

Eating

When discussing the culinary prowess of the Western European nations, Germany is not usually the first name to leap off the tongue, but the culinary revolution that's been simmering here for years under the layers of sausage-cabbage-and-carbs is finally bubbling to the surface. Up and down the country you'll find chefs playing up local, seasonal produce and making healthy, creative street food. There are exciting riffs on vegetarian and vegan food, and organic everything. Some wines these days can rival the French and Italian old-timers. Dig in and drink up – you might just be surprised.

ALEKSANDAR TODOROVIC/SHUTTERSTOCK ©

Drinking & Nightlife

Germany sure knows how to have a good time. Check out Berlin's boundless freedom of expression and open exploration of sex and celebration; wild all-night clubs pumping to electro and techno; the towering tankards, Dirndl-clad waitresses, and oompah bands of Bavaria's beer halls and gardens. Though quieter in rural parts, major towns and cities keep drinks and good vibes flowing at chic cocktail bars, rollicking pubs and skyline-gazing roof terraces.

Entertainment

Fabulously ornate concert halls where the greatest of composers once waved a baton (we're talking Beethoven, Brahms, Bach and Co. here); theatres staging boundary-crossing productions; born-again industrial warehouses devoted to alternative arts; and dark, poster-smothered jazz dens that swing after midnight – entertainment in Germany

★ Best Eating & Drinking

Esszimmer, Munich (p120)

Bratwursthäusle, Nuremberg (p195)

Restaurant Genuss-Atelier, Dresden (p183)

Prater Garten, Berlin (p79)

Tantris, Munich (p119)

Zum Roten Ochsen, Dresden (p148)

Louisengarten, Dresden (p184)

Chinesischer Turm, Munich (p121)

is as rich as it is varied and exciting. For major venues you'll need to book ahead (usually possible online), with occasional last-minute discounts available.

From left: Mountain biking (p160), Black Forest; Potsdamer Platz (p67), Berlin

Plan Your Trip
Month by Month

FOOTTOO/SHUTTERSTOCK ©

February

The German Carnival is still a good excuse for a party. Ski resorts are at their busiest thanks to school holidays, so make reservations.

☆ Berlin Film Festival

Stars, directors and critics sashay down the red carpet for two weeks of screenings and glamour parties at the Berlinale, one of Europe's most prestigious celluloid festivals.

🍷 Karneval/Fasching

The pre-Lenten season is celebrated with street partying, parades, satirical shows and general revelry. Big parties are held in Cologne, the Black Forest and Munich.

March

Days start getting longer and the first inkling of spring is in the air. Fresh herring hits menus, especially along the coastal regions, and dishes prepared with *Bärlauch* (wild garlic) are all the rage.

April

Even if you stopped believing in the Easter Bunny long ago, there's no escaping him in Germany. Meanwhile, nothing epitomises the arrival of spring more than the first crop of white asparagus. Germans go nuts for it.

⊙ Maifest

Villagers celebrate the end of winter on 30 April by chopping down a tree for a *Maibaum* (Maypole). painting, carving and decorating it, then staging a merry revel with traditional costumes, singing and dancing.

May

One of the loveliest months, often surprisingly warm and sunny, perfect for ringing in beer-garden season. Plenty of public holidays, which Germans turn into extended weekends or miniholidays, resulting in busy roads and lodging shortages.

Above:Oktoberfest (p100), Munich

✥ Karneval der Kulturen

Hundreds of thousands of revellers celebrate Berlin's multicultural tapestry with parties, exotic nosh and a fun parade of flamboyantly dressed dancers, DJs, artists and musicians shimmying through the streets of Kreuzberg (p78).

☉ Labour Day

On 1 May, a public holiday, some cities host political demonstrations for workers' rights. In Berlin, past protests have taken on a violent nature, although now it's mostly a big street fair.

☉ Muttertag

Mothers are honoured on the second Sunday of May, much to the delight of florists, sweet shops and greeting-card companies. Make restaurant reservations far in advance.

June

Germany's festival pace quickens, while gourmets can rejoice in the bounty of fresh, local produce in the markets. Life moves outdoors: the summer solstice means the sun doesn't set until around 9.30pm.

☉ Vatertag

Father's Day, now also known as *Männertag* (Men's Day), is essentially an excuse for men to get liquored up with the blessing of the missus. It's always on Ascension Day.

☕ Christopher Street Day

No matter your sexual persuasion, come out and paint the town pink at major LGBTIQ+ pride celebrations in Berlin and Cologne.

July

School's out for the summer and peak travelling season begins, so you'd better be the gregarious type. Whether you're headed to the mountains or the coast, book accommodation in advance. It won't be the Med, but swimming is now possible in lakes, rivers, and the Baltic and North Seas.

Above: Christopher Street Day (p221) celebrations

August

Germany's hottest month is often cooled by afternoon thunderstorms. It's the season for *Pfifferlinge* (chanterelle mushrooms) and fresh berries, which you can pick in the forests.

🍷 Wine Festivals

With grapes ripening to a plump sweetness, wine festivals have tastings, folkloric parades, fireworks and the election of local and regional wine queens. Dürkheimer Wurstmarkt (www.duerkheimer-wurst markt.de) is one of the biggest and most famous.

September

Often a great month weather-wise – sunny but not too hot. The main travel season is over but it's still busy thanks to wine and autumn festivals. Trees may start turning into a riot of colour towards the end of the month.

🏃 Berlin Marathon

Sweat it out with the other 50,000 runners or just cheer 'em on during Germany's biggest street race, at which nine world records have been set since 1977.

☉ Erntedankfest

Rural towns celebrate the harvest with decorated church altars, *Erntedankzug* (processions) and villagers dressed in folkloric garments.

🍷 Oktoberfest

Munich's legendary beer-swilling party (p100) gets started around mid-September. Enough said.

October

Children are back in school and most people at work as days get shorter, colder and wetter. Trade-fair season kicks off, affecting lodging prices and availability in Frankfurt, Cologne, Berlin, Hamburg and other cities. Tourist offices, museums and attractions keep shorter hours. Some close for winter.

November

This can be a dreary month mainly spent indoors. However, queues at tourist sights are short, and theatre, concert, opera and other cultural events are plentiful. Bring warm clothes and rain gear.

✨ St Martinstag

This festival (10–11 November) honours 4th-century St Martin, known for his humility and generosity. It sees a lantern procession and a re-enactment of the famous scene where the saint cuts his coat in half to share with a beggar, followed by a feast of stuffed roast goose.

December

Cold and sun-deprived days are brightened by Advent, the four weeks of festivities preceding Christmas, celebrated with enchanting markets, illuminated streets, Advent calendars, candle-festooned wreaths, home-baked cookies and other rituals. The ski resorts usually get their first dusting of snow.

☉ Nikolaustag

On the eve of 5 December, German children put their boots outside the door hoping that St Nick will fill them with sweets and small toys overnight. Ill-behaved children, though, may find only a prickly rod left behind by St Nick's helper, Knecht Ruprecht.

🎁 Christmas Markets

Mulled wine, spicy gingerbread cookies, shimmering ornaments – these and lots more are typical features of German Christmas markets, held from late November until late December. Nuremberg's Christkindlesmarkt (p195) is especially famous.

✨ Silvester

New Year's Eve is called 'Silvester', in honour of the 4th-century pope under whom the Romans adopted Christianity as their official religion. The new year is greeted with fireworks launched by thousands of amateur pyromaniacs.

Plan Your Trip
Get Inspired

YULIA GRIGORYEVA/SHUTTERSTOCK ©

Read

Grimms Märchen (Grimms Fairy Tales; 1812) Jacob and Wilhelm Grimm's fairy tales, now shared with children worldwide.

Mr Norris Changes Trains (1935) and **Goodbye to Berlin** (1939) Usually published together as *The Berlin Stories*, these two novellas by Christopher Isherwood chronicle early-1930s Berlin, and went on to inspire the musical and film *Cabaret*.

The Rise & Fall of the Third Reich (1960) William Shirer's definitive tome about Nazi Germany remains powerful.

Watch

Das Boot (1981) Dives into the claustrophobic world of WWII U-boat warfare.

Good Bye, Lenin! (2003) Drama-comedy about a young East Berliner protecting his ailing mother from the knowledge that the Wall has fallen.

Das Leben der Anderen (The Lives of Others; 2006) Academy Award winner; unmasks the pervasiveness and destructiveness of East Germany's Stasi.

Babylon Berlin (2017) Sumptuous detective drama series, set in pre-WWII Berlin.

Listen

Ring of the Nibelung (1848–74) Richard Wagner's epic opera cycle.

The Threepenny Opera (1928) Runaway hit musical by Brecht and Weill.

Lili Marleen (1944) No song is more evocative of wartime Germany than Marlene Dietrich's haunting, dreamy *Lili Marleen*, released to demoralise enemy soliders.

Atem (1973) Groundbreaking album by electronic music pioneers Tangerine Dream.

Sehnsucht (1994) Industrial metal band Rammstein's international breakthrough album.

Above: Rammstein performance

Plan Your Trip
Five-Day Itineraries

Best of the East

Despite over two decades of a reunified Germany, the former GDR (DDR in German) still maintains it's own unique character. This five-day taster, including the capital Berlin and fascinating Dresden, will show you the East's history and its resurrection from the bad days of Soviet dominance.

Berlin (p35) Kick off in Berlin, the country's capital, and visit the Reichstag, the Brandenburg Gate and Museumsinsel (Museum Island).
🚌 S-Bahn 40 mins or train 24 mins to Potsdam

Potsdam (p85) The town has several palaces and parks, but the main draw here is Schloss Sanssouci, the private retreat of King Friedrich the Great.
🚌 3-4½ hrs to Dresden (from Berlin)

Dresden (p173) Frauenkirche is the top attraction here, destroyed during WWII but rebuilt between 1994 and 2005.

The Historic South

This neat, kid-friendly itinerary is jam-packed with scenic and historic sights, ideal for time-poor folks who want the big-name attractions. It's an easy five days, but you might find yourself lingering an extra night or two en route.

Nuremberg (p187) Castle walls, steam trains, Nazi history and handmade toys: what will you take in first?
🚌 1¼ hrs to Munich

Rothenburg ob der Tauber (p199) Few German villages are as picture-book pretty as this perfectly preserved medieval marvel.
🚌 1 hr 20 mins to Nuremberg

Munich (p97) Explore myriad museums, sample beer gardens galore or spend a sombre day in Dachau, outside town.
🚌 2 hrs to Füssen

Füssen (p136) End your trip with a fairy-tale stop at Schloss Neuschwanstein, Germany's most visited hilltop castle.

FROM LEFT: SEANPAVONEPHOTO/GETTY IMAGES ©; © BAYERISCHE SCHLÖSSERVERWALTUNG WWW.SCHLOESSER.BAYERN.DE/ANDREW MONTGOMERY/LONELY PLANET ©

Plan Your Trip
10-Day Itinerary

Along the Rhine & Moselle

The Rhine and Moselle rivers in Germany's far west cut through mountains and valleys carpeted in vines, passing hilltop castles and quaintly historical towns and villages along the way.

① **Cologne** (p211) Climb the 509 steps to the top of Cologne's stunning cathedral's south tower and explore the unique Römisch-Germanisches Museum. 🚃 1 hr to Koblenz

② **Koblenz** (p237) Wander Koblenz' pretty rebuilt Altstadt and marvel at the confluence of the Moselle and Rhine. 🚃 ½ hr to Bacharach

Cochem (p250) Gateway to the Moselle Valley and a popular cruise terminus. Check out its 11th-century castle, the Reichsburg. 🚃 35 mins to Traben

③ **Bacharach** (p232) This is one of the Rhine's quaintest villages and certainly worth a stopover. 🚢 50 mins to Rüdesheim

⑤

④ **Rüdesheim** (p230) Enjoy spectacular views of the Rhine and some of Germany's finest wines. 🚃 1½ hrs to Cochem

⑥ **Traben-Trarbach** (p251) Sample crisp Moselle wines in these twin villages straddling the Rhine and visit the Buddha Museum. 🚃 1½ hrs to Trier

⑦ **Trier** (p255) World Heritage Site Trier boasts Germany's finest Roman monuments such as the Kaiserthermen baths and a Colusseum-style amphitheatre.

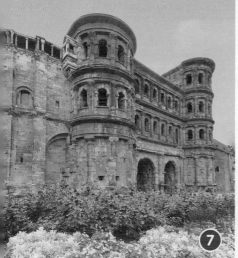

Plan Your Trip
Two-Week Itinerary

Southern Ring

This circular route around the two states of Bavaria and Baden-Württemberg takes in the essence of Germany's south, a place of romantic castles, unsurpassed beer and historical city centres, all backed by the snow-dusted peaks of the Barvarian Alps.

To Frankfurt

Heidelberg (p139) Wander the streets of this university town (Germany's first), well known for its baroque Altstadt. 🚌 3½ hrs to Rothenburg ob der Tauber

5

4

Baden-Baden (p165) Bathe in the thermal waters of this luxe spa town boasting Germany's most celebrated aqua minerals. 🚌 1¾ hrs to Heidelberg

3

Triberg (p170) Sample the Black Forest's most famous exports – cuckoo clocks and gateau. 🚌 1¼ hrs to Baden-Baden

MATT MUNRO/LONELY PLANET ©

3

From Frankfurt

6

7

Nuremberg (p187) Important WWII sites, handmade toys and a rich railroading history await, before you return to Munich.
🚆 1¼ hrs to Munich

Rothenburg ob der Tauber (p199) This irrepressibly photogenic village will have you swooning for its chocolate-box architecture and cobbled lanes.
🚆 1 hr 20 mins to Nuremberg

Munich (p97) In three days, explore Marienplatz, the Residenz and the Pinakotheken, Munich's clutch of world-class galleries. Drink beer!
🚆 2 hrs to Füssen

1

Füssen (p136) Like everyone else, you're here to explore Schloss Neuschwanstein, Germany's top attraction: inspiration for Disney's iconic castle. 🚆 6 hrs to Triberg

2

1

7

Plan Your Trip
Family Travel

WESTEND61/GETTY IMAGES ©

The Low-Down

Practically all hotels can provide cots (cribs), though sometimes there's a small charge. Some properties allow small children to stay in their parents' room free of charge if they don't require extra bedding.

As long as they're not running wild, children are generally welcome in German restaurants, especially in informal cafes, bistros, pizzerias or *Gaststätten* (inns). Many offer a limited *Kindermenü* (children's menu) or *Kinderteller* (children's dishes).

Breastfeeding in public is commonly practised, although most women are discreet about it.

Children under 12 years or shorter than 1.5m (59 inches) must ride in the back seat in cars (including taxis) and use a car seat or booster appropriate for their weight. Taxis are not equipped with car seats, and you should bring your own car seat or reserve one early if hiring a car.

On trains children under 15 years travel free if accompanied by at least one parent or grandparent, as long they're registered on your ticket at the time of purchase. Children under six always travel free and without a ticket.

Kidding Around

Kids might already have seen in picture books many of the things that make the country so special: enchanting palaces and legend-shrouded castles, medieval towns and half-timbered villages, Viking ships and Roman ruins. This is the birthplace of the Brothers Grimm and their famous fairy tales. If you follow the Fairy-Tale Road (the Romantic Road; p202), you even get to see Sleeping Beauty's castle and Hamelin, the town of Pied Piper fame.

Outdoor Activities

The great outdoors yields endless variety in Germany. Tourist offices can recommend walking trails suitable for families, including stroller-friendly paths, or can hook you up with a local guide. Also ask

PAN VEGA/SHUTTERSTOCK ©

about kid-geared activities like geocaching, animal-spotting safaris and nature walks.

Germany's beaches and lakes are beautifully clean and usually devoid of big waves and dangerous undercurrents, although water temperatures rarely exceed 21°C (70°F). Many have a *Strandbad* (lido) with change rooms, playgrounds, splash zones, slides, ping-pong tables, restaurants and boat rentals.

All ski resorts have ski schools with English-speaking instructors who initiate kids in the art of the snow plough in group or private lessons. All of them, of course, have plenty of off-piste fun as well: snow-shoeing, sledding, walking and ice skating.

Need to Know

Baby food, formulas, milk Buy in supermarkets and pharmacies (drugstores)

Changing facilities Rare; best bring a towel to be safe

★ Best Museums & Theme Parks

Chocolate Museum (p219), Cologne

Museum für Naturkunde (p66), Berlin

Deutsches Museum (p115), Munich

Deutsche Bahn Museum (p192), Nuremberg

Cots (cribs) Available upon request in most hotels, especially midrange and top-end ones; best to reserve in advance

Highchairs & kids' menus Standard in most restaurants

Nappies (diapers) Widely available in supermarkets and pharmacies (drugstores)

Strollers Bring your own

Transport Discounts widely available; bring your own car seat or reserve one early if hiring a car

From left: Tobogganing fun; Schokoladenmuseum (p219), Cologne

Fernsehturm (p66)

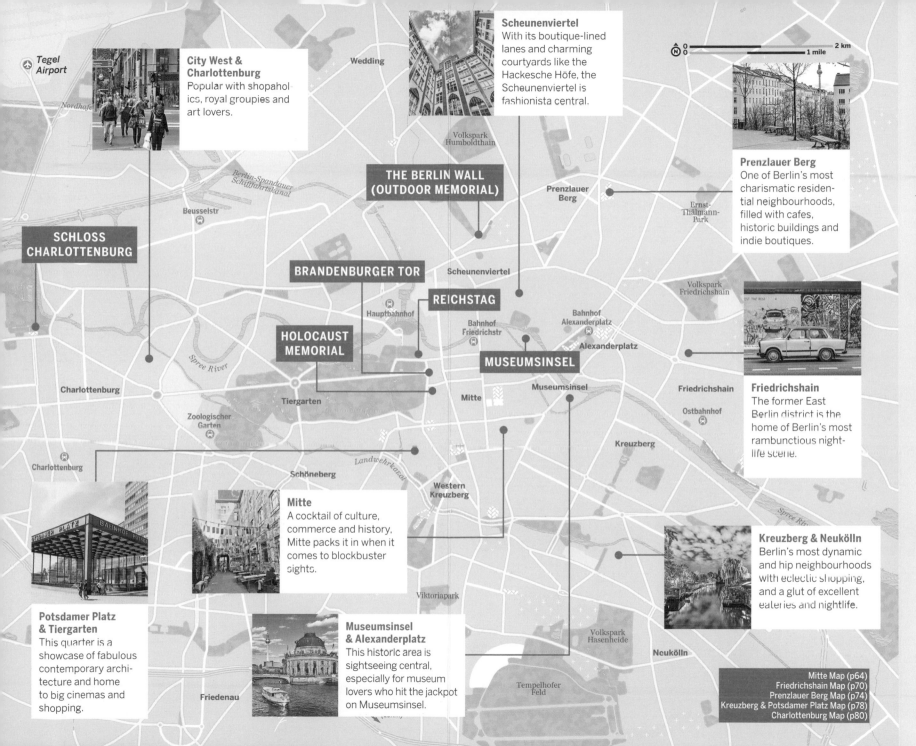

City West & Charlottenburg
Popular with shopaholics, royal groupies and art lovers.

Scheunenviertel
With its boutique-lined lanes and charming courtyards like the Hackesche Höfe, the Scheunenviertel is fashionista central.

Prenzlauer Berg
One of Berlin's most charismatic residential neighbourhoods, filled with cafes, historic buildings and indie boutiques.

THE BERLIN WALL (OUTDOOR MEMORIAL)

SCHLOSS CHARLOTTENBURG

BRANDENBURGER TOR

REICHSTAG

HOLOCAUST MEMORIAL

MUSEUMSINSEL

Friedrichshain
The former East Berlin district is the home of Berlin's most rambunctious nightlife scene.

Mitte
A cocktail of culture, commerce and history, Mitte packs it in when it comes to blockbuster sights.

Kreuzberg & Neukölln
Berlin's most dynamic and hip neighbourhoods with eclectic shopping, and a glut of excellent eateries and nightlife.

Potsdamer Platz & Tiergarten
This quarter is a showcase of fabulous contemporary architecture and home to big cinemas and shopping.

Museumsinsel & Alexanderplatz
This historic area is sightseeing central, especially for museum lovers who hit the jackpot on Museumsinsel.

Mitte Map (p64)
Friedrichshain Map (p70)
Prenzlauer Berg Map (p74)
Kreuzberg & Potsdamer Platz Map (p78)
Charlottenburg Map (p80)

Berlin

In the past century alone, Berlin staged a revolution, was bombed to bits, torn in two then ultimately reunited. History aside, Berliners (understandably) love a good time. Ways to entertain yourself here are endless – from bars to techno temples, beer gardens, cocktail caverns, cabaret shows and symphonies! A hotbed of creativity, Berlin's post-Wall abundance of spaces and its irrepressible, free-wheeling spirit give rise to a culture that thrives on experimentation and new ideas. High-brow, low-brow and everything in between – the full arc of expression is welcomed here.

Berlin in Two Days

Kick off day one at the **Reichstag** (p39) then stroll south to the **Brandenburg Gate** (p41), Berlin's most recognisable structure. Further south lies the famous **Holocaust Memorial** (p57) and **Potsdamer Platz** (p67), the city's heart. **Checkpoint Charlie** (p62) is a short distance away. You could spend the entire second day at the **Museumsinsel** (p50) taking in world-class repositories of the past such as the **Pergamonmuseum** (p46), **Neues Museum** (p47) and the **Bode-Museum** (p49).

Berlin in Four Days

Start day three at the **Gedenkstätte Berliner Mauer** (p43) and the **Mauerpark** (p68). Take a whirlwind tour of **Schloss Charlottenburg** (p71) before heading to the Kurfürstendamm for a spot of shopping. Day four might begin at the Jewish Museum (p69) before heading to the **East Side Gallery** (p43), the longest piece of the Wall to have survived.

Previous page: Berliner Dom (p49) and the DDR Museum (p67) on the Spree River
BERLINPICTURES/SHUTTERSTOCK ©

BERLIN

Berliner Dom (p49)

Museumsinsel (p46)

Spree River

DDR Museum (p67)

Fernsehturm (p66)

Arriving in Berlin

Tegel Airport TXL express bus to Alexanderplatz (40 minutes) and bus X9 for City West €2.60; taxi €20 to €25.

Schönefeld Airport Airport-Express trains to central Berlin twice hourly (20 to 30 minutes) and S9 train every 20 minutes for Friedrichshain and Prenzlauer Berg €3.20; taxi €40.

Hauptbahnhof Main train station served by S-Bahn, U-Bahn, tram, bus and taxi.

Zentraler Omnibus Bahnhof (ZOB) The central bus station is on the western city edge. U-Bahn U2 to city centre €2.60; taxi €18.

Sleeping

Outside of high season, around holidays and during major trade shows it's generally not necessary to book accommodation in advance.

For more information on the best neighbourhood to stay in, see p83.

SERGIY PALAMARCHUK/SHUTTERSTOCK ©

Reichstag

Reinstated as the home of the German parliament in 1999, the late 19th-century Reichstag is one of Berlin's most iconic buildings.

Great For...

☑ Don't Miss

Free auto-activated audioguides provide info on the building, landmarks and the workings of parliament.

Beginnings

It's been burned, bombed, rebuilt, buttressed by the Wall, wrapped in plastic and finally brought back from the dead by Norman Foster: 'turbulent history' just doesn't do it when describing what this most famous of Berlin's landmarks has endured. This neo-baroque edifice was finished in 1894 to house the German Imperial Diet. It served its purpose until 1933 when it was badly damaged by fire in an arson attack carried out by Marinus van der Lubbe, a young Dutch communist. This shocking event conveniently gave Hitler a pretext to tighten his grip on the German state. In 1945 the building was a major target for their Red Army, who raised the red flag in an act that became a symbol of the Soviet defeat of the Nazis.

MB/BIRDY/GETTY IMAGES ©

❶ Need to Know

Map p64; www.bundestag.de; Platz der Republik 1, Visitors Centre, Scheidemannstrasse; ◷lift 8am midnight, last entry 9.45pm, Visitors Centre 8am-8pm Apr-Oct, to 6pm Nov-Mar; ☐100, ⓢBrandenburger Tor, Hauptbahnhof, ⓊBrandenburger Tor, Bundestag) **FREE**

✕ Take a Break

For quick feeds, **Berlin Pavillon** (Map p64; ☏030-2065 4737; www.berlin-pavillon.de; Scheidemannstrasse 1; dishes €4.50-9; ◷8am-9pm) is handy.

★ Top Tip

For guaranteed access, make free ticket reservations online before you leave home. All visitors must show ID to enter.

The Cold War Years

Although in West Berlin, the Reichstag found itself very near the dividing line between East and West Berlin and from the early 1960s, the Berlin Wall. With the West German government sitting safely in faraway Bonn, this grand façade lost its purpose and in the 1950s some in West Berlin thought it should be demolished. However, the wrecking balls never got their day and the Reichstag was restored, albeit without a lot of its earlier decorations.

Reunification & Norman Foster

Almost a year after the Wall came down, the official reunification ceremony was symbolically held at the Reichstag which, it was later decided, would become the seat of the German Bundestag (parliament)

once again. Before Norman Foster began his reconstruction work, the entire Reichstag was spectacularly wrapped in plastic sheeting by the Bulgarian-American artist Christo in the summer of 1995. The following four years saw the erection of Foster's now-famous glittering glass cupola, the centrepiece of the visitor experience today. It is the Reichstag's most distinctive feature, serviced by lift and providing fabulous 360-degree city views and the opportunity to peer down into the parliament chamber. To reach the top, follow the ramp spiralling up around the dome's mirror-clad central cone. The cupola was a spanking new feature, but Foster's brief also stipulated that some parts of the building were to be preserved. One example is the Cyrillic graffiti left by Soviet soldiers in 1945.

Brandenburger Tor

A symbol of division during the Cold War, the landmark Brandenburg Gate now epitomises German reunification and often serves as a picturesque backdrop for festivals and concerts.

Great For...

☑ **Don't Miss**

The north wing of the gate houses a quiet room for peaceful contemplation.

Beginnings

Commissioned by Prussian emperor Friedrich Wilhelm II (r 1888–1918), architect Carl Gotthard Langhans found inspiration in Athens' Acropolis for this elegant triumphal arch. It was completed in neo-classical sandstone in 1791 as the royal city gate, and a suitably regal entrance to the grand avenue of Unter den linden (which once led to the palace of the Prussian royals). It is crowned by the *Quadriga*, Johann Gottfried Schadow's sculpture of the winged goddess of victory piloting a chariot drawn by four horses. After trouncing the Prussians in 1806, Napoleon famously kidnapped Victory and held her hostage in Paris until she was freed by plucky Prussian general Ernst von Pfuel in 1815.

The gate overlooks Pariser Platz

ⓘ Need to Know

Brandenburg Gate; Map p64; Pariser Platz;
Ⓢ Brandenburger Tor, Ⓤ Brandenburger Tor

✕ Take a Break

There are plenty of cafes along Unter
den Linden.

★ Top Tip

Visit after dark when the gate is lit up in
dramatic fashion.

Two and a half years later, it wasn't the
Russians who took pickaxes to the hated
concrete but the East Berliners themselves.

Restoration

In the early years of the new millennium
the Brandenburg Gate was restored to its
former glory, and reopened in 2002 on the
12th anniversary of German reunification.
No longer open to traffic (which had actually caused more damage than WWII) the
cobbled area around is usually busy with
tourists all day long.

Pariser Platz

The Brandenburg Gate, today a symbol of
German unity, stands sentinel over Pariser
Platz. This harmoniously proportioned
square is once again framed by banks as
well as the US, British and French embassies, just as it was during its 19th-century
heyday.

Cold War Divide

The Brandenburg Gate survived the Red
Army's 1945 onslaught more or less intact,
though it stood in an area decimated by
shelling. In a rare example of cooperation
between East and West Berlin, both sides
contributed to a post-war patch up job on
the structure. However, from the 1960s
it became a symbol of a divided city (and
continent) as it was located so close to
the Berlin Wall on the western side. In the
1970s and '80s visitors could climb to the
top to peer into the socialist utopia of East
Berlin. On 12 June 1987, it was here that
Ronald Reagan addressed his most famous
Cold War words to the Soviets when he
said: 'Mr Gorbachov – tear down this wall!'.

My God, Help Me To Survive This Deadly Love by Dimitri Vrubel

ГОСПОДИ ! ПОМОГИ МНЕ ВЫЖИТЬ

СРЕДИ ЭТОЙ СМЕРТНОЙ ЛЮБВИ

MEiN GOTT HiLE MiR DiESE TÖDLiCHE LiEBE ZU ÜBERLE

The Berlin Wall

For 29 years the Berlin Wall was the most potent symbol of the Cold War. Surprisingly few of its reinforced concrete slabs remain in today's reunited Berlin (the longest section to survive intact is located at the East Side Gallery).

Great For...

☑ Don't Miss

Other hidden pieces of the Wall still stand in Berlin. Ask the tourist offices about locations.

Construction

Shortly after midnight on 13 August 1961, East German soldiers and police began rolling out miles of barbed wire that would soon be replaced with prefab concrete slabs. The wall was a desperate measure taken by the German Democratic Republic (GDR) government to stop the sustained brain and brawn drain it had experienced since its 1949 founding. Around 3.6 million people had already left for the West, putting the GDR on the verge of economic and political collapse.

Demise

The Wall's demise in 1989 came as unexpectedly as its construction. Once again the GDR was losing its people in droves, this time via Hungary, which had opened its borders with Austria. Something had to give. It did on 9 November 1989 when a GDR

Gedenkstätte Berliner Mauer

MERTEN SNIJDERS/GETTY IMAGES ©

Gedenkstätte Berliner Mauer

⑤ Nordbahnhof

ⓘ Need to Know

Track down remaining fragments of the Wall across the city using Memorial Landscape Berlin Wall (www.berlin-wall -map.com)

✕ Take a Break

Not far from the outdoor memorial is the famous Konnopke's Imbiss (p75).

★ Top Tip

There's a great view from the Documentation Centre's viewing platform.

and integrates an original section of Wall, vestiges of the border installations and escape tunnels, a chapel and a monument Multimedia stations, panels, excavations and a Documentation Centre provide context, and explain what the border fortifications looked like and how they shaped the everyday lives of people on both sides of it.

spokesperson (mistakenly, it later turned out) announced during a press conference that all travel restrictions to the West would be lifted. When asked when, he said simply, 'Immediately'. Amid scenes of wild partying, the two Berlins came together again.

Over the course of 1990 the Wall almost disappeared, some bits smashed up and flogged to tourists, other sections carted off to museums, parks, embassies, exhibitions and even private gardens across the globe.

Gedenkstätte Berliner Mauer

The **outdoor memorial** (Map p74; ☏030-467 986 666; www.berliner-mauer-gedenkstaette. de; ☉Visitor & Documentation Centre 10am-6pm Tue-Sun, open-air exhibit 8am-10pm daily; ⑤Nordbahnhof, Eberswalder Strasse) **FREE** extends for 1.4km along Bernauer Strasse

East Side Gallery

Most of the Wall was quickly dismantled, but along Mühlenstrasse, paralleling the Spree, a 1.3km stretch became the **East Side Gallery** (Map p70; www.eastsidegallery-berlin.de; ☉24hr; Ⓤ Warschauer Strasse, ⑤ Ostbahnhof, Warschauer Strasse) **FREE**, the world's largest open-air mural collection. In more than 100 paintings, dozens of artists translated the era's euphoria and optimism into a mix of political statements and artistic visions.

Birgit Kinder's *Test the Best,* showing a Trabi car bursting through the Wall; *My God, Help Me To Survive This Deadly Love* by Dimitri Vrubel (pictured above left), which has Erich Honecker and Leonid Brezhnev locking lips; and Thierry Noir's bright cartoon faces are all shutterbug favourites.

The Berlin Wall

The construction of the Berlin Wall was a unique event in human history, not only for physically bisecting a city but for becoming a dividing line between competing ideologies and political systems. It's this global impact and universal legacy that continues to fascinate people decades after its triumphant tear-down. Fortunately, some of original Wall segments and other vestiges remain, along with museums and memorials, to help fathom the realities and challenges of daily life in Berlin during the Cold War.

Our illustration points out the top highlights you can visit to learn about different aspects of these often tense decades. The best place to start is the ❶ **Gedenkstätte Berliner Mauer**, for an excellent introduction to what the inner-city border looked liked and what it meant to live in its shadow. Reflect upon what you've learned while relaxing along the former death strip, now the ❷ **Mauerpark**, before heading to the emotionally charged exhibit at the ❸ **Tränenpalast**, an actual border-crossing pavilion. Relive the euphoria of the

Tränenpalast
This modernist 1962 glass-and-steel border pavilion was dubbed 'Palace of Tears' because of the many tearful farewells that took place outside the building as East Germans and their Western visitors had to say goodbye.

Brandenburger Tor
People around the world cheered as East and West Berliners partied together atop the Berlin Wall in front of the iconic city gate, which today is a photogenic symbol of united Germany.

Potsdamer Platz
Nowhere was the death strip as wide as on the former no man's land around Potsdamer Platz, from which sprouted a new postmodern city quarter in the 1990s. A tiny section of the Berlin Wall serves as a reminder.

Checkpoint Charlie
Only diplomats and foreigners were allowed to use this border crossing. Weeks after the Wall was built, US and Soviet tanks faced off here in one of the hottest moments of the Cold War.

Wall's demise at the **④ Brandenburger Tor**, then marvel at the revival of **⑤ Potsdamer Platz**, which was nothing but death-strip wasteland until the 1990s. The Wall's geopolitical significance is the focus at **⑥ Checkpoint Charlie**, which saw some of the tensest moments of the Cold War. Wrap up by finding your favourite mural motif at the **⑦ East Side Gallery**.

It's possible to explore these sights by using a combination of walking and public transport, but a bike ride is the best method for gaining a sense of the former Wall's erratic flow through the central city.

FAST FACTS

Beginning of construction 13 August 1961
Fall of the Wall 9 November 1989
Total length 155km
Height 3.6m
Weight of each segment 2.6 tonnes
Number of watchtowers 300

Remnants of
the Wall →

Gedenkstätte Berliner Mauer
Germany's central memorial to the Berlin Wall and its victims exposes the complexity and barbaric nature of the border installation, along a 1.4km stretch of the barrier's course.

Alexanderplatz

Alexanderstr

Mauerpark
Famous for its flea market and karaoke, this popular park actually occupies a converted section of the death strip. A 30m segment of surviving Wall is now an official practice ground for budding graffiti artists.

East Side Gallery
Paralleling the Spree for 1.3km, this is the longest Wall vestige. After its collapse, more than a hundred international artists expressed their feelings about this historic moment in a series of colourful murals.

Bode-Museum (p49)

CANADASTOCK/SHUTTERSTOCK ©

Museumsinsel

Berlin's Museumsinsel (Museum Island) is a treasure trove of 600,000 years of art, artefacts and architecture spread across five museums. It's a Unesco-listed highlight and essential Berlin viewing.

Great For..

☑ Don't Miss

There are fine views of the Museumsinsel from the upstairs cafe terrace at the Humboldt-Box.

Pergamonmuseum

Opening a fascinating window onto the ancient world, the palatial three-wing complex of the **Pergamonmuseum** (Map p64; ☎030-266 424 242; www.smb.museum; Bodestrasse 1-3; adult/concession/under 18yr €12/6/free; ⊗10am-6pm Fri-Wed, to 8pm Thu; ☐100, 200, TXL, ⓢHackescher Markt, Friedrichstrasse, Ⓤ Friedrichstrasse) unites a rich feast of classical sculpture and monumental architecture from Greece, Rome, Babylon and the Middle East, including the radiant-blue Ishtar Gate from Babylon, the Roman Market Gate of Miletus and the Caliph's Palace of Mshatta. Renovations put the namesake Pergamon Altar off limits until 2023. Budget at least two hours for this amazing place and be sure to pick up the free and excellent audioguide.

Interior, Pergamonmuseum

ℹ️ Need to Know

If you are planning to visit all five museums, the three-day pass (adult/concession €24/12) is a good deal.

✕ Take a Break

Each of the five museums has its own cafe.

★ Top Tip

Buy tickets for the Neues Museum and the Pergamonmuseum online at www.smb.museum.

century AD). Merchants and customers once flooded through here onto the market square of this Roman trading town (in today's Turkey) that functioned as a link between Asia and Europe.

Aside from the caliph's palace, a major standout upstairs in the Islamic collection is the 17th-century Aleppo Room from the house of a Christian merchant in Syria, with its richly painted, wood-panelled walls. If you look closely, you can make out *The Last Supper* and *Mother and Child* amid all the ornamentation (straight ahead, to the right of the door).

Neues Museum

David Chipperfield's reconstruction of the bombed-out **New Museum** (Map p64; 📞030-266 424 242; www.smb.museum; Bodestrasse 1-3; adult/concession/under 18yr €12/6/free; ⏱10am-6pm Fri-Wed, to 8pm Thu; 🚌100, 200, TXL, 🟢Hackescher Markt, Friedrichstrasse, Ⓤ Friedrichstrasse) is now the residence of Queen Nefertiti, the show-stopper of the Egyptian Museum that also features mummies, sculptures and sarcophagi. Pride

The Pergamon unites three major collections, the Antikensammlung (Collection of Classical Antiquities), the Museum für Islamische Kunst (Museum of Islamic Art) and the Vorderasiatisches Museum (Museum of Near Eastern Antiquities). The temporary entrance first leads you to the last of these, into the world of Babylon during the reign of King Nebuchadnezzar II. It's impossible not to be awed by the reconstructed Ishtar Gate, the Processional Way leading up to it and the facade of the king's throne hall. All are sheathed in glazed bricks glistening in radiant blue and ochre. The strutting lions, horses and dragons, which represent major Babylonian gods, are so striking that you can almost hear the roaring and fanfare.

Another key exhibit on the ground floor is the giant Market Gate of Miletus (2nd

of place of the Museum of Pre- and Early History in the same building goes to Trojan antiquities, a Neanderthal skull and the 3000-year-old 'Berliner Goldhut', a golden conical hat. Skip the queue by buying your timed ticket online.

Altes Museum

A curtain of fluted columns gives way to the Pantheon-inspired rotunda of the grand neoclassical **Old Museum** (Map p64; ☎030-266 424 242; www.smb.museum; Am Lustgarten; adult/concession/under 18 €10/5/free; ☻10am-6pm Tue, Wed & Fri-Sun, to 8pm Thu; ☐100, 200, TXL, ⑤Friedrichstrasse, Hackescher Markt, ⑪Friedrichstrasse), which houses a prized antiquities collection. In the downstairs galleries, sculptures, vases, tomb reliefs and jewellery shed light on various facets of life in ancient Greece, while upstairs the focus

is on the Etruscans and Romans. Top draws include the *Praying Boy* bronze sculpture, Roman silver vessels, an 'erotic cabinet' (over 18s only!) and portraits of Caesar and Cleopatra.

Alte Nationalgalerie

The Greek temple–style **Old National Gallery** (Map p64; ☎030-266 424 242; www.smb.museum; Bodestrasse 1-3; adult/concession €10/5; ☻10am-6pm Tue, Wed & Fri-Sun, to 8pm Thu; ☐100, 200, TXL, ⑤Hackescher Markt) is a three-storey showcase of 19th-century European art. To get a sense of the period's virtuosity, pay special attention to the moody landscapes by Romantic heart-throb Caspar David Friedrich, the epic canvases by Franz Krüger and Adolf Menzel glorifying Prussia, the Gothic fantasies of Karl Friedrich Schinkel,

Alte Nationalgalerie

and the sprinkling of French and German impressionists.

Bode-Museum

On the northern tip of Museumsinsel, the **Bode-Museum** (Map p64; ☎030-266 424 242; www.smb.museum; cnr Am Kupfergraben & Monbijoubrücke; adult/concession/under 18 €12/6/free; ☺10am-6pm Tue, Wed & Fri-Sun, to 8pm Thu; ⑤Hackescher Markt, Friedrichstrasse) houses a comprehensive collection of European sculpture from the early Middle Ages to the 18th century,

JULIE WOODHOUSE/GETTY IMAGES ©

including priceless masterpieces by Tilman Riemenschenider, Donatello and Giovanni Pisano. Other rooms host a precious coin collection and a smattering of Byzantine art, including sarcophagi and ivory carvings.

Berliner Dom

Pompous yet majestic, an Italian Renaissance–style former royal court church (1905), the **Berlin Cathedral** (Map p64; ☎ticket office 030-2026 9136; www.berlinerdom.de; Am Lustgarten; adult/concession €7/5; ☺9am-8pm Apr-Sep, to 7pm Oct-Mar; ☐100, 200, TXL, ⑤Hackescher Markt) does triple duty as house of worship, museum and concert hall. Inside it's gilt to the hilt and outfitted with a lavish marble-and-onyx altar, a 7269-pipe Sauer organ and elaborate royal sarcophagi. Climb up the 267 steps to the gallery for glorious city views.

Humboldt-Box

This futuristic five-floor **structure** (Map p64; ☎030-2927 8248; www.humboldt-box.com; Schlossplatz 5; ☺10am-7pm Mar-Nov, to 6pm Dec-Feb; ☐100, 200, TXL, ⓤHausvogteiplatz) **FREE** opens up a window on the Berlin City Palace, to be called 'Humboldt-Forum', whose reconstruction has been underway since 2013. On display are interactive teasers from each future resident – the Ethnological Museum, the Museum of Asian Art and the Central Library – along with a fantastically detailed model of the historic city centre.

Museumsinsel

A HALF-DAY TOUR

Navigating around this five-museum treasure repository can be daunting, so we've created this itinerary to help you find the must-see highlights while maximising your time and energy. You'll need at least four hours and a Museumsinsel ticket for entry to all museums.

Start in the Altes Museum where you can admire the roll call of antique gods guarded by a perky bronze statue called the ❶ **Praying Boy**, the poster child of a prized collection of antiquities. Next up, head to the Neues Museum for your audience with ❷ **Bust of Queen Nefertiti**, the star of the Egyptian collection atop the grand central staircase.

One more floor up, don't miss the dazzling Bronze Age ❸ **Berliner Goldhut** (room 305). Leaving the Neues Museum, turn left for the Pergamonmuseum. With the namesake altar off limits until at least 2023, the first major sight you'll see is the ❹ **Ishtar Gate**. Upstairs, pick your way through the Islamic collection, past carpets, prayer niches and a caliph's palace facade to the intricately painted ❺ **Aleppo Room**.

Jump ahead to the 19th century at the Alte Nationalgalerie to zero in on paintings by ❻ **Caspar David Friedrich** on the 3rd floor and precious sculptures such as Schadow's ❼ **Statue of Two Princesses** on the first floor. Wrap up your explorations at the Bode-Museum, reached in a five-minute walk. Admire the foyer with its equestrian statue of Friedrich Wilhelm, then feast your eyes on European sculpture without missing masterpieces by ❽ **Tilman Riemenschneider**.

FAST FACTS

Oldest object 700,000-year-old Paleolithic hand axe at Neues Museum

Newest object A piece of barbed wire from the Berlin Wall at Neues Museum

Oldest museum Altes Museum, 1830

Most popular museum on Museumsinsel Neues Museum (777,000 visitors)

Total Museumsinsel visitors (2017) 2.33 million

Sculptures by Tilman Riemenschneider (Bode-Museum)
Dazzling detail and great emotional expressiveness characterise the wooden sculptures by late-Gothic master carver Tilman Riemenschneider, as in his portrayal of *St Anne and Her Three Husbands* from around 1510.

Spree River

Entrance

❽

Bode-Museum

Georgenstrasse

M1 & 12 Tram stop

Dorotheenstrasse

M1 & 12 Tram stop

Bust of Queen Nefertiti (Room 210, Neues Museum)
In the north dome, fall in love with Berlin's most beautiful woman – the 3330-year-old Egyptian queen Nefertiti, she of the long graceful neck and timeless good looks – despite the odd wrinkle and a missing eye.

Unter den Linden

Aleppo Room
(Room 16, Pergamonmuseum)
A highlight of the Museum of Islamic Art, this richly painted, wood-panelled reception room from a Christian merchant's home in 17th-century Aleppo, Syria, combines Islamic floral and geometric motifs with courtly scenes and Christian themes.

Ishtar Gate
(Room 9, Pergamonmuseum)
Draw breath as you enter the 2600-year-old city gate to Babylon, which has soaring walls sheathed in radiant blue-glazed bricks and adorned with ochre reliefs of strutting lions, bulls and dragons representing Babylonian gods.

Pergamonmuseum

Spree River

Paintings by Caspar David Friedrich
(Top Floor, Alte Nationalgalerie)
A key artist of the romantic period, Caspar David Friedrich put his own stamp on landscape painting with his dark, moody and subtly dramatic meditations on the boundaries of human life versus the infinity of nature.

Alte Nationalgalerie

Entrance

Entrance

Entrance

Statue of Two Princesses
(1st Floor, Alte Nationalgalerie)
Johann Gottfried Schadow captures Prussian princesses (and sisters) Luise and Friederike in a moment of intimacy and thoughtfulness in this double marble statue, created in 1795 at the height of the neoclassical period.

Neues Museum

Bodestrasse

Altes Museum

Entrance

Berliner Dom

Lustgarten

Berliner Goldhut
(Room 305, Neues Museum)
Marvel at the Bronze Age artistry of the Berlin Gold Hat, a ceremonial gold cone embossed with ornamental bands believed to have been used in predicting the best times for planting and harvesting.

Praying Boy (Room 5, Altes Museum)
The top draw at the Old Museum is the *Praying Boy*, ancient Greece's 'Next Top Model'. The life-size bronze statue of a young male nude is the epitome of physical perfection and was cast around 300 BC in Rhodes.

Schloss Charlottenburg

This exquisite baroque pile is the finest of Berlin's nine remaining royal palaces. Inspired by Versailles, it backs up against an idyllic park, complete with carp pond, rhododendron-lined paths, two smaller palaces and a mausoleum.

Great For...

❶ Need to Know

Map p80; ☑030-320 910; www.spsg.de; Spandauer Damm 10-22; ☉hours vary by building; 🚌M45, 109, 309, Ⓤ Richard-Wagner-Platz, Sophie-Charlotte-Platz)

★ **Top Tip**

Each building charges separate admission but a day pass called charlottenburg+Combined Ticket (adult/concession €17/13) is available.

We can guarantee that your camera will have a love affair with this late-baroque jewel. The palace itself is clad in a subtle yellow, typical of the royal Hohenzollern family, and wonderfully adorned with slender columns and geometrically arranged windows. An ornate copper-domed tower overlooks the forecourt and the imposing equestrian statue of the 'Great Elector' Friedrich Wilhelm. There's a lot to see here so allow at least three hours.

Altes Schloss

Also known as the Nering-Eosander Building after its two architects, the Altes Schloss is the central, and oldest, section of the palace. It is fronted by Andreas Schlüter's grand equestrian statue of the *Great Elector* (1699). Inside, the baroque living quarters of Friedrich I and Sophie-Charlotte are an extravaganza

in stucco, brocade and overall opulence. Highlights include the Oak Gallery, a wood-panelled festival hall draped in family portraits; the charming Oval Hall overlooking the park; Friedrich I's bedchamber, with the first-ever proper bathroom in a baroque palace; and the Eosander Chapel, with its trompe l'œil arches. The king's passion for priceless china is reflected in the dazzling Porcelain Chamber, which is weighed down with almost 3000 pieces of exquisite Chinese and Japanese blueware. Upstairs you will find paintings, vases, tapestries, weapons, porcelain, a 2600-piece silver table setting and many other items the Prussian royals found essential for their lifestyle.

Neuer Flügel

Arguably the most beautiful rooms at Charlottenburg are located in the Neuer

Mausoleum, Schlossgarten Charlottenburg

Flügel (New Wing). The flamboyant private chambers of King Frederick the Great (r 1740–1786)were designed in 1746 by star architect Georg Wenzeslaus von Knobelsdorff. Standouts include the White Hall banquet room, the gilded Golden Gallery and the paintings by Watteau, Pesne and other 18th-century French masters. In the same wing, the apartments of Queen Luise (1776–1810), wife of King Friedrich Wilhelm III, are decked out with lavish chandeliers, furniture and hand-painted silk wall coverings.

Neuer Pavillon

Returning from a trip to Italy, Friedrich Wilhelm III (r 1797–1848) commissioned Karl

Friedrich Schinkel to design this petite summer refuge modelled on a villa in Naples. Today, the minipalace is a sparkling backdrop for masterpieces by such Schinkel-era painters as Caspar David Friedrich and Eduard Gaertner, as well as by the sculptor Christian Daniel Rauch. Ground-floor rooms brim with original Biedermeier furniture.

Schlossgarten

The expansive park behind Schloss Charlottenburg is part formal French, part unruly English and all idyllic playground. Hidden among the shady paths, flower beds, lawns, mature trees and carp pond are two smaller royal buildings, the sombre Mausoleum and the charming Belvedere. It's a fantastic place for strolling, jogging or lazing on a sunny afternoon. In the summer months take a picnic to enjoy on the grass.

Belvedere

This pint-size palace with the distinctive cupola got its start in 1788 as a teahouse for Friedrich Wilhelm II. Here he enjoyed reading, music and holding spiritual sessions with the mystical Order of the Rosicrucians. These days, the late-rococo vision by Carl Gotthard Langhans makes an elegant backdrop for porcelain masterpieces by the royal manufacturer KPM.

Mausoleum

In the Schlosspark, west of the carp pond, the neoclassical Mausoleum (1810; pictured left) was conceived as the final resting place of Queen Luise but twice expanded to make room for other royals, including Luise's husband Friedrich Wilhelm III and Emperor William I and his wife Augusta. Their ornate marble sarcophagi are great works of art. More royals are buried in the crypt (closed to the public).

> ☑ **Don't Miss**
>
> Combine a visit to the palace with a spin round the local museums.

> ✕ **Take a Break**
>
> **Kleine Orangerie** (Map p80; ☏030-322 2021; mains €6-15; ⊗10am-6pm Tue-Sun) is located near the entrance to the palace park.

© STIFTUNG PREUSSISCHE SCHLÖSSER UND GÄRTEN BERLIN BRANDENBURG/ PHOTOGRAPHER: WOLFGANG PFAUDER

BARTEK KUZIA/500PX ©

Holocaust Memorial

A short stroll from the Brandenburg Gate, this vast memorial to Europe's Jews who were murdered by the Nazis leaves few untouched. The design, hundreds of concrete columns rising from the ground, creates an unforgettable effect.

Great For

☑ Don't Miss

Worthwhile audioguides are available from the Ort der Information.

Inaugurated in 2005, this football-field-sized memorial (the official name is the Memorial to the Murdered Jews of Europe) by American architect Peter Eisenman consists of 2711 sarcophagi-like concrete columns rising from 19,000 sq m of undulating ground (pictured above). The memorial has no designated entrance or exit – you're free to access this maze at any point and make your individual journey through it. The design is purposefully disorientating, the columns at slightly different heights than those around them and the walkways creating a claustrophobic effect. At busy times many visitors can be seen sitting on the smaller blocks in contemplation of the memorial's meaning. Some have criticised the memorial for not including others murdered by the Nazis, such as homosexuals, Roma and people

Entrance to the memorial from the Ort der Information

SVEN NORDBRUM/GETTY IMAGES ©

ℹ Need to Know

Map p64; ☎030-2639 4336; www.
stiftung-denkmal.de; Cora-Berliner-Strasse 1;
audioguide €3; ⊘24hr; ⑤Brandenburger Tor,
Ⓤ Brandenburger Tor **FREE**

✕ Take a Break

Although you have to pay to get up there,
the café at Panoramapunkt (p67) has
unrivalled views over Mitte.

★ Top Tip

Visit after dark when the columns are
dramatically uplit.

Ort der Information

For context, visit the subterranean Ort der
Information (Information Centre) whose
exhibits are thought-provoking at the very
least. The entrance is on the eastern side of
the memorial, near Cora-Berliner-Strasse.

What's Nearby

It's ironic that the **Site of Hitler's bunker**
(Führerbunker; Map p64; cnr In den Minis-
tergärten & Gertrud-Kolmar-Strasse; ⊘24hr;
⑤Brandenburger Tor, ⓊBrandenburger Tor) is
located only a short walk southeast of the
Holocaust Memorial. As Berlin burnt and
Soviet tanks advanced relentlessly towards
the city centre, it was here that Adolf Hitler
committed suicide on 30 April 1945, alongside Eva Braun, his long-time companion,
hours after their marriage. The bodies were
never found. Today, a modern parking lot
just off Gertrud-Kolmar-Strasse covers the
site, revealing its dark history only via an
information panel with a diagram of the vast
bunker network, construction data and the
site's post-WWII history.

with disabilities, though other memorials
have been built to these groups.

Conception & Construction

A holocaust memorial was a long time
in the making, the idea having been put
forward in the 1980s. It wasn't until 1994
that a competition for the design was
launched, with the winning artist to receive
a budget of €25 million. The two short-
listed designs were eventually vetoed by
Chancellor Kohl and a new competition
was announced in 1996. The next year Peter Eisenman's design was announced as
winner though the original plan had 4,000
pillars. Construction began in 2003 and
was opened to the public in May 2005. It's
estimated around three million visitors
walk through the memorial every year,
making it one of Berlin's top attractions.

Beach bar on the Spree River

JEAN-PIERRE LESCOURRET/GETTY IMAGES ©

Berlin Nightlife

With its well-deserved reputation as one of Europe's primo party capitals, Berlin offers a thousand-and-one scenarios for getting your cocktails and kicks (or wine or beer, for that matter).

Great For

☑ **Don't Miss**

Café am Neuen See (see p79) is one of Berlin's best beer gardens.

Bars & Cafes

Berlin is a notoriously late city: bars stay packed from dusk to dawn and beyond, and some clubs don't hit their stride until 4am. The lack of a curfew meant a tradition of binge drinking was never created.

Edgier, more underground venues cluster in Kreuzberg, Friedrichshain, Neukölln and up-and-coming outer boroughs like Wedding (north of Mitte) and Lichtenberg (past Friedrichshain). Places in Charlottenburg, Mitte and Prenzlauer Berg tend to be quieter and close earlier. Some proprietors have gone to extraordinary lengths to come up with special design concepts.

The line between cafe and bar is often blurred, with many changing stripes as the hands move around the clock. Alcohol, however, is served pretty much all day. Cocktail bars are booming in Berlin and

A Berlin cocktail bar

BRUNO EHRS/GETTY IMAGES ©

2002, Berlin also jumped on the 'sandwagon' with the opening of its first beach bar, Strandbar Mitte, in a prime location on the Spree River. Many that followed have since been displaced by development, which has partly fuelled the latest trend: rooftop bars.

Clubbing

Over the past 25 years, Berlin's club culture has put the city firmly on the map of hedonists. With more than 200 venues, finding one to match your mood isn't difficult. Electronic music in its infinite varieties continues to define Berlin's after dark action but other sounds like hip-hop, dancehall, rock, swing and funk have also made inroads. The edgiest clubs have taken up residence in power plants, transformer stations, abandoned apartment buildings and other repurposed locations. The scene is in constant flux as experienced club owners look for new challenges and a younger generation of promoters enters the scene with new ideas and impetus.

several new arrivals have measurably elevated the 'liquid art' scene. Dedicated drinking dens tend to be elegant cocoons with mellow lighting and low sound levels. A good cocktail will set you back between €10 and €15.

Although still lower than in other major capital cities, drinks prices have crept up over the last couple of years.

Beaches & Outdoor Drinking

Berliners are sun cravers. As soon as the first rays spray their way into spring, outdoor tables show up faster than you can pour a pint of beer. The most traditional places for outdoor chilling are, of course, the beer gardens, with long wooden benches set up beneath leafy old chestnuts and cold beer and bratwurst on the menu. In

Historical Highlights

This walk checks off Berlin's blockbuster landmarks as it cuts right through the historic city centre, Mitte ('Middle'). This is the birthplace and glamorous heart of Berlin, a high-octane cocktail of culture, architecture and commerce.

Start Reichstag
Distance 3.5km
Duration 3 hours

Classic photo of the neo-classical Brandenburger Tor.

2 The only remaining gate of Berlin's 18th-century town wall, the **Brandenburger Tor** (p40) has became a cheery symbol of German reunification.

3 Unter den Linden has been Berlin's showpiece road since the 18th century.

1 The 1894 **Reichstag** (p38) is the historic anchor of the federal government quarter. The glass dome was added in the 1990s.

Take a Break Einstein Unter den Linden (www.einstein-udl.com/en; Unter den Linden 42; mains €16-25; ⏰7am-11pm Mon-Fri, from 8am Sat & Sun) is a good spot for people-watching, as well as a break over coffee and cakes.

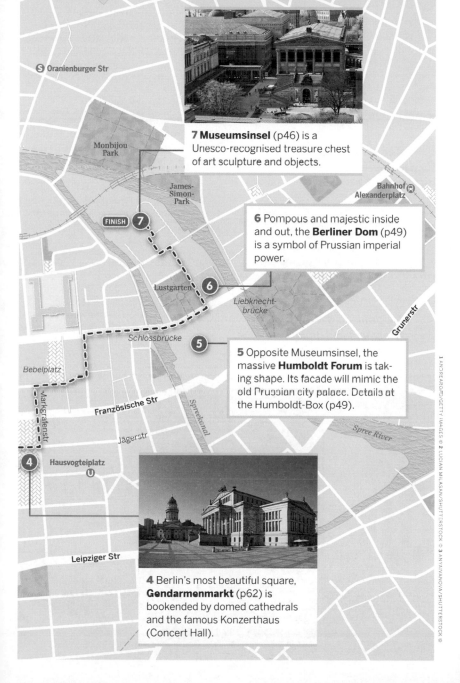

7 Museumsinsel (p46) is a Unesco-recognised treasure chest of art sculpture and objects.

6 Pompous and majestic inside and out, the **Berliner Dom** (p49) is a symbol of Prussian imperial power.

5 Opposite Museumsinsel, the massive **Humboldt Forum** is taking shape. Its facade will mimic the old Prussian city palace. Details at the Humboldt-Box (p49).

4 Berlin's most beautiful square, **Gendarmenmarkt** (p62) is bookended by domed cathedrals and the famous Konzerthaus (Concert Hall).

⑤ Oranienburger Str

Monbijou Park

James-Simon-Park

Bahnhof ⓡ Alexanderplatz

FINISH ⑦

Lustgarten ⑥

Liebknecht-brücke

Grunerstr

Schlossbrücke ⑤

Bebelplatz

Markgrafenstr

Französische Str

Spreekanal

Jägerstr

Spree River

④ Hausvogteiplatz ⓤ

Leipziger Str

⊙ SIGHTS

Berlin is split into 12 official Bezirke (districts; for example, Mitte, Prenzlauer Berg, Kreuzberg), which are subdivided into individual Kieze (neighbourhoods). Key sights such as the Brandenburger Tor and Museumsinsel cluster in the walkable historic city centre – Mitte – which also cradles the fashion-centric Scheunenviertel around Hackescher Markt.

⊙ Unten den Linten

**Deutsches
Historisches Museum**   Museum

(German Historical Museum; Map p64; ☎030-203 040; www.dhm.de; Unter den Linden 2; adult/concession/child under 18 incl IM Pei Bau €8/4/free; ☉10am-6pm; ▣100, 200, Ⓤ Hausvogteiplatz, Ⓢ Hackescher Markt) If you're wondering what the Germans have been up to for the past 1500 years, take a spin around the baroque Zeughaus,

> **the principal gateway for foreigners and diplomats between the two Berlins**
>
> Checkpoint Charlie

formerly the Prussian arsenal and now home of the German Historical Museum. Upstairs, displays concentrate on the period from the 6th century AD to the end of WWI in 1918, while the ground floor tracks the 20th century all the way through to the early years after German reunification.

⊙ Friedrichstrasse

Gendarmenmarkt   Square

(Map p64; Ⓤ Französische Strasse, Stadtmitte) This graceful square is bookended by the domed German and French cathedrals and punctuated by a grandly porticoed concert hall, the **Konzerthaus** (☎030-203 092 333; www.konzerthaus.de; Gendarmenmarkt 2). It was named for the Gens d'Armes, an 18th-century Prussian regiment consisting of French Huguenot refugees.

Checkpoint Charlie   Historic Site

(Map p78; cnr Zimmerstrasse & Friedrichstrasse; ☉24hr; Ⓤ Kochstrasse) FREE Checkpoint Charlie was the principal gateway for foreigners and diplomats between the two Berlins from 1961 to 1990. Unfortunately,

WAVE, MOVIES/SHUTTERSTOCK®

this potent symbol of the Cold War has degenerated into a tacky tourist trap, though a free open-air exhibit that illustrates milestones in Cold War history is one redeeming aspect.

Museum für Kommunikation Berlin

Museum

(Map p78; ☑030-202 940; www.mfk-berlin.de; Leipziger Strasse 16; adult/concession/child under 17 €5/3/free; ☉9am-8pm Tue, 9am-5pm Wed-Fri, 10am-6pm Sat & Sun; ⊠200, ⓤMohrenstrasse, Stadtmitte) Three cheeky robots welcome you to this elegant, neo-baroque museum, which takes you on an entertaining romp through the evolution of communication, from smoke signals to smartphones. Admire such rare items as a Blue Mauritius stamp or one of the world's first telephones, test milestones in communication techniques, or ponder the impact of information technology on our daily lives.

◎ Scheunenviertel

Hackesche Höfe

Historic Site

(Hackesche Courtyards; Map p64; ☑030-2809 8010; www.hackesche-hoefe.com; enter from Rosenthaler Strasse 40/41 or Sophienstrasse 6; ⊠M1, ⓢHackescher Markt, ⓤWeinmeisterstrasse) The Hackesche Höfe is the largest and most famous of the courtyard ensembles peppered throughout the Scheunenviertel. Built in 1907, the eight interlinked *Höfe* reopened in 1996 with a congenial mix of cafes, galleries, shops and entertainment venues. The main entrance on Rosenthaler Strasse leads to Court I, prettily festooned with art nouveau tiles, while Court VII segues to the romantic Rosenhöfe with a sunken rose garden and tendril-like balustrades.

Hamburger Bahnhof – Museum für Gegenwart

Museum

(Contemporary Art Museum; Map p64; ☑030-266 424 242; www.smb.museum; Invalidenstrasse 50-51; adult/concession €10/5, free 4-8pm 1st Thu of the month; ☉10am-6pm Tue, Wed & Fri, to 8pm Thu, 11am-6pm Sat & Sun; ⊠M5, M8, M10, ⓢHauptbahnhof, ⓤHauptbahnhof) Berlin's

⌐➤⌐ Sachsenhausen Concentration Camp

About 35km north of Berlin, **Sachsenhausen** (Memorial & Museum Sachsenhausen; ☑03301-200 200; www.stiftung-bg.de; Strasse der Nationen 22, Oranienburg; ☉8.30am-6pm mid-Mar–mid-Oct, to 4.30pm mid-Oct–mid-Mar, museums closed Mon mid-Oct–mid-Mar; Ⓟ; ⓢOranienburg) **FREE** was built by prisoners and opened in 1936 as a prototype for other camps. By 1945, some 200,000 people had passed through its sinister gates, most of them political opponents, Jews, Roma people and, after 1939, POWs. Tens of thousands died here from hunger, exhaustion, illness, exposure, medical experiments and executions. A tour of the memorial site with its remaining buildings and exhibits will leave no one untouched.

Thousands more succumbed during the death march of April 1945, when the Nazis evacuated the camp in advance of the Red Army. Note the memorial plaque to these victims as you walk towards the camp from S-Bahnstation Oranienburg (at the corner of Strasse der Einheit and Strasse der Nationen).

ITZAVU/SHUTTERSTOCK ©

contemporary art showcase opened in 1996 in an old railway station, whose grandeur is a great backdrop for this Aladdin's cave of paintings, installations, sculptures and video art. Changing exhibits span the arc of post-1950 artistic movements – from conceptual art and pop art to minimal art and

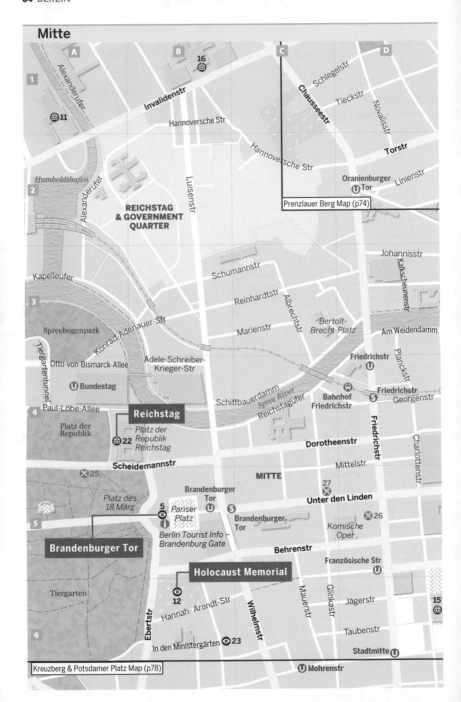

Mitte

REICHSTAG & GOVERNMENT QUARTER

Prenzlauer Berg Map (p74)

Humboldthafen

Spreebogenpark

Tiergarten

Platz der Republik

Platz des 18 März

Pariser Platz

Berlin Tourist Info – Brandenburg Gate

Reichstag

Brandenburger Tor

Holocaust Memorial

MITTE

Komische Oper

Kreuzberg & Potsdamer Platz Map (p78)

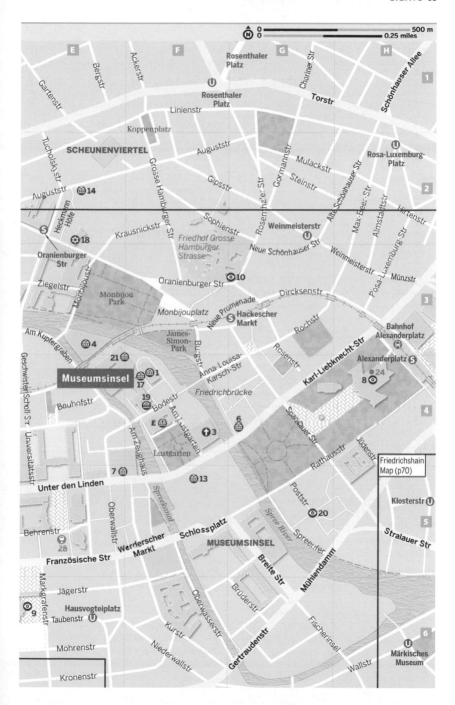

Mitte

Fluxus – and include seminal works by such major players as Andy Warhol, Cy Twombly, Joseph Beuys and Robert Rauschenberg.

Museum für Naturkunde
Museum

(Museum of Natural History; Map p64; ☑030-2093 8591; www.naturkundemuseum.berlin; Invalidenstrasse 43; adult/concession incl audioguide €8/5; ⊘9.30am-6pm Tue-Fri, 10am-6pm Sat & Sun; ⬤; ☒M5, M8, M10, 12, ⓊNaturkundemuseum) Fossils and minerals don't quicken your pulse? Well, how about Tristan, the T-Rex? His skeleton is among the best-preserved in the world and, along with the 12m-high *Brachiosaurus branchai*, part of the Jurassic superstar line-up at this highly engaging museum. Elsewhere you can wave at Knut, the world's most famous dead polar bear; marvel at the fragile bones of an ultrarare *Archaeopteryx* protobird, and find out why zebras are striped.

Neue Synagoge
Synagogue

(Map p64; ☑030-8802 8300; www.centrum judaicum.de; Oranienburger Strasse 28-30; adult/concession €5/4, audioguide €3; ⊘10am-6pm Mon-Fri, to 7pm Sun, closes 3pm Fri & 6pm Sun Oct-Mar; ☒M1, ⓊOranienburger Tor, ⓈOranienburger Strasse) The gleaming gold dome of the Neue Synagoge is the most visible symbol of Berlin's revitalised Jewish community. The 1866 original was Germany's largest synagogue but its modern incarnation is not so much a house of worship (although prayer services do take place), as a museum and place of remembrance called Centrum Judaicum. The dome can be climbed from April to September (adult/concession €3/2.50).

Alexanderplatz

Fernsehturm
Landmark

(TV Tower; Map p64; ☑030-247 575 875; www.tv-turm.de; Panoramastrasse 1a; adult/child €15.50/9.50, fast track online ticket €19.50/12; ⊘9am-midnight Mar-Oct, 10am-midnight Nov-Feb, last ascent 11.30pm; ☒100, 200, TXL, ⓊAlexanderplatz, ⓈAlexanderplatz) Germany's tallest structure, the TV Tower has been soaring 368m high since 1969 and is as iconic to Berlin as the Eiffel Tower is to Paris. On clear days, views are stunning from the observation deck (with bar) at 203m or from the upstairs **Sphere restaurant** (www.tv-turm.de/en/bar-restaurant; mains lunch €10.50-18, dinner €12.50-28; ⊘10am-11pm; 🕾) at 207m, which makes one revolution per hour.

DDR Museum
Museum

(GDR (East Germany) Museum; Map p64;
☎030-847 123 731; www.ddr-museum.de;
Karl-Liebknecht-Strasse 1, adult/concession
€9.80/6; ⊗10am-8pm Sun-Fri, to 10pm Sat;
🚊100, 200, TXL, Ⓢ Hackescher Markt) This
touchy-feely museum does an insightful
and entertaining job of pulling back the
iron curtain on daily life in socialist East
Germany. You'll learn how kids were put
through collective potty training, engi-
neers earned little more than farmers, and
everyone, it seems, went on nudist holidays. A perennial crowd-pleaser among
the historic objects on display is a Trabi,
the tinny East German standard car – sit
in it to take a virtual spin around an East
Berlin neighbourhood.

◎ Potsdamer Platz & Tiergarten

This new quarter, forged from ground once
bisected by the Berlin Wall, is a showcase
of fabulous contemporary architecture and
home to big cinemas and shopping. Culture
lovers should not skip the Kulturforum
museums, especially the Gemäldegalerie,
which sits right next to the world-class
Berliner Philharmonie. The leafy Tiergarten,
with its rambling paths, monuments and
hidden beer gardens, makes for a perfect
sightseeing break.

Europe's fastest lift, **Panoramapunkt**
(Map p78; ☎030-2593 7080; www.panorama
punkt.de; Potsdamer Platz 1; adult/concession
€7.50/6, without wait €11.50/9; ⊗10am-8pm
Apr-Oct, to 6pm Nov-Mar; 🚊M41, 200, Ⓢ Potsdamer Platz, Ⓤ Potsdamer Platz), yo-yoes up
and down the red-brick postmodern Kollhof
Tower. From the bi-level viewing platform at
a lofty 100m, you can pinpoint the sights,
make a java stop in the 1930s-style cafe,
enjoy sunset from the terrace and check
out the exhibit that peels back the layers of
the quarter's history.

Tiergarten
Park

(Strasse des 17 Juni; 🚊100, 200, Ⓢ Potsdamer
Platz, Brandenburger Tor, Ⓤ Brandenburger
Tor) Berlin's rulers used to hunt boar and

pheasants in the rambling Tiergarten until
garden architect Peter Lenné landscaped
the grounds in the 19th century. Today it's
one of the world's largest urban parks (pictured p69), popular for strolling, jogging,
picnicking, frisbee tossing and, yes, nude
sunbathing and gay cruising (especially
around the Löwenbrücke).

Topographie des Terrors
Museum

(Topography of Terror; Map p78; ☎030-2545
0950; www.topographie.de; Niederkirchner
Strasse 8; ⊗10am-8pm, grounds close at dusk
or 8pm at the latest; 🚊M41, Ⓢ Potsdamer Platz,
Ⓤ Potsdamer Platz) FREE In the spot where
the most feared institutions of Nazi Germany once stood (including the Gestapo
headquarters and the SS central command), this compelling exhibit chronicles
the stages of terror and persecution, puts
a face on the perpetrators and details
the impact these brutal institutions had
on all of Europe. A second exhibit outside
zeroes in on how life changed for Berlin
and its people after the Nazis made it
their capital.

Gemäldegalerie
Gallery

(Gallery of Old Masters; Map p78; ☎030-266 424
242; www.smb.museum/gg; Matthäikirchplatz;
adult/concession/under 18 €10/5/free; ⊗10am-
6pm Tue, Wed & Fri, to 8pm Thu, 11am-6pm Sat
& Sun; ♿; 🚊M29, M48, M85, 200, Ⓢ Potsdamer
Platz, Ⓤ Potsdamer Platz) This museum ranks
among the world's finest and most comprehensive collections of European art,
with about 1500 paintings spanning the arc
of artistic vision from the 13th to the 18th
century. Wear comfy shoes when exploring
the 72 galleries: a walk past masterpieces
by Titian, Dürer, Hals, Vermeer, Gainsbor-
ough and many more Old Masters covers
almost 2km. Don't miss the Rembrandt
Room (Room X).

◎ Prenzlauer Berg

Prenzlauer Berg doesn't have any
blockbuster sights, and most of what it
does have is concentrated in the pretty
southern section around Kollwitzplatz.

LGBTIQ+ Berlin

Generally speaking, Berlin's gayscape runs the entire spectrum from mellow cafes, campy bars and cinemas to saunas, cruising areas, clubs with darkrooms and all-out sex venues. In fact, sex and sexuality are entirely everyday matters to the unshockable city folks and there are very few, if any, itches that can't be quite openly and legally scratched. As elsewhere, gay men have more options for having fun, but grrrrls of all stripes won't feel left out either.

Blu (www.blu.fm) Online and freebie-print magazine with searchable, up-to-the-minute location and event listings.

L-Mag (www.l-mag.de) Bimonthly magazine for lesbians.

Siegessäule (www.siegessaeule.de) Free weekly lesbigay 'bible'.

Christopher Street Day (p23) celebrations
SERGEY KOHL/SHUTTERSTOCK ©

The neighbourhood does include the city's most important exhibit on the Berlin Wall, the Gedenkstätte Berliner Mauer (Berlin Wall Memorial; p43), which begins in Wedding and stretches for 1.4km all the way into Prenzlauer Berg.

Mauerpark   Park
(Map p74; www.mauerpark.info; btwn Bernauer Strasse, Schwedter Strasse & Gleimstrasse; ⛲M1, M10, 12, ⓊEberswalder Strasse) With its wimpy trees and anaemic lawn, Mauerpark is hardly your typical leafy oasis, especially given that it was forged from a section of

Cold War–era death strip (a short stretch of Berlin Wall survives). It's this mystique combined with an unassuming vibe and a hugely popular Sunday flea market and karaoke show that has endeared the place to locals and visitors alike.

◎ Friedrichshain

This notorious party district also has a serious side, especially when it comes to blockbuster vestiges of the GDR era such as the East Side Gallery (p43), and **Karl-Marx-Allee** (Map p70; ⓊStrausberger Platz, Weberwiese, Frankfurter Tor) **FREE**. Sights are spread out and best reached by public transport.

Volkspark
Friedrichshain   Park
(Map p74; bounded by Am Friedrichshain, Friedenstrasse, Danziger Strasse & Landsberger Allee; ◐24hr; ⛲142, 200, ⛲21, M4, M5, M6, M8, M10, ⓊSchillingstrasse) Berlin's oldest public park has provided relief from urban life since 1840, but has been hilly only since the late 1940s, when wartime debris was piled up here to create two 'mountains' – the taller one, Mont Klamott **FREE**, rises 78m high. Diversions include expansive lawns for lazing, tennis courts, a half-pipe for skaters, a couple of handily placed beer gardens and an outdoor cinema.

Computerspiele-
museum   Museum
(Computer Games Museum; Map p70; ☏030-6098 8577; www.computerspielemuseum.de; Karl-Marx-Allee 93a; adult/concession €9/6, after 6pm €7/5; ◐10am-8pm; ⛲240, 347, ⓊWeberwiese) No matter if you grew up with Nimrod, Pac-Man, World of Warcraft or no games at all, this well-curated museum takes you on a fascinating trip down computer-game memory lane while putting the industry's evolution into historical and cultural context. Colourful and engaging, it features interactive stations amid hundreds of original exhibits, including an ultrarare 1972 Pong arcade machine and its twisted modern cousin, the 'PainStation' (must be over 18 to play…).

SVETLANA TURCHENICK/SHUTTERSTOCK ©

Tiergarten (p67)

⊚ Kreuzberg & Neukölln

Kreuzberg and Neukölln are home to Berlin's most colourful hangs, with a gritty, global-village atmosphere flavoured by a burgeoning roster of eclectic eateries, bars, nightlife and indie shopping.

Jüdisches Museum   Museum
(Jewish Museum; Map p78; ☑030-2599 3300; www.jmberlin.de; Lindenstrasse 9-14; adult/ concession €8/3, audioguide €3; ☺10am-8pm; ⑪Hallesches Tor, Kochstrasse) In a landmark building by American-Polish architect Daniel Libeskind, Berlin's Jewish Museum offers a chronicle of the trials and triumphs in 2000 years of Jewish life in Germany. The exhibit smoothly navigates all major periods, from the Middle Ages via the Enlightenment to the community's post-1990 renaissance. Find out about Jewish cultural contributions, holiday traditions, the difficult road to emancipation, outstanding individuals (eg Moses Mendelssohn and Levi Strauss) and the fates of ordinary people.

Tempelhofer Feld   Park
(www.gruen-berlin.de/tempelhofer-feld; enter via Oderstrasse, Tempelhofer Damm or Columbiadamm; ☺sunrise to sunset; ⑪; ⑪Paradestrasse, Boddinstrasse, Leinestrasse, Tempelhof, Ⓢ Tempelhof) ⚑ FREE The airfield of Tempelhof Airport, which so gloriously handled the Berlin airlift of 1948–49, has been repurposed as one of the largest urban parks in the world. In this non-commercial open-sky adventure playground, cyclists, bladers and kite-surfers whisk along the tarmac, while fun zones include the **Luftgarten** (☑0152 2255 9174; www.luftgarten-berlin.de; enter Columbiadamm; ☺11am-midnight or later Apr-Oct, weather permitting; ⑪Boddinstrasse) beer garden, barbecue areas, bike rentals, an artsy mini-golf course, a skatepark, an outdoor classroom, art installations, and urban gardening projects. More than two dozen panels provide historical background information.

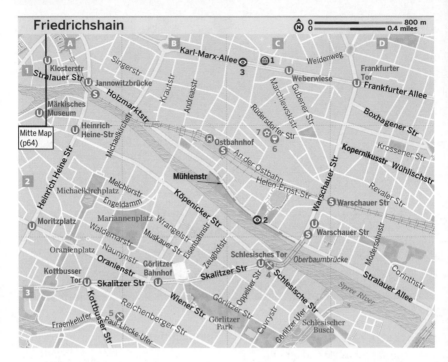

Schöneberg

Though devoid of blockbuster sights, Schöneberg has a few niche museums that are worth your while.

Museum der Unerhörten Dinge Museum

(Museum of Unheard of Things; ☏030-781 4932, 0175 410 9120; www.museumderunerhoerten dinge.de; Crellestrasse 5-6; ☺3-7pm Wed-Fri; ⓤKleistpark, Ⓢ Julius-Leber-Brücke) FREE 'Every object tells a story' could be the motto of this kooky collection of curiosities. Find madness nibbling at your psyche as you try to find the meaning in displays about Swiss cowpat-worshippers or Goethe's stone rose. It may all be a mind-bending spoof or a complete exercise in irony by founder Roland Albrecht. But one thing's certain: it will challenge the way you look at museums.

Schwules Museum Museum

(Gay Museum; Map p78; ☏030-6959 9050; www. schwulesmuseum.de; Lützowstrasse 73; adult/

concession €7.50/4; ☺2-6pm Mon, Wed, Fri & Sun, to 8pm Thu, to 7pm Sat; ☐M29, ⓤNollendorfplatz, Kurfürstenstrasse) In a former print shop, this nonprofit museum is one of the largest and most important cultural institutions documenting LGBTIQ+ culture around the world, albeit with a special focus on Berlin and Germany. It presents changing exhibits on gay icons, artists, gender issues and historical themes and also hosts film screenings and discussions to keep things dynamic.

Charlottenburg

The glittering heart of West Berlin during the Cold War, Charlottenburg is a big draw for shopaholics, royal groupies and art lovers. Its main sightseeing attraction is Schloss Charlottenburg (p52), with its park and adjacent art museums. About 3.5km southeast of here, the City West area, around Zoologischer Garten (Zoo Station), is characterised by Berlin's

Friedrichshain

biggest shopping boulevard, the Kurfürstendamm. After dark, the many fine restaurants and bars in this sedate and well-heeled borough teem with locals as well as tourists overnighting in the area's abundant hotels.

Kaiser-Wilhelm-Gedächtniskirche Church

(Kaiser Wilhelm Memorial Church; Map p80; ☎030-218 5023; www.gedaechtniskirche.com; Breitscheidplatz; ⊙church 9am-7pm, memorial hall 10am-6pm Mon-Sat, noon-5.30pm Sun; 🚌100, 200, Ⓤ Zoologischer Garten, Kurfürstendamm, Ⓢ Zoologischer Garten) FREE Allied bombing in 1943 left only the husk of the west tower of this once magnificent neo-Romanesque church standing. Now an antiwar memorial, it stands dignified amid the roaring traffic. Historic photographs displayed in the Gedenkhalle (Hall of Remembrance), at the bottom of the tower, help you visualise the former grandeur of this 1895 church. The adjacent octagonal hall of worship, added in 1961, has glowing midnight-blue glass walls and a giant 'floating' Jesus.

Story of Berlin Museum

(Map p80; ☎030-8872 0100; www.story-of-berlin.de; Kurfürstendamm 207-208, enter via Ku'damm Karree mall; adult/concession/child €12/9/5; ⊙10am-8pm, last admission 6pm; 🚌X9, X10, 109, 110, M19, M29, TXL, Ⓤ Uhlandstrasse) This engaging museum breaks 800 years of Berlin history into bite-size chunks that are easy to swallow but substantial enough to be satisfying. Each of the 23 rooms uses sound, light, technology and original objects to zero in on a specific theme or epoch in the city's history, from its founding in 1237 to the fall of the Berlin Wall. Tickets include a 45-minute tour (in

English) of a still-functional 1970s atomic bomb shelter beneath the building.

Zoo Berlin Zoo

(Map p80; ☎030-254 010; www.zoo-berlin.de; Hardenbergplatz 8; adult/child €15.50/8, with aquarium €21/10.50; ⊙9am-6.30pm Apr-Sep, to 6pm Mar & Oct, to 4.30pm Nov-Feb; 🚌100, 200, Ⓢ Zoologischer Garten, Ⓤ Zoologischer Garten, Kurfürstendamm) Berlin's zoo holds a triple record as Germany's oldest (since 1844), most-species-rich and most-popular animal park. Top billing at the moment goes to a pair of bamboo-devouring pandas on loan from China. The menagerie includes nearly 20,000 critters representing 1500 species, including orangutans, koalas, rhinos, giraffes and penguins. Public feeding sessions take place throughout the day – check the schedule online and by the ticket counter.

⊕ ACTIVITIES

Berlin's main appeal lies undeniably in its urban charisma, but if you've had your fill of sightseeing and partying, there are plenty of easy ways to let off some steam. In summer, swimming, bicycling and running are popular diversions, while in the colder month you can join locals in cheering on their favourite sports teams.

⊕ TOURS

Guided tours are a great way for getting a quick Berlin primer and plenty of companies are happy to show you around on foot or by bus, boat or bike – and in English! If you're short on time, let the sights whoosh by on a bus tour. Aside from traditional

Best Berlin Blogs

It's no secret that Berlin is a fast-changing city, so it's only natural that the food scene is also developing at lightning speed. Fortunately there are a number of passionate foodies keeping an eye on new openings and developments and generously sharing them on their (English-language) blogs. If you read German, also check out Mit Vergnügen (www.mitvergnuegen.com), Berlin Ick Liebe Dir (www.berlin-ick-liebe-dir.de) and GastroInferno (www.gastroinferno.com).

Berlin Food Stories (www.berlinfood stories.com) Excellent up-to-the-minute site by a dedicated food lover who keeps tabs on new restaurants and visits each one several times before writing honest, mouth-watering reviews. Also runs food tours – see the website for dates.

Stil in Berlin (www.stilinberlin.de) One of the longest-running city blogs (since 2006), Mary Sherpe's 'baby' keeps track of developments in food, fashion, style and art.

CeeCee (www.ceecee.cc) Stylish blog on what's hot and what's not across Berlin's culinary and cultural spectrum.

I Heart Berlin (www.iheartberlin.de) Long-running blog spreads the love about cool places and upcoming events.

Eatler (www.eatler.de) Irreverent and opinionated blog on restaurant openings and closings and emerging trends.

two- or three-hour spins, there are hop-on, hop-off tours as well as the handy bus lines 100 and 200 that let you see major landmarks for the price of a public transport ticket. Look for flyers in the hotel lobby or at tourist offices.

If you prefer sightseeing at a slower pace, join a walking tour. All run introductory spins around blockbuster and offbeat sights as well as themed tours (eg Third Reich, Cold War, Sachsenhausen, Potsdam).Walking tours are offered by the following companies.

Original Berlin Walks (030-301 9194; www.berlinwalks.de; adult/concession from €14/12)

New Berlin Tours (www.newberlintours.com; tours adult/concession from €14/12; free tour 10am, 11am, noon, 2pm & 4pm)

Brewer's Berlin Tours (0177 388 1537; www.brewersberlintours.com; adult/concession €15/12)

Insider Tour Berlin (030-692 3149; www.insidertour.com; adult/concession €14/12)

Alternative Berlin Tours (0162 819 8264; www.alternativeberlin.com; tours €12-35).

If you prefer to cover more ground, consider the following operators, who each offer a roster of similar tours.

Berlin on Bike (Map p74; 030-4373 9999; www.berlinonbike.de; Knaackstrasse 97, Kulturbrauerei, Court 4; tours incl bike adult/concession €24/20, bike rental per 24hr €10; 8am-8pm mid-Mar–mid-Nov, 10am-4pm Mon-Sat mid-Nov–mid-Mar; M1, Eberswalder Strasse)

Fat Tire Tours Berlin (Map p64; 030-2404 7991; www.fattiretours.com/berlin; Panoramastrasse 1a; adult/concession/under 12 incl bicycle from €28/26/14; Alexanderplatz, Alexanderplatz)

In fine weather, the most leisurely way to see the city is from its canals or rivers aboard a boat cruise, such as those offered by the following companies.

Reederei Riedel (030-6796 1470; www.reederei-riedel.de; tours from €14; Mar-Oct)

Stern und Kreisschiffahrt (030-536 3600; www.sternundkreis.de; tours from €15; Mar-Dec).

There are also all sorts of fascinating niche tours, including a Bowie Walk with **Berlin Music Tours** (0172 424 2037; www.musictours-berlin.com; Bowie walk €19; noon Sat & Sun Apr-Oct, 11.30am Nov-Mar) or a sustainable Berlin tour with **Green Me** (www.greenmeberlin.com; public tours per person €30-50, private tours on request) 🐾.

🔒 SHOPPING

Berlin is a great place to shop, and we're definitely not talking malls and chains. The city's appetite for the individual manifests in small neighbourhood boutiques and buzzing markets that are a pleasure to explore.

KaDeWe
Department Store

(Map p80; 📞030-212 10; www.kadewe.de; Tauentzienstrasse 21-24; ⊗10am-8pm Mon-Thu, to 9pm Fri, 9.30am-8pm Sat; Ⓤ Wittenbergplatz) Continental Europe's largest department store has been going strong since 1907 and boasts an assortment so vast that a pirate-style campaign is the best way to plunder its bounty. If pushed for time, at least hurry up to the legendary 6th-floor gourmet-food hall. The name, by the way, stands for *Kaufhaus des Westens* (department store of the West).

LP12 Mall of Berlin
Mall

(Map p78; www.mallofberlin.de; Leipziger Platz 12; ⊗10am-9pm Mon-Sat; 📶; 🚌200, Ⓤ Potsdamer Platz, Ⓢ Potsdamer Platz) This sparkling retail quarter is tailor-made for black-belt mall rats. More than 270 shops vie for your shopping euros, including flagship stores by Karl Lagerfeld, Hugo Boss, Liebeskind, Marc Cain, Muji and other international high-end brands, alongside the usual high-street chains like Mango and H&M. Free mobile-phone recharge stations in the basement and on the 2nd floor.

Bikini Berlin
Mall

(Map p80; 📞030-5549 6455; www.bikini berlin.de; Budapester Strasse 38-50; ⊗shops 10am-8pm Mon-Sat, bldg 9am-8.30pm Mon-Sat, noon-6pm Sun; 📶; 🚌100, 200, Ⓤ Zoologischer Garten, Ⓢ Zoologischer Garten) Germany's first concept mall opened in 2014 in a smoothly rehabilitated 1950s' architectural icon nicknamed 'Bikini' because of its design: 200m-long upper and lower

 Berlin Loves to Boogie

Since the 1990s, Berlin's club culture has taken on near-mythical status and, to no small degree, contributed to the magnetism of the German capital. It has incubated trends and sounds, launched the careers of such internationally renowned DJs as Paul van Dyk, Ricardo Villalobos, Ellen Allien and Paul Kalkbrenner, and put Berlin firmly on the map of global music fans who turn night into day in the over 200 clubs in this curfew-free city.

What distinguishes the Berlin scene from other party capitals is a focus on independent, non-mainstream niche venues, run by owners or collectives with a creative rather than a corporate background. The shared goal is to promote a diverse, inclusive and progressive club culture rather than to maximise profit. This is also reflected in a door policy that strives to create a harmonious balance in terms of age, gender and attitude.

TOMML/GETTY IMAGES ©

sections separated by an open floor, now chastely covered by a glass facade. Inside are three floors of urban indie boutiques, short-lease pop-up 'boxes' for up-and-comers, and an international street-food court.

FLEA MARKETS

Flea markets are like urban archaeology: you'll need plenty of patience and luck when sifting through other people's

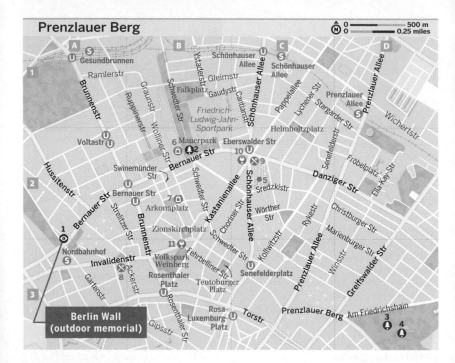

Prenzlauer Berg

cast-offs, but oh, the thrill, when you finally unearth a piece of treasure! Berlin's numerous hunting grounds set up on weekends (usually Sunday) year-round – rain or shine – and are also the purview of fledgling local fashion designers and jewellery makers. The most famous market is the weekly **Flohmarkt am Mauerpark** (Map p74; www.flohmarktimmauerpark.de; Bernauer Strasse 63-64; ☻9am-6pm Sun; ☐M1, M10, 12, Ⓤ Eberswalder Strasse) in Prenzlauer Berg, which is easily combined with a visit to nearby **Trödelmarkt Arkonaplatz** (Map p74; www.troedelmarkt-arkonaplatz.de; Arkonaplatz; ☻10am-4pm Sun; ☐M1, M10, Ⓤ Bernauer Strasse).

⊗ EATING

Berlin's food scene is growing in leaps and bounds and maturing as beautifully as a fine Barolo. Sure, you can still get your fill of traditional German comfort staples, from sausage to roast pork knuckle, but

it's the influx of experimental chefs from around the globe that makes eating in the capital such a delicious and exciting experience.

⊗ Mitte

Katz Orange International €€

(Map p74; ☑030-983 208 430; www.katz orange.com; Bergstrasse 22; mains €17-24; ☻6-11pm; ☐M8, Ⓤ Rosenthaler Platz) ✿ With its holistic farm-to-table menu, stylish country flair and top-notch cocktails, the 'Orange Cat' hits a gastro grand slam. It will have you purring for such favourites as Duroc pork that's been slow-roasted for 12 hours (nicknamed 'candy on bone'). The setting in a castle-like former brewery is stunning, especially in summer when the patio opens.

Ki-Nova International €€

(Map p78; ☑030-2546 4860; www.ki-nova. de; Potsdamer Strasse 2; mains €9-17; ☻11.30am-11pm Mon-Fri, 1-11pm Sat, 1-9pm Sun;

Prenzlauer Berg

◉ **Sights**
  1 Gedenkstätte Berliner Mauer A2
  2 Mauerpark B2
  3 Mont Klamott D3
  4 Volkspark Friedrichshain D3

◉ **Activities, Courses & Tours**
  5 Berlin on Bike C2

◉ **Shopping**
  6 Flohmarkt im Mauerpark B2

  7 Trödelmarkt Arkonaplatz B2

⊗ **Eating**
  8 Katz Orange A3
  9 Konnopke's Imbiss C2

◉ **Drinking & Nightlife**
  10 Prater Garten C2
  11 Weinerei Forum B3

🖼📷; 🚌200, Ⓤ Potsdamer Platz, Ⓢ Potsdamer Platz) 🍴 The name of this lunchtime favourite hints at the concept: 'ki' is Japanese for energy and 'nova' Latin for new. 'New energy' in this case translates into health-focused yet comforting bites starring global and regional superfoods from kale to cranberries. The contempo interior radiates urban warmth with heavy plank tables, black tiled bar, movie stills and floor-to-ceiling windows.

Cookies Cream Vegetarian €€€

(Map p64; ☎030-2749 2940; www.cookies cream.com; Behrenstrasse 55; mains €25, 3-/4-course menu €49/59; ⊗6pm-midnight Tue-Sat; 🍴; Ⓤ Französische Strasse) In 2017, this perennial local favourite became Berlin's first flesh-free restaurant to enter the Michelin pantheon, on its 10th anniversary no less. Its industrial look and clandestine location are as unorthodox as the compositions of head chef Stephan Hentschel. The entrance is off the service alley of the Westin Grand Hotel (past the chandelier, ring the bell).

Pauly Saal German €€€

(Map p64; ☎030-3300 6070; www.paulysaal. com; Auguststrasse 11-13; 3-/4-course lunches €69/85, 7-course dinners €115; ⊗noon-2pm & 6-9.30pm Tue-Sat, bar to 2.30am; 🚇M1, Ⓢ Oranienburger Strasse, Ⓤ Oranienburger Tor) Since taking the helm at this Michelin-starred outpost, Arne Anker has given the cuisine a youthful and light edge while following the seasonal-regional credo. Only multicourse menus are served,

even at lunch. The venue itself – in the edgy-art-decorated gym of a former **Jewish girls' school** (Jüdische Mädchenschule; Map p64; www.maedchenschule.org; Auguststrasse 11-13; ⊗hours vary) 𝗙𝗥𝗘𝗘 in a Bauhaus building – is simply stunning.

⊗ Prenzlauer Berg

Konnopke's Imbiss German €

(Map p74; ☎030-442 7765; www.konnopke -imbiss.de; Schönhauser Allee 44a; sausages €1.60-2.90; ⊗10am-8pm Mon-Fri, 11.30am-8pm Sat; 🚇M1, M10, M13, Ⓤ Eberswalder Strasse) Brave the inevitable queue at this famous sausage kitchen, ensconced in the same spot below the elevated U-Bahn tracks since 1930, but now equipped with a heated pavilion and an English menu. The 'secret' sauce topping is classic *Currywurst* and comes in a four-tier heat scale from mild to wild.

⊗ Kreuzberg & Friedrichshain

Burgermeister Burgers €

(Map p70; ☎030-2388 3840; www.burger -meister.de; Oberbaumstrasse 8; burgers €3.50-4.80; ⊗11am-3am Mon-Thu, 11am-4am Fri, noon-4am Sat, noon-3am Sun; Ⓤ Schlesisches Tor) It's green, ornate, a century old and... it used to be a toilet. Now it's a burger joint beneath the elevated U-Bahn tracks. Get in line for the plump all-beef patties (try the Meisterburger with fried onions, bacon and barbecue sauce) tucked between a brioche bun and paired with thickly cut cheese fries. Fast-food heaven!

Cocolo
Ramenbar   Japanese €

(Map p70; ☏030-9833 9073; www.kuchi.de;
Paul-Lincke-Ufer 39-40; soups €9-12;
☺noon-11pm Mon-Sat, 6pm-midnight Sun;
☏; Ⓤ Kottbusser Tor) For some of Berlin's
top Japanese soups, follow locals to this
lantern-lit canal-side charmer, where
homemade noodles, fresh vegetables
and toppings from egg to wakame bathe
in a richly flavoured pork broth. The
heart-warming winter dish is also a nice
good-weather nosh, best enjoyed on the
terrace with canal views.

Schöneberg

Cafe Einstein
Stammhaus   Austrian €€€

(Map p78; ☏030-2639 1917; www.cafeein
stein.com; Kurfürstenstrasse 58; breakfast
€7-15, mains dinner €19-32; ☺8am-midnight;
Ⓤ Nollendorfplatz) In the former home
of silent-movie star Henny Porten, this
Vienna-style cafe is the living room of
moneyed, genteel types reading the
morning paper over black coffee or
tucking into *Wiener Schnitzel* at night. The
'Einstein breakfast' is a prime pick any
time of day (served until 6pm). Marble
tabletops, jumbo-sized mirrors and high
stucco-trimmed ceilings add to the sophisticated vibe.

Charlottenburg

Benedict   Breakfast €€

(☏030-994 040 997; www.benedict-breakfast.
de; Uhlandstrasse 49; breakfast €7.50-18;
☺24hr; ☏; Ⓤ Spichernstrasse) It's 4am or
4pm and you're in the mood for blueberry
pancakes or eggs benedict? No problem.
At this upbeat restaurant, breakfast – and
only breakfast! – is served, no matter
where the hands of the clock. Portions
are as huge as the selection, which
takes inspiration from around the world,
from classic German spreads to American steak and eggs via North African
shakshuka.

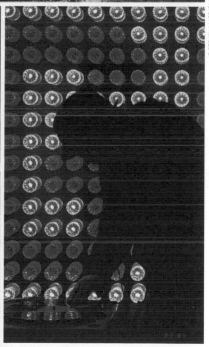

From left: Swimming by the Spree; Friedrichshain nightclub; Beach bar; DJ

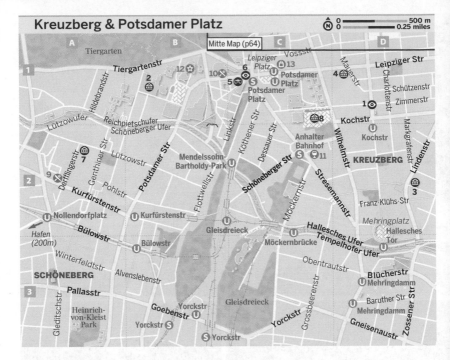

Kreuzberg & Potsdamer Platz

Mitte Map (p64)

500 m
0.25 miles

Good Friends
Chinese €€

(Map p80; ☑030-313 2659; www.good friends-berlin.de; Kantstrasse 30; 2-course weekday lunch €7-7.70, dinner mains €8-21; ☺noon-1am; ⑤Savignyplatz) Good Friends is widely considered Berlin's best Cantonese restaurant. The ducks dangling in the window are merely a nod to a menu long enough to confuse Confucius, including plenty of authentic homestyle dishes (on a separate menu). If steamed chicken feet prove too challenging, you can always fall back on sweet-and-sour pork or fried rice with shrimp.

● DRINKING & NIGHTLIFE

From cocktail lairs and concept bars, craft beer pubs to rooftop lounge, the next thirst parlour is usually within stumbling distance.

● Mitte

Rooftop Terrace
Bar

(Map p64; ☑030-460 6090; www.roccoforte hotels.com; Behrenstrasse 37, Hotel de Rome; ☺3-11pm Mon-Fri, from noon Sat & Sun May-Sep, weather permitting; ☎; ☐100, 200, TXL, ⑪Hausvogteiplatz) A hushed, refined ambience reigns at the rooftop bar of the exclusive Hotel de Rome, where you can keep an eye on the Fernsehturm (TV Tower), historic landmarks and the construction projects along Unter den Linden. It's a chill spot for an afternoon coffee, a glass of homemade ginger lemonade or sunset cocktails with bar snacks.

Solar Lounge
Bar

(Map p78; ☑0163 765 2700; www.solar-berlin.de; Stresemannstrasse 76; ☺6pm-2am Sun-Thu, to 3am Fri & Sat; ⑤Anhalter Bahnhof) Watch the city light up from this 17th-floor glass-walled sky lounge above a posh restaurant. With its

Kreuzberg & Potsdamer Platz

dim lighting, soft black leather couches and breathtaking panorama, it's a great spot for sunset drinks or a date. Getting there aboard an exterior glass lift is half the fun. The entrance is behind the Pit Stop auto shop.

Café am Neuen See   Beer Garden
(Map p80; ☑030-254 4930; www.cafeamneuen see.de; Lichtensteinallee 2; ☺restaurant 9am-11pm, beer garden noon-late Mon-Fri, 11am-late Sat & Sun; ☻; ☐200, Ⓤ Zoologischer Garten, ⓈZoologischer Garten, Tiergarten) Next to an idyllic lake in Tiergarten, this restaurant gets jammed year-round for its sumptuous breakfast and seasonal fare, but it really comes into its own during beer garden season. Enjoy a microvacation over a cold one and a pretzel or pizza, then take your sweetie for a spin in a rowing boat. Children's playground, too.

⊖ Prenzlauer Berg & Friedrichshein

Berghain/Panorama Bar   Club
(Map p70; www.berghain.de; Am Wriezener Bahnhof; ☺Fri-Mon; ⓈOstbahnhof) Only world-class DJs heat up this hedonistic bass-junkie hellhole, found inside a labyrinthine ex-powerplant. Hard-edged minimal techno dominates the ex-turbine hall (Berghain) while house dominates at Panorama Bar, one floor up. Long lines, strict door, no cameras. Check the website for midweek concerts and record-release parties at the main venue and the adjacent **Kantine am Berghain** (admission varies; ☺hours vary).

Prater Garten   Beer Garden
(Map p74; ☑030-448 5688; www.pratergar ten.de; Kastanienallee 7-9; snacks €2.50-7.50; ☺noon-late Apr-Sep, weather permitting; ☻; ☐M1, 12, Ⓤ Eberswalder Strasse) Berlin's oldest beer garden has seen beer-soaked days and nights since 1837. It is still a charismatic spot for guzzling a custom-brewed Prater pilsner (self-service) beneath the ancient chestnut trees. Kids can romp around the small play area.

Weinerei Forum   Wine Bar
(Map p74; ☑030-440 6983; www.weinerei.com; Fehrbelliner Strasse 57; ☺10am-midnight; ☎; ☐M1, Ⓤ Rosenthaler Platz) After 8pm, this living-room-style cafe turns into a wine bar that works on the honour principle: you 'rent' a wine glass for €2, then help yourself to as much vino as you like and at the end decide what you want to pay. Please be fair to keep this fantastic system going.

⊖ Kreuzberg & Neukölln

Griessmühle   Club
(www.griessmuehle.de; Sonnenallee 221; ☺club from 10pm Fri & Sat; ⓈSonnenallee) Hugging an idyllic canal in Neukölln, Griessmühle is a sprawling indoor–outdoor space with a funky garden strewn with tree houses, Trabis (GDR-era cars) and flower beds. The project by the ZMF artist collective woos attitude-free electro lovers with an events roster that includes not only parties and concerts but also a monthly flea market, movie nights and ping-pong parties.

Charlottenburg

Klunkerkranich

Bar

(www.klunkerkranich.de; Karl-Marx-Strasse 66; ⊗4pm-2am; 🚇; ⓤRathaus Neukölln) In the warmer months, vibes, views and sounds are the ammo of this club-garden-bar combo on the rooftop parking deck of the Neukölln Arcaden shopping mall. It's a great place for day-to-night drinking and chilling to local DJs or bands. Sustenance is provided. Check the website – these folks come up with new ideas all the time (gardening workshops anyone?).

🍷 Schöneberg & Charlottenburg

Monkey Bar

Bar

(Map p80; ☑030-120 221 210; www.monkey barberlin.de; Budapester Strasse 40; ⊗noon-2am; 🚇; 🚌100, 200, ⓢZoologischer Garten, ⓤZoologischer Garten) On the 10th floor of the 25hours Hotel Bikini Berlin, this mainstream-hip 'urban jungle' delivers

fabulous views of the city and Zoo Berlin while the menu gives prominent nods to tiki concoctions (great Mai Tai!) and gin-based cocktail sorcery. Come early for chilled sundowners on the sweeping terrace. Different DJs spin nightly Friday to Sunday, from 4pm.

Möve im Felsenkeller

Pub

(☑030-781 3447; Akazienstrasse 2; ⊗4pm-midnight Mon-Sat; ⓤEisenacher Strasse) An artist hang-out since the 1920s, this woodsy Old Berlin pub is where Jeffrey Eugenides penned his bestseller *Middlesex* (upstairs, at the round table in the corner). A stuffed seagull dangles from the ceiling of the storied haunt where you can choose from six beers on tap.

Hafen

Bar

(Map p78; ☑030-211 4118; www.hafen-berlin.de; Motzstrasse 19; ⊗from 7pm; ⓤNollendorfplatz) This 'Harbour' has been a friendly stop to dock at for about a quarter of a century.

Charlottenburg

It's still a good place to ease into the night with dancing, theme parties, drinking and flirting.

⭐ ENTERTAINMENT

Berlin's cultural scene is lively, edgy and the richest and most varied in the German-speaking world. With three state-supported opera houses, five major orchestras – including the world-class **Berliner Philharmoniker** (Map p78; ☑tickets 030-2548 8999; www.berliner-philharmoniker.de; Herbert-von-Karajan-Strasse 1; tickets €21-290; ☒M29, M48, M85, 200, ⓢPotsdamer Platz, ⓤPotsdamer Platz) – scores of theatres, cinemas, cabarets and concert venues, Berlin is replete with entertainment options.

ℹ️ INFORMATION

Visit Berlin (www.visitberlin.de), the Berlin tourist board, operates five walk-in offices, info desks at the airports, and a **call centre** (☑030-2500 2333; ⊗9am-6pm Mon-Fri) whose multilingual staff field general questions and make hotel and ticket bookings.

Alexanderplatz (☑030-250 025; lobby Park Inn, Alexanderplatz 7; ⊗7am-9pm Mon-Sat, 8am-6pm Sun; ☒100, 200, TXL, ⓤAlexanderplatz, ⓢAlexanderplatz)

Brandenburger Tor (Map p64; ☑030-250 023; Pariser Platz, Brandenburger Tor, south wing; ⊗9.30am-7pm Apr-Oct, to 6pm Nov-Mar; ⓢBrandenburger Tor, ⓤBrandenburger Tor)

Central Bus Station (ZOB) (Masurenallee 4-6; ⊗8am-8pm Mon, Fri & Sat, to 4pm Tue-Thu & Sun; ⓢMesse Nord/ICC)

Europa-Center (Map p80; ☑030-2500 2333; Tauentzienstrasse 9, Europa-Center, ground fl; ⊗10am-8pm Mon-Sat; ☒100, 200, ⓤKurfürstendamm, Zoologischer Garten, ⓢZoologischer Garten)

Hauptbahnhof (☑030-250 025; Hauptbahnhof, Europaplatz entrance, ground fl; ⊗8am-10pm; ⓢHauptbahnhof, ⊠Hauptbahnhof)

ℹ️ GETTING THERE & AWAY

AIR

Until completion of the Berlin Brandenburg Airport (due in 2020, currently 8 years behind schedule), flights continue to land at Berlin's **Tegel Airport** (TXL; www.berlin-airport.de; ☒Flughafen Tegel), about 8km northwest of the city centre, and at **Schönefeld Airport** (SXF; www.berlin-airport.de; ⊠Airport-Express, RE7 & RB14, ⓢS9, S45), about 24km southeast.

BUS

Travelling to Berlin by coach has become easy, affordable and popular. Buses are comfortable, clean and air-conditioned; some offer free on-board wi-fi and sell snacks and soft drinks.

Having gobbled up much of its competitors, **Flixbus** (www.flixbus.de) is now the main operator with only **Eurolines** (www.eurolines.de) holding its own, at least for now. A handy intercity bus search engine is www.busradar.com.

TRAIN

Berlin is well connected by **Deutsche Bahn** (☐01806 99 66 33; www.bahn.de) rail services throughout Germany and to popular European destinations, including Prague, Warsaw and Amsterdam.

While all long-distance trains converge at the Hauptbahnhof, some also stop at other stations such as Spandau, Ostbahnhof, Gesundbrunnen and Südkreuz.

Europe's biggest long-distance coach company Flixbus has also launched Flixtrain (www.flixtrain.de). Since August 2017, its mamba-green carriages trundle from Berlin to Stuttgart with stops in Frankfurt and Heidelberg, among others. Prices are generally much lower than Deutsche Bahn's. Trains depart from many Berlin train stations, including Haupbahnhof, Ostbahnhof and Bahnhof Zoo.

 GETTING AROUND

TO/FROM THE AIRPORT
TEGEL

TXL express bus to Alexanderplatz (40 minutes) and bus X9 for CityWest (eg Zoo station, 20 minutes), €2.80; taxi €25.

SCHÖNEFELD

Airport-Express trains (RB14 or RE7) to central Berlin twice hourly (30 minutes), and S9 trains every 20 minutes for Friedrichshain and Prenzlauer Berg, €3.40; taxi to city centre €45 to €50.

PUBLIC TRANSPORT

Berlin's comprehensive public transport system is administered by BVG and consists of the U-Bahn (subway), the S-Bahn (light rail), buses and trams. For full information and a handy journey planner, go to www.bvg.de.

For most rides you need an AB ticket (€2.80) valid for two hours with transfers permitted in the direction of travel. If you're taking more than two trips per day, a *Tageskarte* (day pass) is good value (€7).

U-BAHN

Most efficient way to travel; operates 4am to 12.30am and all night Friday, Saturday and public holidays. From Sunday to Thursday, half-hourly night buses take over in the interim.

S-BAHN

Less frequent than U-Bahn trains but with fewer stops, and thus useful for longer distances. Same operating hours as the U-Bahn.

BUS & TRAM

Buses are slow but useful for sightseeing on the cheap and run frequently 4.30am to 12.30am; half-hourly night buses in the interim. MetroBuses (designated eg M1, M19) operate 24/7.

Trams operate only in the eastern districts; MetroTrams (designated eg M1, M2) run 24/7.

TAXI

Can be hailed or ordered by phone (030-20 20 20) or smartphone app. Taxi ranks are ubiquitous in the centre.

Where to Stay

Berlin offers the gamut of places to rest your weary head: from a former bank, boat or factory, in the home of a silent-movie diva or in a 'flying bed'. Too off-beat? Every major international chain has a showcase property here.

Neighbourhood	Atmosphere
Mitte	Close to major sights; great transport links; top hotels and restaurants; can be touristy and expensive.
Museumsinsel & Alexanderplatz	Supercentral sightseeing quarter; easy transport access; mainstream shopping; large and new hotels; no nightlife.
Potsdamer Platz & Tiergarten	Cutting-edge architecture; high-end hotels; top museums; next to huge Tiergarten city park; limited eating options and no nightlife.
Scheunenviertel	Hipster; trendy, historic, central; boutique hotels; indie shopping; strong cafe scene; street art; can be pricey and busy.
City West & Charlottenburg	Great shopping; stylish bars and quality restaurants; good-value lodging; historic B&Bs; far from key sights and happening nightlife.
Kreuzberg & Neukölln	Vibrant arty, underground and multicultural party quarter; best for bar-hopping and clubbing; foodie scene; street art; gritty, noisy and busy; away from main sights.
Friedrichshain	Student and family quarter; nightlife; superb Cold War–era sights; transport difficult in some areas and limited sleeping options.
Prenzlauer Berg	Clean residential area; lively cafe and restaurant scene; indie boutiques; limited late-night action; few essential sights.

POTSDAM

Potsdam

Potsdam, on the Havel River just 25km southwest of central Berlin, is the capital and crown jewel of the federal state of Brandenburg. Easily reached by S-Bahn, the former Prussian royal seat is the most popular day trip from Berlin, luring visitors with its splendid gardens and palaces that garnered Unesco World Heritage status in 1990.

Headlining the roll call of royal pads is Schloss Sanssouci, the private retreat of King Friedrich II (Frederick the Great). He was also the mastermind behind many of Potsdam's other fabulous parks and palaces, which miraculously survived WWII.

Potsdam in One Day

If, like many visitors, you only have a day to spend in delightful Potsdam, a visit to the city's magnificent palaces should form the bulk of your itinerary. See **Schloss Sanssouci** (p88) with its spectacular gardens, **Schloss Cecilienhof** (p92), where the 1945 Potsdam Agreement deciding the post-war fate of Germany was signed, and the neighbouring **Marmorpalais** (p92), famed for its magnificent marble halls.

Potsdam in Two Days

If you're able to spend some more time in this attractive city, once the seat of Prussian kings, you'll have time to round out your Potsdam experience. Take a one-hour tour of Potsdam's wonderfully reconstructed **Stadtschloss** (p92), now home to the Brandenburg State Parliament, followed by a stroll around the delightfully contrasting **Dutch** (Holländisches Viertel; p92) and **Russian Quarters** (Alexandrowka; p92) and a visit to the sombre, off-the-beaten-track **Memorial Leistikowstrasse** (KGB Prison; p93).

Previous page: A typical red-brick house in Holländisches Viertel (Dutch Quarter; p92)

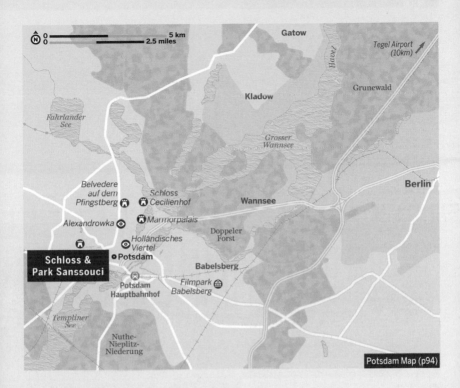

Potsdam Map (p94)

Arriving in Potsdam

Potsdam-Charlottenhof and **Potsdam-Sanssouci** are served by Regional trains (30 min) from Berlin Hauptbahnhof and Zoologischer Garten.

Potsdam Hauptbahnhof is served by the S7 from central Berlin (40 minutes, €3.30).

You need a ticket covering zones A, B and C (€3.40) for either service.

Sleeping

Most people visit Potsdam on a day trip from Berlin, but there are actually some extremely charming historical private hotels that would make an overnight stay quite enjoyable. All room rates are subject to a 5% tourist tax in addition to VAT (business travellers are exempt).

Neues Palais, Park Sanssouci

Schloss & Park Sanssouci

Potsdam's chief draws are the summer palaces and parks of Sanssouci, built and laid out in the 18th and 19th centuries. The park is huge and the sights numerous so choose what you want to see carefully.

Great For...

☑ Don't Miss

One of the joys of visiting Potsdam's palaces are the walks through exquisite parkland in between.

Schloss Sanssouci

Frederick the Great's famous summer **palace** (Map p94; adult/concession incl tour or audioguide €12/8; ⏰10am-5.30pm Tue-Sun Apr-Oct, to 5pm Nov & Dec, to 4.30pm Jan-Mar; 🚌614, 650, 695) was designed by Georg Wenzeslaus von Knobelsdorff in 1747; the rococo jewel sits daintily above vine-draped terraces with the king's grave nearby. Admission is limited and by timed ticket only; book online to guarantee entry. Otherwise, only city tours booked through the tourist office guarantee entry to the Schloss.

Standouts on the audioguided tours include the Konzertsaal (Concert Hall), whimsically decorated with vines, grapes and even a cobweb where sculpted spiders frolic. The king himself gave flute recitals here. Also note the intimate Bibliothek

Schloss Sanssouci

ⓘ Need to Know

Map p94; ☑0331-969 4200; www.spsg.de; Maulbeerallee; day pass to all palaces adult/concession €19/14; ⓢvaries by palace; ⓡ606, 695

✕ Take a Break

Picnic in one of the parks or try **Drachenhaus** (Map p94; ☑0331-505 3808; www.drachenhaus.de; Maulbeerallee 4; mains €10-25; ⓢ11am-7pm daily Apr-Oct, noon-6pm Tue-Sun Nov, Dec & Mar, noon-6pm Sat & Sun Jan & Feb)

★ Top Tip

Book your timed ticket to Schloss Sanssouci online to avoid wait times and/or disappointment. You can buy a one-day pass (€19) to all of Potsdam's palaces.

(library), lidded by a gilded sunburst ceiling, where the king would seek solace amid 2000 leather-bound tomes ranging from Greek poetry to the latest releases by his friend Voltaire. Another highlight is the Marmorsaal (Marble Room), an elegant white Carrara marble symphony modelled after the Pantheon in Rome.

As you exit the palace, don't be fooled by the Ruinenberg, a pile of classical 'ruins' looming in the distance: they're merely a folly conceived by Frederick the Great.

Neues Palais

The final palace commissioned by Frederick the Great, the **Neues Palais** (New Palace; Map p94; Am Neuen Palais; adult/concession incl tour or audioguide €8/6; ⓢ10am-5.30pm Mon & Wed-Sun Apr-Oct, to

5pm Nov-Dec, to 4.30pm Jan-Mar; ⓡ605, 606, 695, ⓢPotsdam Charlottenhof) has made-to-impress dimensions, a central dome and a lavish exterior capped with a parade of sandstone figures. The interior attests to the high level of artistry and craftsmanship of the 18th century. It's an opulent symphony of ceiling frescoes, gilded stucco ornamentation, ornately carved wainscoting and fanciful wall coverings alongside paintings (by Antoine Pesne, for example) and richly crafted furniture.

The palace was built in only six years, largely to demonstrate the undiminished power of the Prussian state following the bloody Seven Years' War (1756-63). The king himself rarely camped out here, preferring the intimacy of Schloss Sanssouci and using it for representational purposes only. Only the last German Kaiser, Wilhelm II, used it as a residence until 1918.

Chinesisches Haus

The 18th-century fad for the Far East is poignantly reflected in the **Chinese House** (Map p94; Am Grünen Gitter; adult/concession €4/3; ⊙10am-5.30pm Tue-Sun May-Oct; 🚌605, 606, 🚋91). The cloverleaf-shaped shutterbug favourite sports an enchanting exterior of exotically dressed gilded figures sipping tea, dancing and playing musical instruments amid palm-shaped pillars. Inside is a precious collection of Chinese and Meissen porcelain.

Bildergalerie

The **Bildergalerie** (Gallery of Old Masters; Map p94; Im Park Sanssouci 4; adult/concession €6/5; ⊙10am-5.30pm Tue-Sun May-Oct; 🚌650, 695) is the oldest royal museum in Germany and shelters a prized collection of Old Masters,

including works by Peter Paul Rubens and Caravaggio's *Doubting Thomas*.

The interior of the elongated hall with its gilded barrel-vaulted ceiling and patterned marble floors is perhaps just as impressive as the mostly large-scale paintings that cover practically every inch of wall space.

Neue Kammern

The **Neue Kammern** (New Chambers; Map p94; Park Sanssouci; adult/concession incl tour or audioguide €6/5; ⊙10am-5.30pm Tue-Sun Apr-Oct; 🚌614, 650, 695) were originally an orangery and later a guesthouse. The rococo interior drips in opulence, most notably in the Ovidsaal, a grand ballroom with a gilded relief, and in the Jasper Hall, drenched in precious stones and lidded by a Venus fresco.

Römische Bäder, Park Charlottenhof

Frederick's Postmortem Odyssey

Frederick the Great so loved Sanssouci he gave specific instructions to be buried – next to his beloved dogs – on the highest terrace of the vineyards in front of the palace. Alas, his nephew and successor Friedrich Wilhelm II blithely ignored his request, putting him instead next to his father, the 'Soldier King' Friedrich Wilhelm I, in a nearby church. In WWII the sarcophagi of both father and son were moved by German soldiers for safekeeping and, after the war, ended up in the ancestral Hohenzollern castle in southern Germany. Only after reunification, in 1991, did Frederick the Great get his final wish, being reburied in the exact spot he'd personally picked out more than 250 years before. It's marked by a simple gravestone.

What's Nearby?

Laid out by Peter Lenné for Friedrich Wilhelm IV, **Park Charlottenhof** (Geschwister-Scholl-Strasse 34a; ⑤Potsdam Charlottenhof Bahnhof) FREE segues imperceptibly from Park Sanssouci but gets far fewer visitors. Buildings here reflect the king's passion for Italy. The small neoclassical **Schloss Charlottenhof** (Charlottenhof Palace; tours adult/concession €6/5; ⊙tours 10am-5.30pm Tue-Sun May-Oct; 🚌605, 606, 610, X5, 🚋91, 94, 98), for instance, was modelled after a Roman villa. It was designed by Karl Friedrich Schinkel, who, aided by his student Ludwig Persius, also dreamed up the so-called **Römische Bäder** (Roman Baths; adult/concession €5/4; ⊙10am-5.30pm Tue-Sun May-Oct) in Park Charlottenhof. Despite the name, it's actually a romantic cluster of 15th-century Italian country-estate buildings (pictured left), complete with vine-draped pergola.

Getting There

Regional trains From Berlin Hauptbahnhof and Zoologischer Garten, trains arrive at Potsdam Hauptbahnhof (p95); some continue to Potsdam Charlottenhof and Sanssouci.

S-Bahn S7 from central Berlin.

Bus 614 and 695 go from Potsdam Hauptbahnhof straight to Schloss Sanssouci.

★ **Top Tip**

Park Sanssouci is open from dawn till dusk and no admission is charged, but avoid visiting on Mondays when most palaces are closed.

© STIFTUNG PREUSSISCHE SCHLOSSER UND GARTEN BERLIN-BRANDENBURG/ PHOTOGRAPHER: HANS BACH

✕ **Take a Break**

Try **Potsdam zur Historischen Mühle** (Map p94; ☎0331-281 493; www.moevenpick-restaurants.com; Zur Historischen Muhle 2; mains €11-20; ⊙8am-10pm; P🍴; 🚌614, 650, 695), which serves international favourites, and has a beer gardon and chidren's playground.

SIGHTS

Altstadt

Although much of Potsdam's historic town centre fell victim to WWII bombing and socialist town planning, it's been nicely restored and is worth exploring on foot. A landmark is the baroque **Brandenburger Tor** (Map p94; Luisenplatz; 🚌606, 631, 🚊91), a triumphal arch built to commemorate Frederick the Great's 1763 victory in the Seven Years' War. It's the gateway to pedestrianised Brandenburger Strasse, the main commercial drag, which links with the scenic Holländisches Viertel (Dutch Quarter).

Holländisches Viertel   Area

(Dutch Quarter; Map p94; www.hollaendisches viertel.net; Mittelstrasse; 🚌606, 631) This picturesque cluster of 134 gabled red-brick houses was built around 1730 for Dutch workers invited to Potsdam by Friedrich Wilhelm I. The entire district has been done up beautifully and brims with galleries, boutiques, cafes and restaurants; Mittelstrasse is especially scenic. Further up Friedrich-Ebert-Strasse is the Nauener Tor (Nauen Gate, 1755), a fanciful city gate.

**Potsdamer
Stadtschloss**   Historic Building

(Landtag Brandenburg, Potsdam City Palace; Map p94; 📞0331-966 1260; www.stadtschloss-pots dam.org; Alter Markt; 🕙usually 8am-5pm Mon-Fri; 🚌631, 🚊93, 98) **FREE** One of Potsdam's newest landmarks is this replica of the 18th-century Prussian City Palace that was partly destroyed in WWII and completely removed by East German town planners in 1960. It reopened in 2014 as the new home of the Brandenburg state parliament. Of the original building, only the ornate Fortuna Portal remains; it now forms the main entrance to the compound, sections of which (including the rooftop terrace and the staircase designed by Knobelsdorff) are open to the public.

Neuer Garten Area

North of the Potsdam old town, the winding lakeside Neuer Garten (New Garden) is laid out in natural English style on the western shore of the Heiliger See. It gets a lot less busy than Park Sanssouci (p91) and is a fine place in which to relax. A couple of palaces provide cultural diversions.

Marmorpalais   Palace

(Marble Palace; Map p94; 📞0331-969 4550; www.spsg.de; Im Neuen Garten 10; tours adult/ concession €6/5; 🕙10am-5.30pm Tue-Sun May-Oct & Sat & Sun Apr, to 4pm Sat & Sun Jan-Mar; 🚌603) As the name suggests, the early-neoclassical Marmorpalais is a symphony in colourful marble on floors, walls, ceilings and fireplaces. The palace was built in 1792 as a summer retreat for Friedrich Wilhelm II by Carl von Gontard and overlooks the Heiliger See. The most fanciful rooms are the Konzertsaal (concert hall), designed to resemble an antique temple, and the Turkish-tent-style Orientalisches Kabinett (Oriental Cabinet) upstairs.

Schloss Cecilienhof   Palace

(Map p94; 📞0331-969 4200; www.spsg.de; Im Neuen Garten 11; conference room adult/conces-sion €8/6, royal quarters €6/5; 🕙10am-5.30pm Tue-Sun Apr-Oct, to 5pm Nov-Dec, to 4.30pm Tue Jan-Mar; 🚌603) This English-style country palace, completed in 1917 for Crown Prince Wilhelm and his wife Cecilie, was the last residence built by the Hohenzollern clan. Their private quarters can be seen on a tour, but the site is mostly famous for hosting the 1945 Potsdam Conference where Stalin, Truman and Churchill (and later his successor Clement Attlee) hammered out Germany's post-war fate and incidentally laid the foundation for the Cold War.

Alexandrowka & Pfingstberg

North of the Altstadt, Potsdam slopes up to the Pfingstberg past a Russian colony, a Russian Orthodox church and a Jewish cemetery.

Alexandrowka   Area

(Map p94; 📞0331-817 0203; www.alexandrowka. de; Russische Kolonie; museum adult/concession/ under 14 €3.50/3/free; 🕙museum 10am-6pm Tue-Thu, Sat & Sun, to 9pm Fri mid-May–mid-Sep,

10am-5pm Fri-Sun Nov-Dec, 10am-6pm Tue-Sun Mar–mid-May & mid-Sep–Oct, closed Jan & Feb; P; 92, 96) One of Potsdam's most unusual neighbourhoods, Alexandrowka is a Russian colony that was a gift from Friedrich Wilhelm III to his close friend Tsar Alexander in 1820. The first residents were the singers of a Russian military choir who had delighted the king. Descendants of the original settlers still live in the chalet-like wooden houses surrounded by gardens and orchards. Learn more at the pretty little museum with nearby garden cafe.

Belvedere auf dem Pfingstberg
Palace

(Map p94; ☏0331-2005 7930; www.pfingst berg.de; Pfingstberg; adult/concession €4.50/ 3.50, audioguides €1; ☉10am-6pm daily Apr-Oct, to 4pm Sat & Sun Mar & Nov; P; 92, 96) For splendid views over Potsdam and surrounds, ascend the spiralling wrought-iron staircases of this twin-towered palace, commissioned by Friedrich Wilhelm IV and modelled on an Italian Renaissance-style villa. There's a small exhibit chronicling the history of the building and the 1801 Pomonatempel just below it. The latter was Karl Friedrich Schinkel's very first architectural commission at age 19.

Memorial Leistikowstrasse (KGB Prison)
Memorial

(Map p94; ☏0331-201 1540; www.gedenks taette-leistikowstrasse.de; Leistikowstrasse 1; ☉10am-6pm Tue-Sun; 92) FREE Now a memorial site, Potsdam's central remand prison for Soviet Counter Intelligence – colloquially known as 'KGB prison' – is a particularly sinister Cold War relic. All sorts of real or alleged crimes could land you here, including espionage, desertion, insubordination or Nazi complicity. Using letters, documents, photographs, personal items and taped interviews, exhibits outline the fate of individuals.

TOURS

Potsdam per Pedales
Cycling

(Map p94; ☏0331-8871 9917; www.potsdam per-pedales.de; Babelsberger Strasse 10; adult/

Birthplace of European Cinema

Film buffs will know that Potsdam is famous not merely for its palaces but also for being the birthplace of European film production. For it was here, in the suburb of Babelsberg, about 4km west of the city centre, that the venerable UFA Studio was founded in 1912. A few years later, it was already producing such seminal flicks as *Metropolis* and *Blue Angel.* Continuing as DEFA (Deutsche Filmakademie) in GDR times, the dream factory was resurrected as Studio Babelsberg after reunification and has since produced or coproduced such international blockbusters as *Inglourious Basterds*, *The Grand Budapest Hotel* and *The Hunger Games.*

There are two ways to plug into the Potsdam film experience. In town, handsome baroque royal stables now house the **Filmmuseum Potsdam** (Map p94; ☏0331-271 8112; www.filmmuseum-potsdam. de; Breite Strasse 1a; adult/concession €5/4; ☉10am-6pm Tue-Sun; 631, 93, 98), which presents an engaging romp through German movie history with an emphasis on the DEFA period. In Babelsberg, next to the actual film studios, **Filmpark Babelsberg** (☏0331-721 2750; www.filmpark-babelsberg.de; Grossbeerenstrasse 200; adult/concession/ child €22/18/15; ☉10am-6pm Apr-Sep, to 5pm Oct; P; 601, 690, S Potsdam Hauptbahnhof, Babelsberg) is a movie-themed amusement park with plenty of shows and behind-the-scenes tours.

Filmmuseum Potsdam

Potsdam

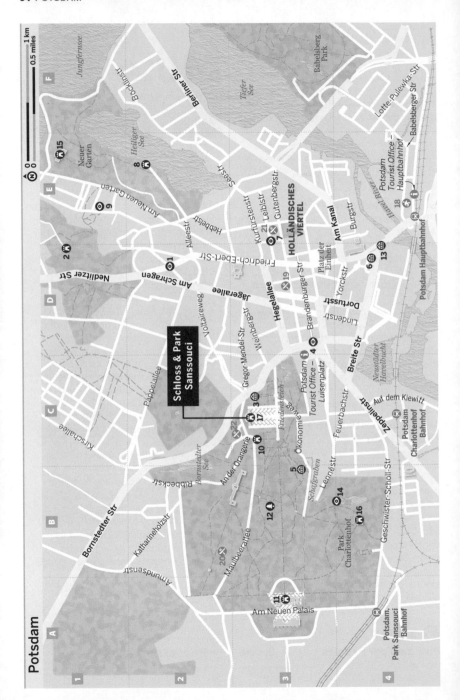

Potsdam

concession per day from €11/9, e-bike €25/20; ⊙7am-7pm Mon-Fri, 9.30am-7pm Sat & Sun Apr-Oct, 8am-7pm Mon-Fri, 9.30am-7pm Sun Nov-Mar; Ⓢ Potsdam Hauptbahnhof) This outfit rents quality bicycles and offers guided and self-guided bike tours.

✗ EATING

Potsdam's Altstadt brims with atmospheric eating options, especially in the Holländisches Viertel (p92). For cafes and fast food, head to the pedestrianised Brandenburger Strasse. However, even the centre gets very quiet at night.

Brasserie zu Gutenberg   French €€

(Map p94; ☎0331-7403 6878; www.brasserie-zu-gutenberg.de; Jägerstrasse 10; mains €9-28; ⊙noon-midnight; ☐604, 609, 638, ☐92, 96) This charming little brasserie with dark-wood tables and chocolate-brown banquettes is great for a hearty meal, perhaps featuring a steak cooked on the lava grill, or the signature coq au vin with a glass of fine Bordeaux. If you just need a little sustenance, order a *Flammkuchen* (Alsatian pizza), crêpes or *croque-monsieur* (fried ham and cheese sandwich).

Maison Charlotte   French €€€

(Map p94; ☎0331-280 5450; www.maison-charlotte.de; Mittelstrasse 20; Flammkuchen €8.50-14.50, mains €24.50-25.50, 3-/4-course menus €44/53; ⊙noon-11pm; ☐604, 609, 638, ☐92, 96) There's a rustic lyricism to the French country cuisine in this darling Dutch Quarter bistro, no matter whether your appetite runs towards a simple *Flammkuchen*, Breton fish soup or a multicourse menu. Bon vivants on a budget come for the daily lunch special (€7.50), which includes a glass of wine; it's best enjoyed on the patio in summer.

ⓘ INFORMATION

Potsdam Tourist Office (Map p94; ☎0331-2755 8899; www.potsdam-tourism.com; ⊙9.30am-6pm Mon-Sat) is located inside the train station. There's another office at **Luisenplatz** (Map p94; Luisenplatz 3; ⊙9.30am-6pm Mon-Sat year-round & 10am-4pm Sun Apr-Oct; ☐605, 631, 650). Because most people visit Potsdam on a day trip from Berlin, at night, the town can get pretty quiet, especially outside the busy summer months.

ⓘ GETTING THERE & AROUND

Regional trains leaving from Berlin Hauptbahnhof and Zoologischer Garten take about 25 minutes to reach Potsdam Hauptbahnhof; some continue on to Potsdam Charlottenhof and Potsdam Sanssouci, which are actually closer to Park Sanssouci (p91). The S7 from central Berlin makes the trip in about 40 minutes. You need a ticket covering zones ABC (€3.40) for either service.

Buses and trams operate throughout Potsdam. Buses for Sanssouci (lines 614 and 695) leave from right outside Potsdam Hauptbahnhof.

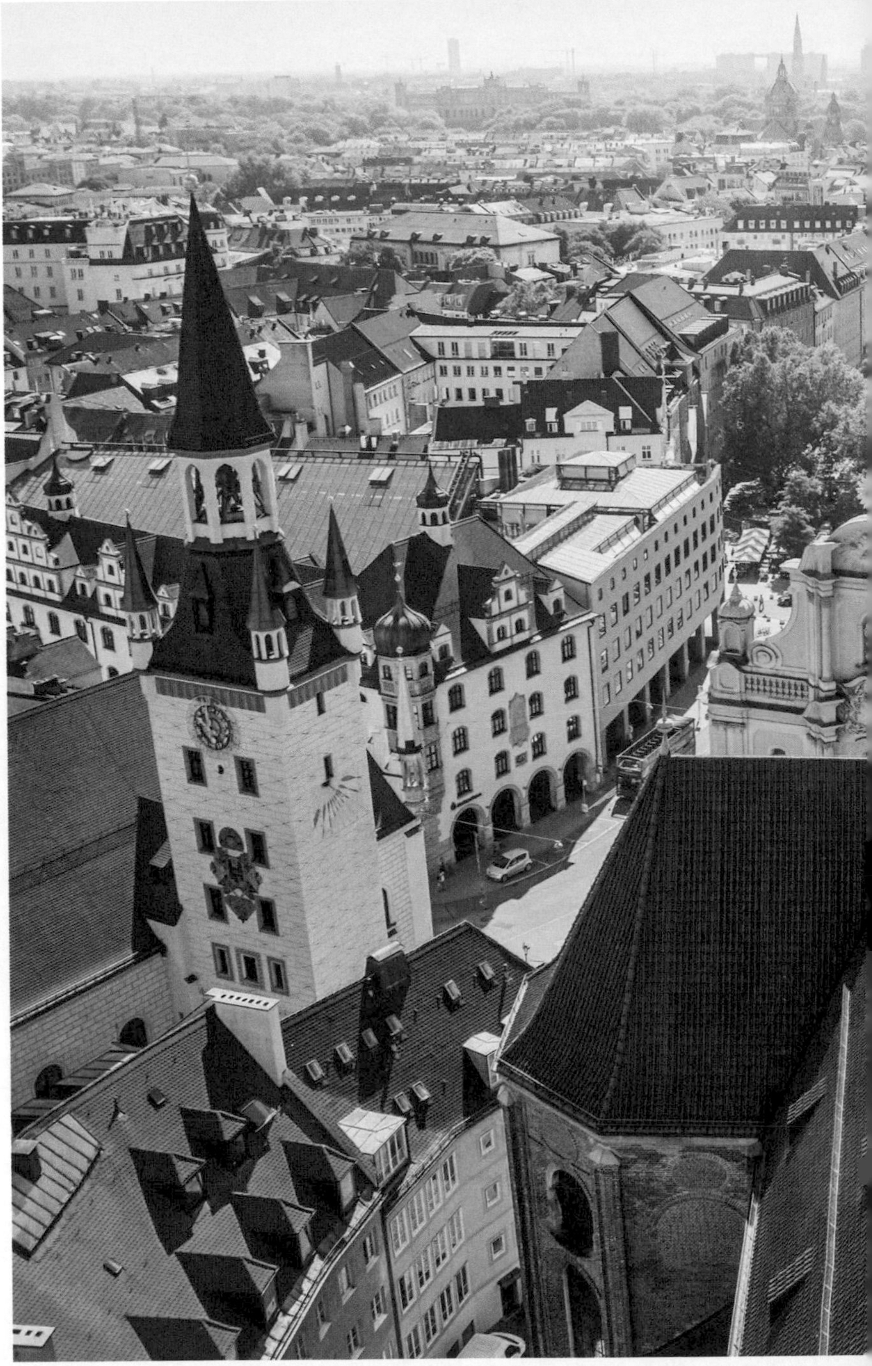

MUNICH

Munich

Munich is the natural habitat of well-heeled power dressers and Lederhosen-clad thigh-slappers, Mediterranean-style street cafes and Mitteleuropa beer halls, highbrow art and high-tech industry. Germany's unofficial southern capital is a flourishing success story that revels in its own contradictions.

Munich's walkable centre retains a small-town air but holds some world-class sights, especially galleries and museums. Throw in royal Bavarian heritage, an entire suburb of Olympic legacy and a kitbag of dark tourism, and it's clear why it's a favourite. You can seek out the past but hit the town once you're done.

Munich in Two Days

Start your day with breakfast at the **Viktualienmarkt** (p110) then cross the **Marienplatz** (p106) for a tour of the royal splendour of the **Residenz** (p110). Take a break in the English Garden, then spend the afternoon admiring technical achievements at the **Deutsches Museum** (p115). Finish the day at a typical Munich beer hall. Your second day can be devoted entirely to the top-notch museums and galleries in the Kunstareal.

Munich in Four Days

Start day three at **BMW World** (p113) and the **BMW Museum** (p113) followed by a clamber up the **Olympic Tower** (p113) at the **Olympiapark** (p113). In the afternoon head to **Nymphenburg** (p112) to see one of Bavaria's finest palaces. Finish off at one of the city's superb beer gardens. Board the S-Bahn on day four for trips to Starnberg and Dachau.

Previous page:Munich skyscape

Munich Altstadt Map (p108)
Central Munich Map (p116)

Arriving in Munich

Munich Airport Located about 30km northeast of the city, Munich's airport handles flights from all European capitals, tourist hotspots and some long-haul destinations.

Hauptbahnhof Situated at the western end of the city centre, Munich's main train station is a major terminus receiving local, national and international services.

Central Bus Station Located on the Stammstrecke with easy access to the rest of the city.

Allgäu Airport Some services touting themselves as flights to Munich actually land at Allgäu Airport near Memmingen, over 100km away.

Sleeping

Munich has the full range of accommodation options you would expect from a major city in Western Europe. Luxury hotels dot the centre, midrange places gather near the Hauptbahnhof. Room rates tend to be higher than in the rest of Bavaria, and they skyrocket during the Oktoberfest. However, midrange accommodation is cheaper here than in other major European cities.

A typical Oktoberfest beer tent

Oktoberfest

The world's most famous beer festival (held mid-September to early October) is an event only ever described in superlatives – biggest, most visited, longest-running...the list goes on. Come and join six million beer lovers for Munich's most raucous annual party.

Great For...

☑ Don't Miss

Dress the part: buy or hire some Bavarian Lederhosen (men) or a Dirndl (women).

Oktoberfest's Beginnings

It all started as an elaborate wedding toast – and turned into the world's biggest collective booze-up. In October 1810 the future king, Bavarian Crown Prince Ludwig I, married Princess Therese and the newlyweds threw an enormous party at the city gates, complete with a horse race. The next year Ludwig's fun-loving subjects came back for more. The festival was extended and, to fend off autumn, was moved forward to September. As the years rolled on, the racehorses were dropped and sometimes the party had to be cancelled, but the institution called Oktoberfest was here to stay.

F.CADIOU/GETTY IMAGES ©

❶ Need to Know

Oktoberfest (www.oktoberfest.de) is served by its own U-Bahn station called Theresienwiese.

✖ Take a Break

Bring a picnic to the Oktoberfest – the food is as pricey as the beer.

★ Top Tip

Hotels book out quickly and prices skyrocket, so reserve a year in advance if you can. If not, try booking a room in another part of Bavaria and coming by train.

Dirndl, Lederhosen & Wies'nbier

Nearly two centuries later, this 16-day extravaganza draws more than six million visitors a year to celebrate a marriage of good cheer and outright debauchery. A special dark, strong beer (*Wies'nbier*) is brewed for the occasion, and Müncheners spend the day at the office in Lederhosen and Dirndl in order to hit the festival right after work. No admission fee is charged, but most of the fun costs something.

Oktoberfest Traditions

On the meadow called Theresienwiese (Wies'n for short), 15 minutes' walk from the Hauptbahnhof, a temporary city is erected, consisting of beer tents, amusements and rides – just what drinkers need after several frothy ones! The action kicks off with the Brewer's Parade at 11am on the first day of the festival. The parade begins at Sonnenstrasse and winds its way to the fairgrounds via Schwanthalerstrasse. At noon, the lord mayor stands before the thirsty crowds at Theresienwiese and, with due pomp, slams a wooden tap into a cask of beer. As the beer gushes out, the mayor exclaims, 'O'zapft ist'e!' (It's tapped!). The next day resembles the opening of the Olympics, as a young woman on horseback leads a parade of costumed participants from all over the world.

Head to the popular **Bier & Oktoberfestmuseum** (Beer & Oktoberfest Museum; Map p108; www.bier-und-oktoberfestmuseum. de; Sterneckerstrasse 2; adult/concession €4/2.50; ⏱1-6pm Tue-Sat; Ⓢ Isartor, Ⓢ Isartor) to learn all about Bavarian suds and the world's most famous booze-up. The four floors heave with old brewing vats, historic photos and some of the earliest Oktoberfest regalia. The 14th-century building has some fine medieval features, including painted ceilings and a kitchen with an open fire.

Residenz

Home to Bavaria's Wittelsbach rulers from 1508 until WWI, the Residenz is Munich's number one attraction. The Residenzmuseum takes up around half of the palace – allow around two hours to do it justice.

Great For...

❶ Need to Know

Map p108; www.residenz-muenchen.de; Max-Joseph-Platz 3; ⊘varies between individual attractions; ⓤOdeonsplatz

★ **Top Tip**

Outside the summer months, visit the Residenz in the afternoon when the Cuvilliés-Theater is open.

Residenzmuseum

Tours of the **Residenzmuseum** (Map p108; 📞089-290 671; Residenzstrasse 1; adult/ concession/under 18yr €7/6/free; ⊗9am-6pm Apr–mid-Oct, 10am-5pm mid-Oct–Mar, last entry 1hr before closing) kick off at the Grottenhof (Grotto Court), home of the wonderful Perseusbrunnen (Perseus Fountain), with its namesake holding the dripping head of Medusa. Next door is the famous Antiquarium (pictured), a barrel-vaulted hall smothered in frescoes and built to house the Wittelsbach's enormous antique collection. It's widely regarded as the finest Renaissance interior north of the Alps.

Upstairs are the Kurfürstenzimmer (Electors Rooms), with some stunning Italian portraits and a passage lined with two dozen views of Italy, painted by local romantic artist Carl Rottmann. Also up

here are François Cuvilliés' Reiche Zimmer (Ornate Rooms), a six-room extravaganza of exuberant rococo carried out by the top stucco and fresco artists of the day; they're a definite museum highlight. More rococo magic awaits in the Ahnengallery (Ancestors Gallery), with 121 portraits of the rulers of Bavaria in chronological order.

The Hofkapelle, reserved for the ruler and his family, is stunning but not as memorable as the exquisite Reiche Kapelle (Ornate Chapel) with its blue-and-gilt ceiling, inlaid marble and 16th-century organ. This chapel was reserved for court residents in the reign of the Wittelsbachs – the Bavarian rulers who lived in the Residenz from 1385 to 1918. Considered the finest rococo interiors in southern Germany, another spot to linger longer is the Steinzimmer (Stone Rooms), the

Antiquarium

emperor's quarters awash in intricately patterned and coloured marble

Schatzkammer der Residenz

The palace's **Treasury** (adult/concession/under 18yr €7/6/free; ⊙9am-6pm Apr-mid-Oct, 10am-5pm mid-Oct–Mar, last entry 1hr before closing) is a veritable banker's bonus worth of jewel-encrusted bling from yesteryear, from golden toothpicks to finely crafted

★ **Top Tip**

Four giant bronze lion statues guard the entrance to the Residenz, supported by pedestals adorned with a half-human, half-animal face. If you wait a moment, you'll see why the lion have remarkably shiny noses: scores of people walk by and casually rub one or all four noses, to bring wealth and good luck.

swords, miniatures in ivory to gold-entombed cosmetics trunks. The 1250 incredibly intricate and attractive items on display come in every precious material you could imagine, including rhino horn, lapis lazuli, crystal, coral and amber.

Cuvilliés-Theater

Commissioned by Maximilian III in the mid-18th century, François Cuvilliés fashioned one of Europe's finest **rococo theatres** (adult/concession/under 18yr €3.50/2.50/free; ⊙2-6pm Mon-Sat, 9am-6pm Sun Apr-Jul & Sep–mid-Oct, 9am-6pm daily Aug, 2-5pm Mon-Sat, 10am-5pm Sun Nov-Mar; 🎭Nationaltheater). Famous for hosting the premiere of Mozart's opera *Idomeneo*, restoration work in the mid noughties revived the theatre's former glory and its stage once again hosts high-brow musical and operatic performances. Access is limited to the auditorium, where you can take a seat and admire the four tiers of loggia (galleries), dripping with rococo embellishment, at your leisure.

Hofgarten

Office workers catching some rays during their lunch break, stylish mothers pushing prams, seniors on bikes, a gaggle of chatty nuns – everybody comes to the **Hofgarten** (Map p108). The formal court gardens, with fountains, radiant flower beds, lime tree–lined gravel paths and benches galore, sit just north of the Residenz. Paths converge at the Dianatempel, a striking octagonal pavilion honouring the Roman goddess of the hunt. Enter the gardens from Odeonsplatz.

LAVINTAR/SHUTTERSTOCK ©

✗ **Take a Break**

Cafe Luitpold (Map p108; www.cafe-luitpold.de; Briennerstrasse 11; mains €10-19; ⊙8am-7pm Mon, to 11pm Tue-Sat, 9am-7pm Sun; 🛜; Ⓤ Odeonsplatz) is one of the best places in central Munich for a light lunch.

⊙ SIGHTS

Munich's major sights cluster around the Altstadt, with the main museum district just north of the Residenz. However, it will take another day or two to explore bohemian Schwabing, the sprawling Englischer Garten, and trendy Haidhausen to the east. Northwest of the Altstadt you'll find cosmopolitan Neuhausen, the Olympiapark, and another of Munich's royal highlights – Schloss Nymphenburg.

⊙ Altstadt

Asamkirche   Church

(Map p108; Sendlinger Strasse 32; ⊙9am-6pm; ⑤Sendlinger Tor, ⑪Sendlinger Tor) Though pocket sized, the late-baroque Asamkirche, built in 1746, is as rich and epic as a giant's treasure chest. Its creators, the brothers Cosmas Damian Asam and Egid Quirin Asam, dug deep into their considerable talent box to swathe every inch of wall space with gilt garlands and docile cherubs, false marble and oversized barley-twist columns.

Münchner Stadtmuseum   Museum

(City Museum; Map p108; www.muenchner
-stadtmuseum.de; St-Jakobs-Platz 1; adult/
concession/child €7/3.50/free, audioguide
free; ⊙10am-6pm Tue-Sun; ⑤Marienplatz,
⑪Marienplatz) Installed for the city's 850th birthday (2008), the Münchner Stadt-museum's Typisch München (Typically Munich) exhibition – taking up the whole of a rambling building – tells Munich's story in an imaginative, uncluttered and engaging way. Exhibits in each section represent something quintessential about the city; a booklet/audioguide relates the tale behind them, thus condensing a long and tangled history into easily digestible themes.

Marienplatz   Square

(Map p108; ⑤Marienplatz, ⑪Marienplatz) The epicentral heart and soul of the Altstadt, Marienplatz is a popular gathering spot and packs a lot of personality into a compact frame. It's anchored by the **Mariensäule** (St Mary's Column), built in 1638 to celebrate victory over Swedish forces during the

Interior, Asamkirche

Thirty Years' War. This is the busiest spot in all Munich, throngs of tourists swarming across its expanse from early morning till late at night. Many walking tours leave from here.

Neues Rathaus   Historic Building
(New Town Hall; Map p108; Marienplatz; S Marienplatz, U Marienplatz) The soot-blackened façade of the neo-Gothic Neues Rathaus is festooned with gargoyles, statues and a dragon scaling the turrets; the tourist office is on the ground floor. For pinpointing Munich's landmarks without losing your breath, catch the lift up the 85m-tall tower.

Altes Rathaus   Historic Building
(Old Town Hall; Map p108; Marienplatz; S Marienplatz, U Marienplatz) The eastern side of Marienplatz is dominated by the Altes Rathaus. Lightning got the better of the medieval original in 1460 and WWII bombs levelled its successor, so what you see is really the third incarnation of the building designed by Jörg von Halspach of Frauenkirche fame. On 9 November 1938 Joseph Goebbels gave a hate-filled speech here that launched the nationwide Kristallnacht programs.

Frauenkirche   Church
(Church of Our Lady; Map p108; www.muenchner-dom.de; Frauenplatz 1; 7.30am-8.30pm; S Marienplatz) The landmark Frauenkirche, built between 1468 and 1488, is Munich's spiritual heart and the Mt Everest of its churches. No other building in the central city may stand taller than its onion-domed twin towers, which reach a skyscraping 99m. The south tower can be climbed, but has been under urgent renovation for several years.

Jüdisches Museum   Museum
(Jewish Museum; Map p108; www.juedisches-museum-muenchen.de; St-Jakobs-Platz 16; adult/child €6/3; 10am-6pm Tue-Sun; Sendlinger Tor, U Sendlinger Tor) Coming to terms with its Nazi past has not historically been a priority in Munich, which is why the opening of the Jewish Museum in 2007 was hailed

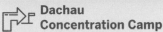

Dachau Concentration Camp

Officially called the **KZ-Gedenkstätte Dachau** (Dachau Memorial Site; 08131-669 970; www.kz-gedenkstaette-dachau.de; Peter-Roth-Strasse 2a, Dachau; 9am-5pm) FREE, this was the Nazis' first concentration camp, built by Heinrich Himmler in March 1933 to house political prisoners. All in all, it 'processed' more than 200,000 inmates, killing at least 43,000, and is now a haunting memorial. Expect to spend two to three hours here.

Start at the visitors centre, which houses a bookshop, a cafe and a tour-booking desk where you can pick up an audioguide (€4). Tours (€3.50; 2½ hours) also run from here at 11am and 1pm (extra tours run at 12.15pm on Sunday between July and September).

You enter the compound itself through the Jourhaus, originally the only entrance. Set in wrought iron, the chilling slogan 'Arbeit Macht Frei' (Work Sets You Free; pictured) hits you at the gate.

The museum, at the southern end of the camp, screens (four times daily) a 22-minute English-language documentary that uses mostly post-liberation footage to outline what took place here. Either side of the small cinema extends an exhibition relating the camp's harrowing story, from a relatively orderly prison for religious inmates, leftists and criminals to an overcrowded concentration camp racked by typhus, and its eventual liberation by the US Army in April 1945.

The Jourhaus gate
SERGIO MENDOZA HOCHMANN/GETTY IMAGES ©

Munich Altstadt

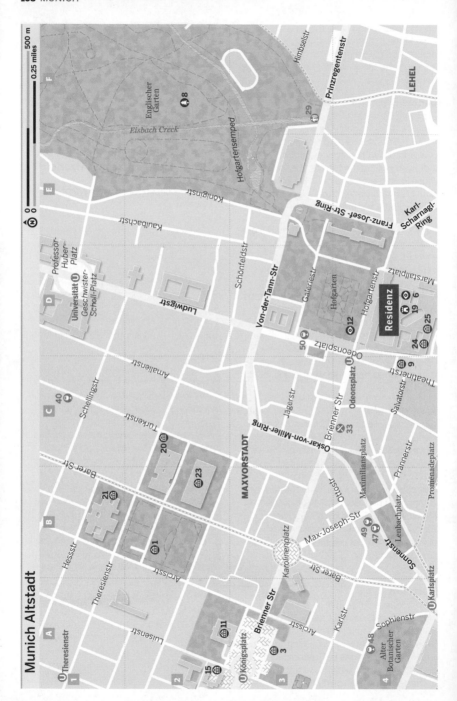

0   N   0.25 miles
0   500 m

A B C D E F

1 2 3 4

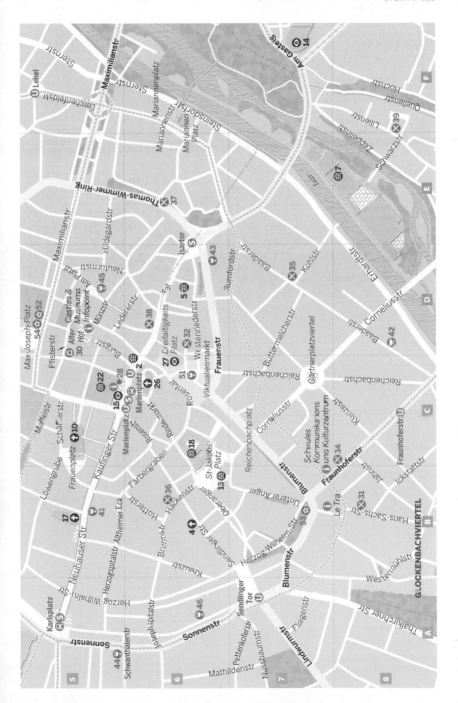

Munich Altstadt

as a milestone. The permanent exhibition offers an insight into Jewish history, life and culture in the city. The Holocaust is dealt with, but the focus is clearly on contemporary Jewish culture.

St Peterskirche
Church

(Church of St Peter; Map p108; Rindermarkt 1; church free, tower adult/child €3/2; ☺tower 9am-6pm Mon-Fri, from 10am Sat & Sun; Ⓤ Marienplatz, Ⓢ Marienplatz) Some 306 steps divide you from the best view of central Munich from the 92m tower of St Peterskirche, central Munich's oldest church (1150). Inside awaits a virtual textbook of art through the centuries. Worth a closer peek are the Gothic St-Martin-Altar, the baroque ceiling fresco by Johann Baptist Zimmermann and rococo sculptures by Ignaz Günther.

Michaelskirche
Church

(Church of St Michael; Map p108; www.st-mich ael-muenchen.de; Kaufingerstrasse 52; crypt €2; ☺crypt 9.30am-4.30pm Mon-Fri, to 2.30pm Sat & Sun; Ⓠ Karlsplatz, Ⓢ Karlsplatz, Ⓤ Karlsplatz) It stands quiet and dignified amid the retail frenzy out on Kaufingerstrasse, but to fans of Ludwig II, the Michaelskirche is the ultimate place of pilgrimage. Its dank crypt is the final resting place of the Mad King, whose humble tomb is usually drowned in flowers.

Viktualienmarkt
Market

(Map p108; ☺Mon-Fri & morning Sat; Ⓤ Marien- platz, Ⓢ Marienplatz) Fresh fruit and vege- tables, piles of artisan cheeses, tubs of exotic olives, hams and jams, chanterelles and truffles – Viktualienmarkt is a feast of flavours and one of central Europe's finest gourmet markets.

Feldherrnhalle
Historic Building

(Field Marshalls Hall; Map p108; Residenz-strasse 1; UOdeonsplatz) Corking up Ode-onsplatz' southern side is Friedrich von Gärnter's Feldherrnhalle, modelled on the Loggia dei Lanzi in Florence. The structure pays homage to the Bavarian army and positively drips with testosterone; check out the statues of General Johann Tilly, who kicked the Swedes out of Munich during the Thirty Years' War; and Karl Philipp von Wrede, an ally turned foe of Napoleon.

It was here on 9 November 1923 that police stopped the so-called Beer Hall Putsch, Hitler's attempt to bring down the Weimar Republic (Germany's government after WWI). A fierce skirmish left 20 people, including 16 Nazis, dead. A plaque in the pavement of the square's eastern side commemorates the police officers who perished in the incident.

⊙ Maxvorstadt & the Englischer Garten

Alte Pinakothek
Museum

(Map p108; ☑089-238 0516; www.pinakothek.de; Barer Strasse 27; adult/concession/child €7/5/free, Sun €1, audioguide €4.50; ⊙10am-8pm Tue, to 6pm Wed Sun; ☐Pinakotheken, ☐Pinakotheken) Munich's main repository of Old European Masters is crammed with all the major players who decorated canvases between the 14th and 18th centuries. This neoclassical temple was masterminded by Leo von Klenze and is a delicacy even if you can't tell your Rembrandt from your Rubens. The collection is world famous for its exceptional quality and depth, especially when it comes to German masters.

Pinakothek der Moderne
Museum

(Map p108; ☑089-2380 5360; www.pinakothek.de; Barer Strasse 40; adult/child €10/free, Sun €1; ⊙10am-6pm Tue, Wed & Fri-Sun, to 8pm Thu; ☐Pinakotheken, ☐Pinakotheken) Germany's largest modern-art museum unites four significant collections under a single roof: 20th-century art, applied design from the 19th century to today, a graphics collection and an architecture museum. It's housed in a spectacular building by Stephan Braunfels, whose four-storey interior centres on a vast eye-like dome letting soft natural light filter throughout the blanched-white galleries.

Museum Brandhorst
Gallery

(Map p108; www.museum-brandhorst.de; Theresienstrasse 35a; adult/concession/child €7/5/free, Sun €1; ⊙10am-6pm Tue, Wed & Fri-Sun, to 8pm Thu; ☐Maxvorstadt/Sammlung Brandhorst, ☐Pinakotheken) A big, bold and aptly abstract building (pictured p120), clad entirely in vividly multihued ceramic tubes, the Brandhorst jostled its way into the Munich Kunstareal in a punk blaze of colour mid-2009. Its walls, its floor and occasionally its ceiling provide space for some of the most challenging art in the city. It includes some instantly recognisable 20th-century images by Andy Warhol, whose work dominates the collection.

Englischer Garten
Park

(English Garden; Map p108; UUniversität) The sprawling English Garden is among Europe's biggest city parks – it even rivals London's Hyde Park and New York's Central Park for size – and is a popular playground for locals and visitors alike. Stretching north from Prinzregentenstrasse for about 5km, it was commissioned by Elector Karl Theodor in 1789 and designed by Benjamin Thompson, an American-born scientist working as an adviser to the Bavarian government.

Neue Pinakothek
Museum

(Map p108; ☑089-2380 5195; www.pinakothek.de; Barer Strasse 29; adult/child €7/free, Sun €1; ⊙10am-6pm Thu-Mon, to 8pm Wed; ☐Pinakotheken, ☐Pinakotheken) The Neue Pinakothek harbours a well-respected collection of 19th- and early-20th-century paintings and sculpture, from rococo to *Jugendstil* (art nouveau). All the world-famous household names get wall space here, including crowd-pleasing French impressionists such as Monet, Cézanne and

No Wave Goodbye

Possibly the last sport you might expect to see being practised in Munich is surfing, but go to the southern tip of the Englischer Garten at Prinzregentenstrasse and you'll see scores of people leaning over a bridge to cheer on wetsuit-clad daredevils as they hang 10 on an **artificially created wave in the Eisbach** (Map p108; www.eisbachwelle.de; Prinzregentenstrasse; 🚊Nationalmuseum/ Haus der Kunst). It's only a single wave, but it's a damn fine one. A decade ago park authorities attempted to ban this watery entertainment, but a successful campaign by surfers saw plans to turn the wave off shelved.

Surfing the Eisbach
POLINA SHESTAKOVA/SHUTTERSTOCK ©

Degas as well as Van Gogh, whose boldly pigmented *Sunflowers* (1888) radiates cheer.

Glyptothek   Museum
(Map p108; www.antike-am-koenigsplatz.mwn. de; Königsplatz 3; adult/child €6/free, Sun €1; ⊙10am-5pm Fri-Sun, Tue & Wed, to 8pm Thu; 🚊Königsplatz, Ⓤ Königsplatz) If you're a fan of classical art or simply enjoy the sight of naked guys without noses (or other pertinent body parts), make a beeline for the Glyptothek. One of Munich's oldest museums, it's a feast of art and sculpture from ancient Greece and Rome amassed by Ludwig I between 1806 and 1830, and it opens a surprisingly naughty window onto the ancient world. Tickets for the museum

are also valid for the **Antikensammlungen** (Antique Collection; Königsplatz 1; adult/child €6/free, Sun €1; ⊙10am-5pm Tue & Thu-Sun, to 8pm Wed).

Lenbachhaus   Museum
(Municipal Gallery; Map p108; ☑089-2333 2000; www.lenbachhaus.de; Luisenstrasse 33; adult/child incl audioguide €10/5; ⊙10am-8pm Tue, to 6pm Wed-Sun; 🚊Königsplatz, Ⓤ Königsplatz) With its fabulous wing added by noted architect Norman Foster, this glorious gallery is the go-to place to admire the vibrant canvases of Kandinsky, Franz Marc, Paul Klee and other members of ground-breaking modernist group Der Blaue Reiter (The Blue Rider), founded in Munich in 1911.

◉ South of Altstadt

Deutsches Museum –
Verkehrszentrum   Museum
(Transport Museum; Map p116; www.deutsches -museum.de/verkehrszentrum; Am Bavariapark 5; adult/child €7/3; ⊙9am-5pm; Ⓤ Theresien- wiese) An ode to the Bavarian obsession with getting around, the Transport Museum explores the ingenious ways humans have devised to transport things and each other. From the earliest automobiles to famous race cars and high-speed ICE trains, the collection is a virtual trip through transport history.

◉ Olympiapark

Schloss
Nymphenburg   Palace
(Map p116; www.schloss-nymphenburg.de; castle adult/child €6/free, all sites €11.50/ free; ⊙9am-6pm Apr–mid-Oct, 10am-4pm mid-Oct–Mar; 🚊Schloss Nymphenburg) This commanding palace and its lavish gardens sprawl around 5km northwest of the Altstadt. Begun in 1664 as a villa for Electress Adelaide of Savoy, the stately pile was extended over the next century to create the royal family's summer residence. Franz Duke of Bavaria, head of the once-royal Wittelsbach family, still occupies an apartment here.

BMW Welt

BMW Welt Notable Building

(BMW World; Map p116; ☏089-125 016 001; www.bmw-welt.de; Am Olympiapark 1; tours adult/child €7/5; ⏱7.30am-midnight Mon-Sat, from 9am Sun; ⓤOlympiazentrum) FREE Next to the Olympiapark, the glass-and-steel, double-cone tornado spiralling down from a dark cloud the size of an aircraft carrier holds BMW Welt, truly a petrolhead's dream. Apart from its role as a prestigious car pick-up centre, this king of showrooms acts as a shop window for BMW's latest models and a show space for the company as a whole.

Olympiapark Sportsground

(Olympic Park; Map p116; www.olympiapark.de; stadium tour adult/concession €8/6; ⏱stadium tours 11am, 1pm & 4pm Apr-Oct; ⓤOlympiazentrum) The area to the north of the city where soldiers once paraded and the world's first Zeppelin landed in 1909 found a new role in the 1960s as the Olympiapark. Despite being built for the 1972 Olympic Summer Games, it has quite a small-scale feel.

When the sky is clear you'll have Munich at your feet against the breathtaking back-drop of the Alps from the top of the 290m **Olympiaturm** (Olympic Tower; adult/child €7/5; ⏱9am-midnight).

BMW Museum Museum

(Map p116; www.bmw-welt.de; Am Olympiapark 2; adult/child €10/7; ⏱10am-6pm Tue-Sun; ⓤOlympiazentrum) This silver, bowl-shaped museum comprises seven themed 'houses' that examine the development of BMW's product line and include sections on motorcycles and motor racing. Even if you can't tell a head gasket from a crankshaft, the interior design – with its curvy retro feel, futuristic bridges, squares and huge backlit wall screens – is reason enough to visit.

ⓐ ACTIVITIES

Walk on the Roof Walking

(Map p116; adult/concessions €43/33; ⏱2.30pm Apr-Oct) Can't make it to the Alps for a high-altitude clamber? No matter. Just head to the Olympic Stadium for a walk on the roof. Yup, the roof; that famously contorted steel and Plexiglas confection is ready for its

Lake Starnberg

Around 25km southwest of Munich, glittering Lake Starnberg (Starnberger See) was once the haunt of Bavaria's royal family but now provides a bit of easily accessible R&R for anyone looking to escape the hustle of the Bavarian capital.

At the northern end of the lake, the affluent, century-old town of Starnberg is the northern gateway to the lake district but lacks any lasting allure, meaning most visitors head straight on to other towns or sites along the lake's edge. The train station is just steps from the lakeshore, where you'll find cruise-boat landing docks, pedal-boat hire and lots of strolling day-trippers. Besides Lake Starnberg, the area comprises the Ammersee and the much smaller Pilsensee, Wörthsee and Wesslinger See. Naturally, the region attracts water-sports enthusiasts, but it also has enough history to satisfy those who enjoy exploring the past.

Lake Starnberg in winter
SUSAZOOM/SHUTTERSTOCK ©

close-up. Just like in the mountains, you'll be roped and hooked up to a steel cable as you clamber around under the eagle-eyed supervision of an experienced guide showering you with fascinating details about the stadium's architecture and construction.

⊙ TOURS

BMW Plant Tours
Tours

(Map p116; ☎089-125 016 001; www.bmw -welt.com; adult/child €9/6; ☉in English

11.30am & 2pm Mon-Fri, in German 6pm; ⓊPetuelring) If you like cars, don't miss a tour of BMW's state-of-the-art plant. The tours in English and German last 2½ hours and take in the entire production process. Booking well ahead is essential, especially in summer.

Radius Tours & Bike Rental
Tours

(Map p116; ☎089-543 487 7740; www.radius tours.com; Arnulfstrasse 3, Hauptbahnhof; ☉8.30am-8pm; ⓇHauptbahnhof, ⓊHauptbahnhof, ⓈHauptbahnhof) Entertaining and informative English-language tours include the two-hour Discover Munich walk (€15), the fascinating 2½-hour Third Reich tour (€17.50), and the three-hour Bavarian Beer tour (€36). The company also runs popular excursions to Neuschwanstein, Salzburg and Dachau and has hundreds of bikes for hire (€14.50 per day).

New Europe Munich
Walking

(Map p108; www.neweuropetours.eu; ☉tours 10am, 10.45am & 2pm; ⓈMarienplatz, ⓊMarienplatz) Departing from Marienplatz, these free English-language walking tours tick off all Munich's central landmarks in three hours. Guides are well informed and fun, though they are under pressure at the end of the tour to get as much as they can in tips. The company also runs (paid) tours to Dachau (€24) and Neuschwanstein (€40).

Vespa Munich
Tours

(Map p116; ☎0151-517 251 69; www.vespa munich.com; Dom-Pedro-Strasse 26; full-day tour €59; ☉office 10am-2pm daily, pick-ups 9am-6pm; ⓇLeonrodplatz) Book in advance, pick up your Vespa and spend the day bombing around Munich guided by the GPS unit provided. It's the latest fun way to see the city, but good luck on those freeways!

City Bus 100
Bus

(Map p116; www.mvv-muenchen.de) Ordinary city bus that runs from the Hauptbahnhof to the Ostbahnhof via 21 sights, including the Residenz and the Pinakothek museums.

🔒 SHOPPING

Munich Readery   Books

(Map p116; www.readery.de; Augustenstrasse 104; ⊙11am-8pm Mon-Fri, 10am-6pm Sat; ⓤTheresienstrasse) With Germany's biggest collection of secondhand English-language titles, the Readery is the place to go for holiday reading matter. In fact we think this might be the only such second-hand bookshop between Paris and Prague. The shop holds events such as author readings, and there's a monthly book club. See the website for details.

Holareidulijö   Clothing

(Map p116; www.holareidulijoe.com; Schellingstrasse 81; ⊙noon-6.30pm Tue-Fri, 10am-1pm Sat May-Sep, 2-6pm Thu & Fri, 11am-1pm Sat Oct-Apr; ⓈSchellingstrasse) This rare secondhand traditional-clothing store (the name is a phonetic yodel) is worth a look. Apparently, wearing hand-me-down Lederhosen greatly reduces the risk of chafing.

Porzellan Manufaktur
Nymphenburg   Ceramics

(Map p116; ☎089-1791 970; www.nymphenburg.com; Nördliches Schlossrondell 8; ⊙10am-5pm Mon-Fri; ⓈSchloss Nymphenburg) Traditional and contemporary porcelain masterpieces by the royal manufacturer. Prices are high.

Flohmarkt im
Olympiapark   Market

(Map p116; Olympiapark; ⊙7am-4pm Fri & Sat; ⓈOlympiapark West) Large flea market held outside the Olympiastadion most Fridays and Saturdays.

Manufactum   Homewares

(Map p108; www.manufactum.de; Dienerstrasse 12; ⊙9.30am-7pm Mon-Sat; ⓈMarienplatz, ⓇMarienplatz) Anyone with an admiration for top-quality design from Germany and further afield should make a beeline for this store. Last-a-lifetime household items compete for shelf space with retro toys, Bauhaus lamps and times-gone-by stationery. The stock changes according to the season.

Munich for Children

(Tiny) hands down, Munich has plenty of activities to please little ones.

Deutsches Museum (Map p108; ☎089-217 9333; www.deutsches-museum.de; Museumsinsel 1; adult/child €12/4; ⊙9am-5pm; ⓈDeutsches Museum) The highly interactive 'Kinderreich' is ideal for kids aged three to eight.

Tierpark Hellabrunn (Hellabrunn Zoo; ☎089-625 080; www.tierpark-hellabrunn.de; Tierparkstrasse 30; adult/child €15/6; ⊙9am-6pm Apr-Sep, to 5pm Oct-Mar; ☒52 from Marienplatz, ⓇTiroler Platz, ⓤThalkirchen) Petting baby goats should make for some unforgettable memories.

SeaLife (Map p116; www.visitsealife.com; Willi-Daume-Platz 1; adult/child gate prices €17.95/14.50; ⊙10am-5pm Mon-Fri, to 6pm Sat & Sun; ⓈOlympiazentrum) For a fishy immersion, head to this new attraction in the Olympiapark (p113).

Paläontologisches Museum (Palaeontological Museum; Map p116; www.palmuc.de; Richard-Wagner-Strasse 10; ⊙8am-4pm Mon-Thu, to 2pm Fri; ☒Königsplatz, ⓤKönigsplatz) [FREE] Dino fans will gravitate here.

Museum Mensch und Natur (Museum of Humankind & Nature; Map p116; www.mmn-muenchen.de; Schloss Nymphenburg; adult/child €3.50/2.50; ⊙9am-5pm Tue, Wed & Fri, to 8pm Thu, 10am-6pm Sat & Sun; ☒Schloss Nymphenburg) Budding scientists will find plenty to marvel at.

Spielzeugmuseum (Toy Museum; Map p108; www.toymuseum.de; Marienplatz 15; adult/child €4/1; ⊙10am-5.30pm; ⓈMarienplatz, ⓤMarienplatz) It's a bit look-but-don't-touch here, but kids should still get a kick out of it

Münchner Marionettentheater (Map p108; ☎089-265 712; www.muema-theater.de; Blumenstrasse 32; ⊙3pm Mon, Wed & Fri, 8pm Sat; ☒Müllerstrasse) The adorable marionettes performing here have enthralled generations of wee ones.

Central Munich

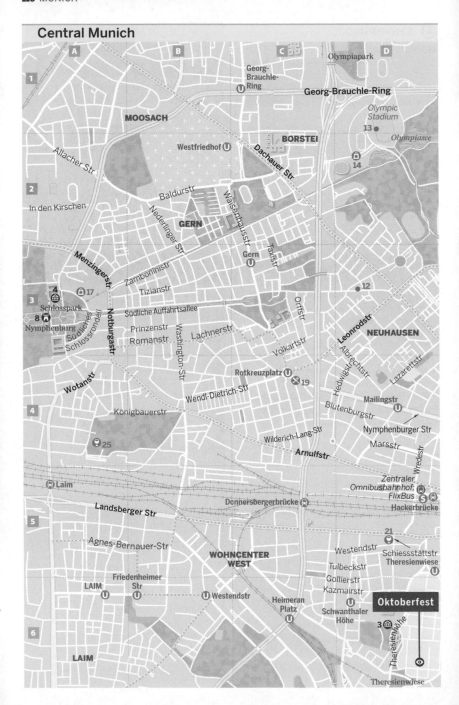

Olympiapark

Georg-Brauchle-Ring

Georg-Brauchle-Ring

MOOSACH

Olympic Stadium

13

Olympiasee

BORSTEI

Westfriedhof Ⓤ

Allacher Str

In den Kirschen

Baldurstr

Dachauer Str

14

GERN

Waisenhausstr

Nederlinger Str

Menzinger str

Zamboninistr

Gern Ⓤ

Taxistr

Tizianstr

17

Schlosspark

Südliche Auffahrtsallee

Ortstr

12

Nymphenburg

8

Prinzenstr

Notburgastr

Romanstr

Lachnerstr

Washington-Str

Volkartstr

Leonrodstr

NEUHAUSEN

Albrechtstr

Hedwigstr

Lazarettstr

Südliches Schlossrondell

Wotanstr

Rotkreuzplatz Ⓤ

19

Wendl-Dietrich-Str

Mailingstr

Königbauerstr

Blutenburgstr

Nymphenburger Str

Marsstr

Wredestr

25

Wilderich-Lang-Str

Arnulfstr

Zentraler
Omnibusbahnhof;
FlixBus

Laim

Landsberger Str

Dennersbergerbrücke

Hackerbrücke

21

Agnes-Bernauer-Str

Westendstr

Schiessstättstr

Theresienwiese

WOHNCENTER
WEST

Tulbeckstr

Gollierstr

LAIM

Friedenheimer Str

Kazmairstr

Oktoberfest

Westendstr

Heimeran
Platz

Schwanthaler
Höhe

3

Theresienhöhe

LAIM

Theresienwiese

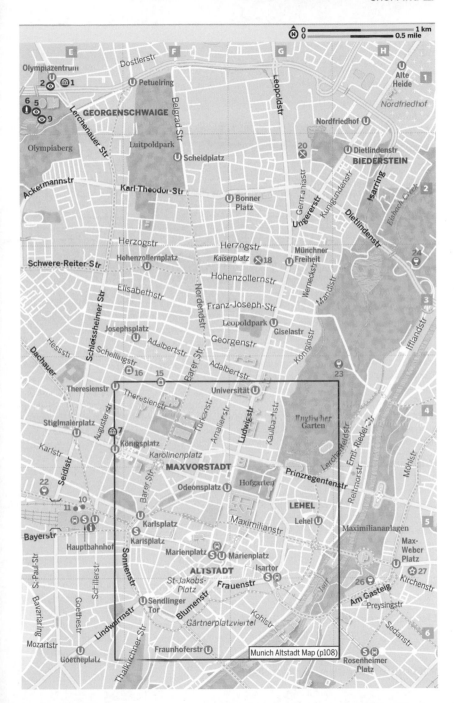

Central Munich

EATING

Munich has southern Germany's most exciting restaurant scene. In Munich's kitchens the best dishes make use of fresh regional, seasonal and organic ingredients. The Bavarian capital is also the best place between Vienna and Paris for internationally flavoured dining, especially for Italian, Afghan, Vietnamese and Turkish food, and even vegetarians can look forward to something other than noodles and salads.

Bratwurstherzl   Franconian €
(Map p108; Dreifaltigkeitsplatz 1; mains €7-12; ☺10am-11pm Mon-Sat; Ⓢ Marienplatz, Ⓤ Marienplatz) Cosy panelling and an ancient vaulted brick ceiling set the tone of this Old Munich tavern with a Franconian focus. Homemade organic sausages are grilled to perfection on an open beechwood fire and served on heart-shaped pewter plates. They're best enjoyed with a cold one from the Hacker-Pschorr brewery.

Eiscafé Sarcletti   Gelato €
(Map p116; www.sarcletti.de; Nymphenburger Strasse 155; ☺9am-11.30pm May-Aug, shorter hours Sep-Apr; Ⓤ Rotkreuzplatz) Ice-cream addicts have been getting their gelato fix at this Munich institution since 1879. Choose from more than 50 mouth-watering flavours, from not-so-plain vanilla to buttermilk and mango.

Fraunhofer   Bavarian €€
(Map p108; ☏089-266 460; www.fraunhofer theater.de; Fraunhoferstrasse 9; mains €5-20; ☺4.30pm-1am; ⎘; Ⓤ Müllerstrasse) With its screechy parquet floors, stuccoed ceilings, wood panelling and virtually no trace that the last century even happened, this wonderfully characterful inn is perfect for exploring the region with a fork. The menu is a seasonally adapted checklist of southern German favourites but also features at least a dozen vegetarian dishes and the odd exotic ingredient. Cash only.

Prinz Myshkin   Vegetarian €€
(Map p108; ☏089-265 596; www.prinzmyshkin. com; Hackenstrasse 2; mains €9-20; ☺11am-12.30am; ⎘; Ⓢ Marienplatz, Ⓤ Marienplatz) This place is proof, if any were needed, that the vegetarian experience has well and truly left the sandals, beards and lentils era. Ensconced in a former brewery, Munich's premier meat-free dining spot occupies a gleamingly whitewashed, vaulted space

where health-conscious eaters come to savour imaginative dishes such as curry-orange-carrot soup, unexpectedly good curries and 'wellness desserts'.

Weisses Brauhaus
Bavarian €€

(Map p108; ☑089-290 1380; www.weisses -brauhaus.de; Tal 7; mains €7-20; ⊗8am-12.30am; ⑤Marienplatz, ⑪Marienplatz) One of Munich's classic beer halls, this place is charged in the evenings with red-faced, ale-infused hilarity, with Alpine whoops accompanying the rabble-rousing oompah band. The *Weisswurst* (veal sausage) here sets the standard for the rest to aspire to; sluice down a pair with the unsurpassed Schneider *Weissbier*, but only before noon. Understandably very popular and reservations are recommended after 7pm.

Cochinchina
Asian €€

(Map p116; ☑089-3898 9577; www.cochin china.de; Kaiserstrasse 28; mains around €20; ⊗11.30am-2.30pm & 6pm-midnight; 🐾; ⑪Münchner Freiheit) Bearing an old name for southern Vietnam, this cosmopolitan Asian fusion restaurant is Munich's top place for Vietnamese and Chinese concoctions. The food is consumed in a dark, dramatically exotic space devoted to the firefly and splashed with colour in the shape of Chinese vases and lamps. The traditional *pho* soup is southern Germany's best.

Königsquelle
European €€

(Map p108; ☑089-220 071; www.koenigsquelle. com; Baaderplatz 2; mains €10-27; ⊗5pm-1am Sun-Fri, from 7pm Sat; ☕Isartor, Ⓡisartor, ⑤Isartor) This wood-panelled Munich institution is well loved for its attentive service, expertly prepared food and dark, well-stocked hardwood bar. It contains what must be the Bavarian capital's best selection of malt whiskies, stacked high behind the bar. The only-just decipherable handwritten menu hovers somewhere mid-Alps, with anything from schnitzel to linguine and goat's cheese to cannelloni to choose from.

Vegelangelo
Vegetarian €€

(Map p108; ☑089-2880 6836; www.vegelan gelo.de; Thomas-Wimmer-Ring 16; mains €13-19, set menu €22-34; ⊗noon-2pm Tue-Thu, 6pm-late Mon-Sat; 🐾; ☕Isartor, ⑤Isartor) Reservations are compulsory at this petite veggie spot, where Indian odds and ends, a piano and a small Victorian fireplace distract little from the superb meat-free cooking, all of which can be converted to suit vegans. There's a set-menu-only policy Friday and Saturday. No prams allowed and no tap water served, but it does accept Bitcoin.

Bamyan
Afghan €€

(Map p108; www.bamyan.de; Hans-Sachs-Strasse 3; mains €9.50-20; ⊗5pm-1am Sun-Fri, from 11.30am Sat; ☕Müllerstrasse) The terms 'happy hour', 'cocktail' and 'chilled vibe' don't normally go together with the word 'Afghan', but that's exactly the combination you get at this exotic hang-out, named after the Buddha statues infamously destroyed by the Taliban in 2001. The gastro-award-winning Central Asian soups, kebabs, rice and lamb dishes, and big salads are eaten at handmade tables inlaid with ornate metalwork.

Wirtshaus in der Au
Bavarian €€

(Map p108; ☑089-448 1400; www.wirtshaus inderau.de; Lilienstrasse 51; mains €10-22; ⊗5pm-midnight Mon-Fri, from 10am Sat & Sun; ☕Deutsches Museum) This Bavarian tavern's simple slogan is 'Beer and dumplings since 1901', and it's this time-honoured staple – dumplings – that's the speciality here. (The tavern even runs a dumpling-making course in English.) Once a brewery, the space-rich dining area has chunky tiled floors, a lofty ceiling and a crackling fireplace in winter. When spring springs, the beer garden fills.

Tantris
International €€€

(Map p116; ☑089-361 9590; www.tantris.de; Johann-Fichte-Strasse 7; menu from €100; ⊗noon-3pm & 6.30pm-1am Tue-Sat Oct-Dec, closed Tue Jan-Sep; 🐾; ⑪Dietlindenstrasse) Tantris means 'the search for perfection' and here, at one of Germany's most famous restaurants, it's not far off it. The interior design is full-bodied '70s – all postbox reds, truffle blacks and illuminated yellows. The food is sublime and the service is sometimes as unobtrusive as it is efficient. The wine cellar is probably Germany's best. Reservations essential.

Esszimmer   Mediterranean €€€

(Map p116; ☑089-358 991 814; www.bmw -welt.com; BMW Welt, Am Olympiapark 1; 4/5 courses €130/145; ⊗from 7pm Tue-Sat; ❄🛜; Ⓤolympiazentrum) It took Bobby Bräuer, head chef at the gourmet restaurant at BMW World, just two years to gain his first Michelin star. Munich's top dining spot is the place to sample high-octane French and Mediterranean morsels, served in a trendy dark and veneered dining room above the i8s and 7 Series.

🍷 DRINKING & NIGHTLIFE

Munich is a great place for boozers with scores of raucous beer halls, snazzy hotel lounges and chestnut-canopied beer gardens. Likewise, the city's club scene is jumping, second only to Berlin. Whether your musical tastes run to disco or dance hall, house or punk, techno or punk-folk, you'll find a place to throw some shapes. Doormen tend be strict and cover charges can hover around €15 at bigger venues. If you look under 30, bring ID. Don't expect much action before 1am.

Hofbräuhaus   Beer Hall

(Map p108; ☑089-2901 36100; www.hofbrau haus.de; Am Platzl 9; ⊗9am-midnight; 🚋Kam-merspiele, Ⓢmarienplatz, Ⓤmarienplatz) Even if you don't like beer, every visitor to Munich should make a pilgrimage to the mother-ship of all beer halls, if only once. Within this major tourist attraction (pictured), you'll discover a range of spaces in which to do your *Mass* lifting: the horse chestnut–shaded garden, the main hall next to the oompah band, tables opposite the industri-al-scale kitchen and quieter corners.

Augustiner Bräustuben   Beer Hall

(Map p116; ☑089-507 047; www.braeustuben. de; Landsberger Strasse 19; ⊗10am-midnight;

From left: Gingerbread souvenirs; Museum Brandhorst (p111); Chinesischer Turm; Hofbräuhaus

🚇Holzapfelstrasse) Depending on the wind direction, the bitter-sweet aroma of hops envelops you as you approach this traditional beer hall inside the Augustiner brewery. The Bavarian fare is superb, especially the *Schweinshaxe* (pork knuckle). Due to the location, the atmosphere in the evenings is slightly more authentic than that of its city-centre cousins, with fewer tourists at the long tables.

Chinesischer Turm Beer Garden

(Map p116; ☎089-383 8730; www.chinaturm.de; Englischer Garten 3; ⊙10am-11pm late Apr-Oct; 🚇Chinesischer Turm, 🚇Tivolistrasse) This one's hard to ignore because of its English Garden location and pedigree as Munich's oldest beer garden (open since 1791). Camera-toting tourists and laid-back locals, picnicking families and businessmen sneaking a sly brew, all clomp around the wooden pagoda (pictured below), showered by the strained sounds of an oompah band.

Schumann's Bar Bar

(Map p108; ☎089-229 060; www.schumanns. de; Odeonsplatz 6-7; ⊙8am-3am Mon-Fri, 6pm-3am Sat & Sun; ⑤Odeonsplatz) Urbane and sophisticated, Schumann's shakes up Munich's nightlife with libational flights of fancy and an impressive range of concoctions. It's also good for weekday breakfasts. Cash only.

Alter Simpl Pub

(Map p108; ☎089-272 3083; www.altersimpl. com; Türkenstrasse 57; ⊙11am-3am Mon-Fri, to 4am Sat & Sun; 🚇Schellingstrasse) Thomas Mann and Hermann Hesse used to knock 'em back at this well-scuffed and wood-panelled thirst parlour. A bookish ambience still pervades, making this an apt spot at which to curl up with a weighty tome over a few Irish ales. The curious name is an abbreviation of the satirical magazine *Simplicissimus*.

Pacha Club

(Map p108; www.pacha-muenchen.de; Maximiliansplatz 5; ⊙7pm-6am Thu, 11pm-6am Fri & Sat; 🚇Lenbachplatz) One of a gaggle of clubs at Maximiliansplatz 5, this nightspot with its cherry logo is one of Munich's hottest nights out, with the DJs spinning their stuff till well after sunrise.

Allianz Arena

> *watch one of Germany's best soccer teams triumph in a futuristic stadium*

Harry Klein Club

(Map p108; ☎089-4028 7400; www.harry kleinclub.de; Sonnenstrasse 8; ☺from 11pm; ⓡKarlsplatz, ⓢKarlsplatz, ⓤKarlsplatz) Follow the gold-lined passageway off Sonnenstrasse to what some regard as one of the best *Elektro-clubs* in the world. Nights here are an amazing alchemy of electro sound and visuals, with live video art projected onto the walls Kraftwerk-style and blending to awe-inspiring effect with the music.

MilchundBar Club

(Map p108; www.milchundbar.de; Sonnenstrasse 27; ☺10pm-7am Mon-Thu, 11pm-9am Fri & Sat; ⓡSendlinger Tor, ⓤSendlinger Tor) One of the hottest addresses in the city centre for those who like to spend the hours between supper and breakfast boogying to an eclectic mix of nostalgia hits during the week and top DJs at the weekends.

Augustiner Keller Beer Garden

(Map p116; www.augustinerkeller.de; Arnulfstrasse 52; ☺10am-1am Apr-Oct; 👪; ⓡHopfenstrasse) Every year this leafy 5000-seat beer garden, about 500m west of the Hauptbahnhof, buzzes with fairy-lit thirst-quenching activity from the first sign that spring may have *gesprungen*. The ancient chestnuts are thick enough to seek refuge under when it rains, or else lug your mug to the actual beer cellar. Small playground.

Rote Sonne Club

(Map p108; www.rote-sonne.com; Maximiliansplatz 5; ☺from 11pm Thu-Sun; ⓡLenbachplatz) Named for a 1969 Munich cult movie starring it-girl Uschi Obermaier, the Red Sun is a fiery nirvana for fans of electronic sounds. A global roster of DJs keeps the dance floor packed and sweaty until the sun rises.

Baader Café Cafe

(Map p108; www.baadercafe.de; Baaderstrasse 47; ☺9.30am-1am Sun-Thu, to 2am Fri & Sat; 📶; ⓡFraunhoferstrasse) Around since the mid-'80s, this literary think-and-drink place lures all sorts, from short skirts to tweed jackets, who linger over daytime coffees and nighttime cocktails. It's normally packed, even on winter Wednesday mornings, and is popular among Brits who come for the authentic English breakfast.

❽ ENTERTAINMENT

As you might expect from a major metropolis, Munich's entertainment scene is lively and multifaceted, though not particularly edgy. You can hobnob with high society at the opera, hang with the kids at an indie club, catch a flick alfresco or watch one of Germany's best soccer teams triumph in a futuristic stadium.

FC Bayern München   Football
(☏089-6993 1333; www.fcbayern.de; Allianz Arena, Werner-Heisenberg-Allee 25, Fröttmaning; Ⓤ Fröttmaning) Germany's most successful team both domestically and on a European level plays home games at the impressive Allianz Arena (pictured left), built for the 2006 World Cup. Tickets can be ordered online.

Bayerische Staatsoper   Opera
(Bavarian State Opera, Map p108; ☏089-2185 1025; www.staatsoper.de; Max-Joseph-Platz 2, Ⓖ Nationaltheater) One of the world's best opera companies, the Bavarian State Opera performs to sell-out crowds at the Nationaltheater in the Residenz and puts the emphasis on Mozart, Strauss and Wagner. In summer it hosts the prestigious **Opernfestspiele** (Opera Festival; www.muenchner-opern-festspiele.de; ☺Jul). The opera's house band is the Bayerisches Staatsorchester, in business since 1523 and thus Munich's oldest orchestra.

Münchner
Philharmoniker   Classical Music
(Map p108; ☏089-480 985 500; www.mphil.de; Rosenheimer Strasse 5; ☺mid-Sep–Jun; Ⓖ Am Gasteig) Munich's premier orchestra regularly performs at the **Gasteig Cultural Centre** (Map p108; ☏tickets 089-548 181 81; www.gasteig.de; Rosenheimer Strasse 5; Ⓖ Am

Top 10 Munich Beer Halls & Gardens

Augustiner Bräustuben (p120) Sample Augustiner at the source in the brewery's own pub.

Augustiner-Grossgaststätte (Map p108; ☏089-2318 3257; www.augustiner-restaurant.com; Neuhauser Strasse 27; ☺9am-11.30pm) A traditional beer hall.

Hofbräuhaus (p120) Arguably the world's best-known beer hall.

Hofbräukeller (Map p116; ☏089-459 9250; www.hofbraeukeller.de; Wiener Platz; ☺10am-midnight; Ⓖ Wiener Platz) A less touristy option.

Braunauer Hof (Map p108; www.wirtshaus-im-braunauer-hof.de; Frauenstrasse 42; ☺10am-midnight Mon-Sat, to 10pm Sun; Ⓖ Isartor, Ⓢ Isartor) On the edge of the Altstadt, this beer temple has a quirky beer garden out back.

Hirschau (Map p116; www.hirschau-muenchen.de; Gysslingstrasse 15; ☺noon-11pm Mon-Fri, from 11am Sat & Sun; Ⓤ Dietlindenstrasse) Huge beer garden in the Englischer Garten.

Hirschgarten (Map p116; www.hirschgarten.de; Hirschgarten 1, ☺11.30am-1am; Ⓖ Kriemhildenstrasse, Ⓢ Laim) Join an incredible 8000 drinkers!

Chinesischer Turm (p121) Enjoy some Munich lager in the shadow of a faux Chinese pagoda.

Park-Cafe (Map p108; www.parkcafe089.de; Sophienstrasse 7; ☺11am-11pm; Ⓖ Lenbachplatz) Less touristy beer garden in the Old Botanical Gardens.

Viktualienmarkt (Map p108; Viktualienmarkt 6; ☺9am-10pm; Ⓤ Marienplatz, Ⓢ Marienplatz) Popular outdoor spot surrounded by market stalls.

Waldwirtschaft Grosshesselohe (☏089-7499 4030; www.waldwirtschaft.de; Georg-Kalb-Strasse 3; ☺10am-10.30pm; ♿; Ⓖ Grosshesselohe/Isartalbahnhof.) Rural bliss and superb beer on Munich's outskirts.

 LGBTIQ+ Munich

Homosexuality is legal in Bavaria, but the scene, even in Munich, is tiny compared to, say, Berlin or Cologne. Homosexuality is widely accepted, and LGBTIQ+ travellers will experience no hostility in the capital. There are websites aplenty, but most are in German only. Try www. gay-web.de or, for women, www.lesarion. de. The **Schwules Kommunikations und Kulturzentrum** (Map p108; ☎089-856 346 400; www.subonline.org; Müllerstrasse 14; ⊗7-11pm Sun-Thu, to midnight Fri, 8pm-1am Sat; 圓Müllerstrasse) in the city centre is a gay information agency. Lesbians can also turn to **Le Tra** (Map p108; ☎089-725 4272; www.letra.de; Angertorstrasse 3; ⊗2.30-5pm Mon & Wed; 圓Müllerstrasse).

BIRGIT KORBER/EYEEM/GETTY IMAGES ©

Gasteig). Book tickets early, as performances usually sell out.

Jazzclub Unterfahrt im Einstein
Live Music

(Map p116; ☎089-448 2794; www.unterfahrt. de; Einsteinstrasse 42; ⊗from 9pm; UMax-Weber-Platz) Join a diverse crowd at this long-established, intimate club for a mixed bag of acts ranging from old bebop to edgy experimental. The Sunday open-jam session is legendary.

INFORMATION

Castles & Museums Infopoint (Map p108; ☎089-2101 4050; www.infopoint-museen -bayern.de; Alter Hof 1; ⊗10am-6pm Mon-Sat; UMarienplatz, SMarienplatz) Central

information point for museums and palaces throughout Bavaria.

Tourist Office branches include **Hauptbahnhof** (Map p116; ☎089-21 800; www.muenchen.de; Bahnhofplatz 2; ⊗9am-8pm Mon-Sat, 10am-6pm Sun; 圓Hauptbahnhof, UHauptbahnhof, SHauptbahnhof) and **Marienplatz** (Map p108; ☎089-2339 6500; www.muenchen.de; Marienplatz 2; ⊗9am-7pm Mon-Fri, to 4pm Sat, 10am-2pm Sun; UMarienplatz, SMarienplatz).

CITY TOUR CARD

The **Munich City Tour Card** (www.city-tourcard-muenchen.com; 1/3 days €12.90/24.90) includes all public transport in the *Innenraum* (Munich city – zones 1 to 4, marked white on transport maps) and discounts of between 10% and 50% for over 80 attractions, tours, eateries and theatres. These include the Residenz, the BMW Museum and the Bier & Oktoberfestmuseum. It's available at some hotels, tourist offices, Munich public transport authority (MVV) offices and U-Bahn, S-Bahn and DB vending machines.

GETTING THERE & AWAY

AIR

Munich Airport (MUC; ☎089-975 00; www. munich-airport.de), aka Flughafen Franz-Josef Strauss, is second in importance only to Frankfurt for international and domestic connections. The main carrier is Lufthansa, but over 80 other companies operate from the airport's two runways, from major carriers such as British Airways and Emirates to minor operations such as Luxair and Air Malta.

Only one major airline from the UK doesn't use Munich's main airport – Ryanair flies into Memmingen's **Allgäu Airport** (FMM; ☎08331-984 2000; www.allgaeu-airport.de; Am Flughafen 35, Memmingen), 125km to the west.

BUS

The **Zentraler Omnibusbahnhof** (Central Bus Station, ZOB; Map p116; www.muenchen-zob.de; Arnulfstrasse 21; SHackerbrücke) next to the Hackerbrücke S-Bahn station handles the vast majority of international and domestic coach services. There's a Eurolines/Touring office, a supermarket and various eateries on the 1st floor; buses depart from ground level.

The main operator out of the ZOB is now low-cost coach company **Flixbus** (Map p116; ☑030 300 137 300; www.flixbus.com; Zentraler Omnibusbahnhof, Arnulfstrasse 21), which links Munich to countless destinations across Germany and beyond.

A special Deutsche Bahn (DB) express coach leaves for Prague (€70, 4¾ hours, three daily) from the ZOB.

TRAIN

Train connections from Munich to destinations in Bavaria are excellent and there are also numerous services to more distant cities within Germany and around Europe. All services leave from the Hauptbahnhof.

Staffed by native English speakers, **EurAide** (www.euraide.de; Desk 1, Reisezentrum, Hauptbahnhof; ☺10am-7pm Mon-Fri Mar-Apr & Aug-Dec, 9.30am-8pm May-Jul; ⓇHauptbahnhof, ⓊHauptbahnhof, ⓈHauptbahnhof) is a friendly agency based at the Hauptbahnhof that sells all DB (Deutsche Bahn) products, makes

reservations and creates personalised rail tours of Germany and beyond.

Connections from Munich:

Baden-Baden €80, four hours, hourly (change in Mannheim)

Berlin €150, 5¼ hours, hourly

Cologne €147, 4½ hours, hourly

Nuremberg €40-60, one hour, twice hourly

GETTING AROUND

TO/FROM THE AIRPORT

Munich Airport Linked by S-Bahn (S1 and S8) to the Hauptbahnhof. The trip costs €10.80, takes about 40 minutes and runs every 20 minutes almost 24 hours a day. The Lufthansa Airport Bus shuttles at 20-minute intervals between the airport and Arnulfstrasse, next to the Hauptbahnhof, between 5.15am and 7.55pm. The trip takes about 45 minutes and costs €10.50 (return €17). A taxi from Munich Airport to the Altstadt costs €50 to €70.

Nationaltheater (p123)

ANDREW MONTGOMERY/LONELY PLANET ©

Allgäu Airport The Allgäu Airport Express also leaves from Arnulfstrasse at the Hauptbahnhof, making the trip up to seven times a day. The journey takes one hour 40 minutes and the fare is €13 (return €19.50).

PUBLIC TRANSPORT

Munich's efficient public-transport system is composed of buses, trams, the U-Bahn and the S-Bahn. It's operated by MVV (www.mvv-muenchen.de), which maintains offices in the U-Bahn stations at Marienplatz, the Hauptbahnhof, Sendlinger Tor, the Ostbahnhof and Poccistrasse. Staff hand out free network maps and timetables, sell tickets and answer questions. Automated trip planning in English is best done online. The U-Bahn and S-Bahn run almost 24 hours a day, with perhaps a short gap between 2am and 4am. Night buses and trams operate in the city centre.

S-Bahn Best for journeys to the outlying areas of the city and for quick dashes along the 11km Stammstrecke (central route served by all lines between Pasing and Ostbahnhof).

U-Bahn Best for middle-distance trips from one part of the city centre to another.

Bus Best for short journeys in the city centre, especially on line 100 between the Ostbahnhof and the Hauptbahnhof.

Tram Best for short trips between various parts of the city centre. Faster than buses.

TICKETS AND FARES

The city-of-Munich region is divided into four zones, with most places of visitor interest (except Dachau and the airport) conveniently clustering within the white *Innenraum* (inner zone).

Single tickets cost €2.70. Children aged between six and 14 pay a flat €1.40 regardless of the length of the trip. Day passes are €6.70 for individuals and €12.80 for up to five people travelling together; a weekly pass called an IsarCard costs €15.40. Bikes cost €3 to take aboard and may only be taken on U-Bahn and S-Bahn trains, but not during the 6am – 9am and 4pm – 6pm rush hours.

Bus drivers sell single tickets and day passes, but tickets for the U-Bahn and S-Bahn and other passes must be purchased from vending machines at stations or MVV offices. Tram tickets are available from vending machines on board. Most tickets must be stamped (validated) at station platform entrances and on board buses and trams before use. The fine for getting caught without a valid ticket is €40.

🛎️ Where to Stay

Luxury hotels dot the centre, midrange places gather near the Hauptbahnhof. Room rates tend to be high, and they skyrocket during the Oktoberfest. However, midrange accommodation is cheaper here than in other major European cities.

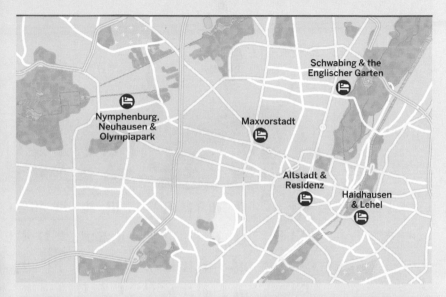

Neighbourhood	Atmosphere
Altstadt & Residenz	Central and near all the sights and best restaurants. No need to use public transport a great deal. Always busy with large groups of tourists and can be expensive.
Haidhausen & Lehel	Quiet, tranquil neighbourhood vibe and just a short ride into the Altstadt. Not much choice.
Maxvorstadt	Instant access to the Kunstareal and a short ride or walk to the Altstadt. Virtually no places to stay.
Nymphenburg, Neuhausen & Olympiapark	Near some of the city's biggest draws and tend to be cheaper. You will need to use public transport quite heavily.
Schwabing & the Englischer Garten	Elegant but buzzing location and just a hop from the tranquillity of Munich's biggest park. Some areas in the studenty south of the neighbourhood can be noisy night and day.

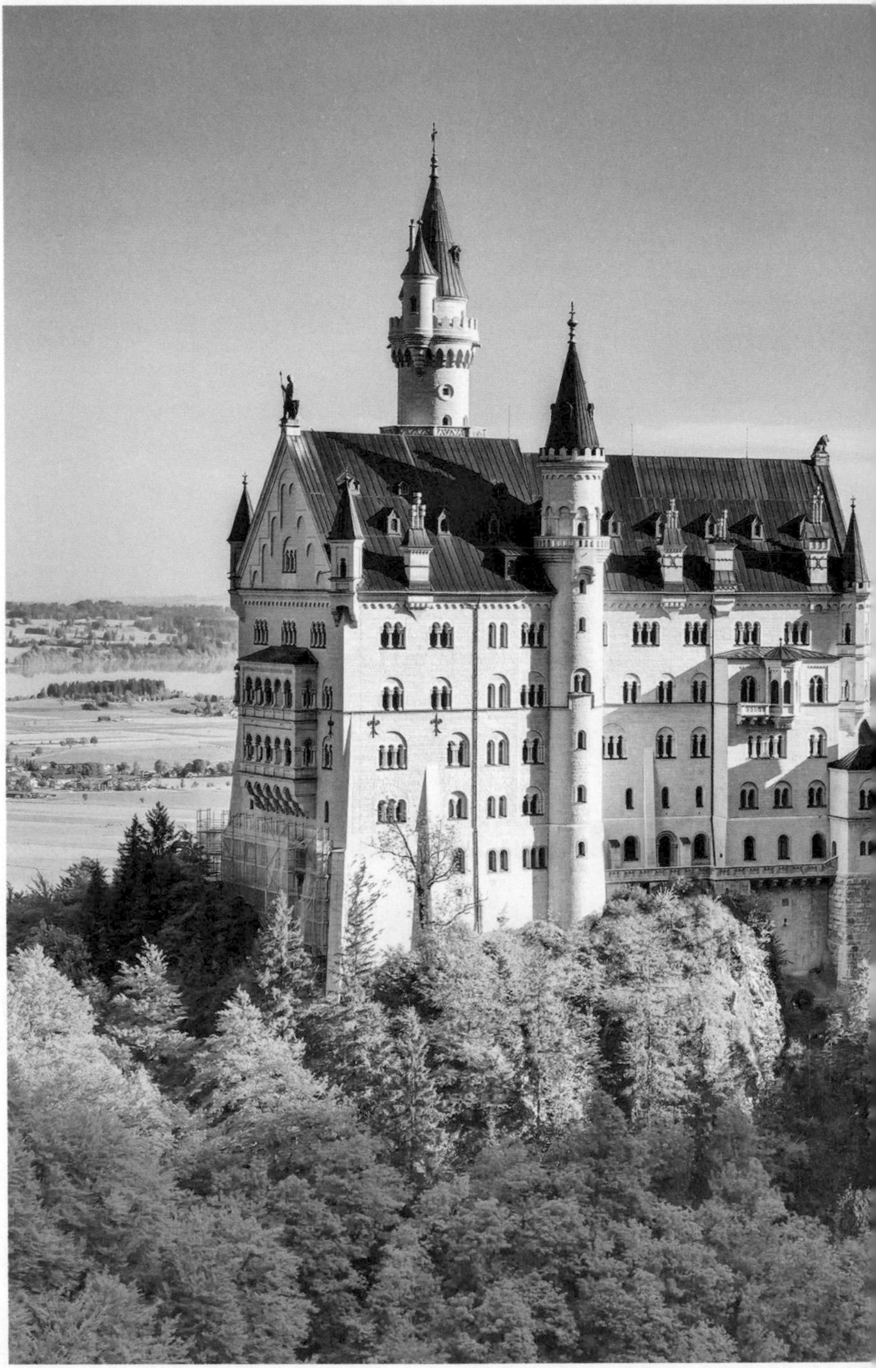

NOPPASIN / SHUTTERSTOCK ©

NEUSCHWANSTEIN

Neuschwanstein

At the southern end of the Romantic Road, the castle of Neuschwanstein, commissioned by King Ludwig II, and his less well-known ancestral home, Schloss Hohenschwangau, are highlights of any trip to Germany. The country's most popular tourist attraction lures tourists in droves all year long, many on day trips from Munich. In the summer months the place is overrun so try to arrive early or come outside of July and August to avoid the biggest crowds. Having toured Ludwig II's fantasy palaces, the nearest town to the castles is tourist-busy Füssen, worth half a day's exploration.

Arriving in Neuschwanstein

Füssen train station This is the closest train station to the castles, which handles services to/from Munich. The first train leaves Munich at 4.48am (€28.40, change in Kaufbeuren), reaching Füssen at 6.49am. Otherwise, direct trains leave Munich once every two hours throughout the day.

Hohenschwangau bus station The bus station for Neuschwanstein and surrounds is called Hohenschwangau and is served from Füssen train station by RVO buses 78 and 73 at least once an hour.

Sleeping

Accommodation in the area is surprisingly good value and the tourist office (p137) can help track down private rooms from as low as €30 per person.

Map labels:

Forggensee

Schwangau

Romantische Str

See Füssen Enlargement

Füssen

Horn

Alterschrofen

Pöllat

Schloss Neuschwanstein

Hohenschwangau Village

Schwansee

Schloss Hohenschwangau

Marienbrücke

Hohenschwangau Ticket Centre

Museum der Bayerischen Könige

Alpsee

Tegelberg

Älpeleskopf (1579m)

Füssen enlargement:
Füssen
Hauptbahnhof
Tourist Office
Beim Olivenbauer
Restaurant Ritterstub'n
Zum Franziskaner
Hohes Schloss
0 — 250 m

0 — 1 km
0 — 0.5 miles

Tronsaal (Throne Room; p134), Schloss Neuschwanstein

The four-metre high chandelier, Thronsaal (Throne Room; p134)

Schloss Neuschwanstein

Appearing through the mountainous forest like a mirage, Schloss Neuschwanstein was the model for Disney's Sleeping Beauty Castle. King Ludwig II drew the blueprints for this fairy-tale pile himself. He envisioned it as a giant stage on which to recreate the world of Germanic mythology, inspired by the operatic works of his friend Richard Wagner.

Great For...

Schloss Neuschwanstein ◉

● Hohenschwangau Village

◉
Schloss Hohenschwangau

Alpsee

❶ Need to Know

⤢tickets 08362-930 830; www.neusch wanstein.de; adult/child €13/free, incl Hohenschwangau €25/free; ⊘9am-6pm Apr–mid-Oct, 10am-4pm mid-Oct–Mar

★ **Top Tip**

Arrive as early as 8am to make sure you bag a ticket for that day.

Construction

Built as a romantic medieval castle, work on the grey-white granite pile started in 1869 but was an anachronism from the start: at the time of Ludwig's death in 1886, the first high-rises had pierced New York's skyline. However, despite his love for the old-fashioned look, the palace had plenty of high-tech features, including a hot-air heating system and running water. Like so many of the king's grand schemes, Neuschwanstein was never finished. For all the coffer-depleting sums spent on it, the king spent just over 170 days in residence.

The Interior

Completed sections include Ludwig's Tristan and Isolde–themed bedroom, dominated by a huge Gothic-style bed crowned with intricately carved cathedral-like spires; a gaudy artificial grotto (another allusion to *Tannhäuser*); and the Byzantine-style **Thronsaal** (Throne Room; pictured p132) with an incredible mosaic floor containing over two million stones. The painting opposite the (throneless) throne platform depicts another castle dreamed up by Ludwig that was never built. The most impressive room is the **Sängersaal** (Minstrels' Hall), whose frescos depict scenes from the opera *Tannhäuser*.

Schloss Hohenschwangau

King Ludwig II grew up at the sun-yellow Schloss Hohenschwangau and later enjoyed summers here until his death in 1886. His father, Maximilian II, built this palace in a neo-Gothic style atop 12th-century ruins left by Schwangau knights. Far less showy than Neuschwanstein, Hohenschwangau has a distinctly lived-in feel where every piece of

Schloss Hohenschwangau

furniture is a used original. After his father died, Ludwig's main alteration was having stars, illuminated with hidden oil lamps, painted on the ceiling of his bedroom.

Castle Tickets & Tours

Schloss Neuschwanstein and Hohenschwangau can only be visited on guided tours (in German or English), which last about 35 minutes each (Hohenschwangau is first). Strictly timed tickets are available from the **ticket centre** (☑08362-930 830; www.hohenschwangau.de; Alpenseestrasse 12; ⊙7.30am-5pm Apr–mid-Oct, 8.30am-3pm mid Oct–Mar) at the foot of the castles.

☑ **Don't Miss**

The excellent Museum der Bayerischen Könige (p136) is a short walk from the castle ticket office.

A.ESPILLA/SHUTTERSTOCK ©

Enough time is left between tours for the steep 30- to 40-minute walk between the castles. All Munich's tour companies run day excursions out to the castles.

Ludwig II, the Fairy-tale King

Ludwig II was a sensitive soul, fascinated by romantic epics, architecture and music, but his parents, Maximilian II and Marie, took little interest in his musings and he suffered a lonely and joyless childhood. In 1864, at 18 years old, the prince became king.

Ludwig was an enthusiastic leader initially, but Bavaria's days as a sovereign state were numbered, and he became a puppet king after the creation of the German Reich in 1871. Ludwig withdrew completely, to drink, draw up castle plans and view concerts and operas. His obsession with lavish projects eventually spelled his undoing.

Contrary to popular belief, it was only Ludwig's purse – and not the state treasury – that was being bankrupted. However, by 1886 his mountain of debt and erratic behaviour had put him at odds with his cabinet. The king, it seemed, needed to be 'managed'.

In 1886, several ministers and relatives arranged a hasty psychiatric test that diagnosed Ludwig as mentally unfit to rule (this was made easier by the fact that his brother had been declared insane years earlier). That June, he was removed to Schloss Berg on Lake Starnberg. A few days later the dejected bachelor and his doctor took a Sunday-evening lakeside walk and were found several hours later, drowned in just a few feet of water.

No one knows with certainty what happened that night. The circumstantial evidence was conflicting and incomplete. Conspiracy theories abound. That summer the authorities opened Neuschwanstein to the public to help pay off Ludwig's huge debts. King Ludwig II was dead, but the myth, and a tourist industry, had been born.

✕ **Take a Break**

Several restaurants line the road that runs from the ticket office to the castles.

Füssen

Nestled at the foot of the Alps, tourist-busy Füssen is the southern climax of the Romantic Road, with the nearby castles of Neuschwanstein and Hohenschwangau the highlight of many a southern Germany trip. But having 'done' the country's most popular tourist route and seen Ludwig II's fantasy palaces, there are several other reasons to linger longer in the area. The town of Füssen is worth half a day's exploration and, from here, you can easily escape from the crowds into a landscape of gentle hiking trails and Alpine vistas.

◉ SIGHTS

Museum der Bayerischen Könige   Museum

(Museum of the Bavarian Kings; www.museum derbayerischenkoenige.de; Alpseestrasse 27; adult/child €11/free; ⊘9am-5pm) Palace-fatigued visitors often head straight for the bus stop, coach park or nearest beer after a tour of the castles, most overlooking this worthwhile museum, installed in a former lakeside hotel 400m from the castle ticket office (heading towards Alpsee lake). The architecturally stunning museum is packed with historical background on Bavaria's former first family and well worth the extra legwork.

The big-window views across the stunningly beautiful lake (a great picnic spot) to the Alps are almost as stunning as the Wittelsbach bling on show, including Ludwig II's famous blue-and-gold robe.

A detailed audioguide is included in the ticket price.

Hohes Schloss   Castle, Gallery

(Magnusplatz 10; adult/child €6/free; ⊘galleries 11am-5pm Tue-Sun Apr-Oct, 1-4pm Fri-Sun Nov-Mar) The Hohes Schloss (pictured below), a late-Gothic confection and one-time retreat of the bishops of Augsburg, towers over Füssen's compact historical centre. The north wing of the palace contains the Staatsgalerie (State Gallery), with regional paintings and sculpture from the 15th and 16th centuries. The Städtische Gemäldegalerie (City Paintings Gallery) below is a showcase of 19th-century artists.

Hohes Schloss

MARKUS LANGE/ROBERTHARDING/GETTY IMAGES ©

The inner courtyard is a masterpiece of illusionary architecture dating back to 1499; you'll do a double take before realising that the gables, oriels and windows are not quite as 3D as they seem.

EATING

Beim Olivenbauer
Austrian, Italian $$

(☑08362-6250; www.beim-olivenbauer.de; Ottostrasse 7; mains €8-19; ⏱11.30am-11.30pm) The Tyrol meets the Allgäu at this fun eatery, its interior a jumble of Doric columns, mismatched tables and chairs, multihued paint and assorted rural knick-knackery. Treat yourself to a wheel of pizza and a glass of Austrian wine, or go local with a plate of *Maultaschen* (pork-and-spinach ravioli) and a mug of local beer.

Zum Franziskaner
Bavarian $$

(Kemptener Strasse 1; mains €6.50-18; ⏱11.30am-10pm) This popular restaurant specialises in *Schweinshaxe* (pork knuckle) and schnitzel, prepared in more varieties than you can imagine. There's some choice for noncarnivores such as *Käsespätzle* (rolled cheese noodles) and salads. When the sun shines the outdoor seating shares the pavement with the 'foot-washing' statue.

Restaurant Ritterstub'n
German $$

(☑08362-7759; www.restaurant-ritterstuben. de; Ritterstrasse 4; mains €10-18.50; ⏱11.30am-10pm Tue-Sun) This convivial pit stop has value-priced salads, snacks, lunch specials, fish, schnitzel and gluten-free dishes, and even a cute kids' menu. The medieval knight theme can be a bit grating but does little to distract from the filling food when you arrive hungry from the peaks.

INFORMATION

The **tourist office** (☑08362-938 50; www. fuessen.de; Kaiser-Maximilian-Platz; ⏱9am-5pm Mon-Fri, 9.30am-3.30pm Sat) is a very professionally run operation where staff field questions about the castles with a smile.

ℹ GETTING THERE & AWAY

If you want to do the castles in a single day from Munich, you'll need to start very early. The first train leaves Munich at 4.48am (€28.40, change in Kaufbeuren), reaching Füssen at 6.49am. Otherwise, direct trains leave Munich once every two hours throughout the day.

The **Deutsche Touring** (www.touring.de, www.romantic-road.com) **Romantic Road Coach** (www.romanticroadcoach.de) leaves from outside Füssen train station (stop 3) at 8am. It arrives in Füssen at 8.30pm.

ℹ GETTING AROUND

RVO buses 78 and 73 (www.rvo-bus.de) serve the castles from Füssen Bahnhof (€4.40 return, eight minutes, at least hourly). Buy tickets from the driver.

Taxis wait outside Füssen Bahnhof. The fare to the castles is around €12.

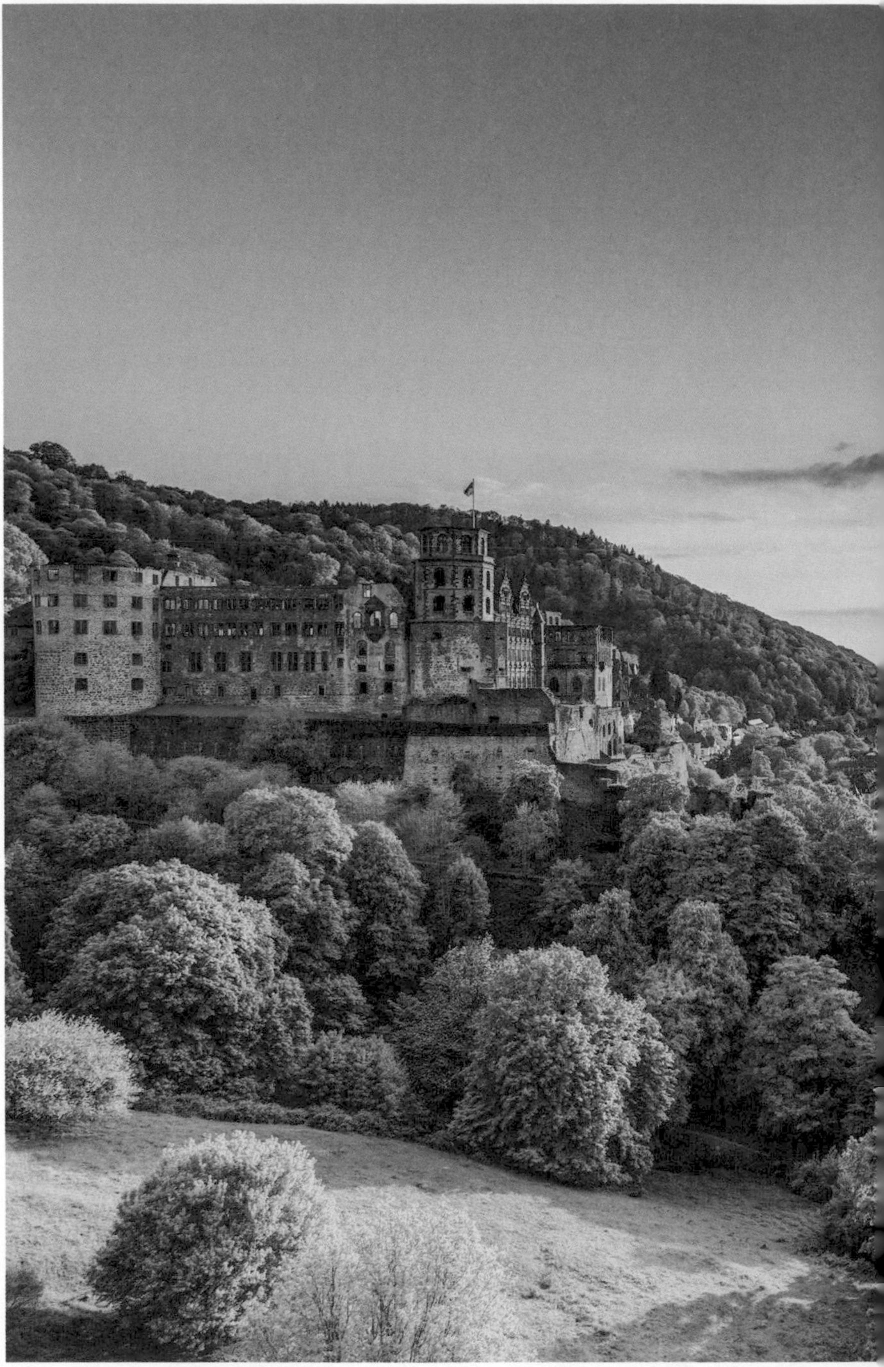

HEIDELBERG

Heidelberg

Surrounded by forest 93km south of Frankfurt, Germany's oldest and most famous university town is renowned for its baroque Altstadt, spirited student atmosphere, beautiful riverside setting and evocative half-ruined hilltop castle, which together draw 11.8 million visitors a year. They follow in the footsteps of the late 18th- and early 19th-century romantics, most notably the poet Goethe. Britain's William Turner also loved Heidelberg, which inspired him to paint some of his greatest landscapes.

Heidelberg in One Day

This compact city can be easily appreciated in a day. Start your explorations of the town's impressive Altstadt from **Marktplatz** (p142), where you can pop into the tourist office for suggested local walks, or just wander the cobblestoned streets and lanes. Head to the **Kurpfälzisches Museum** (p146) for a thorough briefing on local history, and wander the 2.5km **Philosophenweg** (p146) for wonderful views of the city and its imposing **castle** (p144). Castle visits should be considered essential.

Getting Around

Getting around Heidelberg on public transport is easy – the tourist office can supply you with a Linienplan transport map.

The city's network of trams and buses is operated by VRN (www.vrn.de).

Standard single bus/tram tickets cost €1.70; short-trip tickets for up to three trips are €1.40. A Ticket 24, valid for 24 hours in up to three zones, costs €6.70. Tickets are sold at tram-stop ticket machines and by bus drivers.

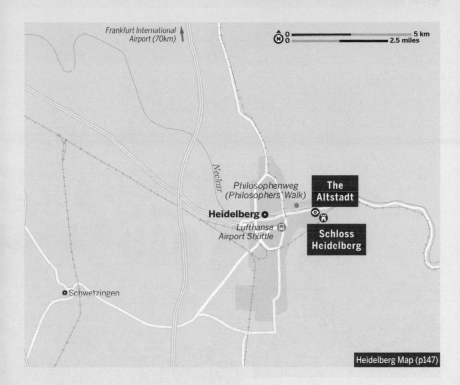

Frankfurt International
Airport (70km)

5 km
2.5 miles

Neckar

*Philosophenweg
(Philosophers' Walk)*

Heidelberg ○

*Lufthansa
Airport Shuttle*

**The
Altstadt**

**Schloss
Heidelberg**

○ Schwetzingen

Heidelberg Map (p147)

Arriving in Heidelberg

Hauptbahnhof Handles all local and
national train services.

Frankfurt airport The nearest airport
is at Frankfurt, reached by regular
Lufthansa bus.

Sleeping

Heidelberg's popularity means finding a
bed can be tricky. Booking ahead is ad-
visable any time of year, but particularly
in summer and during the Christmas
season.

Karl-Theodor-Brücke

The Altstadt

The highlight of any visit to Heidelberg is a stroll through the streets of its well-preserved Altstadt, a red-roofed townscape of remarkable architectural unity. Built pretty much from scratch during the 18th century, it emerged from WWII almost completely unscathed.

Great For

☑ Don't Miss

Next to the Universitätsmuseum, the Alte Aula is a neo-Renaissance hall whose rich decoration dates from 1886.

Marktplatz

The **Marktplatz** (Map p147) is the focal point of Altstadt street life. The **Hercules fountain** – that's him up on top of the pillar – in the middle is where petty criminals were chained and left to face the mob in the Middle Ages.

Heiliggeistkirche

For bird's-eye views, climb 208 stairs to the top of the tower of Heidelberg's famous **church** (Map p147; ☎06221-980 30; www.ekihd.de; Marktplatz; tower adult/child €2/1; ☺church 11am-5pm Mon-Sat, from 12.30pm Sun, tower 11am-5pm Mon-Sat, from 12.30pm Sun Apr-Oct, 11am-3pm Fri & Sat, from 12.30pm Sun Nov-Mar), constructed between 1344 and 1441, which was shared by Catholics and Protestants from 1706 until 1936 (it's now Protestant).

Graffiti, Studentenkarzer (student jail)

ATLANTIDE PHOTOTRAVEL/GETTY IMAGES ©

ⓘ Need to Know

The Altstadt is served by its own S-Bahn station (Altstadt).

✕ Take a Break

The Zum Roten Ochsen (p148) tavern is located at the eastern end of the Altstadt.

★ Top Tip

The Heidelberg Card (one/two/four days €13/15/17) is worth buying from a tourist office (p149) if you intend visiting most of Heidelberg's museums.

Studentenkarzer

From 1823 to 1914, students convicted of misdeeds such as public inebriation, loud nocturnal singing, freeing the local pigs or duelling were sent to this **student jail** (Map p147; ☑06221-541 2813; www.uni-heidelberg.de; Auginergasse 2; adult/child incl Universitätsmuseum €3/2.50; ☉10am-6pm Tue-Sun Apr-Oct, to 4pm Mon-Sat Nov-Mar) for at least 24 hours. Judging by the inventive wall graffiti (pictured above), some found their stay highly amusing. Delinquents were let out to attend lectures or take exams. In certain circles, a stint in the Karzer was considered a rite of passage.

Universitätsmuseum

The three-room **University Museum** (Map p147; www.uni-heidelberg.de; Grabengasse 1; adult/child incl Studentenkarzer €3/2.50; ☉10am-6pm Tue-Sun Apr-Sep, to 4pm Tue-Sat Oct-Mar), inside the Alte Universität building, has paintings, portraits, documents and photos recording the university's mostly illustrious history. Only the signs on the Third Reich period are in English but the admission fee includes an English audioguide.

Alte Brücke

Alte Brücke (Karl-Theodor-Brücke; Map p147), Heidelberg's 200m-long 'old bridge' (pictured above left), built in 1786, connects the Altstadt with the river's right bank and the Schlangenweg (Snake Path), whose switchbacks lead to the Philosophenweg (Philosophers' Walk). Next to the tower gate on the Altstadt side of the bridge, look for the brass sculpture of a monkey holding a mirror. It's the 1979 replacement of the 17th-century original sculpture.

Schloss Heidelberg

Schloss Heidelberg

Towering over the Altstadt, Heidelberg's ruined Renaissance castle cuts a romantic figure, especially from across the Neckar River when illuminated at night. It's one of the most idyllic spots in Germany, but also one with a tumultuous past.

Palatinate princes, stampeding Swedes, rampaging French, Protestant reformers and lightning strikes – this Renaissance pile has seen the lot. Its turbulent history, lonely beauty and changing moods helped inspire the German Romantic movement two centuries ago. Goethe and Mark Twain are its most illustrious visitors to date.

Attractions

The Schlosshof, the castle's central courtyard, is hemmed by Gothic and Renaissance buildings so elaborate they often elicit visitor oohs and aahs. The most eye-catching façade belongs to the Friedrichsbau, which is festooned with life-size sculptures of kings and emperors. Psalm 118 is inscribed on the front in Hebrew. Another breath-taking feature are the far-reaching views over the Neckar River and the Altstadt rooftops.

Great For

☑ **Don't Miss**

The cafe next to the Grosses Fass is a good place to sample German wine.

Bergbahn (funicular railway)

❶ Need to Know

Map p147; ☎06221-658 880; www.schloss
-heidelberg.de; Schlosshof 1; adult/child incl
Bergbahn €7/4, tours €5/2.50, audioguide
€5; ⊗grounds 24hr, castle 8am-6pm, English
tours hourly 11.15am-4.15pm Mon-Fri, from
10.15am Sat & Sun Apr-Oct, fewer tours
Nov-Mar

✗ Take a Break

There's a cafe next to the Grosses
Fass or pack a picnic to enjoy in the
Schlossgarten.

★ Top Tip

In summer visit in the evening when
admission charges don't apply.

With a capacity of 228,000L, the Grosses
Fass is the world's largest wine cask. It was
fashioned from 130 oak trees. Describing
it as being 'as big as a cottage' Mark Twain
bemoaned its emptiness and mused on its
possible functions as a dance floor and a
gigantic cream churn.

The surprisingly interesting Deutsches
Apotheken-Museum off the Schlosshof
traces the history of Western pharmacology, in which Germany played a central role.
Exhibits include pharmacies from the early
1700s and the Napoleonic era.

The grassy and flower-filled Schlossgarten on the hillside south and east of the
castle is a lovely spot for a stroll.

Visiting

Tickets are only required between 8am
and 5.30pm – after this you can stroll

the grounds for free. The only way to see
the less-than-scintillating interior is by
tour – multilingual audioguides that cite
Goethe's poems and Mark Twain's stories
can be hired at the ticket office (to the
right as you enter the gardens from the
Bergbahn). Except for the museum, the
entire Schloss is wheelchair accessible
though the cobblestones make for rough
going.

Getting There

To reach the red sandstone hulk perched
about 80m above the Altstadt, you can
either make the long slog up the steep,
cobbled Burgweg in around ten minutes,
or take the Bergbahn (funicular railway;
pictured above). This was opened in
1890 and services run every ten minutes
from the Kornmarkt stop. Schloss tickets
include the ride on the Bergbahn.

⊙ SIGHTS

Heidelberg's Altstadt runs along the left (south) bank of the Neckar River from Bismarckplatz east to the hillside Schloss. One of Europe's longest pedestrian zones, the 1600m-long Hauptstrasse, runs east–west through the Altstadt. It's about 200m south of the Neckar, and passes a series of picturesque public squares, many with historic or modern fountains. Superb views of the town extend from the north (right) bank of the Neckar in Neuenheim.

Kurpfälzisches Museum · Museum

(Map p147; www.museum-heidelberg.de; Hauptstrasse 97; adult/child Tue-Sat €3/1.80, Sun €1.80/1.20; ⊙10am-6pm Tue-Sun) The city-run Palatinate Museum chronicles Heidelberg's eventful past, particularly the Roman period – exhibits include original wood beams from a 3rd-century bridge. To learn about really ancient history, check out the replica of the 600,000-year-old jawbone of *Homo heidelbergensis* (Heidelberg Man), unearthed some 18km southeast in 1907 (the original is stored at the university's palaeontology institute). Most of the museum's late 15th- to 20th-century paintings and sculptures are by artists from or associated with the region.

Jesuitenkirche · Church

(Map p147; www.heidelberg-neckartal.de; Schulgasse 4; church free, Schatzkammer adult/child €3/2.50; ⊙church 9.30am-6pm May-Sep, to 5pm Oct-Apr, Schatzkammer 10am-5pm Tue-Sat, from 1pm Sun Jun-Oct, Sat & Sun Nov-May) Rising above an attractive square just east of Universitätsplatz, the red-sandstone Jesuits' church, with an all-white interior, is a fine example of 18th-century baroque. The *Schatzkammer* (treasury) displays precious religious artefacts. Look out for regular concerts.

Philosophenweg · Trail

(Philosophers' Walk; Neckar River north bank) Winding past monuments, towers, ruins, a beer garden, and an enormous *Thingstätte* (amphitheatre) built by the Nazis in 1935, the 2.5km-long Philosophers' Walk has captivating views of Heidelberg's Schloss, especially at sunset when the city is bathed in a reddish glow. Access is easiest via the steep Schlangenweg from Alte Brücke (p143). Don't attempt to drive up as the road is narrow and there's nowhere to turn around at the top.

✪ ACTIVITIES

Solarschiff · Cruise

(Map p147; www.hdsolarschiff.com; Alte Brücke; adult/child €9/3.50; ⊙10am-6pm Tue-Sun Mar-Oct) ⫟ One of the most peaceful ways to appreciate Heidelberg's charms is to get out on the river. Solarschiff's solar-powered boat is silent – all you hear during a 50-minute cruise, apart from onboard commentary in English and German, are the water and the distant sounds of the city.

✪ TOURS

Tourist Office Walking Tours · Walking

(Map p147; www.heidelberg-marketing.de; adult/child €9/7; ⊙English tours 10.30am Thu-Sat Apr-Oct) English-language tours (1½ hours) taking in the Altstadt's highlights depart from the Marktplatz tourist office (p149).

✪ EATING

The Altstadt, especially around Steingasse and Untere Strasse, is chock-full of restaurants, cafes, pubs and beer gardens. Cosy restaurants frequented by locals are tucked away on the side streets south of the Hauptstrasse and west of the Kornmarkt.

Many of Heidelberg's traditional pubs are also atmospheric places to dine on hearty German cuisine.

Joe Molese · Diner €

(Map p147; www.joemolese.com; Steingasse 16a; dishes €5-12; ⊙noon-11pm) Sandwiches – like pastrami, tomato and honey-mustard vinaigrette; brie, arugula and truffle oil; or wild smoked salmon with lemon juice and olive oil – are the standout at Joe's, but it also

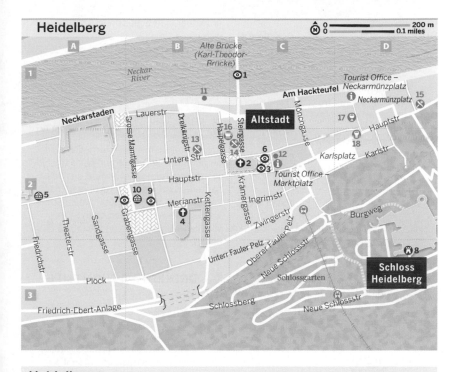

Heidelberg

◉ **Sights**

✪ **Activities, Courses & Tours**

✖ **Eating**

◎ **Drinking & Nightlife**

has fantastic salads, chicken drumsticks, burgers and buffalo wings. Black-and-white chequer-board tiling and fire-engine-red walls give it a souped-up New York deli vibe. Cash only.

Schnitzelbank   German €€

(☏06221-211 89; www.schnitzelbank-heidelberg.de; Bauamtsgasse 7; mains €15-22; ⊗5pm-11.30pm Mon-Fri, from 11.30am Sat & Sun, bar to 1am) Small and often jam-packed, this cosy wine tavern has you sampling the local tipples (all wines are regional) and cuisine. You'll be crouching on wooden workbenches from the time when this was still a cooperage. It's these benches that give the place its name, incidentally, not the veal and pork schnitzel on the menu.

Café Weinstube Burkardt
Cafe €€

(Map p147; ☎06221-166 620; www.facebook.
com/cafeburkardt; Untere Strasse 27; mains €12-
23.50; ⊙kitchen 11.30am-2pm & 6-10pm, cafe
9am-11pm) Charming Burkardt's has a superb selection of wines from the Heidelberg
region available by the glass, and first-rate
food, such as risotto with asparagus and
mushrooms or apricot and lamb ragout.
The courtyard abuts the house where
Friedrich Ebert, German President during
the Weimar Republic, was born.

'S' Kastanie
European €€€

(☎06221-728 0343; www.restaurant-s-kastanie.
de; Elisabethenweg 1; 2-course lunch menu €10,
3-/4-/5-course dinner menus €43/46.50/58,
mains €17-29.50; ⊙11.30am-2.30pm & 6-10pm
Wed-Fri, 5-10pm Sat, 11.30am-8pm Sun; 🚗) A
panoramic terrace provides sweeping views
of the river at this gorgeous 1904-built
former hunting lodge with stained glass
and timber panelling, set in the forest near
the castle. Chef Sven Schönig's stunning
creations include octopus carpaccio with
grilled watermelon and cauliflower mousse

or feather-light goat's cheese soufflé with
wild-garlic sauce. Vegetarian and vegan
choices are available.

Zur Herrenmühle Heidelberg
German €€€

(Map p147; ☎06221-602 909; www.herren
muehle.net; Hauptstrasse 239; mains €28.50-
36, 3-/4-course menus €62/68; ⊙6-9.30pm
Mon-Sat, noon-4pm & 6-9.30pm Sun) A flour
mill from 1690 has been turned into an
elegant and highly cultured place to enjoy
refined 'country-style' cuisine, such as
saffron-crusted dorade royale with baby
spinach and creamed potato, beneath
weighty, 300-year-old wooden beams
with candles flickering on the tables. Book
ahead.

🍷 DRINKING & NIGHTLIFE

Zum Roten Ochsen
Pub

(Red Ox Inn; Map p147; www.roterochsen.de;
Hauptstrasse 217; ⊙5pm-midnight Mon-
Wed, from 11.30am Thu-Sat) Fronted by a
red-painted, blue-grey-shuttered facade,
Heidelberg's most historic student pub

Marktplatz (p142)

has black-and-white frat photos on the dark wooden walls and names carved into the tables. Along with German luminaries, visitors who've raised a glass here include Mark Twain, John Wayne and Marilyn Monroe. Live piano plays from 7.30pm, with plenty of patrons singing along.

KulturBrauerei   Microbrewery
(Map p147; www.heidelberger-kulturbrauerei. de; Leyergasse 6; ☺7am-11pm) With its wood-plank floor, chairs from a Spanish monastery, black iron chandeliers and an enchanting beer garden, this brewpub is an atmospheric spot to taste the house brews, including many seasonal specialities, and local dishes such as homemade sausages with cream cheese, radish and dark bread.

Chocolaterie Yilliy   Cafe
(Map p147; www.chocolaterie-heidelberg.de; Haspelgasse 7; ☺10am-8pm) Especially when the weather's chilly, this is a wonderful spot to warm up with a wickedly thick house-speciality hot chocolate in flavours like hazelnut, Cointreau, chilli or praline. The airy space has a laid-back lounge-room vibe, with a book swap, piano, regular acoustic gigs and rotating exhibitions by local artists.

❂ ENTERTAINMENT

The city's effervescent cultural scene includes concerts, films, and dance and theatre performances. Venues sell tickets online, or buy them from **Zigaretten Grimm** (☏06221-209 09; www.duerninger.de; Sophienstrasse 11; ☺9am-7pm Mon-Fri, 10am-5pm Sat).

Karlstorbahnhof   Arts Centre
(☏06221-978 911; www.karlstorbahnhof.de; Am Karlstor 1; ☺Sep-Jul) Within an old train station, beloved cultural centre Karlstorbahnhof has an art-house cinema screening original-language films; theatre, cabaret and comedy performances (some in English); a nightclub hosting DJs and parties; and a diverse range of concerts. It's 100m east of the Karlstor, the towering stone gate at the eastern end of the Altstadt.

❶ INFORMATION

The Heidelberg Card (one/two/four days €15/17/19) entitles you to unlimited public transport use, free admission to the Schloss (including the Bergbahn cogwheel railway) and discounts for museums, tours and more. A two-day family card for up to two adults and three children costs €36. Pick one up from a tourist office:

Tourist Office – Hauptbahnhof (☏06221-5844 444; www.heidelberg-marketing.de; Willy-Brandt-Platz 1; ☺9am-7pm Mon-Sat, 10am-6pm Sun Apr-Oct, 9am-6pm Mon-Sat Nov-Mar) Right outside the main train station.

Tourist Office – Marktplatz (Map p147; Marktplatz 10; ☺8am-5pm Mon-Fri) At the Rathaus (Town Hall) in the old town.

Tourist Office – Neckarmünzplatz (Map p147; ☏06221-5840 244; Obere Neckarstrasse 31; ☺9am-6pm Mon-Sat, 10am-5pm Sun Apr-Oct, 10am-5pm Mon-Sat Nov-Mar) By the river on Neckarmünzplatz.

❶ GETTING THERE & AWAY

TRAIN

From the **Hauptbahnhof** (Willy-Brandt-Platz), 3km west of the Schloss, there are up to three services per hour to/from Frankfurt (€19.90 to €29.90, one to 1½ hours) and Stuttgart (€23.90 to €39.90, 40 minutes to one hour), as well as S-Bahn services to Mannheim (€5.80, 30 minutes, two per hour) and Speyer (€10.90, 50 minutes, every 30 minutes). From Mannheim you can connect to German Wine Route towns.

BUS

The fastest way to reach Frankfurt airport is the **Lufthansa Airport Shuttle** (☏06152-976 9099; www.frankfurt-airport-shuttles.de; Crowne Plaza Hotel, Kurfürsten-Anlage 1-3; one-way €24; ☺5am-6.30pm). It runs every 90 minutes; journey time is one hour.

To get to Frankfurt-Hahn airport, you can take the **Hahn Express** (☏06204-608 2400; www.holger-tours.de; one-way €22) (2¼ hours, five daily), which stops at the Hauptbahnhof.

THE BLACK
FOREST

The Black Forest

Home of the cuckoo clock, the Schwarzwald (Black Forest) gets its name from its dark, slightly sinister canopy of evergreens: this is where Hansel and Gretel encountered the wicked witch. The vast expanse of hills, valleys, rivers and forests stretch from the swish spa town of Baden-Baden to the Swiss border, and from the Rhine almost to Lake Constance.

A short walk from most towns and you will be in the middle of quiet countryside dotted with traditional farmhouses and amiable dairy cows, perhaps, or in a thick forest.

The Black Forest in Two Days

To really see the Black Forest, you need to hit the trails. Tourist offices are invaluable resources, as is the online planner at www.wanderservice-schwarzwald.de.

If time is limited, journey between Baden-Baden, the region's northern gateway, and Freiburg – with its 11th century **Freiburger Münster** (p154) – to the south. Baden-Baden's therapeutic waters (p156) have soothed weary wanderers for centuries. The Black Forest is also where you'll find many **walks** (p158).

The Black Forest in One Week

Serious nature lovers should allocate at least a week to explore this vast and beautiful part of Germany, home of the Schwarzwaldverein (www.schwarzwald-verein.de), where well-trodden paths criss-cross the deepest reaches of the Black Forest and snuggle away little villages like Schiltach, Triberg and Gutach. Highlights include the steep Murg Valley, Titisee and 1493m **Feldberg Steig** (p161).

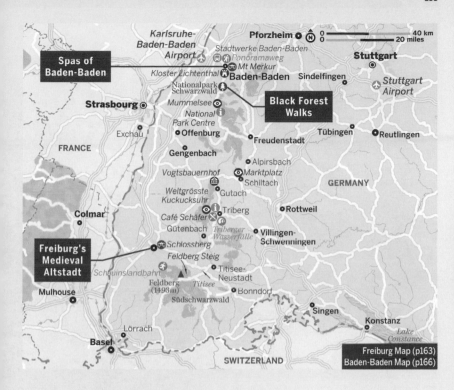

Freiburg Map (p163)
Baden-Baden Map (p166)

Arriving in the Black Forest

Karlsruhe-Baden-Baden Airport
Handles mainly budget flights. 15km
from Baden-Baden.

Stuttgart International Airport A major hub for Germanwings. 13km south
of the city.

Freiburg Hauptbahnhof The main train
station for accessing the Black Forest
handles local and national services.

Sleeping

Charismatic hotels abound in Freiburg's
Altstadt but it's wise to book ahead
in summer. The **tourist office** (p164)
offers a booking service (€3) and has a
list of good-value private guesthouses.

Baden-Baden is crammed with hotels,
but bargains are rare. The **tourist office**
(p167) has a room reservation service,
for a 10% fee.

Historisches Kaufhaus, Münsterplatz

Freiburg's Medieval Altstadt

Sitting plump at the foot of the Black Forest's wooded slopes and vineyards, Freiburg is a sunny, cheerful university town, its medieval Altstadt a story-book tableau of gabled town houses, cobblestone lanes and cafe-rimmed plazas.

Great For...

☑ **Don't Miss**

Look out for pavement mosaics in front of many shops denoting what is sold there.

Freiburger Münster

With its lacy spires, cheeky gargoyles and intricate entrance portal, Freiburg's 11th-century **minster** (Map p163; www.freiburgermuenster.info; tower adult/concession €2/1.50; ⊘10am-5pm Mon-Sat, 1-7pm Sun, tower 9.30am-5pm Mon-Sat, 1-5pm Sun) cuts an impressive figure above the central market square (Münsterplatz; pictured above). It has dazzling kaleidoscopic stained-glass windows that were mostly financed by medieval guilds and a high altar with a masterful triptych by Dürer protégé Hans Baldung Grien. Square at the base, the tower becomes an octagon higher up and is crowned by a filigreed 116m-high spire. On clear days you can spy the Vosges Mountains in France.

Martinstor

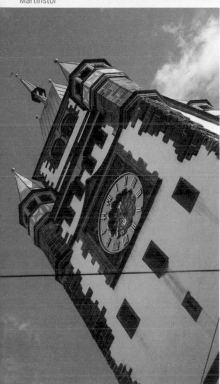

CONSSUELLA/SHUTTERSTOCK ©

Münsterplatz
Freiburger ⊚
Münster
⊚ *Historisches*
Kaufhaus
Schlossbergring
⊚
Augustinermuseum Schlossberg

❶ Need to Know

Freiburger Münster is closed for visits during services (exact times are available at the info desk inside).

✗ Take a Break

There is a cafe overlooking the cloister at the Augustinermuseum where you can sip a drink and soak up the monastic vibe.

★ Top Tip

A €7 ticket is available which is valid for all museums in Freiburg.

Closer to the ground, near the main portal in fact, note the medieval wall measurements used to ensure that merchandise (eg loaves of bread) were of the requisite size.

Augustinermuseum

Dip into the past as represented by artists working from the Middle Ages to the 19th century at this superb **museum** (Map p163; ☑0761-201 2501; www.freiburg.de; Augustinerplatz 1; adult/concession/child €7/5/free; ⊙10am-5pm Tue-Thu, Sat & Sun, to 7pm Fri) in a sensitively modernised monastery. The Sculpture Hall on the ground floor is especially impressive for its fine medieval sculpture and masterpieces by Renaissance artists Hans Baldung Grien and Lucas Cranach the Elder. Head upstairs for eye-level views of mounted gargoyles.

Historisches Kaufhaus

Facing the Münster's south side and embellished with polychrome tiled turrets is the arcaded brick-red **Historisches Kaufhaus**, an early 16th-century merchants' hall (pictured above). The coats of arms on the oriels and the four figures above the balcony symbolise Freiburg's allegiance to the House of Habsburg.

City Gates

Freiburg has two intact medieval gates. The **Martinstor** (Map p163; Martin's gate) rises above Kaiser Joseph-Strasse, while the 13th-century **Schwabentor** (Map p163; Schwabenring), is a massive city gate with a mural of St George slaying the dragon and tram tracks running under its arches.

Caracalla Spa

ROMAN BARAKIN/SHUTTERSTOCK ©

Spas of Baden-Baden

Baden-Baden's air of old-world luxury and curative waters have attracted royals, the rich and celebrities over the years – Obama and Bismarck, Queen Victoria and Victoria Beckham included.

Great For...

☑ Don't Miss

Baden-Baden is criss-crossed with walking trails – one leads 3km to the 11th-century Altes Schloss.

Friedrichsbad

If it's the body of Venus and the complexion of Cleopatra you desire, abandon modesty (and clothing) to wallow in thermal waters at **Friedrichsbad** (Map p166; ☑07221-275 920; www.carasana.de; Römerplatz 1; 3hr ticket €25, incl soap-&-brush massage €37; ☺9am-10pm, last entry 7pm), a palatial 19th-century marble-and-mosaic-festooned spa. As Mark Twain put it, 'after 10 minutes you forget time; after 20 minutes, the world', as you slip into the regime of steaming, scrubbing, hot–cold bathing and dunking in the Roman-Irish bath.

Friedrichsbad

JWACKENHUT/GETTY IMAGES ©

ⓘ **Need to Know**

Bus 205 runs hourly between the Bahnhof and the airport, less frequently at weekends.

✕ **Take a Break**

Weinstube im Baldreit (p167) is one of the best places to eat in town.

★ **Top Tip**

Drink Baden-Baden's mineral-rich water for free at the Fettquelle near Römerplatz.

Kaiserallee 3; ⊙10am-5pm Mon-Sat, 2-5pm Sun) was built in 1839 as an attractive addition to the Kurhaus (p166). The 90m-long portico is embellished with 19th-century frescoes of local legends. Baden-Baden's elixir of youth, some say, is the free curative mineral water that gushes from a faucet linked to the Fried-richsbad spring.

What's Nearby

The sublime **casino** (Map p166; ☑07221-302 40; www.casino-baden-baden.de; Kaiserallee 1; admission €5, guided tour €7; ⊙2pm-2am Sun-Thu, to 3.30am Fri & Sat, guided tours 9.30-11.45am Apr-Oct, 10am-11.30am Nov-Mar) seeks to emulate – indeed, outdo – the gilded splendour of Versailles. Marlene Dietrich called it 'the most beautiful casino in the world'. Gents must wear a jacket and tie. If you're not much of a gambler and want to simply marvel at the opulence, hook onto a 40-minute guided tour.

Under the same roof is super-stylish restaurant The Grill and upscale club Bernstein, where the dance floor heaves with beautiful people.

Caracalla Spa

Modern, glass-fronted **Caracalla Spa** (Map p166; ☑07221-275 940; www.carasana. de; Römerplatz 11; 2/3hr €16/19, day ticket €23; ⊙8am-10pm, last admission 8pm) has a cluster of indoor and outdoor pools, grottos and surge channels, making the most of the mineral-rich spring water. For those who dare to bare, saunas range from the rustic 'forest' to the roasting 95°C 'fire' variety.

Trinkhalle

Standing proud above a manicured park, this neoclassical **pump room** (Map p166;

Walking the Westweg (p161)

Black Forest Walks

As locals will tell you, the essence of visiting the Black Forest is getting geared up and hitting the many trails that criss-cross the region. Well-marked routes take you to some of the most picturesque areas in the region, some far from the main tourist hotspots.

Great For...

❶ Need to Know

Outdoor-equipment shops are widespread in southern Germany and stock high-quality gear.

★ **Top Tip**

Make use of the Schwarzwald Verein's free tour planner at www.wanderservice -schwarzwald.de.

If you do decide to pull on walking boots and get out there, local tourist information offices in towns on or near the trails can help out with guides and maps.

It's also worth checking out Schwarz-waldverein (www.schwarzwaldverein.de), whose well-marked paths reach even the darkest depths of the Black Forest. They produce maps and guides, have over 500 qualified hiking guides on their books, can arrange luggage transfer between overnight stays and oversee 24,000km of hiking trails across the region. They also look after the Black Forest's mountain-biking routes.

The Black Forests trails have a simple marking system. A red, blue-red or white-red diamond signifies you are on a long-distance path, a blue diamond means you're hiking on a regional trail and a yellow diamond marks a local route. Trails are pretty easy to follow with arrows and signposts at strategic points.

From gentle half-day strolls to multiday treks, we've cherry-picked the region for a few of our favourites.

Panoramaweg

If you want to appreciate Baden-Baden and the northern Black Forest from its most photogenic angles, this 40km-long high-level ridge trail weaves past waterfalls and viewpoints, through orchards and woodland. If you don't fancy doing the whole route in one go it can be easily split up into sections measuring five to seven kilometres.

Gütenbach-Simonswäldertal

Tucked-away Gütenbach, 22km south of Triberg, is the trailhead for one of the Black Forest's most beautiful half-day hikes

Wutachschlucht

(13km). From here a forest trail threads to Balzer Herrgott, where a sandstone figure of Christ has grown into a tree. Walking downhill from here to the Simonswälder Valley, fir-draped hills rise like a curtain before you. Return by veering north to Teich-schlucht gorge, where a brook cascades through primeval forest lined with sheer cliffs and moss-strewn boulders. Head upstream to return to Gütenbach.

Westweg

Up for a bit of an adventure? This famous long-distance trail, marked with a red diamond, stretches for 280km from Pforzheim in the Northern Black Forest to Basel in Switzerland. Highlights include the steep Murg Valley, Titisee and Feldburg. See www.westweg.de for maps and further details.

Wutachschlucht

This wild gorge, carved out by a fast-flowing river (pictured left) and flanked by near-vertical rock faces, lies near Bonndorf, close to the Swiss border and 15km east of Schluchtsee. The best way to experience its unique microclimate, where you might spot orchids, ferns, rare butterflies and lizards, is on this 14km-long trail leading from Schattenmühle to Wutachmühle. For more details, visit the website www.wutachschlucht.de.

Feldberg Steig

Orbiting Feldberg, the Black Forest's highest peak at 1493m, this 12km-long walk traverses a nature reserve that's home to chamois and wildflowers. On clear days the views of the Alps are glorious. It's possible to snowshoe part of the route in winter.

Martinskapelle

A scenic and easy-going walk, this 10km loop kicks off at a hilltop chapel called the Martinskapelle, which sits 11km southwest of Triberg. The well-marked path wriggles through forest to tower-topped Brendturm (1149m) which rewards walkers with views reaching from Feldberg to the Vosges and the Alps when the weather is playing ball. Continue via Brendhäusle and Rosseck for stunning vistas of the mountains and forest.

What's Nearby

Finally approved in 2014, the Black Forest National Park (p171) is ideal for all sorts of outdoor activities. The main information centre in Ruhestein is the best place to start when striking out into this wonderful piece of (now strictly protected) central European landscape.

> ☑ **Don't Miss**
>
> There are over 70 official campsites in the area – great for planning hikes around.

> ✕ **Take a Break**
>
> The Schwarzwaldverein (www.schwarz waldverein.de) maintains a list of over 100 picnic spots along the trails.

Freiburg

Sitting plump at the foot of the Black Forest's wooded slopes and vineyards, Freiburg is a sunny, cheerful university town, its medieval Altstadt a story-book tableau of gabled townhouses, cobblestone lanes and cafe-rimmed plazas. Party-loving students spice up the local nightlife.

Blessed with 2000 hours of annual sunshine, this is Germany's warmest city. Indeed, while neighbouring hilltop villages are still shovelling snow, the trees in Freiburg are clouds of white blossom, and locals are already imbibing in canal-side beer gardens. This eco-trailblazer has shrewdly tapped into that natural energy to generate nearly as much solar power as the whole of Britain, making it one of the country's greenest cities.

◉ SIGHTS

Schlossberg   Viewpoint
(Schlossbergring; cable car one-way/return €3.30/5.50; ☉9am-10pm daily Mar-Oct, closed Tue Nov-Feb) The forested Schlossberg dominates Freiburg. Take the footpath opposite the Schwabentor (p155), leading up through sun-dappled woods, or hitch a ride on the recently restored *Schlossbergbahn* cable car. For serious hikers, several trails begin here including those to St Peter (17km) and Kandel (25km).

The little peak is topped by the ice-cream-cone-shaped *Aussichtsturm* (lookout tower). From here, Freiburg spreads photogenically before you – the spire of the Münster soaring above a jumble of red gables, framed by the dark hills of the Black Forest.

Rathausplatz   Square
(Town Hall Square; Map p163) Join locals relaxing in a cafe by the fountain in chestnut-shaded Rathausplatz, Freiburg's prettiest square. Pull out your camera to snap pictures of the square's ox-blood-red 16th-century Altes Rathaus (Old Town Hall) that houses the tourist office (p164); the step-gabled 19th-century Neues Rathaus

(New Town Hall); and the medieval Martinskirche church with its modern interior.

Archäologisches Museum   Museum
(Map p163; ☎0761-201 2574; www.freiburg.de; Rotteckring 5; adult/concession €4/3; ☉10am-5pm Tue-Sun) This archaeology-focused museum is inside the red-sandstone neo-Gothic Colombischlössle villa. From the skylit marble entrance, a cast-iron staircase ascends to a stash of finds from Celtic grave offerings to Roman artefacts and Stone Age statuettes.

Museum für Stadtgeschichte   Museum
(Map p163; ☎0761-201 2515; Münsterplatz 30; adult/concession €3/2; ☉10am-5pm Tue-Sun) The sculptor Christian Wentzinger's baroque townhouse, east of the Historisches Kaufhaus (p155), now shelters this museum, spelling out in artefacts Freiburg's eventful past. Inside, a wrought-iron staircase guides the eye to an elaborate ceiling fresco.

Museum für Neue Kunst   Gallery
(Map p163; ☎0761-201 2583; Marienstrasse 10; adult/concession €3/2; ☉10am-5pm Tue-Sun) Across the Gewerbekanal from the Altstadt, this gallery highlights 20th-century Expressionist and abstract art, including emotive works by Oskar Kokoschka and Otto Dix.

Haus zum Walfisch   Landmark
(Map p163; House of the Whale; Franziskanerstrasse) The marvellously extravagant Haus zum Walfisch sports a late-Gothic oriel garnished with two impish gargoyles.

◈ EATING

The Altstadt is stacked with cafes, wine taverns, brewpubs and restaurants, many spilling out onto pavement terraces. You can find cheap bites around the Martinstor (p155) and Kartäuserstrasse.

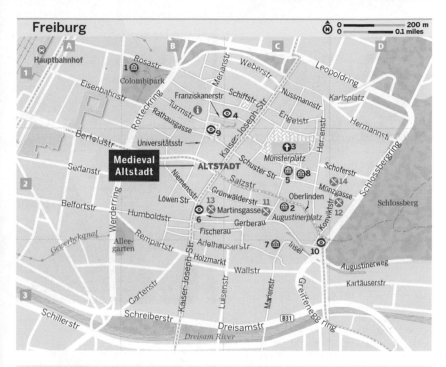

Freiburg

Markthalle   Market €

(Map p163; www.markthalle-freiburg.de; Martinsgasse 235; light meals €4-8; ⊗8am-8pm Mon-Thu, to midnight Fri & Sat) Eat your way around the world – from curry to sushi, oysters to antipasti – at the food counters in this historical market hall, nicknamed 'Fressgässle'.

**Edo's
Hummus Küche**   Vegetarian €

(Map p163; http://edoshummus.com; Atrium Augustinerplatz; light meals €2.50-8.50;

⊗11.30am-9pm Mon-Sat; 🖋) Edo's pulls in the midday crowds with superb home-made hummus served with warm pitta, as well as lentils, fava bean salad and falafel. The basic hummus plate for €4.90 is a meal in itself.

Kreuzblume   International €€€

(Map p163; 🖉0761-311 94; www.hotel kreuz blume.de; Konviktstrasse 31; mains €18-32, 3-course menu €42.50; ⊗6-11pm Wed-Sun; 🖋) On a flower-festooned lane, this pocket-sized restaurant with clever

From left: Cuckoo clocks; A traditional *Bollenhut* bonnet at the Schwarzwälder Freilichtmuseum Vogtsbauernhof (p169); Schiltach (p169)

backlighting, slick monochrome decor and a menu fizzing with bright, sunny flavours attracts a rather food-literate clientele. Each dish combines just a few hand-picked ingredients in bold and tasty ways: apple, celery and chestnut soup, say, or roast duck breast with wild herb salad. Service is tops.

Wolfshöhle Mediterranean €€€
(Map p163; ☑0761-303 03; www.wolfshoehle
-freiburg.de; Konviktstrasse 8; mains €23-49,
3-course lunch/dinner €35/63; ☺noon-2pm &
6-9.30pm Tue-Sat) With tables set up on a
pretty square, Wolfshöhle is a summer-
evening magnet. The menu whisks you off
on a gastronomical tour of the Mediterranean, with well-executed, beautifully
presented dishes listed in the modern,
ingredient-driven way: Jerusalem arti-
choke with black truffle and hazelnut, for
instance, or sea bass with saffron and
clams. The €35, three-course lunch offers
a good introduction.

ℹ INFORMATION

Available at the **tourist office** (Map p163;
☑0761-388 1880; www.visit.freiburg.de;
Rathausplatz 2-4; ☺8am-8pm Mon-Fri, 9.30am-
5pm Sat, 10.30am-3.30pm Sun Jun-Sep, 8am-
6pm Mon-Fri, 9.30am-2.30pm Sat, 10am-noon
Sun Oct-May), the three-day **WelcomeKarte**,
covering all public transport and the **Schau-
inslandbahn** (www.schauinslandbahn.de;
Schauinslandstrasse, Oberried; return adult/
child €12.50/8, one-way €9/6; ☺9am-5pm Oct-
Jun, to 6pm Jul-Sep) cable car, costs €26/16 per
adult/child.

ℹ GETTING THERE & AWAY

AIR

Freiburg shares **EuroAirport** (BSL; ☑France
+33 3 89 90 31 11; www.euroairport.com) with
Basel (Switzerland) and Mulhouse (France);
get there on the **airport bus** (☑0761-500
500; www.freiburger-reisedienst.de; one-way/
return €19.90/39). The airport is 71km south
of Freiburg via the A5 motorway. Low-cost

airline easyJet flies from here to destinations including London, Edinburgh, Berlin, Rome, Amsterdam and Alicante. Ryanair also fly from here to Dublin and London Stansted.

BUS

The airport bus goes hourly from Freiburg's bus station to EuroAirport. It takes roughly an hour.

Südbaden Bus (www.suedbadenbus.de) and RVF (www.rvf.de) operate bus and train links to towns and villages throughout the southern Black Forest. Single tickets for one/two/three zones cost €2.30/4/5.70; a 24-hour Regio24 ticket costs €5.80 for one person and €8.20 for two to five people. Buses depart from the Hauptbahnhof.

TRAIN

Freiburg is on a major north–south rail corridor, with frequent departures from the Hauptbahnhof for destinations such as Basel (€19.10 to €26.60, 45 minutes) and Baden-Baden (€23.70 to €40, 45 minutes to 1½ hours). There's a local connection to Breisach (€5.70, 26 minutes, at least hourly).

ⓘ GETTING AROUND

Bus and tram travel within Freiburg is operated by VAG (www.vag-freiburg.de) and charged at the one-zone rate. Buy tickets from the vending machines or from the driver and validate upon boarding.

Baden-Baden

This Black Forest town boasts grand colonnaded buildings and whimsically turreted art nouveau villas spread across the hillsides and framed by forested mountains.

The bon vivant spirit of France, just across the border, is tangible in the town's open-air cafes, chic boutiques and pristine gardens fringing the Oos River. And with its temple-like thermal baths – which put the *Baden* (bathe) in Baden – and palatial casino (p157), the allure of this grand dame of German spa towns is as timeless as it is enduring.

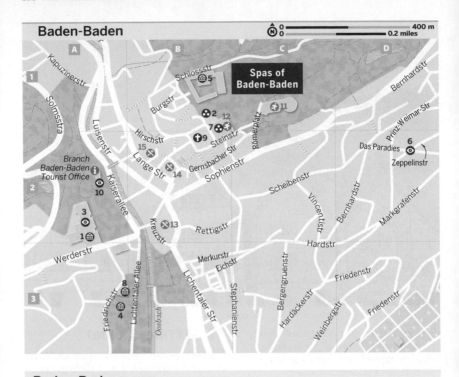

Baden-Baden

◎ SIGHTS

Museum Frieder Burda   Gallery

(Map p166; ☎07221-398 980; www.museum
-frieder-burda.de; Lichtentaler Allee 8b; adult/
concession €13/11; ◷10am-6pm Tue-Sun) A
Joan Miró sculpture guards the front of
this architecturally innovative gallery, designed by Richard Meier. The star-studded
collection of modern and contemporary
art features Picasso, Gerhard Richter and
Jackson Pollock originals; these are com-
plemented by temporary exhibitions. There

are short guided tours (**FREE**) at noon, 2pm
and 4pm on Saturdays.

Previous temporary exhibitions include
the light and space creations of American
artist James Turrell; Die Brücke German expressionist works; and the colour-charged
paintings of contemporary Indian artist
Bharti Kher.

Kurhaus   Landmark

(Map p166; www.kurhaus-baden-baden.de; Kaiserallee 1) Corinthian columns and a frieze of

mythical griffins grace the belle époque facade of the Kurhaus, which towers above well-groomed gardens. An alley of chestnut trees, flanked by two rows of boutiques, links the Kurhaus with Kaiserallee.

Römische Badruinen
Ruins

(Map p166; Römerplatz; adult/child €2.50/1; ◎11am-noon & 3-4pm mid-Mar–mid-Nov) The beauty-conscious Romans were the first to discover the healing properties of Baden-Baden's springs in the city they called Aquae Aureliae. Slip back 2000 years at one of the oldest and best-preserved Roman bathing complexes in the country. Multilingual audioguides are available.

Staatliche Kunsthalle
Gallery

(Map p166; ☑07221-3007 6400; www.kunsthalle -baden-baden.de; Lichtentaler Allee 8a; adult/ concession €7/5, Fri free; ◎10am-6pm Tue-Sun) Sidling up to the Museum Frieder Burda is this sky-lit gallery, which showcases rotating exhibitions of contemporary art in neo-classical surrounds. Previous exhibitions include the immigration-focused works of Nigerian artist Emeka Ogboh and the highly experimental creations of Chinese artist Liang Shuo.

Stiftskirche
Church

(Map p166; Marktplatz; ◎8am-6pm) **FREE** The centrepiece of cobbled Marktplatz is this pink church, a hotchpotch of Romanesque, late Gothic and, to a lesser extent, baroque styles. Its foundations incorporate some ruins of the former Roman baths. Come in the early afternoon to see its stained-glass windows cast rainbow patterns across the nave.

Kloster Lichtenthal
Abbey

(Map p153; Lichtentaler Allee) **Lichtentaler Allee** concludes at the Kloster Lichtenthal, a Cistercian abbey founded in 1245, with an abbey church where generations of the margraves (hereditary princes of the Holy Roman Empire) of Baden lie buried.

✪ EATING

Café König
Cafe €

(Map p166; Lichtentaler Strasse 12; cake €3.50-5, lunch specials €11-19; ◎8.30am-6.30pm) Liszt and Tolstoy once sipped coffee at this venerable cafe, which has been doing a brisk trade in Baden-Baden's finest cakes, tortes, pralines and truffles for over 250 years. Black Forest gateau topped with clouds of cream; fresh berry tarts; or moist nut cakes – oh, decisions!

Weinstube im Baldreit
German €€

(Map p166; ☑07221-231 36; Küferstrasse 3; mains €12.50-19; ◎5-10pm Tue-Sat) Well hidden down cobbled lanes, this wine-cellar restaurant is tricky to find, but worth looking for. Baden-Alsatian fare such as *Flammkuchen* (Alsatian pizza) topped with Black Forest ham, Roquefort and pears is expertly matched with local wines. Eat in the ivy-swathed courtyard in summer, and the vaulted interior in winter.

Nigrum
Gastronomy €€€

(Map p166; ☑07221-397 9008; www.restaurant -nigrum.de; Baldreitstrasse 1; 3-/5-/8-course menu €65/85/115; ◎6pm-midnight Tue-Sat) This dark, seductive, gold-kissed glamour puss of a restaurant has insiders whispering Michelin star. Profound, season-driven flavours here are presented in the new-fangled way according to primary ingredients. The tasting menus don't disappoint – be it braised, meltingly soft Iberian pork cheek or salmon confit with octopus. It's all beautifully cooked and served with flair.

❶ INFORMATION

Main Baden-Baden Tourist Office (☑07221-275 200; www.baden-baden.com; Schwarzwaldstrasse 52, B500; ◎9am-6pm Mon-Sat, to 1pm Sun) Situated 2km northwest of the centre. If you're driving from the northwest (from the A5) this place is on the way into town. Sells events tickets.

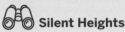 **Silent Heights**

Escape the crowds and enjoy the view at these Baden-Baden lookouts and trails.

Neues Schloss (Map p166; Schlossstrasse) A stately 15th-century residence with views over the rooftops of Baden-Baden to the dark, undulating woods of the Black Forest.

Mt Merkur (funicular one-way/return €2/4; ⏱10am-10pm) Hiking and picnicking high above Baden-Baden at this lookout, reached by funicular.

Florentinerberg (Map p166; Höllengasse) Uplifting views over city and forest-draped hill from these former Roman baths and botanical gardens.

Paradies am Annaberg (Map p166; Das Paradies) Landscaped gardens in the Italian style, with falls and far-reaching forest views.

Panoramaweg A 40km hike starting in Baden-Baden, which dips into the most scenic bits of the northern Black Forest.

Neues Schloss
JUERGEN WACKENHUT/SHUTTERSTOCK ©

Branch Baden-Baden Tourist Office (Map p166; Kaiserallee 3; ⏱10am-5pm Mon-Sat, 2-5pm Sun; 🛈) In the Trinkhalle (p157). Sells events tickets.

🛈 GETTING THERE & AWAY

Karlsruhe-Baden-Baden Airport (Baden Airpark; ☎07229-662 000; www.badenairpark.de), 15km west of Baden-Baden, serves destinations including London Stansted, Edinburgh, Rome and Malaga by Ryanair.

Buses to Black Forest destinations depart from the bus station, next to the **Hauptbahnhof** (Ooser Bahnhofstrasse).

Baden-Baden is on a major north–south rail corridor. Twice-hourly destinations include Freiburg (€23.70 to €40, 45 to 90 minutes) and Karlsruhe (€11 to €16, 15 to 30 minutes).

Baden-Baden is close to the A5 (Frankfurt–Basel autobahn) and is the northern starting point of the zigzagging Schwarzwaldhochstrasse, which follows the B500.

🛈 GETTING AROUND

Local buses run by **Stadtwerke Baden-Baden** (www.stadtwerke-baden-baden. de; Waldseestrasse 24) cost €2/6.40 for a single/24-hour ticket. A day pass for up to five people is €10.60. Bus 201 (every 10 minutes) and other lines link the Bahnhof (train station) with Leopoldsplatz. Bus 205 runs roughly hourly between the Bahnhof and the airport (p168) from Monday to Friday, less frequently at weekends.

Gutach

Slumbering at the foot of thickly wooded hills and identified by its rambling hip-roofed, shingle-clad farmhouses ablaze with geraniums in summer, little Gutach is a fine rural escape for hiking, cycling and family holidays.

One of the village's main claims to fame is that it's the original home of the traditional *Bollenhut* bonnet (topped with pom-poms; the bonnet is a common sight at costumed folk parades).

Gutach is in the side valley that runs south of the Kinzigtal. The B33 runs through it, linking it to Triberg, 13.5km south.

From nearby Hausach there are regular train connections to towns such as Gengenbach (€4.30, 18 minutes) and Triberg (€6.70, 21 minutes).

Vogtsbauernhof   Museum

(Black Forest Open-Air Museum; ☑07831-935
60; www.vogtsbauernhof.org; Wählerbrücke
1, Gutach; adult/concession/child/family
€10/9/5.50/28; ⊙9am-6pm late Mar-early Nov,
to 7pm Aug, last entry 1hr before closing) The
Schwarzwälder Freilichtmuseum spirals
around the Vogtsbauernhof, a self-
contained early-17th-century farmstead.
Farmhouses shifted from their original
locations have been painstakingly reconstructed here, using techniques such as
thatching and panelling, to create this
authentic farming hamlet and preserve
age-old Black Forest traditions. There are
free guided tours at 2.30pm daily in German, and at 1pm daily in July and August
in English.

Explore barns filled with wagons and
horn sleds, Rauchküchen (kitchens for
smoking fish and meat) and the Hippen-
seppenhof (1599), with its chapel and
massive hipped roof constructed from
400 trees. It's a great place for families,
with inquisitive farmyard animals to pet,
artisans on hand to explain their crafts, and
frequent demonstrations covering topics
from sheep shearing to butter-making.

The Vogtsbauernhof is 4.5km north of
Gutach on the B33.

Schiltach

Snuggled up at the foot of wooded hills and
on the banks of the Kinzig and Schiltach
rivers, medieval Schiltach looks too ludi-
crously pretty to be true. The meticulously
restored half-timbered houses (pictured
p165), which once belonged to tanners,
merchants and raft builders, are a riot of
crimson geraniums in summer.

Being at the confluence of the two rivers,
logging was big business here until the
19th century and huge rafts were built to
ship timber as far as the Netherlands. The
willow-fringed banks now attract grey herons
and kids who come to splash in the shallow
waters when the sun's out.

Schiltach Tourist Office (☑07836 5850;
www.schiltach.de; Marktplatz 6; ⊙9am-noon &

⮕ Great Drives in the Black Forest

Driving is a great way to reach the
forest's out-of-the-way corners.

Schwarzwaldhochstrasse (Black Forest
Highway; www.schwarzwaldhochstrasse.
de) Swoon over views of the Vosges
Mountains, forests and lakes such as
Mummelsee on this high-altitude road,
meandering 60km from Baden-Baden
to Freudenstadt on the B500.

Badische Weinstrasse (Baden Wine
Road; www.deutsche-weinstrasse.de) From
Baden-Baden south to Lörrach, this
160km route corkscrews through the
red-wine vineyards of Ortenau, the Pinot
Noir grape country of Kaiserstuhl and
Tuniberg, and the white-wine vines of
Markgräflerland.

Schwarzwald-Tälerstrasse (Black Forest
Valley Road) Twisting 100km from Rastatt
to Alpirsbach, this road dips into the
forest-cloaked hills and half-timbered
towns of the Murg and Kinzig valleys.

Deutsche Uhrenstrasse (German Clock
Road; www.deutscheuhrenstrasse.de) A
320km loop starting in Villingen-
Schwenningen that follows the story of
clockmaking in the Black Forest. Stops
include Furtwangen and cuckoo-crazy
Triberg.

Grüne Strasse (Green Road; www.gruene
strasse.de) Linking the Black Forest
with the Rhine Valley and the French
Vosges, this 160km route zips through
Kirchzarten, Freiburg, Breisach, Colmar
and Münster.

MYIMAGES - MICHA/SHUTTERSTOCK ©

Weltgrösste Kuckucksuhr

2-4pm Mon-Thu, 9am-noon Fri) The tourist office in the Rathaus can help find accommodation and offers free internet access. Local hiking options are marked on an enamel sign just opposite.

Schiltach is on the B294 that runs through the Kinzigtal. Trains run hourly to nearby towns including Gengenbach (€9.50, 36 minutes) to the west and Freudenstadt (€6.80, 29 minutes) to the north.

The Bahnhof is 280m north of the central **Marktplatz**, on the opposite side of the Kinzig River. It's around a five-minute walk.

Triberg

Home to Germany's highest waterfall, heir to the original 1915 Black Forest gateau recipe, and nesting ground of the world's biggest cuckoos, Triberg leaves visitors reeling with superlatives. It was here that in bleak winters past folk huddled in snow-bound farmhouses to carve the clocks that would drive the world cuckoo, and here that in a flash of brilliance the water-fall was harnessed to power the country's first electric street lamps in 1884.

⊙ SIGHTS

Triberger Wasserfälle   Waterfall

(adult/concession €5/4.50) Niagara they ain't but Germany's highest waterfalls do exude their own wild romanticism. The Gutach River feeds the seven-tiered falls, which drop a total of 163m and are illuminated until 10pm. A paved trail accesses the cascades. Pick up a bag of peanuts at the ticket counter to feed the tribes of inquisitive red squirrels. Entry is cheaper in winter. The falls are located in central Triberg.

Weltgrösste Kuckucksuhr   Landmark

(Map p153; World's Largest Cuckoo Clock; www.dold-urlaub.de; Untertalstrasse 28, Schonach; adult/child €2/1; ⊙10am-noon & 1-5pm Tue-Sun) A rival to the hotly contested giant-cuckoo-clock crown, the so-called 'world's oldest-largest cuckoo clock' kicked into gear in

1980 and took local clockmaker Joseph Dold three years to build by hand. A Dold family member is usually around to explain the mechanism.

EATING

From the cafe where you can dig into the original Black Forest gateau to old-school taverns dishing up German grub to pizzerias – you'll find plenty of choice on and around the main drag, Hauptstrasse.

Café Schäfer   Cafe €

(☑07722-4465; www.cafe-schaefer-triberg. de; Hauptstrasse 33; cakes €3-4; ⓧ9am-6pm Mon, Tue, Thu & Fri, 8am-6pm Sat, 11am-6pm Sun) Confectioner Claus Schäfer uses the original 1915 recipe for Black Forest gateau to prepare this sinful treat that layers chocolate cake perfumed with cherry brandy, whipped cream and sour cherries and wraps it all in more cream and shaved chocolate. Trust us, it's worth the calories.

INFORMATION

Triberg markets itself as *Das Ferienland* (The Holiday Region). See www.dasferienland.de, an online portal with information on the town and the wider region.

Triberg Tourist Office (☑07722-866 490; www.triberg.de; Wallfahrtstrasse 4; ⓧ9am-5pm Mon-Fri, 10am-5pm Sat & Sun) Inside the Schwarzwald-Museum. Stocks walking (€3), cross-country ski trail (€2) and mountain bike (€6.90) maps.

GETTING THERE & AROUND

From the Bahnhof, 1.5km north of the centre, the *Schwarzwaldbahn* train line loops southeast to

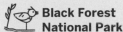 Black Forest National Park

An outdoor wonderland of heather-speckled moors, glacial cirque lakes, deep valleys, mountains and near-untouched coniferous forest, the **Black Forest National Park** (☑07449-929 980; www.nationalpark-schwarzwald.de; Schwarzwaldhochstrasse 2, Bühlertal; ⓧ9am-noon & 2-3.30pm Mon-Thu, 9am-noon Fri; ⓟ) is the Schwarzwald at its wildest and untamed best. Nature is left to its own devices in this 100-sq-km pocket in the northern Black Forest, tucked between Baden-Baden and Freudenstadt and centred on the Schwarzwaldhochstrasse (Black Forest Highway), the Murg Valley and Mummelsee (the lookout tower is open 10.30am-5pm on weekends).

Hiking and cycling trails abound, as do discovery paths geared towards children. Stop at this visitor centre or at the **National Park Centre** (☑07449-9299 8444; Ruhestein; ⓧ10am-6pm Tue-Sun May-Sep, to 5pm Oct-Apr) in Ruhestein for the low-down and to pick up maps. Details of guided tours and online maps are also available on the website.

Konstanz (€27.50, 1½ hours, hourly), and northwest to Offenburg (€13.50, 46 minutes, hourly).

Bus 7150 travels north through the Gutach and Kinzig valleys to Offenburg; bus 7265 heads south to Villingen via St Georgen. Buses also depart from the for Marktplatz, and the nearby town of Schonach (hourly).

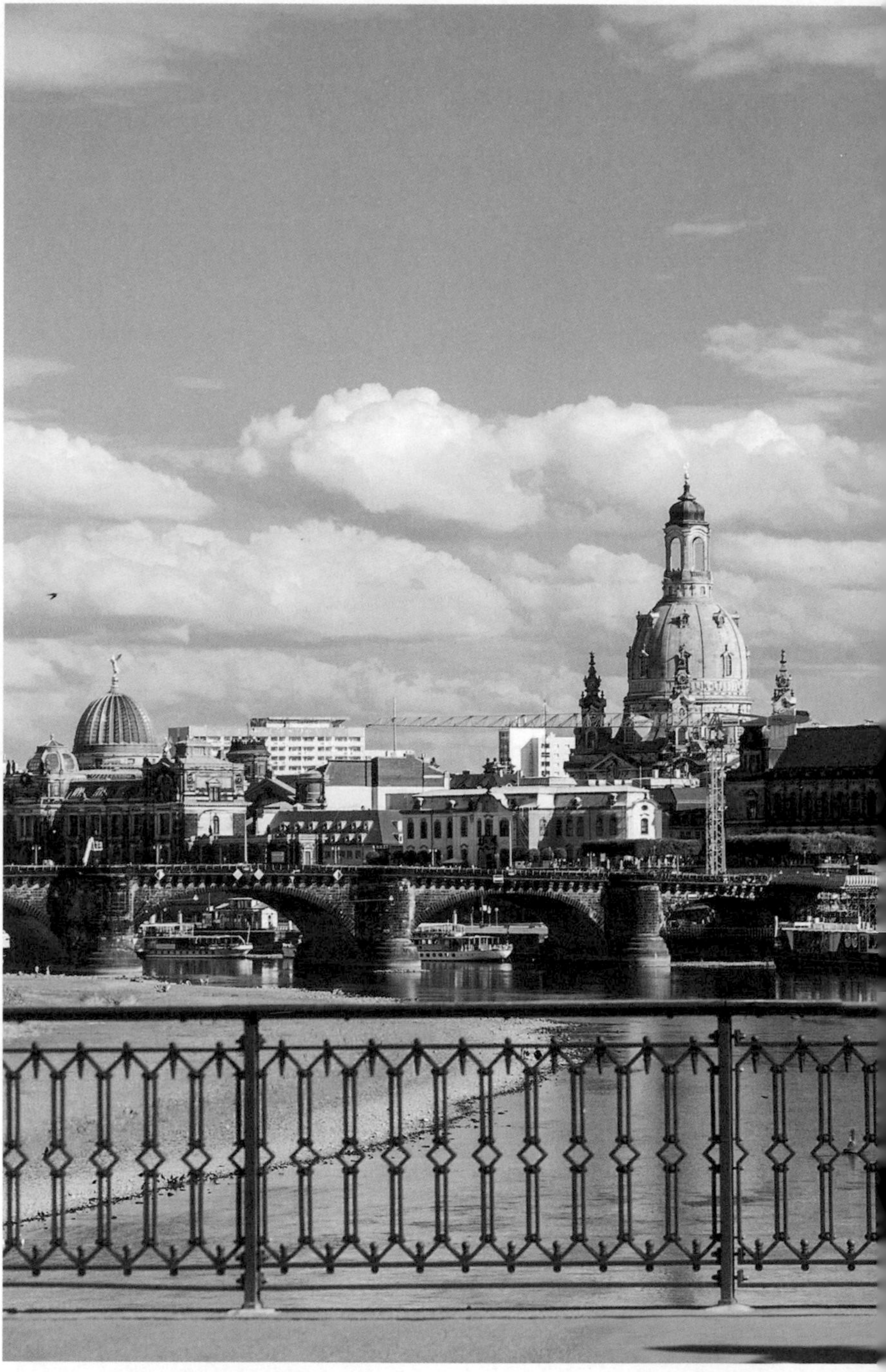

DRESDEN

Dresden

There are few city silhouettes more striking than Dresden's. The classic view from the Elbe's northern bank takes in spires, towers and domes belonging to palaces, churches and stately buildings. Dresden's cultural heyday came under the 18th-century reign of Augustus the Strong (August der Starke), whose legacy included many iconic buildings. The devastating fire-bombings of 1945 levelled a great many of these treasures, but most were painstakingly rebuilt. Today, Dresden enjoys a constantly evolving arts and cultural scene and boasts zinging pub and nightlife quarters, especially in the Outer Neustadt.

Dresden in One Day

Begin your explorations in the compact but magnificent baroque Altstadt, with your camera at the ready. Start the day with a wander through Augustus the Strong's **Zwinger palace** (p180), built out of Versailles envy. Allow at least a few hours to explore its superb museums. Next, follow your feet to the neo-Renaissance **Semperoper** (p181) then wander through the spectacular **Residenzschloss** (p178) which took over 50 years to rebuild from the WWII rubble.

Dresden in Two Days

On day two, round out your explorations of the Altstadt with a visit to the **Frauenkirche** (p176), the enduring symbol of the city, rebuilt from a rubble pile between 1994 and 2005, then head to the **Albertinum gallery** (p180) to sample fine art from the 18th century onwards. Cross the beautiful Augustusbrücke to the Innere Neustadt to experience a more down-to-earth side of the city, and round out your explorations with a visit to the **Militärhistorisches Museum Dresden** (p181).

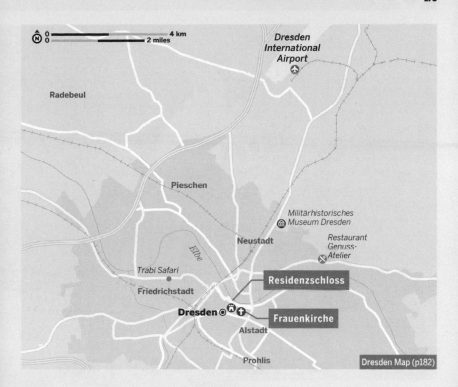

Dresden Map (p182)

Arriving in Dresden

Dresden International Airport handles many domestic flights but only a handful of international connections.

Dresden Hauptbahnhof, to the south of the Altstadt, is served by national and regional trains.

Sleeping

Dresden's centrally located hotels can be both bland and horrendously expensive, with rates among the highest in Germany. Thankfully there are plenty of cheap beds available at the city's superb hostels. Given the efficient tram system, it's also worth looking into cheaper – and often better – hotel options in outlying districts.

Frauenkirche

JORG GREUEL/GETTY IMAGES ©

Frauenkirche

Dresden's top sight, the unmissable Frauenkirche has become a symbol of East Germany's post-communist renewal. Destroyed by Allied bombs in 1945, it was a heap of baroque rubble until rebuilding work began in 1994.

Standing in perfect baroque wedding-cake symmetry on Dresden's pretty Neumarkt, the domed Frauenkirche – Dresden's most beloved symbol – returned to Dresden's cityscape in 2005 after a decade of building work. The original had graced the skyline for two centuries, before collapsing after the WWII bombing raid which turned Dresden into an inferno and destroyed most of the city centre. It had been left as a war memorial – the East German authorities weren't keen on rebuilding churches – but once the GDR's regime had been swept away in 1989, plans for the churche's comeback, which had been drawn up in 1985, were quickly accelerated.

Original Building

The original Frauenkirche dated back to the first half of the 18th century but a church

Great For...

☑ **Don't Miss**

The altar, reassembled from nearly 2000 fragments, is especially striking.

Cafe-lined streets surrounding the Frauenkirche

❶ Need to Know

Map p182; ✆0351-6560 6100; www.frauen
kirche-dresden.de; Neumarkt; audioguide
€2.50, cupola adult/student €8/5; ⊙10am-
noon & 1-6pm Mon-Fri, weekend hours vary)

✕ Take a Break

The Frauenkirche is almost ringed with
cafes (pictured left) that spill out onto
the Neumarkt in summer.

★ Top Tip

At the Visitors Centre you can watch a
useful documentary about the church's
history.

had stood on this spot since the 11th
century. The design you see today replaced
a smaller building and was completed
in 1743. Its most striking feature is the
96m-high dome, made of sandstone and
weighing 12,000 tons. It was a remarkable
feat of engineering for the time, compara-
ble to the dome of St Paul's in London. The
rounded structure is a prominent feature
on the Dresden skyline.

Destruction

Dresden city centre was (in)famously
destroyed in a massive air raid launched by
British and American planes on 13 February
1945. Some 3900 tons of explosives were
hurled down on the city from over 1200
bombers. The resulting firestorm killed
around 25,000 people and left Dresden a
smouldering shell. The Frauenkirche stood

throughout the two days of the raid until
finally collapsing on 15 February.

Resurrection

The reconstruction work cost €180 million
and was financed largely by donations
raised by the Society to Promote the
Reconstruction of the Church of Our Lady
and Dresdner Bank. In a symbolic act of
reconciliation, the cross and orb that tops
the Frauenkirche were created by a British
goldsmith whose father was involved in the
February 1945 air raid.

A spitting image of the original, it may
not bear the gravitas of age but that
only slightly detracts from its festive
beauty inside and out. The cupola can
be climbed. The galleried interior is a
wonderful place for concerts, meditations
and services. Check the website (www.
frauenkirche-dresden.de) for the current
schedule or stop by the Frauenkirche
Visitors Centre.

Residenzschloss

MIKHAIL MARKOVSKIY/SHUTTERSTOCK ©

Residenzschloss

One of the highlights of any visit to Dresden, the Residenzschloss occupies a hefty chunk of the Altstadt. The residence of Saxony's rulers for over 400 years, it's now a treasure chest of the city's art.

History

A fortress of some sort had stood on the site since the 13th century, but following a major fire a new baroque residence was commissioned in the early 18th century by Augustus II the Strong. This was then given a neo-Renaissance makeover in 1914, just in time for Saxony's ruling dynasty to move out at the end of WWI. The palace suffered almost complete destruction in the American and British air raids of February 1945, after which the building was left as a pile of rubble. Some reconstruction began in the 1960s but it wasn't until the end of the Cold War that serious efforts were made to bring the Residenzschloss back to life. Work wasn't completed until 2013.

Dresden's extraordinary city palace now houses multiple precious collections, including the unmissable Historisches

Great For...

☑ **Don't Miss**

In the Historisches Grünes Gewölbe look out for the priceless *Moor with Emerald Cluster.*

Lion head door knocker, Residenzschloss

DIRK FREDER/GETTY IMAGES ©

Elbe River

Terrassenufer

Schlossplatz

Residenzschloss

Grünes Gewölbe (Green Vault), a real-life
Aladdin's Cave spilling over with precious objects wrought from gold, ivory,
silver, diamonds and jewels. The entire
renovated building, including its unique
murals and baroque towers, is quite simply
spectacular.

Collections

If you are intent on seeing everything at the
Residenzschloss, you'll need to set aside a
whole day. There's so much on display that
two separate treasure chambers are needed to show off the extraordinary wealth of
the Saxon rulers' private collections. Established by Augustus II the Strong in 1723, the
Historisches Grünes Gewölbe (Historic
Green Vault; €12) and the **Neues Grünes
Gewölbe** (New Green Vault; adult/child under
17yr incl audioguide €12/free) contain one of

Europe's largest treasure collections and
the former was one of Europe's first public
museums. Sections in the Historisches
Grünes Gewölbe are named after precious
materials such as gold, silver, amber and
ivory. Also housed here is the **Kupfer-
stich-Kabinett**, which counts around half
a million prints and drawings by 20,000
artists (including Dürer, Rembrandt, Mi-
chelangelo, Toulouse-Lautrec and Picasso)
in its possession. Numismatists might want
to drop by the **Münzkabinett** (Coin Cabinet) in the palace tower for a small array of
historic coins and medals.

The **Türckische Cammer** (Turkish
Chamber), one of the richest collections of
Ottoman art outside Turkey, is also here. A
huge three-mast tent made of gold and silk
is one standout among many. The **Riesen-
saal** (Giant's Hall) houses a spectacular
10,000-piece collection of armour, and the
display includes recreations of jousting
tournaments.

◉ SIGHTS

Key sights cluster in the compact Altstadt on the Elbe's south bank, about 1km from the Hauptbahnhof via Prager Strasse, the main pedestrianised shopping strip. From here, Augustusbrücke leads across the river to the Neustadt, with its own major train station (Dresden-Neustadt) and the main pub and party quarter in the Äussere Neustadt (Outer Neustadt).

Zwinger   Palace

(Map p182; ☑0351-4914 2000; www.der-dresd ner-zwinger.de; Theaterplatz 1; ticket for all museums adult/concession €12/9, courtyard free; ⊙6am-10pm Apr-Oct, to 8pm Nov-Mar) A collaboration between the architect Matthäus Pöppelmann and the sculptor Balthasar Permoser, the Zwinger was built between 1710 and 1728 on the orders of Augustus the Strong, who, having returned from seeing Louis XIV's palace

> *the Semperoper opened in 1841 and has hosted premieres of famous works*

at Versailles, wanted something similar for himself. Originally a party palace for royals, the Zwinger has ornate portals that lead into the vast fountain-studded courtyard, which is framed by buildings lavishly festooned with evocative sculpture. Today it houses three superb museums within its baroque walls.

Albertinum   Gallery

(Map p182; ☑0351-4914 2000; www.skd. museum; enter from Brühlsche Terrasse or Georg-Treu-Platz 2; adult/concession/child under 17yr €10/7.50/free; ⊙10am-6pm Tue-Sun) The Renaissance-era former arsenal is the stunning home of the **Galerie Neue Meister** (New Masters Gallery), which displays an array of paintings by some of the great names in art from the 18th century onwards. Caspar David Friedrich and Claude Monet's landscapes compete with the abstract visions of Marc Chagall and Gerhard Richter, all in gorgeous rooms orbiting a light-filled courtyard. There's also a superb sculpture collection spread over the lower floors.

Semperoper

MLENNY/GETTY IMAGES ©

Militärhistorisches
Museum Dresden · Museum

(☏0351-823 2803; www.mhmbw.de; Olbricht-
platz 2; adult/concession €5/3; ⊙10am-6pm
Thu-Sun & Tue, to 9pm Mon; ᤍ7 or 8 to
Stauffenbergallee) Even devout pacifists
will be awed by this engaging museum,
housed in a 19th-century arsenal bisected
by a bold glass-and-steel wedge designed
by Daniel Libeskind. Exhibits have been
updated for the 21st century, so don't
expect a rollcall of military victories or a
parade of weapons. Instead, you'll find
a progressive – and often artistic – look
at the roots and ramifications of war and
aggression.

Semperoper · Historic Building, Opera
(Map p182; ☏0351-320 7360; www.semperoper
-erleben.de; Theaterplatz 2; tour adult/conces-
sion €11/7; ⊙hours vary) One of Germany's
most famous opera houses, the Semperoper (pictured left) opened in 1841 and
has hosted premieres of famous works by
Richard Strauss, Carl Maria von Weber and
Richard Wagner. Guided 45-minute tours
operate almost daily (the 3pm tour is in
English); exact times depend on rehearsal
and performance schedules. Buy advance
tickets online to skip the queue.

TOURS

Trabi Safari · Driving
(☏0351-8990 0110; www.trabi-safari.de;
Bremer Strasse 35; adult/child under 17 €49/
free) Get behind the wheel of the ultimate
GDR-mobile for this 1½-hour guided drive
around the city, taking in sights from all
eras. The price depends on the number of
people in the car; four people to a car is
the best value.

NightWalk
Dresden · Walking
(Map p182; ☏0172 781 5007; www.nightwalk
-dresden.de; Albertplatz; €17; ⊙9pm) See
street art, learn what life was like in East
Germany and visit fun pubs and bars in
the Outer Neustadt on this superfun tour.
NightWalk also has the exclusive rights to

Dresden & WWII

Between 13 and 15 February 1945,
British and American planes unleashed
3900 tonnes of explosives on Dresden
in four huge air raids. Bombs and incen-
diary shells whipped up a mammoth
firestorm, and ashes rained down on villages 35km away. When the blazes had
died down and the dust settled, tens of
thousands of Dresdners had lost their
lives and 20 sq km of this once-elegant
baroque city lay in smouldering ruins.

Historians still argue over whether
this constituted a war crime committed
by the Allies on an innocent civilian
population. Some claim that with the
Red Army at the gates of Berlin, the
war was effectively won, and the Allies
gained little military advantage from the
destruction of Dresden. Others have
said that, as the last urban centre in the
east of the country left intact, Dresden
could have provided shelter for German
troops returning from the east and was
a viable target.

take visitors to the slaughterhouse where
Kurt Vonnegut Jr survived the bombing
of Dresden in 1945, and which he later
immortalised in *Slaughterhouse-Five*.

Sächsische
Dampfschiffahrt · Boating
(Map p182; ☏0351-866 090; www.saech
siche-dampfschiffahrt.de; Terrassenufer; adult/
concession €18.50/11) Ninety-minute Elbe
tours leave from the Terrassenufer dock
several times daily in summer, aboard
the world's oldest fleet of paddle-wheel
steamers. There are also services to Saxon
Switzerland and castles along the river.

Grosse
Stadtrundfahrt · Bus
(Map p182; ☏0351-899 5650; www.stadtrund
fahrt.com; Theaterplatz; day pass adult/conces-
sion €20/18; ⊙9.30am-10pm Apr-Oct, to 8pm

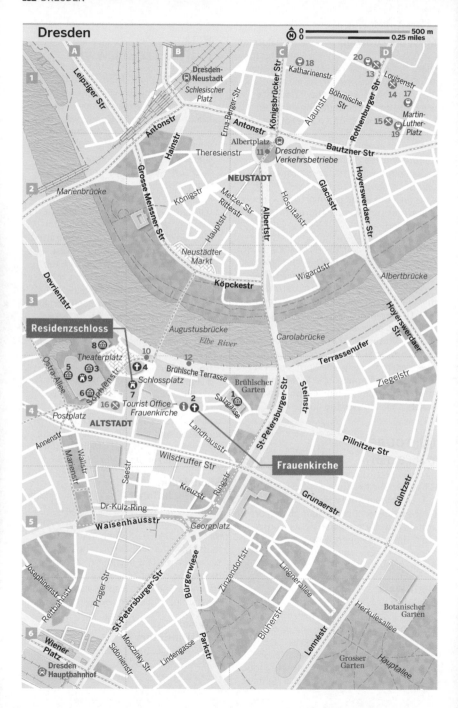

Dresden

0 — 500 m
0 — 0.25 miles
Ⓝ

Dresden

Nov-Mar) This narrated hop-on, hop-off tour, with 22 stops and optional short guided tours, ticks off all the major sights. Buses leave every 15 to 30 minutes.

⊗ EATING

Little India
Indian €€

(Map p182; ☑0351-3232 6400; www.little india-dresden.de; Louisenstrasse 48; mains €10-15; ⊙11am-2.30pm & 5-11pm Tue-Sat, to 10pm Sun;) Bright, minimalist and informal, this fantastic Indian restaurant is a world away from most in Dresden, and its popularity is obvious (be prepared to wait for a table when it's busy). The large menu (available in English) includes superb tandoori dishes and an entire vegetarian section, as well as standard chicken, lamb and pork mains. The naan is heavenly.

Cafe Continental
International €€

(Map p182; ☑0351-272 1722; www.cafe-con tinental-dresden.de; Görlitzer Strasse 1; dishes €6-20; ⊙9am-1am Sun-Thu, to 3am Fri & Sat; ⊚) If the greenly lit openings behind the bar remind you of aquariums, you've hit the nail on the head, for buzzy 'Conti' was a pet store back in GDR days. Today, it's a great place to hit no matter the hour, for anything from cappuccino or cocktails to homemade cakes or a full meal.

Raskolnikoff
International €€

(Map p182; ☑0351-804 5706; www.raskol nikoff.de; Böhmische Strasse 34; mains €10-15; ⊙11am-10.30pm Mon-Sat, from 9am Sun) An artist squat in the 1980s, Raskolnikoff now brims with grown-up artsy-bohemian flair, especially in the sweet little garden at the back, complete with a bizarre water feature. The seasonally calibrated menu showcases the fruits of the surrounding land in globally inspired dishes, including a variety of *pelmeni* (Russian dumplings), which proudly represent the Dostoyevsky character the establishment is named after.

Sophienkeller
Saxon €€

(Map p182; ☑0351-497 260; www.sophien keller-dresden.de; Taschenberg 3; mains €12-20; ⊙11am-1am) The 1730s theme, complete with waitresses trussed up in period garb, may be a bit overcooked, but the local specialities certainly aren't. It's mostly rib-sticking fare, such as the boneless half-duck with red cabbage or the spit-roasted suckling pig. Wash it down with a mug of dark Bohemian Krušovice, and enjoy the ambience of vaulted ceilings in the Taschenbergpalais building.

Restaurant Genuss-Atelier
German €€€

(☑0351-2502 8337; www.genuss-atelier.net; Bautzner Strasse 140; mains €15-27; ⊙5-11pm Wed-Fri, noon-3.30pm & 5-11pm Sat & Sun; ⊟11

Dresden dining

to Waldschlösschen) Lighting up Dresden's culinary scene is this fantastic place that's well worth the trip on the 11 tram. The creative menu is streets ahead of most offerings elsewhere, although the best way to experience the 'Pleasure-Atelier' is to book a surprise menu (three/four/five courses €39/49/59) and let the chefs show off their craft. Reservations essential.

🍷 DRINKING & NIGHTLIFE

Every other door leads into a bar in the centre of Outer Neustandt, at the crossing of Görlitzer Strasse and Louisenstrasse. Some people just plonk themselves down on the pavement and drink in big seated groups...who needs bars?

Bottoms Up   Bar
(Map p182; ☑0351-802 0158; Martin-Luther-Strasse 31; ⊙5pm-5am Mon-Fri, from 10am Sat & Sun) This is one of Neustadt's most popular and happening bars. There's an outside beer garden, cider on tap, choices of beers ranging from fancy Belgian to local German, and a cosy interior that gets packed at night. The weekend brunch is excellent.

Louisengarten   Beer Garden
(Map p182; www.biergarten-dresden.de; Louisenstrasse 43; ⊙4pm-1am Sun-Thu, 3pm-2am Fri & Sat) This boho-flavoured beer garden takes the go-local concept to the limit. Wind down the day with beer (Lenin's Hanf, aka Lenin's Hemp) supplied by the nearby Neustädter Hausbrauerei and grilled meats courtesy of the butcher down the street.

Lloyd's   Bar
(Map p182; ☑0351-501 8775; www.lloyds-cafe-bar.de; Martin-Luther-Strasse 17; ⊙8am-1am) In a quiet corner of the Neustadt, Lloyd's oozes grown-up flair thanks to stylish cream-coloured leather furniture, huge mirrors and fanciful chandeliers. It's a solid pit stop from breakfast to that last expertly poured cocktail; it even does a respectable afternoon tea and cake by the fireplace.

Downtown   Club
(Map p182; ☑0351-811 5592; www.downtown-dresden.de; Katharinenstrasse 11-13; ⊙10pm-late Fri & Sat) This iconic old factory is home to one of Dresden's most popular clubs, a mainstream affair that packs in a young and up-for-it crowd with three floors of dance

action. There's a main floor with hits of the '80s and '90s (you have been warned), an electro lounge and a loft floor with R'n'B sounds.

 INFORMATION

The excellent **Dresden Card** (www.dresden.de/dresdencard) provides free public transport as well as sweeping sightseeing discounts. Various cards are available from the **Tourist Office** (Map p182; ☑0351-501 501; www.dresden.de; QF Passage, Neumarkt 2; ☺10am-7pm Mon-Fri, to 6pm Sat, to 3pm Sun). The one-day Dresden-City-Card (single/family €12/15) is good for transport and discounts to 90 sights, attractions, tours and other participating venues. The two-day version (€37/66) delivers free admission to all state museums with the exception of the Historisches Grünes Gewölbe, and discounts on many others.The Dresden-Regio-Card (from €20/30) includes all this plus discounts to 40 additional sights. All in all, they're excellent value and guarantee big savings if you plan to visit several museums in Dresden.

 GETTING THERE & AWAY

AIR

Dresden International Airport (DRS, ☑0351 881 3360; www.dresden-airport.de; Flughafenstrasse) has flights to many German cities and international destinations including Amsterdam, Zurich, Dubai and Moscow.

The S2 train links the airport with the city centre several times hourly (€2.30, 20 minutes). Taxis are about €20.

TRAIN

Fast trains make the trip to Dresden from Berlin-Hauptbahnhof in two hours (€40) and Leipzig in 1¼ hours (€19.90). The S1 local train runs half-hourly to Meissen (€6.20, 40 minutes) and Bad Schandau in Saxon Switzerland (€6.20, 45 minutes). RE trains connect Dresden with Chemnitz (€16, one hour) via Freiberg (€9.70, 30 to 45 minutes).

⌐⌐ Peeking Behind the Iron Curtain

Pirna is a charming town on the Elbe, famous as Canaletto's home during his years in Saxony, and a friendly and easy-going place today. The big attraction in town is the excellent **DDR Museum** (☑03501-774 842; www.ddr-museum-pirna.de; Rottwerndorferstrasse 45; adult/child €8/6; ☺10am-5pm Tue-Sun Apr-Oct, 10am-5pm Tue-Thu, Sat & Sun Nov-Mar; entry after 3.30pm), in a former army barracks on the outskirts of the town. You can wander around a fully furnished East German apartment, sit in a classroom with GDR president Walter Ulbricht glowering at you, or find out how much a Junge Pioniere youth organisation uniform cost.

To get here, take the S1 from Dresden's Hauptbahnhof to Pirna, walk five minutes to the central bus station (ZOB) and hop on local bus N for 'Geibeltbad/Freizeitzentrum' (€4, 35 minutes).

A Trabi (the standard GDR-era car)
MICHAEL NITZSCHKE/GETTY IMAGES ©

 GETTING AROUND

Buses and trams are run by **Dresdner Verkehrsbetriebe** (DVB; Map p182; ☑0351-857 1011; www.dvb.de/en). Fares within town cost €2.30, and a day pass €6, valid until 4am the following morning. Buy tickets from vending machines at stops or aboard trams, and remember to validate them in the machines provided.

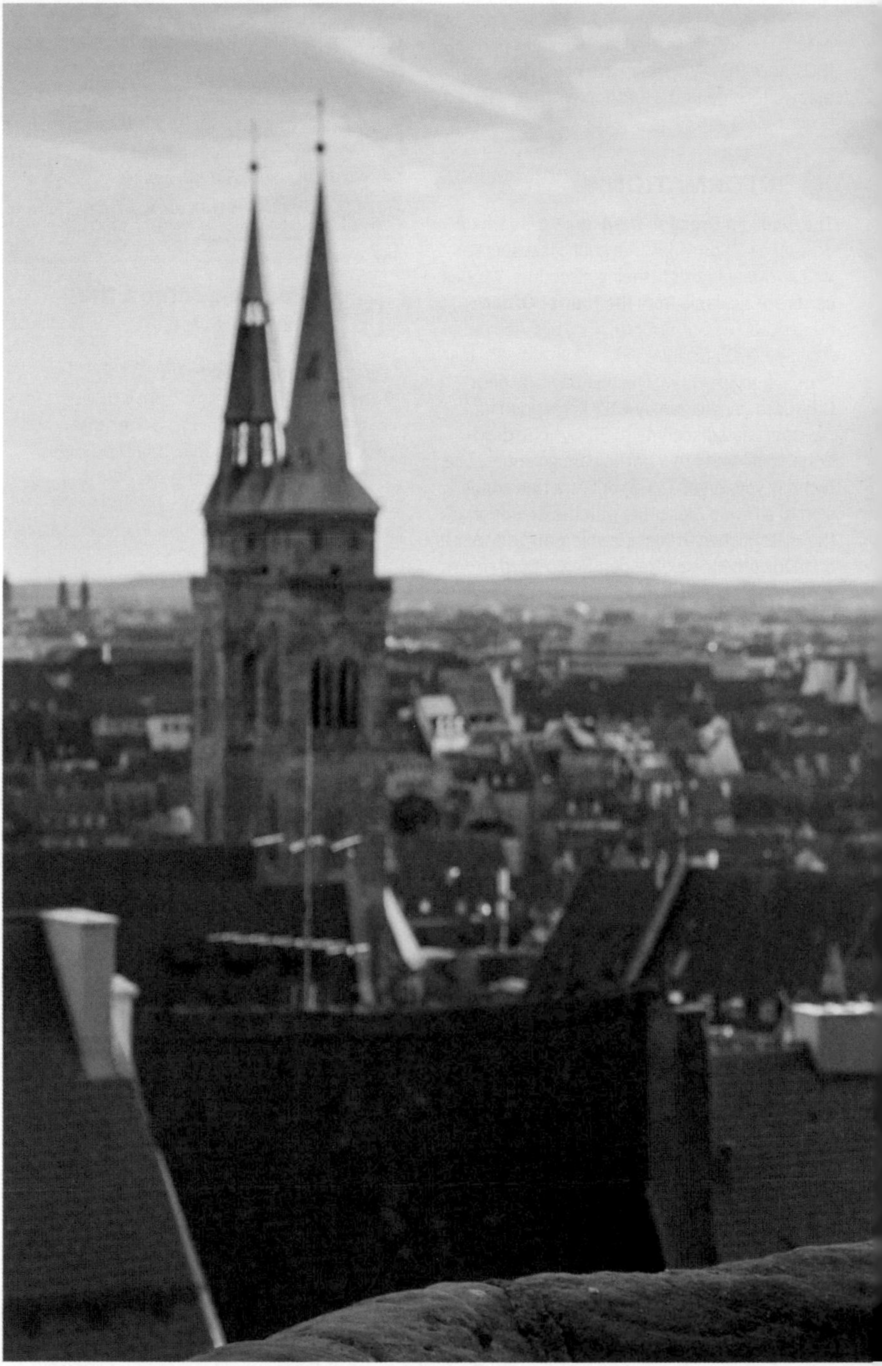

ARAGAMI12345 / 500PX ©

NUREMBERG

Nuremberg

Nuremberg (Nürnberg) is an energetic city where the nightlife is intense and the beer dark as coffee. The city is alive with visitors year-round, but especially during the spectacular Christmas market. For centuries, Nuremberg was the undeclared capital of the Holy Roman Empire and the preferred residence of most German kings. By the 19th century, it had become a powerhouse in the industrial revolution, which the Nazi party saw as a perfect stage for its activities. After the party's demise, the city played host to the war crimes tribunal known as the Nuremberg Trials.

Nuremberg in One Day

Start your explorations at the Hauptmarkt, Nuremburg's main square. Walk north past the old town hall with with its medieval dungeons to 13th-century **St Sebalduskirche** (p190) and onwards to **Stadtmuseum Fembohaus** (p191) to learn about the highs and lows of this important city, then head south to **Albrecht-Dürer-Haus** (p191), where the Renaissance genius lived and worked.

Nuremberg in Two Days

Looming over the scene is the **Kaiserburg** (p190), the castle of medieval knights with its warren of imperial chambers. You can spend hours wandering around the city ramparts, but be sure to save plenty of time to explore the excellent **Germanisches Nationalmuseum** (p191) and fascinating **Memorium Nuremberg Trials** (p192). And for something refreshingly different, Nuremburg's nationally-lauded **Deutsche Bahn Museum** (p192) is a delight for young and old.

Previous page: Nuremberg skyscape
ARAGAMI12345/500PX ©

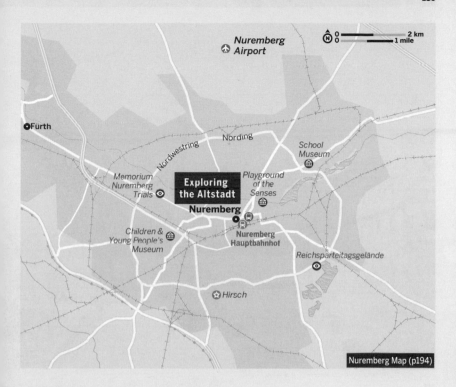

Nuremberg Map (p194)

Arriving in Nuremberg

Albrecht Dürer Airport Handles domestic and some international flights.

Nuremberg Hauptbahnhof Major stop in the city centre served by local and national trains.

Main bus station Important stop for many national and international services. Located in the city centre.

Sleeping

Accommodation gets tight and rates rocket during the Christmas market and the toy fair (trade only) in late January to early February. At other times, cheap rooms can be found, especially if you book ahead. Most accommodation is located within the walls of the Altstadt, but staying outside can bring costs down considerably.

Kaiserburg

CAD. WIZARD/SHUTTERSTOCK/GETTY IMAGES ©

Exploring the Altstadt

Nuremberg has one of the largest and most history-packed old towns in the business and a wander around its crooked, steep lanes, covered bridges and intact city defences is one of the high points of any visit to Bavaria.

Great For...

☑ **Don't Miss**

Ehekarussell Brunnen (Weisser Turm U-Bahn), a grotesque sculptural work depicting six interpretations of marriage.

St Sebalduskirche

Nuremberg's **oldest church** (Map p194; www.sebalduskirche.de; Winklerstrasse 26; ⊘9.30am-4pm Jan-Mar, to 6pm Apr-Dec) was built in rusty pink-veined sandstone in the 13th century. Its exterior is adorned with religious sculptures and symbols; check out the ornate carvings over the Bridal Doorway to the north, showing the Wise and Foolish Virgins. Inside, the bronze shrine of St Sebald (Nuremberg's own saint) is a Gothic and Renaissance master-piece that took its maker, Peter Vischer the Elder, and his two sons more than 11 years to complete.

Stadtmuseum Fembohaus

Offering an entertaining overview of the city's history, highlights of the **Stadtmuseum Fembohaus** (Map p194;

Stadtmuseum Fembohaus

CARGO80/GETTY IMAGES ©

Albrecht-Dürer-Haus 🏛️ 🏰 **Kaiserburg**
🏛️ **Stadtmuseum**
Fembohaus
St Sebalduskirche ⊙
⊙ **Hauptmarkt**

Germanisches
Nationalmuseum
🏛️

🛈 Need to Know

The Altstadt is served by the Weisser Turm and Lorenzkirche U-Bahn stations.

✘ Take a Break

Altstadt-based Bratwursthäusle (p195) is the best place to sample Nuremberg's famous sausages.

★ Top Tip

The two-day Nürnberg+Fürth Card (€25) gives admission to all museums and attractions.

📞0911-231 2595; Burgstrasse 15; adult/child €6/1.50; ⊙10am-5pm Tue-Fri, to 6pm Sat & Sun) include the restored historic rooms of this 16th-century merchant's house.

Albrecht-Dürer-Haus

Dürer, Germany's most famous Renaissance draughtsman, lived and worked at the **Albrecht-Dürer-Haus** (Map p194; 📞0911-231 2568; Albrecht-Dürer-Strasse 39; adult/child €6/1.50; ⊙10am-5pm Tue, Wed & Fri, to 8pm Thu, to 6pm Sat & Sun, to 5pm Mon Jul-Sep) from 1509 until his death in 1528. After a multimedia show, there's an audioguide tour of the four-storey house, which is narrated by 'Agnes', Dürer's wife.

Kaiserburg

This enormous **castle complex** (Map p194; 📞0911-244 6590; www.kaiserburg-nuernberg.de;

Auf der Burg; adult/child incl Sinwell Tower €7/ free, Palas & Museum €5.50/free; ⊙9am-6pm Apr-Sep, 10am-4pm Oct-Mar) above the Altstadt poignantly reflects Nuremberg's medieval might. The main attraction is a tour of the newly renovated Palas (residential wing) to see the lavish Knights' and Imperial Hall, a Romanesque double chapel and an exhibit on the inner workings of the Holy Roman Empire. This segues to the Kaiserburg Museum, which focuses on the castle's military and building history.

Germanisches Nationalmuseum

Spanning prehistory to the early 20th century, the **national museum** (Map p194; 📞0911-133 10; www.gnm.de; Kartäusergasse 1; adult/child €8/5; ⊙10am-6pm Tue & Thu-Sun, to 9pm Wed) is the German-speaking world's biggest and most important museum of Teutonic culture. It features works by German painters and sculptors, an archaeological collection, arms and armour, musical and scientific instruments, and toys.

◎ SIGHTS

Deutsche Bahn Museum   Museum

(Map p194; ☑0800-3268 7386; www.db museum.de; Lessingstrasse 6; adult/child €6/3; ◎9am-5pm Tue-Fri, 10am-6pm Sat & Sun)
Forget Dürer and wartime rallies, Nuremberg is a railway town at heart. Germany's first passenger trains ran between here and Fürth, a fact reflected in the unmissable German Railways Museum. which explores the history of Germany's legendary rail system. The huge exhibition that continues across the road is one of Nuremberg's top sights, especially if you have a soft spot for things that run on rails.

If you have tots aboard, head straight for KIBALA (Kinder-Bahnland – Children's Railway World), a section of the museum where lots of hands-on, interactive choo-choo-themed attractions await. There's also a huge model railway, one of Germany's largest, set in motion every hour by a uniformed controller.

However the real meat of the show are the two halls of locos and rolling stock. The first hall contains Ludwig II's incredible rococo rail carriage, dubbed the 'Versailles of the rails', as well as Bismarck's considerably less ostentatious means of transport. There's also Germany's most famous steam loco, the Adler, built by the Stephensons in Newcastle-upon-Tyne for the Nuremberg–Fürth line. The second hall across the road from the main building houses some mammoth engines, some with their Nazi or Deutsche Reichsbahn insignia still in place.

Memorium Nuremberg Trials   Memorial

(☑0911-3217 9372; www.memorium-nurem berg.de; Bärenschanzstrasse 72; adult/child incl audioguide €6/1.50; ◎9am-6pm Mon & Wed-Fri, 10am-6pm Sat & Sun Apr-Oct, slightly shorter hours Nov-Mar) Göring, Hess, Speer and 21 other Nazi leaders were tried for crimes against peace and humanity by the Allies in Schwurgerichtssaal 600 (Court Room 600) of this still-working courthouse. Today the room forms part of an engaging exhibit detailing the background, progression and impact of the trials using

Dokumentationszentrum, Reichsparteitagsgelände

TRABANTOS/SHUTTERSTOCK ©

film, photographs, audiotape and even the original defendants' dock. To get here, take the U1 towards Bärenschanze and get off at Sielstrasse.

Reichsparteitags-gelände
Historic Site

(Luitpoldhain; ☎0911-231 7538; www.museen. nuernberg.de/dokuzentrum; Bayernstrasse 110; grounds free, Documentation Centre adult/child incl audioguide €6/1.50; ☉grounds 24hr, Documentation Centre 9am 6pm Mon Fri, 10am 6pm Sat & Sun) If you've ever wondered where the infamous B&W images of ecstatic Nazi supporters hailing their Führer were taken, it was here in Nuremberg. Much of the grounds were destroyed during Allied bombing raids, but enough remain to get a sense of the megalomania behind it, espe cially after visiting the excellent Dokumentationszentrum (Documentation Centre; pictured left). It's served by tram 8 from the Hauptbahnhof.

⊙ TOURS

Geschichte für Alle
Cultural

(☎0911-307 360; www.geschichte-fuer-alle.de; adult/concession €8/7) An intriguing range of themed English-language tours by a nonprofit association. The 'Albrecht Dürer' and 'Life in Medieval Nuremberg' tours come highly recommended.

Old Town Walking Tours
Walking

(☎0170-141 1223; www.nuernberg-tours.de; tour €10; ☉1pm May-Oct) English-language oldtown walking tours are run by the tourist office – tours leave from the Hauptmarkt branch (p196) and take two hours.

Nuremberg Tours
Walking

(www.nurembergtours.com; adult/concession €22/19; ☉11.15am Mon, Wed & Sat Apr-Oct) Four-hour walking and public transport tours taking in the city centre and the Reichsparteitagsgelände. Groups meet at the entrance to the Hauptbahnhof.

 Nuremburg for Kids

No city in Bavaria has more for kids to see and do than Nuremberg. Every two months the region even produces a thick 'what's on' magazine called **Frankenkids** (www.frankenkids.de) focusing specifically on things to do with children. Keeping the little ones entertained in these parts really is child's play.

Children & Young People's Museum (☎0911-600 040; www.kindermuseum-nuern berg.de; Michael-Ende-Strasse 17; adult/family €7.50/19.50; ☉2-5.30pm Sat, 10am-5.30pm Sun Sep-Jun) Educational exhibitions and lots of hands-on fun – just a pity it's not open more often.

School Museum (☎0911-530 2574; Äussere Sulzbacher Strasse 62; adult/child €6/1.50; ☉9am-5pm Tue-Fri, 10am-6pm Sat & Sun) Recreated classroom plus school-related exhibits from the 17th century to the Third Reich.

Deutsche Bahn Museum (p192) Feeds the kids' obsession for choo-choos.

Playground of the Senses (www. erfahrungsfeld.nuernberg.de; Wöhrder Wiese; adult/child €8.50/7; ☉9am-6pm Mon-Fri, 1-6pm Sat, 10am-6pm Sun May–mid-Sep) Some 80 hands-on 'stations' designed to educate children in the laws of nature, physics and the human body. Take the U2 or U3 to Wöhrder Wiese.

Playmobil (☎0911-9666 1700; www.play mobil-funpark.de; Brandstätterstrasse 2-10; admission €11.90; ☉10am-6pm mid-Feb–Mar, 9am-6pm Apr, 9am-7pm May–mid-Sep) This theme park has life-size versions of the popular toys. It's located 9km west of the city centre in Zirndorf; take the S4 to Anwanden, then change to bus 151. Free admission if it's your birthday. Special 'Kleine Dürer' (Little Dürer; €2.99) figures are on sale here and at the tourist office.

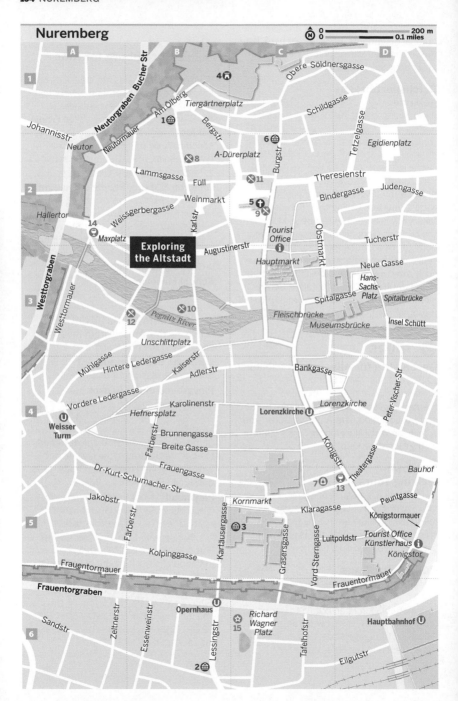

Nuremberg

N

0 ————— 200 m
0 ————— 0.1 miles

Neutorgraben Bucher Str

Obere Söldnersgasse

Tiergärtnerplatz

Am Ölberg

Johannisstr

Neutor

Neutormauer

Bergstr

Schildgasse

Tetzelgasse

Egidienplatz

4

1

6

8

A-Dürerplatz

Burgstr

Lammsgasse

Füll

11

Theresienstr

Bindergasse

Judengasse

Weinmarkt

5

9

Weissgerbergasse

Karlstr

Hallertor

14

Maxplatz

**Exploring
the Altstadt**

Augustinerstr

Tourist
Office

Hauptmarkt

Obstmarkt

Tucherstr

Neue Gasse

Westtorgraben

Westtormauer

12

Pegnitz River

10

Spitalgasse

Hans-
Sachs-
Platz

Spitalbrücke

Fleischbrücke

Museumsbrücke

Insel Schütt

Unschlittplatz

Mühlgasse

Hintere Ledergasse

Kaiserstr

Adlerstr

Bankgasse

Vordere Ledergasse

Karolinenstr

Lorenzkirche

Lorenzkirche

Peter-Vischer-Str

Weisser
Turm

Hefnersplatz

Färberstr

Brunnengasse

Breite Gasse

Königstr

Theatergasse

Bauhof

Dr-Kurt-Schumacher-Str

Frauengasse

7

13

Jakobstr

Färberstr

Kornmarkt

Kartäusergasse

3

Grasergasse

Klaragasse

Vord Sternstrasse

Luitpoldstr

Peuntgasse

Königstormauer

Tourist Office
Künstlerhaus

Königstor

Kolpinggasse

Frauentormauer

Frauentormauer

Frauentorgraben

Sandstr

Zeltnerstr

Essenweinstr

Opernhaus

Lessingstr

Richard
Wagner
Platz

15

Tafelhofstr

Hauptbahnhof

2

Eilgutstr

A B C D

Nuremberg

ⓐ SHOPPING

From late November to Christmas Eve, the Hauptmarkt is taken over by what most regards as Germany's top **Christkindlesmarkt** (Christmas market; www.christkindlesmarkt.de). Yuletide shoppers descend on the 'Christmas City' from all over Europe to seek out unique gifts at the scores of colourful timber trinket stalls that fill the square.

Bier Kontor   Alcohol
(Map p194; An der Mauthalle 2; ⊙11am-2pm & 2.30-7pm Mon-Sat) This small shop just off the tourist drag stocks a whopping 350 types of beer, from local Franconian suds to Hawaiian ales, fruity Belgian concoctions to British porters. And staff really know their stuff when it comes to the amber nectar.

⊗ EATING

Nuremberg has all kinds of cuisines, from Chinese to Croatian, Mexican to Czech. But it's the cosy Franconian taverns serving dark *Landbier* and the city's famous bratwurst that will leave a lasting culinary memory. Eating out is cheaper than in Munich but perhaps slightly pricier than in the rest of Franconia.

Café am Trödelmarkt   Cafe €
(Map p194; Trödelmarkt 42; dishes €4-10; ⊙9am-6pm Mon-Sat, 10am-6pm Sun) A gorgeous place on a sunny day, this multilevel waterfront cafe overlooks the covered Henkersteg bridge. It's especially popular for its

continental breakfasts, and has fantastic cakes, as well as good blackboard lunchtime specials between 11am and 2pm.

Naturkostladen
Lotos   Organic, Buffet €
(Map p194; www.naturkostladen-lotos.de; Am Unschlittplatz 1; dishes €4-9; ⊙9am-6.30pm Mon-Fri, to 5pm Sat; ⊘) Unclog arteries and blast free radicals with a blitz of grain burgers, spinach soup or vegan pizza at this strictly organic health-food shop. The fresh bread and cheese counter is a treasure chest of nutritious picnic supplies.

Albrecht Dürer
Stube   Franconian €€
(Map p194; ⊘0911-227 209; www.albrecht-durer-stube.de; cnr Albrecht-Dürer-Strasse & Agnesgasse; mains €6-15.50; ⊙6pm-midnight Mon-Sat plus 11.30am-2.30pm Fri & Sun) This unpretentious and intimate restaurant has a Dürer-inspired dining room, prettily laid tables, a ceramic stove keeping things toasty and a menu of Nuremberg sausages, steaks, sea fish, seasonal specials, Franconian wine and *Landbier* (regional beer). There aren't many tables so booking ahead at weekends is recommended.

Bratwursthäusle   Franconian €€
(Map p194; http://die-nuernberger-bratwurst.de; Rathausplatz 1; meals €7.50-11.50; ⊙11am-10pm) Seared over a flaming beech-wood grill, the little links sold at this rustic inn next to the Sebalduskirche arguably set the standard across the land. You can dine in the

SACK/GETTY IMAGES ©

Christkindlesmarkt (p195)

timbered restaurant or on the terrace with views of the Hauptmarkt. Service can be flustered at busy times and it's cash only when the bill comes.

Goldenes Posthorn
Franconian €€

(Map p194; ☑0911-225 153; Glöckleinsgasse 2, cnr Sebalder Platz; mains €6-14; ⊙11.30am-11.30pm) Push open the heavy copper door to find a real culinary treat that has hosted royals, artists and professors (including Albrecht Dürer) since 1498. You can't go wrong sticking with the miniature local sausages, but the pork shoulder and also the house speciality – vinegar-marinated ox cheeks – are both good value for money.

🍺 DRINKING & NIGHTLIFE

Franconia is a slightly underrated beer destination, and as the capital, Nuremberg offers some first-rate quaffing. *Landbier* (beers produced in small breweries out in the sticks) and craft beers are definitely the beverages to seek out with

lots of variety on offer. Coffee varies in quality, it has to be said. When it comes to post-sundown frolicking, Nuremberg has everything from mainstream clubs to alternative venues, but specialises in student-y cafe-bar hangouts.

Kettensteg
Beer Garden

(Map p194; Maxplatz 35; ⊙11am-11pm) At the end of the chain bridge and in the shadow of the Halletor you'll find this classic Bavarian beer garden complete with its gravel floor, folding slatted chairs, fairy lights, tree shade and river views. Zirndorfer, Lederer and Tucher beers are on tap and some of the food comes on heart-shaped plates.

Barfüsser Brauhaus
Beer Hall

(Map p194; Königstrasse 60; ⊙11am-1am Mon-Fri, to 2am Sat) This cellar beer hall deep below street level is a popular spot to hug a mug of site-brewed ale, bubbling frothily in the copper kettles that occupy the cavernous vaulted interior. The traditional trappings of the huge quaffing space clash oddly with the polo shirts of the swift-footed waiting staff, but that's our only criticism.

⭐ ENTERTAINMENT

The excellent *Plärrer* (www.plaerrer.de), available at newsstands throughout the city and from the tourist office, is the best source of information on events around town.

Staatstheater — Theatre

(Map p194; ☎0911-231 3808; www.staats theater-nuernberg.de; Richard-Wagner-Platz 2) Nuremberg's magnificent state theatre serves up an impressive mix of dramatic arts. The renovated art nouveau opera house presents opera and ballet, while the Kammerspiele offers a varied program of classical and contemporary plays. The Nürnberger Philharmoniker also performs here.

Hirsch — Live Music

(☎0911-429 414; www.der-hirsch.de; Vogelweih erstrasse 66) This converted factory, 2.5km south of the Hauptbahnhof, hosts live alternative music almost daily, both big-name acts and local names. Take the U1 or U2 to Plärrer, then change to tram 4, alighting at Dianaplatz.

ℹ INFORMATION

Tourist office branches at Hauptmarkt and in the Künstlerhaus sell the Nuremberg Card (€23) with two days of free museum entry and public transport. Staff also offer maps, info and advice.

Tourist Office Hauptmarkt (Map p194; ☎0911-233 60; www.tourismus.nuernberg.de; Hauptmarkt 18; ☺9am-6pm Mon-Sat, 10am-4pm Sun) Hauptmarkt branch of the tourist office. Has extended hours during Christkindlesmarkt which takes place on its doorstep.

Tourist Office Künstlerhaus (Map p194; ☎0911-233 60; www.tourismus.nuernberg.de; Königstrasse 93; ☺9am-7pm Mon-Sat, 10am-4pm Sun) Publishes the excellent *See & Enjoy* booklet, a comprehensive guide to the city.

ℹ GETTING THERE & AWAY

AIR

Nuremberg's **Albrecht Dürer Airport** (NUE; ☎0911-937 00; www.airport-nuernberg.de; Flughafenstrasse), 5km north of the centre, is served by regional and international carriers, including Ryanair, Lufthansa, Air Berlin and Air France.

BUS

Buses to destinations across Europe leave from the main bus station (ZOB) near the Hauptbahnhof. There's a Touring/Eurolines office nearby. Flixbus (www.flixbus.com) links Nuremberg with countless destinations in Germany and beyond. Special Deutsche Bahn express coaches to Prague (from €10, 3½ hours, seven daily) leave from the ZOB.

TRAIN

Nuremberg is connected by train to Berlin (from €80, three to 3½ hours, hourly), Frankfurt (€30 to €60, 2¼ hours, at least hourly), Hamburg (from €80, 4½ hours, hourly) and Munich (€40 and €60, one hour, twice hourly). Services also go to Cheb (€34, 1¾ hours, every two hours), for connections to Prague, and Vienna (from €90, four to 5½ hours, every two hours).

ℹ GETTING AROUND

The best transport around the Altstadt is at the end of your legs. Timed tickets on the VGN bus, tram and U-Bahn/S-Bahn networks cost from €1.30. A day pass costs €8.10. Passes bought on Saturday are valid all weekend.

ROTHENBURG
OB DER TAUBER

Rothenburg ob der Tauber

A medieval gem, Rothenburg ob der Tauber ('above the Tauber River') is a top tourist stop along the Romantic Road. With its web of cobbled lanes, higgledy-piggledy houses and towered walls, the town is the fairy-tale Germany the hordes of Japanese and Korean tourists come to see. Urban conservation orders here are the strictest in Germany – and at times it feels like a medieval theme park – but all's forgiven in the evenings, when the yellow lamplight casts its spell long after the last tour buses have left.

Arriving in Rothenburg ob der Tauber

Rothenburg train station Only handles local services to Steinach, where you can change to services to Würzburg and then Munich.

Romantic Road Coach Stops in the main bus park at the train station and on the more central Schrannenplatz.

Sleeping

At the last count, Rothenburg had around 50 accommodation providers, not bad for a town of just over 11,000 people. Bagging a bed, even in the height of summer, isn't normally a problem, though you'll need to book ahead if you want pillow space in the old town.

Previous page: Restored medieval buildings
BORIS STROUJKO/SHUTTERSTOCK ©

Detwang

Flugplatz
Rothenburg ob
der Tauber

The Romantic Road

Reichsstadtmuseum

Rothenburg ob der Tauber

Rothenburg ob der Tauber Hauptbahnhof

Mittelalterliches Kriminalmuseum

Neusitz

Tauber

N
0 — 1 km
0 — 0.5 mile

Rothenburg ob der Tauber Map (p207)

Aerial view over the town

Schloss Neuschwanstein (p205)

The Romantic Road

Quaint little Rothenburg is just about the most engaging stop on the 350km-long Romantic Road, Germany's most popular touring route. Here we list other highlights of the trip extending from Würzburg to Füssen.

Great For...

ℹ Need to Know

The Romantic Road Coach (p209) runs daily from April to October between Frankfurt and Füssen.

★ **Top Tip**

Consider doing the route by bike for a slower, more bucolic experience.

Würzburg

This scenic town straddles the Main River and is renowned for its art, architecture and delicate wines.

Würzburg was a Franconian duchy when, in 686, three Irish missionaries tried to persuade Duke Gosbert to convert to Christianity and ditch his wife. Gosbert was mulling it over when his wife had the three bumped off. When the murders were discovered decades later, the martyrs became saints and Würzburg was made a pilgrimage city, and, in 742, a bishopric.

For centuries the resident prince-bishops wielded enormous power and wealth, and the city grew in opulence under their rule. Their crowning glory is the Residenz, one of the finest baroque structures in Germany and a Unesco World Heritage Site.

Rothenburg ob der Tauber

This is the Romantic Road's quaintest halt with its ring of medieval town walls, cobbled lanes and old taverns. Visit in the quieter times for a taste of romance minus the tourists.

Dinkelsbühl

Some 40km south of Rothenburg, immaculately preserved Dinkelsbühl proudly traces its roots to a royal residence founded by Carolingian kings in the 8th century. Saved from destruction in the Thirty Years' War and ignored by WWII bombers, this is arguably the Romantic Road's most authentically medieval halt. For a good overall impression of the town, walk along the fortified walls with their 18 towers and four gates.

Würzburg Altstadt

Nördlingen

Charmingly medieval, Nördlingen sees fewer tourists than its better-known neighbours and manages to retain an air of authenticity. The town lies within the Ries Basin, a massive impact crater gouged out by a meteorite more than 15 million years ago. Nördlingen's 14th-century walls, all original, mimic the crater's rim and are almost perfectly circular.

Donauwörth & Harburg

Donauwörth is a medieval rebuild, largely destroyed during WWII. Nearby Schloss

☑ Don't Miss

Renaissance Schloss Weikersheim (www.schloss-weikersheim.de) is one of the finest palaces on the entire Romantic Road.

Harburg looms over the Wörnitz River, its medieval covered parapets, towers, turrets, keep and red-tiled roofs so perfectly preserved they almost seem like a film set. Tours tell the building's long tale and evoke the ghosts that are said to use the castle as a hang-out.

Augsburg

The largest city on the Romantic Road is an engaging stop, though one with a grittier, less-quaint atmosphere than others along the route. Top billing here goes to the Fuggerei, Augsburg's Catholic welfare settlement, the oldest in existence.

Wieskirche

The ecclesiastical climax of the Romantic Road is the baroque Wieskirche located in the village of Wies, just off the B17 between Füssen and Schongau. It's one of Bavaria's best-known baroque churches and a Unesco-listed World Heritage Site. About a million visitors a year flock here to see this monumental opus by the legendary artist-brothers, Dominikus and Johann Baptist Zimmermann.

Neuschwanstein & Hohenschwangau Castles

The Romantic Road comes to a fittingly idyllic crescendo at Germany's most popular tourist attraction, Neuschwanstein (p132) and Hohenschwangau (p134) castles, a felt hat's throw from the Alps.

Füssen

The town of Füssen (p136) is worth half a day's exploration and, from here, you can easily escape from the crowds into a landscape of gentle hiking trails and Alpine vistas.

MICHAEL ABID/500PX ©

✖ Take a Break

The Romantic Road has every kind of dining experience, from gourmet to kebabs.

◉ SIGHTS

Alt-Rothenburger Handwerkerhaus
Historic Building

(Map p207; www.alt-rothenburger-handwerker haus.de; Alter Stadtgraben 26; adult/child €3/1.50; ☺11am-5pm Mon-Fri, from 10am Sat & Sun Easter-Oct, 2-4pm daily Dec) Hidden down a little alley is the Alt-Rothenburger Handwerkerhaus, where numerous artisans – including coopers, weavers, cobblers and potters – have their workshops today, and mostly have had for the house's more than 700-year existence. It's half museum, half active workplace and you can easily spend an hour or so watching the artisans at work.

Deutsches Weihnachtsmuseum
Museum

(Christmas Museum; Map p207; ☎09861-409 365; www.weihnachtsmuseum.de; Herrngasse 1; adult/child/family €4/2.50/7; ☺10am-5pm Easter-Christmas, shorter hours Jan-Easter) If you're glad Christmas comes but once every 365 days, then stay well clear of the Käthe Wohlfahrt Weihnachtsdorf (p208), a Yuletide superstore that also houses this Christmas Museum. This repository of all things 'Ho! Ho! Ho!' traces the development of various Christmas customs and decorations, and includes a display of 150 Santa figures, plus lots of retro baubles and tinsel – particularly surreal in mid-July when the mercury outside is pushing 30°C.

Mittelalterliches Kriminalmuseum
Museum

(Medieval Crime & Punishment Museum; Map p207; www.kriminalmuseum.eu; Burggasse 3; adult/concession €7/4; ☺10am-6pm Apr-Oct, 1-4pm Nov-Mar) The star attractions at this gruesomely fascinating museum are medieval implements of torture and punishment. Exhibits include chastity belts, masks of disgrace for gossips, a cage for cheating bakers, a neck brace for quarrelsome women and a beer-barrel pen for drunks. You can even snap a selfie in the stocks. The museum has 50,000 exhibits, making it the biggest of its kind in Europe.

Rathausturm
Historic Building

(Town Hall Tower; Map p207; Marktplatz; adult/child €2/0.50; ☺9.30am-12.30pm & 1-5pm Apr-Oct, 10.30am-2pm & 2.30-6pm Sun-Thu, to 7pm Fri & Sat Dec, noon-3pm Sat & Sun Jan-Mar & Nov) The Rathaus on Marktplatz was begun in Gothic style in the 14th century and was completed during the Renaissance. Climb the 220 steps of the medieval town hall to the viewing platform of the Rathausturm, to be rewarded with widescreen views of the Tauber.

Reichsstadtmuseum
Museum

(Map p207; www.reichsstadtmuseum. rothenburg.de; Klosterhof 5; adult/child €6/5; ☺9.30am-5.30pm Apr-Oct, 1-4pm Nov-Mar) Highlights of the Reichsstadtmuseum, housed in a former Dominican convent, include the *Rothenburger Passion* (1494), a cycle of 12 panels by Martinus Schwarz, and the oldest convent kitchen in Germany, as well as weapons and armour. Outside the main entrance (on your right as you're facing the museum), you'll see a spinning barrel, where the nuns distributed bread to the poor – and where women would leave babies they couldn't afford to keep.

Stadtmauer
Historic Site

(Town Wall; Map p207) With time and fresh legs, a 2.5km circular walk around the unbroken ring of town walls gives a sense of the importance medieval people placed on defending their settlements. A great lookout point is the eastern tower, the **Röderturm** (Rödergasse; adult/child €2/1; ☺9am-5pm Mar-Oct & Dec), but for the most impressive views head to the western side of town, where a sweeping view of the Tauber Valley includes the Doppelbrücke, a double-decker bridge.

Rothenburg ob der Tauber

(N) 0 — 200 m
0 — 0.1 miles

Rothenburg ob der Tauber

🟠 Sights
1 Alt-Rothenburger Handwerkerhaus	C3
2 Deutsches Weihnachtsmuseum	B3
3 Mittelalterliches Kriminalmuseum	B3
4 Rathausturm	B2
5 Reichsstadtmuseum	A2
6 Röderturm	D3
7 Stadtmauer	D3

🟡 Shopping
8 Käthe Wohlfahrt Weihnachtsdorf	B3

🟢 Eating
9 Gasthof Goldener Greifen	B3
10 Mittermeier	D1
11 Zur Höll	A3

🔵 TOURS

The tourist office runs 1½-hour walking tours (€7; in English) at 2pm from April to October and during Advent. Every evening a lantern-toting *Nachtwächter* (night-watchman) dressed in traditional costume leads an entertaining tour of the Altstadt; English tours (€8) meet at the Rathaus just before 8pm.

🍴 EATING

Rothenburg boasts some excellent Franconian restaurants and taverns as well as plenty of international fast food. The town's speciality is the *Schneeball*, the famous snowball, ribbons of dough loosely shaped into balls, deep-fried then coated in icing sugar or cinnamon.

Bottoms Up For Freedom

In 1631 the Thirty Years' War – pitching Catholics against Protestants – reached the gates of Rothenburg ob der Tauber. Catholic General Tilly and 60,000 of his troops besieged the Protestant market town and demanded its surrender. The town resisted but couldn't stave off the onslaught of marauding soldiers, and the mayor and other town dignitaries were captured and sentenced to death.

And that's about where the story ends and the legend begins. As the tale goes, Rothenburg's town council tried to sate Tilly's bloodthirstiness by presenting him with a 3L pitcher of wine. Tilly, after taking a sip or two, presented the councillors with an unusual challenge, saying, 'If one of you has the courage to step forward and down this mug of wine in one gulp, then I shall spare the town and the lives of the councilmen!' Mayor Georg Nusch accepted – and succeeded! And that's why you can still wander though Rothenburg's wonderful medieval lanes today.

It's pretty much accepted that Tilly was really placated with hard cash. Nevertheless, local poet Adam Hörber couldn't resist turning the tale of the *Meistertrunk* (champion drinker) into a play, which, since 1881, has been performed every Whitsuntide (Pentecost), the seventh Sunday after Easter. It's also re-enacted several times daily by the clock figures (pictured) on the tourist office building.

BILL HEINSOHN/GETTY IMAGES ©

Gasthof
Goldener Greifen   Franconian €€

(Map p207; ☑09861-2281; www.gasthof-greifen-rothenburg.de; Obere Schmiedgasse 5; mains €8-17; ☉11.30am-10pm; ☎) Erstwhile home of Heinrich Toppler, one of Rothenburg's most famous medieval mayors (the dining room was his office), the 700-year-old Golden Griffin is the locals' choice in the touristy centre. A hearty menu of Franconian favourites is served in an austere semimedieval setting and out back in the sunny and secluded garden. There's also a long kids' menu, a rarity in Bavaria.

Zur Höll   Franconian €€

(Map p207; ☑09861-4229; www.hoell.rothenburg.de; Burggasse 8; mains €7-20; ☉5-11pm Mon-Sat) This medieval wine tavern is in the town's oldest original building, with sections dating back to AD 900. The menu of regional specialities is limited but refined, though it's the superb selection of Franconian wines that people really come for.

Mittermeier   Barvarian €€€

(Map p207; ☑09861-945 430; www.villamittermeier.de; Vorm Würzburger Tor 7; mains €10-30; ☉6-10.30pm Tue-Sat; Ⓟ☎) Supporter of the slow food movement and a regular in the Michelin Guide, this hotel restaurant pairs punctilious artisanship with top-notch ingredients, sourced regionally whenever possible. There are five different dining areas including a black-and-white tiled 'temple', an alfresco terrace and a barrel-shaped wine cellar. The wine list is one of the best in Franconia. Book ahead.

🔒 SHOPPING

Käthe Wohlfahrt
Weihnachtsdorf   Decorations

(Map p207; www.wohlfahrt.com; Herrngasse 1; ☉10am-5pm Mon-Sat) With its mind-boggling assortment of Yuletide decorations and ornaments, this huge shop (pictured) lets you celebrate Christmas every day of the year. Many of the

Käthe Wohlfahrt Weihnachtsdorf

items are handcrafted with amazing skill and imagination; prices are correspondingly high. This is the original shop in a chain that has spread across Rothenburg and all of Germany.

ℹ INFORMATION

Tourist Office (Map p207; ☎09861-404 800; www.tourismus.rothenburg.de; Marktplatz 2; ◷9am-6pm Mon-Fri, 10am-5pm Sat & Sun May-Oct, 9am-5pm Mon-Fri, 10am-1pm Sat Nov-Apr) Helpful office running walking tours and offering free internet access.

ℹ GETTING THERE & AWAY

BUS

The **Romantic Road Coach** (www.romantic roadcoach.de) stops in the main bus park at the Hauptbahnhof and on the more central Schrannenplatz.

From April to October this special coach runs daily in each direction between Frankfurt and Füssen (for Neuschwanstein); the entire journey takes around 12 hours. There's no charge for breaking the journey and continuing the next day, but it can get incredibly crowded in summer.

TRAIN

You can go anywhere by train from Rothenburg, as long as it's Steinach. Change there for services to Würzburg (€15.70, one hour and 10 minutes). Travel to and from Munich (from €29, three to four hours) can involve up to three different trains, making a day trip unfeasible.

ℹ GETTING AROUND

The city has five car parks right outside the walls. The town centre is essentially closed to nonresident vehicles, though hotel guests are exempt.

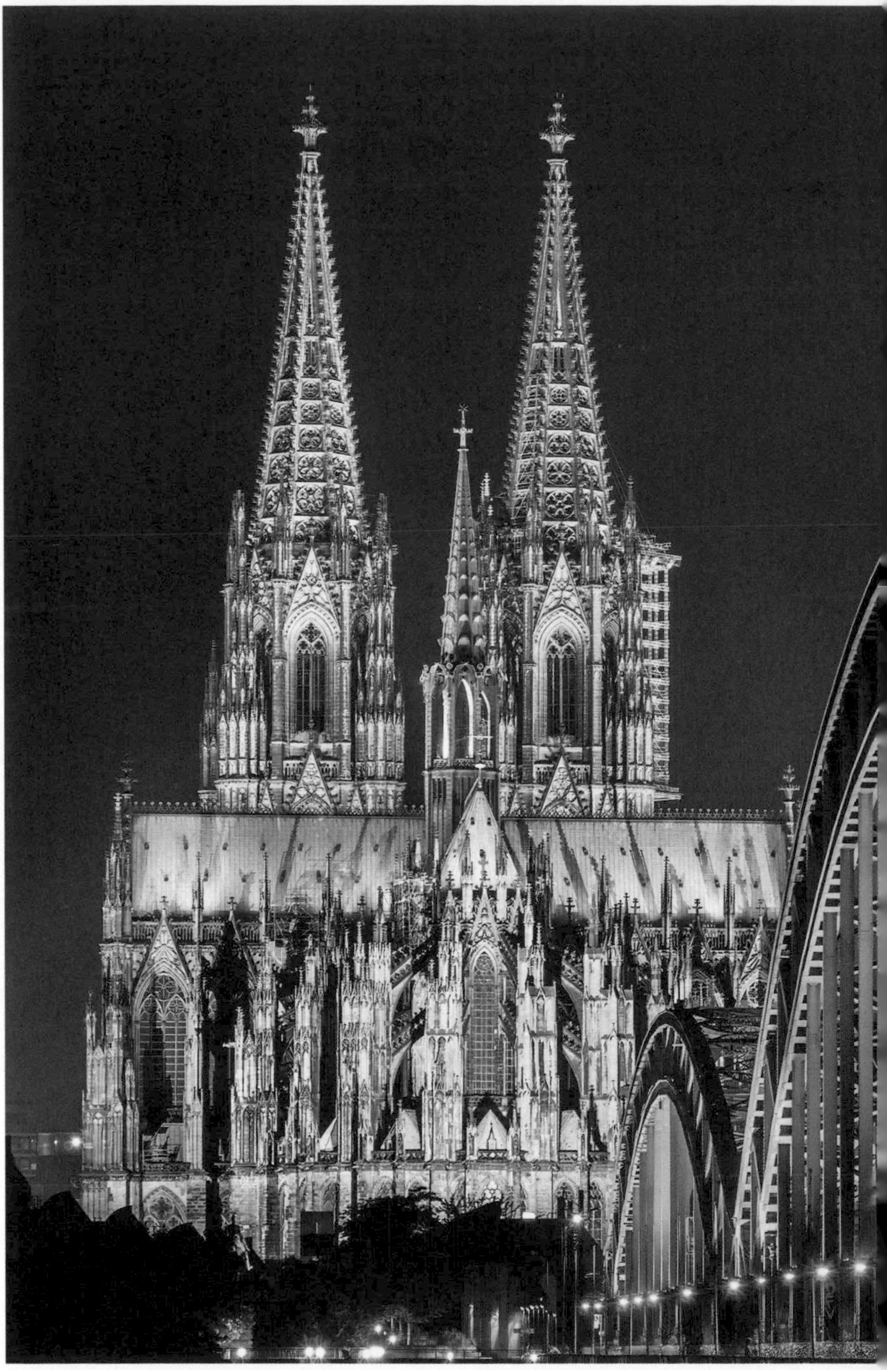

ARNULPH FUHRMANN / 500PX ©

COLOGNE

Cologne

Germany's fourth-largest city was founded by the Romans in 38 BC and grew into a major trading centre; a tradition that continues. Today, Cologne (Köln) offers seemingly endless attractions, led by its famous cathedral, whose filigree twin spires dominate the skyline, and a museum landscape with subjects as diverse as chocolate, sports and Roman history. Visually, the city is like a 3D textbook on history and architecture, which runs the gamut from Roman to medieval, classical, avant-garde and postmodern. After dark, you'll have no trouble finding your people, whoever they are.

Cologne in One Day

Say hello to the gargoyles as you huff and puff up the south tower of the majestic **Cologne Cathedral** (p214) for a full-on city panorama. Have your breath taken away again as you enter this dazzling house of worship, whose loftiness and ancient treasures never fail to amaze, then amble down to the **Wallraf-Richartz-Museum** (p216). After those heavyweight attractions, take a load off on a **boat ride** (p220) on the Rhine before heading down to the irresistible **Schokoladenmuseum** (p219).

Cologne in Two Days

Connect with Cologne's Roman origins at **Römisch-Germanisches Museum** (p216), perhaps also popping into the adjacent **Museum Ludwig** (p217) to check out contemporary art, followed by the **Museum für Angewandte Kunst** (p219) or the sobering **NS-Dokumentationszentrum** (p217). Head to the Belgisches Viertel neighbourhood to lighten the mood with cake or a wine, then poke around the boutiques and galleries of this charismatic quarter before ascending the **KölnTriangle Panorama** (p217) as the sun sets and the city starts to twinkle below.

Previous page: Hohenzollern Brücke (p220) and Kölner Dom (p214)
ARNULPH FUHRMANN/500PX ©

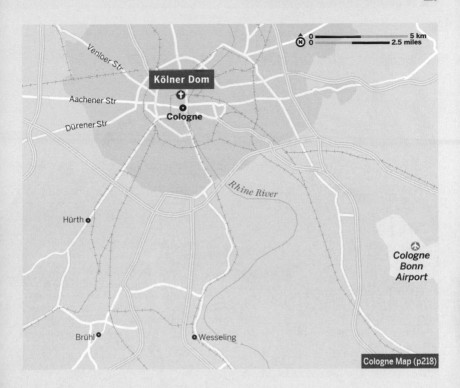

Cologne Map (p218)

Arriving in Cologne

Cologne-Bonn Airport Receives domestic as well as many European flights.

Cologne Hauptbahnhof A major halt on the German rail network handling countless local, regional and national services.

Central bus station Handles national and international coach services. Near the Hauptbahnhof

Sleeping

Cologne often hosts trade shows (especially in spring and autumn) when hotel rates can double or even triple. Otherwise, you'll find good-value options throughout the walkable central area. Note that a 5% city tax is added to your hotel bill (business travellers are exempt).

Kölner Dom

SAIKOW/SHUTTERSTOCK ©

Kölner Dom

Cologne's geographical and spiritual heart – and its single-biggest tourist draw – is the magnificent Kölner Dom (Cologne Cathedral). With its soaring twin spires, this is the Mt Everest of cathedrals, jam-packed with art and treasures.

Great For...

☑ **Don't Miss**

The underground Domforum visitor centre is a good source of info and tickets.

The Dom is Germany's largest cathedral and must be circled to truly appreciate its dimensions. Note how its lacy spires and flying buttresses create a sensation of lightness and fragility despite its mass and height.

This sensation continues inside, where a phalanx of pillars and arches supports the lofty nave. Soft light filters through the medieval stained-glass windows (pictured above right) as well as a much-lauded recent one by contemporary artist Gerhard Richter in the transept. A kaleidoscope of 11,500 squares in 72 colours, Richter's abstract design has been called a 'symphony of light'. In the afternoon especially, when the sun hits it just so, it's easy to understand why.

History

Construction began in 1248 in the French Gothic style but proceeded slowly and was

Stained-glass windows

THABUTTA/SHUTTERSTOCK ©

ⓘ Need to Know

Map p218; ☎0221-9258 4720; www.
koelner-dom.de; Domkloster 4; tower adult/
concession €4/2; ⊙6am-9pm May-Oct, to
7.30pm Nov-Apr, tower 9am-6pm May-Sep, to
5pm Mar, Apr & Oct, to 4pm Nov-Feb; ☐5, 16,
18 Dom/Hauptbahnhof

✕ Take a Break

There are several cafes and restaurants
in and around the Dom's square.

★ Top Tip

To get more out of your visit, invest €1
in the information pamphlet or join a
guided tour.

eventually halted in 1560 when funds ran
out. The half-built church lingered for nearly 300 years and even suffered a stint as
a horse stable and prison when Napoleon
occupied the town. A few decades later, a
generous cash infusion from Prussian King
Friedrich Wilhelm IV finally led to its completion in 1880, 632 years after it started.
Luckily, it escaped WWII bombing raids
with nary a shrapnel wound and has been a
Unesco World Heritage Site since 1996.

Shrine of the Three Kings

The pièce de résistance among the
cathedral's bevy of treasures is the Shrine
of the Three Kings behind the main altar, a
richly bejewelled and gilded sarcophagus
said to hold the remains of the kings who
followed the star to the stable in Bethle-
hem where Jesus was born. The bones

were spirited out of Milan in 1164 as spoils
of war by Emperor Barbarossa's chancellor
and instantly turned Cologne into a major
pilgrimage site.

South Tower

For an exercise fix, climb the 533 steps up
the Dom's south tower to the base of the
steeple. This dwarfed all buildings in Europe
until Gustave Eiffel built a certain tower in
Paris. During your climb up to the 95m-high
viewing platform, take a breather and admire
the 24-tonne Peter Bell (1923), the largest
free-swinging working bell in the world.

Other Highlights

Look for the Gero Crucifix (970), notable
for its monumental size and an emotional
intensity rarely achieved in those early
medieval days; the choir stalls from 1310,
richly carved from oak; and the altar
painting (c 1450) by Cologne artist Stephan
Lochner.

◉ SIGHTS

Plan on a couple of days to explore Cologne's wealth of sights. The city maintains an excellent website (www.museen-koeln.de) with info on most of Cologne's museums. The **MuseumsCard** (per person/family €18/30) is good for one-time admission to all municipal museums on two consecutive days.

The area around Cologne's historical city hall (Altes Rathaus) has been a major construction site while a new U-Bahn line is being built. During this time, massive archaeological excavations have unearthed many new discoveries about Cologne's Roman and Jewish past.

Wallraf-Richartz-Museum & Fondation Corboud   Museum

(Map p218; ☑0221-2212 1119; www.wallraf.museum; Obenmarspforten; adult/concession €9/5.50; ☺10am-6pm Tue-Sun; ☒1, 7, 9 Heumarkt, ☒5 Rathaus) One of Germany's finest art museums, the Wallraf-Richartz presents a primo collection of European art from the 13th to the 19th centuries in a minimalist cube designed by the late OM Ungers. All the marquee names are here – Rubens and Rembrandt to Monet – along with a prized sampling of medieval art, most famously Stefan Lochner's *Madonna in Rose Bower*, nicknamed the 'Mona Lisa of Cologne'.

Römisch-Germanisches Museum   Museum

(Roman Germanic Museum; Map p218; ☑0221-2212 4438; www.roemisch-germanisches-museum.de; Roncalliplatz 4; adult/concession/under 18yr €6.50/3.50/free; ☺10am-5pm Tue-Sun; ☒5, 16, 18 Dom/Hauptbahnhof) Sculptures and ruins displayed outside the entrance are merely the overture to a full symphony of Roman artefacts found along the Rhine. Highlights include the giant Poblicius tomb (AD 30–40), the magnificent 3rd-century Dionysus mosaic, and astonishingly well-preserved glass items. Insight into daily Roman life is gained from toys, tweezers, lamps and jewellery, the designs of which have changed surprisingly little since Roman times.

Museum Ludwig

SPUNK TAXI/SHUTTERSTOCK ©

Museum Ludwig   Museum

(Map p218; ☑0221-2212 6165; www.museum
-ludwig.de; Heinrich-Böll-Platz; adult/concession
€12/8, more during special exhibits; ☉10am-
6pm Tue-Sun; ☒5, 16, 18 Dom/Hauptbahnhof)
A mecca of modern art, Museum Ludwig
(pictured left) presents a tantalising mix of
works from all major genres. Fans of German expressionism (Beckmann, Dix, Kirchner) will get their fill here as much as those
with a penchant for Picasso, American pop
art (Warhol, Lichtenstein) and Russian
avant-garde painter Alexander Rodchenko.
Rothko and Pollock are highlights of the
abstract collection, while Gursky and Till-
manns help make the photography section
a must-stop.

KölnTriangle
Panorama   Viewpoint

(☑02234 992 1555; www.koelntrianglepanorama.
de; Ottoplatz 1; adult/under 12 €3/free; ☉11am-
11pm Mon-Fri, 10am-11pm Sat & Sun May-Sep,
noon-8pm Mon-Fri, 10am-8pm Sat & Sun Oct-Apr;
℗; ⓊKöln Messe/Deutz) The noise of the
city fades to a quiet hum on the viewing
platform, located at a lofty 103m atop the
KölnTriangle office tower on the right Rhine
bank across from the Cologne Cathedral
(p215). The building, with its shiny glass and
aluminum facade, is an eye-catcher in its
own right.

Kolumba   Museum

(Map p218; ☑0221-933 1930; www.kolumba.de;
Kolumbastrasse 4; adult/child €5/free; ☉noon-
5pm Wed-Mon; ☒5 Rathaus) Art, history, architecture and spirituality form a harmonious
tapestry in this spectacular collection of
the Archdiocese of Cologne's religious
treasures. Called Kolumba, the building
encases the ruins of the late-Gothic church
of St Kolumba, its layers of foundations
going back to Roman times, and the Madonna in the Ruins chapel, built on the site
in 1950. Exhibits span the arc of religious
artistry from the early days of Christianity
to the present. Don't miss the 12th-century
carved ivory crucifix.

🏙 Harbour Redux:
Rheinauhafen

London has its Docklands, Düsseldorf
its Medienhafen, Hamburg is building HafenCity and now Cologne has
joined the revitalised-harbour trend
with the Rheinauhafen. South of the
Altstadt, this urban quarter has sprung
up along a 2km stretch between the
Severinsbrücke and Südbrücke bridges.
Dozens of 19th-century brick buildings
have second lives as office, living and
entertainment spaces, juxtaposed with
contemporary designs ranging from
bland to avant-garde. The most dramatic change to Cologne's skyline comes
courtesy of a trio of *Kranhäuser* (crane
houses), huge inverted L-shaped structures that are an abstract interpretation
of historical harbour cranes. There are
some shops, restaurants and cafes as
well as a riverside promenade.

Rheinauhafen

NS-
Dokumentationszentrum   Museum

(NS-DOK; Map p218; ☑0221-2212 6332; www.
museenkoeln.de/ns-dokumentationszentrum;
Appellhofplatz 23-25; adult/concession €4.50/2;
☉10am-6pm Tue-Fri, 11am-6pm Sat & Sun; ☒3,
4, 5, 16, 18 Appellhofplatz) Cologne's Third
Reich history is poignantly and exhaustively
documented, housed in the very building
that served as the headquarters of the local
Gestapo (Nazi secret police). The basement prison, where scores of people were
interrogated, tortured and killed, is now a
memorial site.

Cologne

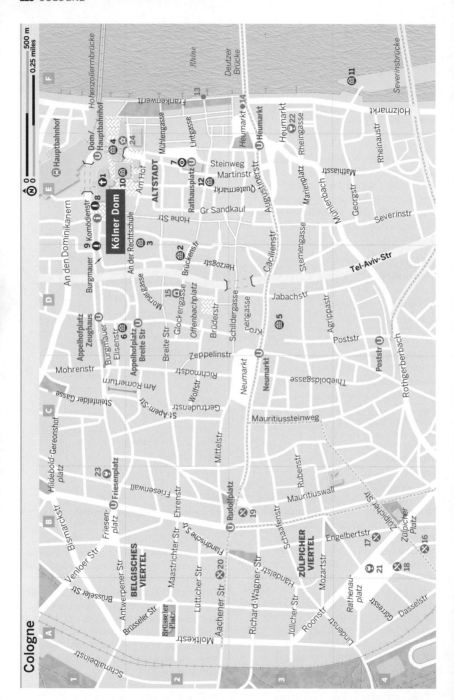

Cologne

Museum für Angewandte Kunst
Museum

(MAKK, Museum of Applied Arts; Map p218; ☑0221-2212 6714; www.makk.de; An der Rechtschule; adult/concession €5/2.50; ☺11am-6pm Tue-Sun; ᠗5, 16, 18 Appellhofplatz, Dom/Hauptbahnhof) If Aalto, Eames and Olivetti are music to your ears, you should swing by the Museum of Applied Arts, which displays a prestigious and extensive collection of classic and innovative objects in its newly reopened Design section. The historical collection upstairs, meanwhile, will remain closed for restoration for the foreseeable future.

Museum Schnütgen
Museum

(Map p218; ☑0221-2212 2310; www.museum-schnuetgen.de; Cäcilienstrasse 29; adult/concession €6/3.50; ☺10am-6pm Tue, Wed & Fri-Sun, to 8pm Thu; P; UNeumarkt) The Museum Schnütgen is an exquisite repository of medieval religious art and sculpture from the Rhineland region presented within the serene ambience of the Romanesque Cäcilienkirche, one of Cologne's oldest churches. Outstanding works include the Parler Bust, a crucifix from St George and the ivory Comb of St Heribert.

Schokoladenmuseum
Museum

(Chocolate Museum; Map p218; ☑0221-931 8880; www.schokoladenmuseum.de; Am

Schokoladenmuseum 1a; adult/student/child €11.50/9/7.50; ☺10am-6pm Tue-Fri, 11am-7pm Sat & Sun, last entry 1hr before closing; ᠗133 Schokoladenmuseum) This boat-shaped, high-tech temple to the art of chocolate making has plenty of engaging exhibits on the 5000-year cultural history of the 'elixir of the gods' (as the Aztecs called it) as well as on the cocoa-growing process. The walk-through tropical forest is a highlight, although most visitors are more enthralled by the glass-walled miniature production facility and a sample at the chocolate fountain.

⊙ ACTIVITIES

Cologne's dense network of bike routes along the Rhine and throughout the city make it a fine place to cycle. Pick up a bike map at the tourist office (p223).

Radstation Köln
Bicycle Rental

(☑0221-139 7190; www.radstationkoeln.de; Breslauer Platz; bikes from three hours/day €6/11; ☺5.30am-10.30pm Mon-Fri, 6.30am-8pm Sat, 8am-8pm Sun; UKöln Dom/Hbf) This bike rental outfit behind the train station also offers excellent three-hour **tours** (Map p218; tours incl bike rental €22.50; ☺1.30pm Apr-Oct; ᠗1, 5, 7, 9 Neumarkt) in English. The website has details.

Cologne for Kids

Cologne is an enjoyable place to visit if you're travelling with little ones. The city has plenty of parks and playgrounds, a zoo, beer gardens with play areas, museums with child-friendly exhibits, and restaurants that welcome tots with special menus.

Schokoladenmuseum (p219) Satisfy everyone's sweet tooth.

Kölner Dom (p215) Imposing at any age.

4711 House of Fragrances (p222) Listen to the Glockenspiel located on the front facade, which plays music every hour.

KD-Panoramafahrt boat tour Fun on the Rhine (see below).

KölnTriangle (p217) Ride the lift 103m up to the viewing platform.

Hohenzollern Bridge Check out the literally tens of thousands love locks.

Praetorium & Roman Sewer (Map p218; www.museenkoeln.de; Kleine Budengasse 2; adult/concession €3.50/3; ⊙10am-5pm Tue-Sun; ᗣ5 Rathaus) Go underground at a Roman governor's palace.

TOURS

KD-Panoramafahrt Boating

(Map p218; ☑0221-258 3011; www.k-d.com; Frankenwerft; adult/concession €10.40/6; ⊙10.30am-6pm Apr-Oct; ᗣ1, 5, 7, 9 Heumarkt, ᗣ5 Rathaus) KD is one of several operators offering one-hour spins on the Rhine taking in the splendid city panorama. Tours leave every 90 minutes from docks in the Altstadt.

EATING

Multicultural Cologne offers culinary journeys around the world. Make tasty discoveries in Belgisches Viertal and the streets in and around Zülpicher Platz and Ehrenstrasse. Sample traditional Rhenish dishes including *Himmel un Ääd* (mashed potato with blood sausage and apple) at atmospheric beer halls. For street-food fans, there's the weekly **Meet & Eat Markt** (Map p218; www.meet-and-eat.koeln; Rudolfplatz; ⊙4-9pm Thu; ᵾRudolfplatz) and the monthly **Street Food Festival** (www.street-food-festival.de; Heliosstrasse 35-37; €2; ⊙noon-10pm Sat, to 8pm Sun, 1st weekend of month Mar-Sep; ᗣ3, 4, 13 Venloer Strasse/Gürtel).

Freddy Schilling Burgers €

(☑0221-1695 5515; www.freddyschilling.de; Kyffhäuserstrasse 34; burgers €7-10; ⊙11.30am-10pm Sun-Thu, to 11pm Fri & Sat; ᗣ9 Dasselstrasse/Bf Süd) A wholewheat bun provides a solid framework for the moist patties made with beef from happy cows and drizzled with Freddy's homemade 'special' sauce. Pair it with a side of hand-cut fries or *Rosis* (butter-and-rosemary-tossed baby potatoes). The vegan burger is a toothsome meat-free alternative.

Engelbät European €

(Map p218; ☑0221-246 914; www.engelbaet.de; Engelbertstrasse 7; crêpes €5.50-9; ⊙11am-midnight Mon-Thu, to 1am Fri & Sat; ᗣ; ᗣ9, 12, 15 Zülpicher Platz) This cosy restaurant-pub is famous for its habit-forming crêpes, which come in 50 varieties – sweet or savoury, meat or vegetarian and vegan. Also popular for its breakfasts (served until 3pm) and salads with homemade dressing.

Salon Schmitz European €€

(Map p218; ☑0221-139 5577; www.salonschmitz.com; Aachener Strasse 28-34; mains from €10; ⊙9am-1am Sun-Thu, open end Fri & Sat; ᗣ1, 7, 12, 15 Rudolfplatz) Spread over three historical row houses, the Schmitz empire is your one-stop shop for excellent food and drink. Greet the day with a lavish breakfast in the retro-hip 1950s and '60s setting of the Salon; order cake, quiche or a hot dish in the Metzgerei, a historical butcher's shop turned deli; or indulge in a fine brasserie-style dinner in the art nouveau–styled Bar.

Bei Oma Kleinmann German €€

(Map p218; ☑0221-232 346; www.beioma kleinmann.de; Zülpicher Strasse 9; mains €13-24; ⊘5pm-midnight Tue-Thu & Sun, to 1am Fri & Sat; ☒9, 12, 15 Zülpicher Platz) Named for its long-time owner, who was still cooking almost to her last day at age 95 in 2009, this perennially booked, graffiti-covered restaurant serves oodles of schnitzel, made either with pork or veal and paired with homemade sauces and sides. Pull up a seat at the small wooden tables for a classic Cologne night out.

Feynsinn International €€

(Map p218; ☑0221-240 9210; www.cafe-feyn sinn.de; Rathenauplatz 7; dinner mains €10-23; ⊘9am-1am Mon-Thu, to 2am Fri, 9.30am-2am Sat, 10am-1am Sun; ☒9, 12 15 Zülpicher Platz) This well-respected Zülpicher Viertel restaurant is an excellent pit stop at any time of the day. Come for extravagant breakfasts, light lunches and creative cakes or a dinner menu that weaves organic seasonal ingredients into sharp-flavoured dishes. Get a table overlooking the park for a meal or just a drink.

DRINKING & NIGHTLIFE

Cologne's huge array of thirst parlours range from grungy to grand. Centres of action include the Altstadt, student-flavoured Zülpicher Viertel, trendy Friesenplatz and Belgisches Viertel, and multicultural Ehrenfeld. Next to Berlin, Cologne has one of the best club scenes for electronic music; the best venues are located outside the Ring.

Odonien Club

(☑0221-972 7009; www.odonien.de; Hornstrasse 85; ⊘beer garden 5pm-late Thu-Sat May-Sep; ⓢNippes) The brainchild of artist Odo Rumpf, this subculture playground is creative lab, beer garden, concert venue, club, art centre, alfresco cinema and urban garden all rolled into one. In summer, there are few more inspiring places to kick back with a cold *Kölsch* than amid Odo's bizarre metal sculptures. On weekends, techno and house electrify the three dance floors.

LGBTIQ+ Cologne

Cologne is one of Germany's most happening and friendly out-and-proud cities. The rainbow flag flies especially proudly in the so-called 'Bermuda Triangle' around Rudolfplatz (especially Schaafenstrasse), which explodes into a non-stop party zone at weekends. Another major romping ground is in Altstadt around Heumarkt (especially Pipinstrasse), which draws older and more sedate folks.

Your top resource: www.patroc.com/gay/cologne.

Cologne Pride in June serves as a warm-up for **Christopher Street Day** (www.colognepride.de; ⊘1st weekend in Jul), which brings more than a million people to Cologne.

Christopher Street Day celebrations
KATERYNA KOGAN/EYEEM/GETTY IMAGES ©

Biergarten Rathenauplatz Beer Garden

(Map p218; ☑0221-801 7349; www.rathenau platz.de/biergarten; Rathenauplatz 30; ⊘noon-11.30pm Apr-Sep; ☒9, 12, 15 Zülpicher Platz) A large, leafy park has one of Cologne's best places for a drink: a community-run beer garden. Tables sprawl under huge old trees, while simple snacks such as salads and very good *Frikadelle* (spiced hamburger) issue forth from a cute little hut.

Brauerei zur Malzmühle Beer Hall

(Map p218; ☑0221-9216 0613; https://brauerei zurmalzmuehle.de; Heumarkt 6; ⊘11.30am-midnight Mon-Thu, to 1.30am Fri, noon-1am Sat, 11am-11pm Sun; ☒1, 5, 7, 9 Heumarkt) Expect

Kölsch Beer

Cologne has its own style of beer, *Kölsch*, which is light, hoppy, slightly sweet and served cool in *Stangen*, skinny, straight glasses that only hold 0.2L. In traditional Cologne beer halls and pubs you don't order beer so much as subscribe; the constantly prowling waiters will keep dropping off the little glasses of beer until you indicate you've had enough by placing a beer mat on top of your glass.

A ceaseless flow of *Stangen* filled with *Kölsch*, along with earthy humour and platters of meaty local foods, are the hallmarks of Cologne's iconic beer halls. Look for the days when each place serves glorious potato pancakes (*Rievkooche* or *Reibekuchen* in the local dialect).

plenty of local colour at this convivial, family-run beer hall, attached to a brewery in business since 1858. It serves the popular *Mühlen Kölsch* which has a robust, malty taste. If you prefer a less potent brew, try the *Koch'sches Malzbier* (malt beer, 2% alcohol). Good menu of traditional Cologne brewpub fare (mains €10 to €22.50).

Päffgen
Beer Hall

(Map p218; ☑0221-135 461; www.paeffgen -koelsch.de; Friesenstrasse 64-66; ⊘10am-midnight Sun-Thu, to 12.30am Fri & Sat; ☒5 Friesenplatz) Busy and boisterous, Päffgen has been pouring *Kölsch* since 1883 and hasn't lost step since. In summer you can enjoy the refreshing brew and local specialities (€4.30 to €15.50) beneath starry skies in the beer garden.

❸ ENTERTAINMENT

With two major orchestras, an opera house and numerous theatres, Cologne has a terrific highbrow cultural scene, along with concerts, musicals and literature and film festivals. For listings consult *Kölner Illus-*

trierte (mainstream, www.koelner.de) and *StadtRevue* (alternative, www.stadtrevue. de). Buy tickets at www.koelnticket.de.

Kölner Philharmonie
Classical Music

(Map p218; ☑0221-280 280; www.koelner-phil harmonie.de; Bischofsgartenstrasse 1; concert tickets €14-48; ⓊKöln Dom/Hbf) The Kölner Philharmonie is a grand modern concert hall that presents a wide range of aural treats, from classical to jazz and chansons. It's also the home base of two world-class classical orchestras, the Gürzenich Orchester and the WDR Sinfonieorchester.

Club Bahnhof Ehrenfeld
Live Music

(http://cbe-cologne.de; Bartholomäus-Schink-Strasse 65/67; ⊘varies; ☒3, 4 Venloer Strasse/ Gürtel, ⓈVenloer Strasse/Gürtel) An institution in Cologne's alternative scene, this club in the hip cross-cultural Ehrenfeld borough has programming as eclectic as the crowd. Depending on the day, dance parties, poetry slams, concerts or flea markets lure punters to three cavernous spaces below the train tracks. Nice beer garden to boot.

ⓐ SHOPPING

Cologne is a popular shopping destination with a fun mix of eccentric boutiques, designer and vintage stores, plus the usual selection of chain and department stores. And, of course, there are classic outlets for its namesake eau de cologne.

4711 House of Fragrances
Perfume

(Map p218; ☑0221-2709 9910; www.4711.com; Glockengasse 4; ⊘9.30am-6.30pm Mon-Fri, to 6pm Sat; ⓊAppellhofplatz) A classic gift for Grandma is a bottle of eau de cologne, invented in, yes, Cologne in the late 18th century. The most famous is 4711, named after the address where it was first created. The building now houses a flagship store and a museum where you can marvel at a giant tapestry and stop by the Fragrance Fountain.

RSZOOM/ALAMY STOCK PHOTO ©

Kölner Philharmonie

INFORMATION

Cologne Tourist Office (Map p218; ☎0221-346 430; www.cologne-tourism.com; Kardinal-Höffner-Platz 1; ⏰9am-8pm Mon-Sat, 10am-5pm Sun; Ⓤ Köln Dom/Hbf)

GETTING THERE & AWAY

AIR

About 18km southeast of the city centre, **Köln Bonn Airport** (CGN; Cologne Bonn Airport; ☎02203-404 001; www.koeln-bonn-airport.de; Kennedystrasse; Köln/Bonn Flughafen) has direct flights to 130 cities and is served by numerous airlines, with destinations across Europe.

The S13, RE6 and RE8 trains connect the airport and the Hauptbahnhof every 20 minutes (€2.80, 15 minutes). Taxis charge about €35.

BUS

Cologne's central bus station near the Hauptbahnhof has been closed to long-distance coaches such as those operated by Flixbus. The nearest stops are 'Köln Nord' in Leverkusen (S6 to/from Cologne's Hauptbahnhof), and 'Köln Süd' at Köln Bonn Airport (S13 to/from Hauptbahnhof).

TRAIN

Cologne's beautiful **Hauptbahnhof** (www.bahnhof.de/bahnhof-de/Köln_Hbf-1032796; Trankgasse 11; 16, 18 Breslauer Platz/Hbf, 5 Dom/Hbf) is a hive of activity with frequent services in all directions, including domestic high-speed ICE trains and international Thalys trains to Brussels (from €59, two hours).

Flixtrain (www.flixtrain.com) also operates a low-cost route to Hamburg via Düsseldorf, the Ruhrgebiet and Münster.

GETTING AROUND

Cologne's mix of buses, *Stadtbahn* (trams), U-Bahn and S-Bahn trains is operated by **KVB** (Kölner Verkehrsbetriebe; ☎01806-50 40 30; www.kvb.koeln) in cooperation with Bonn's system. Short trips (up to four stops) cost €1.90, longer ones €2.40. Day passes are €7.10 for one person and €10 for up to five people travelling together. Buy your tickets from the machines at stations and aboard trams; be sure to validate them. KVB's website has a journey planner.

THE ROMANTIC RHINE VALLEY

The Romantic Rhine Valley

Between Rüdesheim and Koblenz, the Rhine cuts deeply through the slate mountains, meandering between hillside castles and steep vineyards to create a magical mixture of beauty and legend. Idyllic villages appear around each bend, their neat half-timbered houses and Gothic church steeples seemingly plucked from the world of fairy tales. High above the river, these famous medieval castles, some ruined, some restored, some mysterious are all vestiges of a time that was anything but tranquil. Today, 67km of this riverscape is known as the Oberes Mittelrheintal and is protected as a World Heritage Site.

Arriving in the Rhine Valley

Koblenz Hauptbahnhof Handles services from destinations north and from along the Rhine Valley.

Bingen Hauptbahnhof Services from the Rhine Valley and destinations south call in here.

Sleeping

Rüdesheim has hotels in the busy village centre and the peaceful surrounding hills.

Sleeping options in Bacharach range from intimate hotels to hostel accommodation in a 12th-century castle.

Both St Goarshausen and St Goar have hotels and guesthouses. There's a campground at Loreley but it's often full.

Koblenz has a number of chain hotels, but there are also some atmospheric options on both banks of the Rhine.

Previous page: Vineyards, Boppard (p234)
HANS-PETER MERTEN/GETTY IMAGES ©

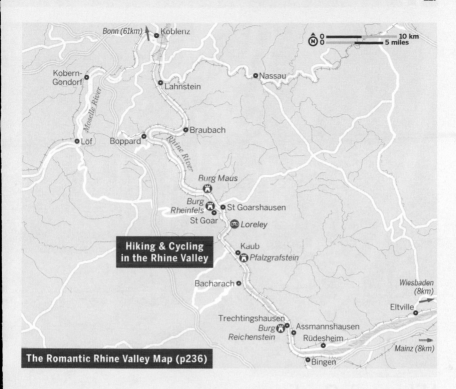

Bonn (61km)
Koblenz
Kobern-Gondorf
Nassau
Lahnstein
Moselle River
Braubach
Löf
Boppard
Rhine River
Burg Maus
Burg Rheinfels
St Goarshausen
St Goar
Loreley

Hiking & Cycling in the Rhine Valley

Kaub
Pfalzgrafstein

Bacharach

Wiesbaden (8km)

Eltville

Trechtingshausen
Burg Reichenstein
Assmannshausen
Rüdesheim

Mainz (8km)

The Romantic Rhine Valley Map (p236)

Bingen

10 km
5 miles

Vineyards, Bingen (p231)

PHILIP KOSCHEL/LOOK-FOTO/GETTY IMAGES ©

Hiking & Cycling in the Rhine Valley

The Rhine Valley is superb territory for hikers and cyclists. There are many options for two-wheelers and boots, and slow travel will enable you to enjoy the best of this beautiful region.

Great For...

☑ **Don't Miss**

A tough hilly stretch of the Rheinsteig between Rüdesheim and Loreley is considered the most invigorating.

Hiking

Two challenging but achingly beautiful long-distance hiking trails run along the Romantic Rhine, with variants continuing downriver to Bonn and upriver to Mainz and beyond. The first is the 199km RheinBurgenWeg (www.rheinburgenweg. com), linking Rolandsbogen, near Bonn, with Bingen, passing some 40 castles. The other is the 320km Rheinsteig (www. rheinsteig.de) which links Wiesbaden with Bonn. It hugs the river valley for most of the way and is considered by many to be one of the best hiking trails in all Germany, and certainly one of its prettiest. And this being the Rhine, no day on the trail would be complete without a wine-tasting session in a wine-producing village or wine cellar. On any stretch of the river a

❶ Need to Know

Try these web resources for more information:

Rhine Cycle Route www.rhinecycle route.eu

BVA BikeMedia www.fahrrad-buecher karten.de

Romantic Germany www.romantic -germany.info

✗ Take a Break

Pack a picnic every day so you can stop anywhere and dine with a view.

★ Top Tip

Tourist offices stock maps and can come up with suggestions for walks and rides.

one-way hike can be turned into a circuit by combining walking with ferries, trains and buses. Other trails which intersect the above two are the Rheinhöhenweg, the Limes-Wanderweg, the Gebückwan-derweg, the Rhine Panorama Way, the Rheingau Riesling Path and several local nature trails.

Cycling

The Rhein-Radweg (www.rheinradweg. eu; Euro Velo route 15) stretches for 1230km (900km of which are in Germany) from Andermatt, Switzerland, to the Hoek van Holland, near Rotterdam. It travels from the source of the Rhein to where it meets the North Sea. Between Bingen and Koblenz it runs along the left (more-or-less west) bank, as well

as on a growing number of sections of the right bank. It links up with two other long-distance bike paths: the 207km Nahe-Hunsrück-Mosel-Radweg (www. naheland-radtouren.de), which follows the Nahe River from Bingen southwest to Trier, and the 311km Mosel-Radweg (www. mosel-radweg.de), which runs along the banks of the Moselle River from Koblenz to Traben-Trarbach, Bernkastel-Kues, Trier and on to Thonville, France. Note that you cannot cycle on several sections of the hiking trails detailed above for safety reasons (usually where they are deemed too narrow to accommodate both riders and walkers).

Bicycles can be taken on regional trains, car ferries and river ferries, making it possible to ride one way (such as down the valley) and take public transport the other. Bike-repair shops are common in large towns, less so in smaller communities. The website www.bettundbike.de helps you find bike-friendly accommodation (hotels and guesthouses with bike storage, bike tools, drying facilities etc). You can search according to town or long-distance cycling trail.

Rüdesheim

Some three million day-tripping coach tourists descend on Rüdesheim each year. The town centre – and especially its most famous feature, a medieval alley known as Drosselgasse – is kitschy and colourful, but there's also wonderful walking in the greater area, which is part of the Rheingau wine region, famed for its superior Rieslings.

◎ SIGHTS & ACTIVITIES

For a stunning Rhine panorama, head up the wine slopes west of Rüdesheim to the Niederwald Monument. Erected between 1877 and 1883, this bombastic monument celebrates the Prussian victory in the Franco-Prussian War and the creation of the German Reich, both in 1871. You can walk up via the Rüdesheimer Berg vineyards – signposted trails include one that begins at the P2 car park (one block above Oberstrasse) – but to save climbing 203 vertical metres, it's faster to glide above the vineyards aboard the 1400m-long **Seilbahn** cable car (Kabinenbahn; Map p236;

www.seilbahn-ruedesheim.de; Oberstrasse 37; adult/child one-way €5.50/3, return €8/4, with Sesselbahn €9/4.50; ◎9.30am-7pm Jul & Aug, to 6pm Mon-Fri, to 7pm Sat & Sun Jun & Sep, shorter hours mid-Mar–May & Oct-Dec).

Weinmuseum   Museum

(Wine Museum; Map p236; ☑06722-2348; www. rheingauer-weinmuseum.de; Rheinstrasse 2; adult/ child incl audioguide €5/3; ◎10am-6pm Mar-Oct) The 1000-year-old Brömserburg castle near the Bingen car-ferry dock now houses this museum (pictured below), filled with winemaking and wine-drinking paraphernalia from Roman times onwards. A six-glass tasting flight costs €14. River views extend from the tower.

Siegfried's Mechanisches Musikkabinett   Museum

(Map p236; ☑06722-492 17; www.smmk.de; Oberstrasse 29; tour adult/child €7.50/4; ◎10am-4pm Mar-Dec) Situated 50m to the left from the top of Drosselgasse, this fun museum has a collection of 350 18th- and 19th-century mechanical musical instruments that play

Weinmuseum

themselves. You'll be shown around on a compulsory 45-minute tour.

ℹ INFORMATION

The **Tourist Office** (Map p236; ☑06722-906 150; www.ruedesheim.de; Rheinstrasse 29a; ⊙9am-6pm Mon-Fri, 10am-4pm Sat & Sun Apr-Sep, shorter hours Oct-Mar) is at the eastern edge of the town centre.

ℹ GETTING THERE & AWAY

Rüdesheim is connected to Bingen by passenger and car ferries.

Trains travel to Wiesbaden (€6.30, 45 minutes, hourly) and Koblenz (€15.10, 80 minutes, hourly).

Bingen

Thanks to its strategic location at the confluence of the Nahe and Rhine rivers, Bingen has been coveted by warriors and merchants since its founding by the Romans in 11 BC. These days it's a busy working town that's less touristy – and less cute – than its smaller neighbours.

◎ SIGHTS

Museum am Strom   Museum
(Map p236; www.bingen.de; Museumsstrasse 3; adult/child €3/2; ⊙10am-5pm Tue-Sun) On Bingen's riverside promenade, this one-time power station now displays exhibits on Rhine romanticism, both engraved and painted. Other highlights include a set of surgical instruments – from scalpels and cupping glasses to saws – left behind by a Roman doctor in the 2nd century AD.

Mäuseturm   Landmark
(Map p236; ⊙closed to the public) The Mouse Tower, on an island near the confluence of the Nahe and Rhine, is where – according to legend – Hatto II, the 10th-century archbishop of Mainz, was devoured alive by mice as punishment for his oppressive rule. In fact, the name is probably a mutation of *Mautturm* (toll tower), which reflects the building's medieval function.

⛴ Getting Around the Rhine Valley

No bridges span the Rhine between Koblenz and Mainz; the only way for drivers to cross the river along this stretch is by *Autofähre* (car ferry).

Services generally operate every 15 or 20 minutes during the day and every 30 minutes early in the morning and late at night.

Car ferry crossings:

Bingen–Rüdesheim (www.bingen -ruedesheimer.de; car & driver €4.50, passenger €1.30, bicycle & rider €2.50, pedestrian €2; ⊙5.30am-9.50pm Sun-Thu, to 12.50am Fri & Sat May-Oct, 5.30am-9.50pm Nov-Apr)

Boppard–Filsen (www.faehre-boppard.de; car & driver €4.50, passenger €1.30, bicycle & rider €2.50, pedestrian €2; ⊙6.30am-10pm Jun-Aug, to 9pm Apr, May & Sep, to 8pm Oct-Mar)

Niederheimbach–Lorch (www.mittel rhein-faehre.de; car & driver €4.50, passenger €1.30, bicycle & rider €2.50, pedestrian €2; ⊙6am-10.50pm Apr-Oct, to 6.50pm Nov-Mar)

Oberwesel–Kaub (www.faehre-kaub.de; car & driver €4.50, passenger €1.30, bicycle & rider €2.50, pedestrian €2; ⊙6am-8pm Mon-Sat, 8am-8pm Sun Apr-Sep, 6am-7pm Mon-Sat, 8am-7pm Sun Oct-Mar)

St Goar–St Goarshausen (www.faehre -loreley.de; car & driver €4.50, passenger €1.30, bicycle & rider €2.50, pedestrian €2; ⊙5.30am-10.30pm Mon-Fri, from 6.20am Sat, from 7.20am Sun May-Sep, shorter hours Oct-Apr)

Passenger-only ferry crossings:

Bingen-Rüdesheim Passenger Ferry (www.bingen-ruedesheimer.de; adult/child €2.50/1.25, bicycle €1.20; ⊙10am-5.30pm Mon-Fri, 8.45am-6.55pm Sat & Sun late Mar-early Nov)

Fährboot (Map p236; www.faehre-kaub. de; Kaub; adult/child €3/1.50; ⊙10am-6pm Tue-Sun Apr-Oct, to 5pm Mar, to 5pm Sat & Sun Nov, Jan & Feb) Serves Pfalzgrafstein (p232)

Pfalzgrafstein Toll Station

Across the river from the village of Kaub, the boat-shaped toll castle **Pfalzgrafstein** (Map p236; ☏06774-745; www.burg-pfalzgrafenstein.de; adult/child €4/2.50, audioguide €1; ☺10am-6pm Tue-Sun mid-Mar–Oct, to 5pm Feb–mid-Mar & Nov), built in 1326, perches on an island in the middle of the Rhine. A once-dangerous rapid here (since modified) forced boats to use the right-hand side of the river, where a chain forced ships to stop and pay a toll. Pick up an audioguide to learn more about its lengthy history. It's reached by the Fährboot passenger ferry, next to Kaub's car ferry dock.

Pfalzgrafstein
ANDREAS JUNG/SHUTTERSTOCK ©

ⓘ GETTING THERE & AWAY

Bingen has two train stations: the Hauptbahnhof, just west of the Nahe in Bingerbrück; and the more central Bahnhof Bingen Stadt, just east of the town centre. Trains from both stations serve Mainz (€10.50, 25 minutes, up to four per hour) and Koblenz (€14.60, 50 minutes, two per hour). Change in Mainz for Wiesbaden.

Passenger ferries (p231) to Rüdesheim leave from the town centre's riverfront promenade; car ferries (p231) dock 1km upriver (east) from the centre.

Bacharach

One of the prettiest of the Rhine villages, tiny Bacharach – 24km downriver from Bingen – conceals its considerable charms behind a 14th-century wall. From the B9, pass through one of the thick arched gateways under the train tracks to reach its medieval old town filled with half-timbered buildings.

◉ SIGHTS & ACTIVITIES

The best way to get a sense of the village and its hillside surrounds is to take a stroll on top of the walls – it's possible to walk almost all the way around the centre.

Peterskirche   Church

(Map p236; Blücherstrasse 1; ☺10am-6pm Mar-Sep, to 4pm Nov-Feb) This late-Romanesque-style Protestant church, completed in 1269, has some columns with vivid capitals – look for the naked woman with snakes sucking her breasts (a warning about the consequences of adultery), at the altar end of the left aisle.

Postenturm   Tower

(Map p236; www.bacharach.de; Blücherstrasse; ☺24hr) FREE Once part of the city's 14th-century fortifications and now surrounded by vineyards, this tower on the upper section of the wall affords panoramic views from the top, reached by scaling 58 steps.

✖ EATING & DRINKING

Zum Grünen Baum   Wine Bar

(Map p236; www.weingut-bastian-bacharach.de; Oberstrasse 63; ☺noon-10pm Apr-Oct, shorter hours Nov-Mar) Dating from 1421, this olde-worlde tavern serves some of Bacharach's best whites; the *Weinkarussel* (€22.50) lets you sample 15 of them. Its nearby **Weingut** (Map p236; ☏06743-937 8530; www.weingut-bastian-bacharach.de; Koblenzer Strasse 1; ☺11am-6pm Fri-Sun Apr-Oct, shorter hours Nov-Mar), by contrast, is state of the art. Owner Friedrich Bastian is a renowned opera singer, so music (and culinary) events take place year-round, including on Bastian's private river island with its own vineyard.

Stübers Restaurant   German €€

(Map p236; ☏06743-1243; www.rhein-hotel-bacharach.de; Langstrasse 50; mains €14-24;

☑5.30-9pm Mon-Sat, noon-2pm & 5.30-9pm Sun early Mar-early Dec; ▥) At the Rhein Hotel, slow food–focused Stübers specialises in regional dishes such as *Rieslingbraten* (Riesling-marinated braised beef) and *Steeger Hinkelsdreck* (chicken-liver pâté with red wine, toasted almonds and grape jelly), with small versions of German favourites for kids. Although the terrace overlooks the Rhine, it's metres from the railway line, so dining inside is a more peaceful experience.

❶ INFORMATION

The **Tourist Office** (Map p236; ☑06743-919 303; www.rhein-nahe-touristik.de; Oberstrasse 10; ☑9am-5pm Mon-Fri, 10am-3pm Sat & Sun Apr-Oct, 9am-1pm Mon-Fri Nov-Mar) has information about the area, including details of day hikes through the vineyards.

❶ GETTING THERE & AWAY

Trains link Bacharach with Koblenz (€11.60, 35 minutes, up to two per hour) and Mainz (€13.70, 40 minutes, up to two per hour).

Loreley & St Goarshausen

The most fabled spot along the Romantic Rhine, Loreley is an enormous, almost vertical slab of slate that owes its fame to a mythical maiden whose siren songs are said to have lured sailors to their deaths in the river's treacherous currents. Heinrich Heine told the tale in his 1824 poem *Die Lorelei*.

The nearby village of St Goarshausen, 2.5km north, is lorded over by the sprawling ruins of Burg Rheinfels, once the mightiest fortress on the Rhine. It's linked by car ferry with its twin across the river, St Goar.

◎ SIGHTS

Loreley
Besucherzentrum   Museum
(Map p236; ☑06771-599 093; www.loreley-be sucherzentrum.de; Loreleyring 7; adult/child €2.50/1.50; ☑10am-5pm Mar-Oct) On the edge of the plateau above the Loreley outcrop, 4km southeast of St Goarshausen, this visitors centre covers the Loreley myth and local flora, fauna, shipping and winemaking traditions through an English-signed multi-media exhibit and German-language 3D film. Major works underway here include new walking trails, an improved viewing platform 190m above the river and a hotel; all are due for completion by late 2019.

Burg Rheinfels   Fortress
(Map p236; ☑06741-7753; www.st-goar.de; Schlossberg 47; adult/child €5/2.50, guided mine tour €7/free; ☑9am-6pm Apr-Oct, to 5pm Mar & Nov, guided mine tours by reservation) Once the mightiest fortress on the Rhine, Burg Rheinfels was built in 1245 by Count Dieter V of Katzenelnbogen as a base for his toll-collecting operations. Its size and labyrinthine layout are astonishing. Kids (and adults) will love exploring the subter-ranean tunnels and galleries, accessed by lantern-lit guided English-language tunnel tours; check the website for schedules. Entry fees are cash only. To reach the sprawling ruins, it's a 550m uphill walk; allow 20 minutes. The complex also incorporates a **hotel** (www.schloss-rheinfels.de).

Burg Maus   Castle
(Burg Peterseck; Map p236; ☑closed to the public) Two rival castles stand either side of the village of St Goarshausen. Burg Peter-seck was built by the archbishop of Trier to counter the toll practices of the powerful Katzenelnbogen family. The latter respond-ed by building a much bigger castle high on the other side of town, Burg Neukatzeneln-bogen (dubbed Burg Katz, meaning 'Cat Castle'). Highlighting the obvious imbalance of power between the Katzenelnbogens and the archbishop, Burg Peterseck was soon nicknamed Burg Maus ('Mouse Castle').

❶ GETTING THERE & AROUND

Koblenz is linked by train with St Goar (€8.30, 25 minutes, hourly) and St Goarshausen (€8.10, 30 minutes hourly). Wiesbaden has trains to/from St Goarshausen (€14.40, one hour, hourly).

From left: Riesling vineyard; Postenturm (p232); Boppard

Mainz has trains to/from St Goar (€14.60, one hour, hourly).

The top of the Loreley outcrop can be reached in the following ways:

Car It's a 4km uphill drive from St Goarshausen.

Shuttle bus One-way from St Goarshausen's Marktplatz costs €2.65; there are up to two buses per hour from 10am to 7pm March to October.

Walk The Treppenweg, a strenuous, 400-step stairway, begins 2.5km upriver from St Goarshausen at the base of the breakwater.

Boppard

Scenically located on a horseshoe bend in the river, Boppard (pronounced bo-*part*) is one of the Romantic Rhine's prettiest towns, not least because its riverfront and historic centre aren't split by the rail line but are both on the same side of the tracks. Many of its charming half-timbered buildings house snug wine taverns serving Riesling from grapes grown nearby, in some of the Rhine's steepest vineyards.

◉ SIGHTS & ACTIVITIES

Outdoor enthusiasts can tackle some superb hillside hiking trails that fan out from Boppard; the tourist office has maps.

Vierseenblick & Gedeonseck The peculiar geography of the Four-Lakes-View panoramic outlook creates the illusion that you're looking at four separate lakes, rather than a single river. The nearby Gedeonseck affords views of the Rhine's hairpin curve. To get up here you can either hike for 1.4km or – to save 240 vertical metres – take the 20-minute **Sesselbahn** (Map p236; ☎06742-2510; http://sesselbahn-boppard.de; Mühltal 12; adult/child one-way €5.50/3, return €8.50/4.50; ◷10am-6pm mid-Apr–Sep, shorter hours Oct & Nov) chairlift over the vines from the upriver edge of town.

Klettersteig This 2½- to three-hour cliff-side adventure hike (a 6.2km round-trip) begins at the upriver edge of town right next to the Sesselbahn. Decent walking or climbing shoes are a must; optional climbing equipment can be rented at the **Aral petrol station** (Map p236; ☎06742-

PFGOLD/SHUTTERSTOCK ©

2447; Koblenzer Strasse 237; climbing equipment hire per day €5, plus €20 deposit; ⊙6am-9pm Mon-Fri, 8am-9pm Sat & Sun). Some vertical sections involve ladders; less vertiginous alternatives are available – except at the Kletterwand, a hairy section with steel stakes underfoot. It's possible to walk back to town via the Vierseenblick.

Hunsrück Trails Germany's steepest scheduled railway route, the **Hunsrück-bahn** (Map p236; www.hunsrueckbahn.de; Hauptbahnhof; adult/child one-way €2.90/1.75, bicycle free; ⊙hourly 10am-6pm Apr-Oct, to 4pm Nov-Mar), travels through five rail tunnels and across two viaducts on its 8km journey from Boppard's Bahnhof to Buchholz (a section continues for 7km from Buchholz to Emmelshausen, though there's little to see here). From Buchholz, many people hike back via the Mörderbachtal to Boppard, but Buchholz is also the starting point for an excellent 17km hike via the romantic Ehrbachklamm (Ehrbach gorge) to Brodenbach (on the Moselle), from where you can take a bus to Koblenz, with connections to Boppard.

Severuskirche Church
(Map p236; Kronengasse; ⊙8am-6pm Apr-Oct, to 5pm Nov-Mar) The impressive late-Romanesque 13th-century Severuskirche is built on the site of Roman military baths. Inside are polychrome wall paintings, a hanging cross from 1225 in the choir, and spiderweb-like vaulted ceilings.

Römer-Kastell Archaeological Site
(Roman Fort, Römerpark; Map p236; cnr Angert-strasse & Kirchgasse; ⊙24hr) FREE A block south of the Marktplatz, the Roman Fort has 55m of original 4th-century Roman wall, and graves from the Frankish era (7th century). A wall panel shows what the Roman town of Bodobrica looked like 1700 years ago.

🍴 EATING & DRINKING

Severus Stube German €€
(Map p236; ☎06742-3218; www.facebook.com/ Severusstube; Untere Marktstrasse 7; mains €10.50-21.50; ⊙5.30-10.30pm Mon, Tue & Thu, to 11pm Fri, 11.30am-2.30pm & 5.30-11pm Sat & Sun Apr-Oct, shorter hours Nov-Mar) Smoked trout roasted in herb butter, pheasant with

Romantic Rhine Valley

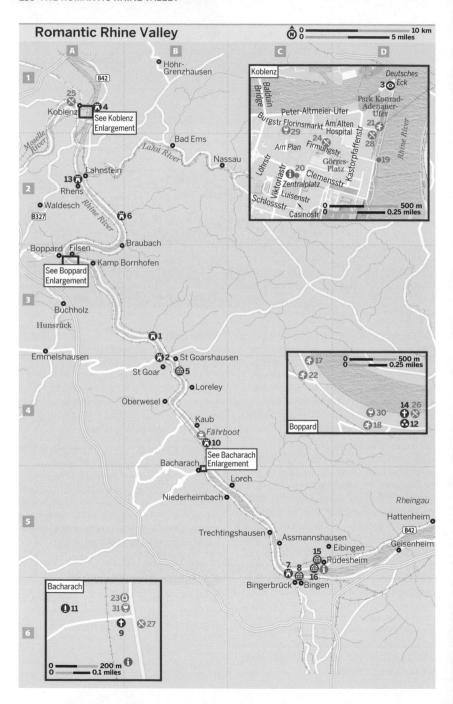

0 10 km
0 5 miles

Koblenz

Deutsches
Eck

3

Park Konrad-
Adenauer-
Ufer

Peter-Altmeier-Ufer

Balduin
Bridge

Burgstr Florinsmarkt
29

Am Alten
Hospital

21

Kastorpfaffenstr

Rhine River

Am Plan

24
Firmungstr

28

Löhrstr

20

Görres-
Platz

19

Viktoriastr

Clemensstr

Zentralplatz

Schlossstr

Luisenstr

Casinostr

0 500 m
0 0.25 miles

Höhr-
Grenzhausen

B42

25

Koblenz 4

See Koblenz
Enlargement

Moselle River

Bad Ems

Lahn River

Nassau

Lahnstein

13

Rhens

Waldesch

Rhine River

B327

6

Boppard Filsen

Braubach

Kamp Bornhofen

See Boppard
Enlargement

Buchholz

Hunsrück

1

Emmelshausen

2 St Goarshausen

St Goar

5

17

0 500 m
0 0.25 miles

22

Loreley

Oberwesel

14 26

30

Boppard

18

12

Kaub

Fährboot

10

Bacharach See Bacharach
Enlargement

Lorch

Niederheimbach

Rheingau

Hattenheim

B42

Trechtingshausen

Assmannshausen

Eibingen

Geisenheim

15

Rüdesheim

7 8

16

Bingerbrück Bingen

Bacharach

23

11

31

27

9

0 200 m
0 0.1 miles

The Romantic Rhine Valley

roast potatoes and bacon, braised beef in horseradish sauce, and warm apple strudel with vanilla custard are among the dishes served at high-backed wooden booths in Severus Stube's cosy, timber-panelled dining room, and on the cobbled laneway in summer. Reservations are recommended.

Weinhaus Heilig Grab   Wine Bar
(Map p236; www.heiliggrab.de; Zelkesgasse 12; ⏰3pm-midnight Wed-Mon) Across the street from the Hauptbahnhof, Boppard's oldest wine tavern, dating back over 200 years, offers a cosy setting for sipping 'Holy Sepulchre' Rieslings. In summer you can sit outside under the chestnut trees, where live music plays on weekends. It also has five **guest rooms** (doubles €73 to €89).

ⓘ GETTING THERE & AWAY

Trains link Boppard with Koblenz (€13.60, 15 minutes, two per hour) and Mainz (€16.40, 1¼ hours, two per hour).

Koblenz

At the confluence of the Rhine and Moselle Rivers and the convergence of three low mountain ranges – the Hunsrück, the Eifel and the Westerwald – the Romans founded a military stronghold they named Confluentes for the site's supreme strategic value. Modern-day Koblenz is a park- and flower-filled city that serves as both the northern gateway to the Romantic Rhine Valley and the northeastern gateway to the Moselle Valley, making it an ideal starting point for exploring the region.

⊚ SIGHTS

Koblenz' Altstadt, most of it rebuilt after WWII, surrounds the northern end of Löhrstrasse, the city's main pedestrian-only shopping street. Its intersection with Altengraben is known as **Vier Türme** (Four Towers) because each of the 17th-century corner buildings sports an ornately carved and painted oriel.

Festung Ehrenbreitstein   Fortress
(Map p236; 0261-6675 4000; www.tor-zum -welterbe.de; adult/child €7/3.50, incl cable car €13.80/6.20, audioguide €2; ⏰10am-6pm Apr-Oct, to 5pm Nov-Mar) On the right bank of the Rhine, 118m above the river, this fortress proved indestructible to all but Napoleonic troops, who levelled it in 1801. To prove a point, the Prussians rebuilt it as one of

Marksburg
SERGEY NOVIKOV/SHUTTERSTOCK ©

⌐⟍⟋⌐ Day Trip to Braubach

High above Braubach are the dramatic towers, turrets and crenellations of the 700-year-old **Marksburg** (Map p236; ☑02627-206; www.marksburg.de; Braubach; adult/child €7/5; ☉10am-5pm mid-Mar–Oct, 11am-4pm Nov–mid-Mar), which is unique among the Rhine fortresses as it was never destroyed. The compulsory tour takes in the citadel, the Gothic hall and the large kitchen, plus a grisly torture chamber, with its hair-raising assortment of pain-inflicting nasties. English tours take place at 3pm and 4pm from mid-March to October.

Europe's mightiest fortifications. There are fabulous views from its ramparts and viewing platform. Inside are several museums, including an excellent regional museum, photography museum and archaeological museum, as well as restaurants, bars and cafes. It's accessible by car, on foot or by **cable car** (Map p236; ☑0261-2016 5850; www.seilbahn-koblenz.de; Rheinstrasse 6; adult/child return €9.90/4.40, incl Festung Ehrenbreitstein €13.80/6.20; ☉9.30am-7pm Jul-Sep, to 6pm Easter-Jun & Oct, 10am-5pm Nov-Easter).

Deutsches Eck   Square
(Map p236) At the point of confluence of the Moselle and the Rhine, the 'German Corner' is dominated by a soaring statue of Kaiser Wilhelm I on horseback, in the bombastic style of the late 19th century. After the original was destroyed in WWII, the stone pedestal remained empty – as a testament to lost German unity – until, post-reunification, a copy was re-erected in 1993. Flowery parks stretch southwest, linking up with a grassy riverfront promenade running southward along the Rhine.

Schloss Stolzenfels   Castle
(Map p236; www.schloss-stolzenfels.de; Schlossweg; adult/child €5/3; ☉10am-6pm mid-Mar–Oct, to 5pm Feb–mid-Mar & Nov) A vision of crenellated towers, ornate gables and medieval-style fortifications, Schloss Stolzenfels rises above the Rhine's left bank 5km south of the city centre. In 1823, the future Prussian king Friedrich Wilhelm IV had the castle – ruined by the French – rebuilt as his summer residence; guests included Queen Victoria. Today, the rooms remain largely as the king left them, with paintings, weapons, armour and furnishings from the mid-19th century. Take bus 650 from the Hauptbahnhof.

⊕ ACTIVITIES
Romantic Old Town
Walking Tour   Walking
(Map p236; ☑0261-194 33; www.koblenz-touristik.de; adult/child €7/3.50; ☉English tours 3pm Sat Apr-Oct) Departing from the **tourist office**, this two-hour tour takes you through the Altstadt, stopping at sights such as the Basilika St Kastor and Liebfrauenkirche, as well as Deutsches Eck. Tours in German run more frequently.

KD Cruises   Boating
(Map p236; ☑0261-310 30; www.k-d.com; Konrad-Adenauer-Ufer; ☉Easter-Oct) KD operates popular cruises from Koblenz along the Rhine to Rüdesheim (one-way/return €42.20/49.20). It also runs trips southwest along the Moselle to Cochem (one-way/return €38.20/44.20).

⊗ EATING & DRINKING
Koblenz has some excellent places to dine, including Michelin-starred establishments. Restaurants congregate in the Altstadt, especially along the streets south of Florinsmarkt, and by the Rhine.

Winninger Weinstube — German €

(Map p236; ☎0261-387 07; www.winninger
-weinstube.de; Rheinzollstrasse 2; mains
€7-14.50; ⊙4pm-midnight Tue-Thu, from noon
Fri-Sun May-Sep, 4-11pm Tue-Sun Oct-Apr; ☜) A
cavernous stone building that once housed
a museum is now a restaurant and wine bar
serving local specialities such as *Koblenzer Saumagen* (stuffed pig's stomach),
Riesling-marinated pork knuckle, liver and
potato dumplings and *Flammkuchen* with
both sweet and savoury topping options.
Wines come from the restaurant's own
vineyard in Winningen just upstream along
the Moselle.

Einstein — Cafe €€

(Map p236; ☎0261-914 4999; www.einstein-ko
blenz.de; Firmungstrasse 30; mains €9.50-24, Sun
brunch €21.90; ⊙9am-10pm Mon-Sat, from 10am
Sun, bar to midnight Sun-Thu, to 2am Fri & Sat)
Grilled calf's liver with masala jus; gilthead,
tiger prawn and lime risotto; ribbon noodles
with feta, spinach and tomatoes; and chocolate cannelloni with almond mascarpone
and orange sorbet are among the choices
at this elegant crimson-toned cafe/bar. It
also has lighter bites like soups and salads.
Book ahead for Sunday's brunch buffet. Live
music often plays on weekends.

Schiller's — European €€€

(Map p236; ☎0261-963 530; www.hotel
-stein.de; Hotel Stein, Mayener Strasse 126;
4-/5-/6-course menus €79/98/119, with paired
wines €107/133/161, 5-course veg menu €89,
with paired wines €124; ⊙6-10pm Tue-Sat)
At the Hotel Stein, 2km north of the city
centre across the Moselle, Michelin-starred
Schiller's utilises premium ingredients like
white asparagus, scampi, foie gras, truffles
and smoked sea urchin roe in its artistically
presented menus (vegetarian menus are
available). Wines are sourced exclusively
from the Moselle and Rhine valleys.

Alte Weinstube Zum Hubertus — Wine Bar

(Map p236; www.weinhaus-hubertus.de;
Florinsmarkt 6; ⊙3.30-11pm Mon, Wed & Thu,
noon-midnight Fri-Sun) Specialising in Rhine
and Moselle wines by the glass and/or
bottle, rustic Alte Weinstube Zum Hubertus
occupies a half-timbered house dating
from 1689, with an open fireplace, antique
furniture and dark-wood panelling. In summer, seating spills onto the square. Classic
German dishes include braised pork.

ℹ GETTING THERE & AWAY

TRAIN

Koblenz has two train stations, the main Hauptbahnhof on the Rhine's left bank about 1km
south of the city centre, and Koblenz-
Ehrenbreitstein on the right bank (right below
Festung Ehrenbreitstein).

Regional trains serve villages on both banks
of the Romantic Rhine, including Bingen (€14.60,
50 minutes, two per hour).

Direct Hauptbahnhof services include:

Bonn (€17, 40 minutes, up to four per hour)

Cologne (€20, 50 minutes, up to three per hour)

Frankfurt (€31, 1½ hours, up to four per hour)

Mainz (€22, one hour, every 30 minutes)

Trier (€24, 1½ to two hours, two per hour)

BUS

Some Romantic Rhine villages are also served
by buses (www.rmv-bus.de) that stop outside
the Hauptbahnhof. Bus 650 goes to Boppard via
Schloss Stolzenfels (€7.10, 40 minutes, two per
hour), while bus 570 goes to Braubach/Marks-
burg (€8.20, 35 minutes, two per hour).

The Fahrplan Rhein-Mosel-Bus services link
Koblenz with Frankfurt-Hahn Airport (€11.50, 1¼
hours, six per day).

BOAT

Several boat companies have docks on
Konrad-Adenauer-Ufer, which runs along the
Rhine south of the Deutsches Eck.

ℹ GETTING AROUND

Bus 1 (€1.90, 13 minutes, two per hour, hourly
after 8pm) links the Hauptbahnhof with the
Deutsches Eck.

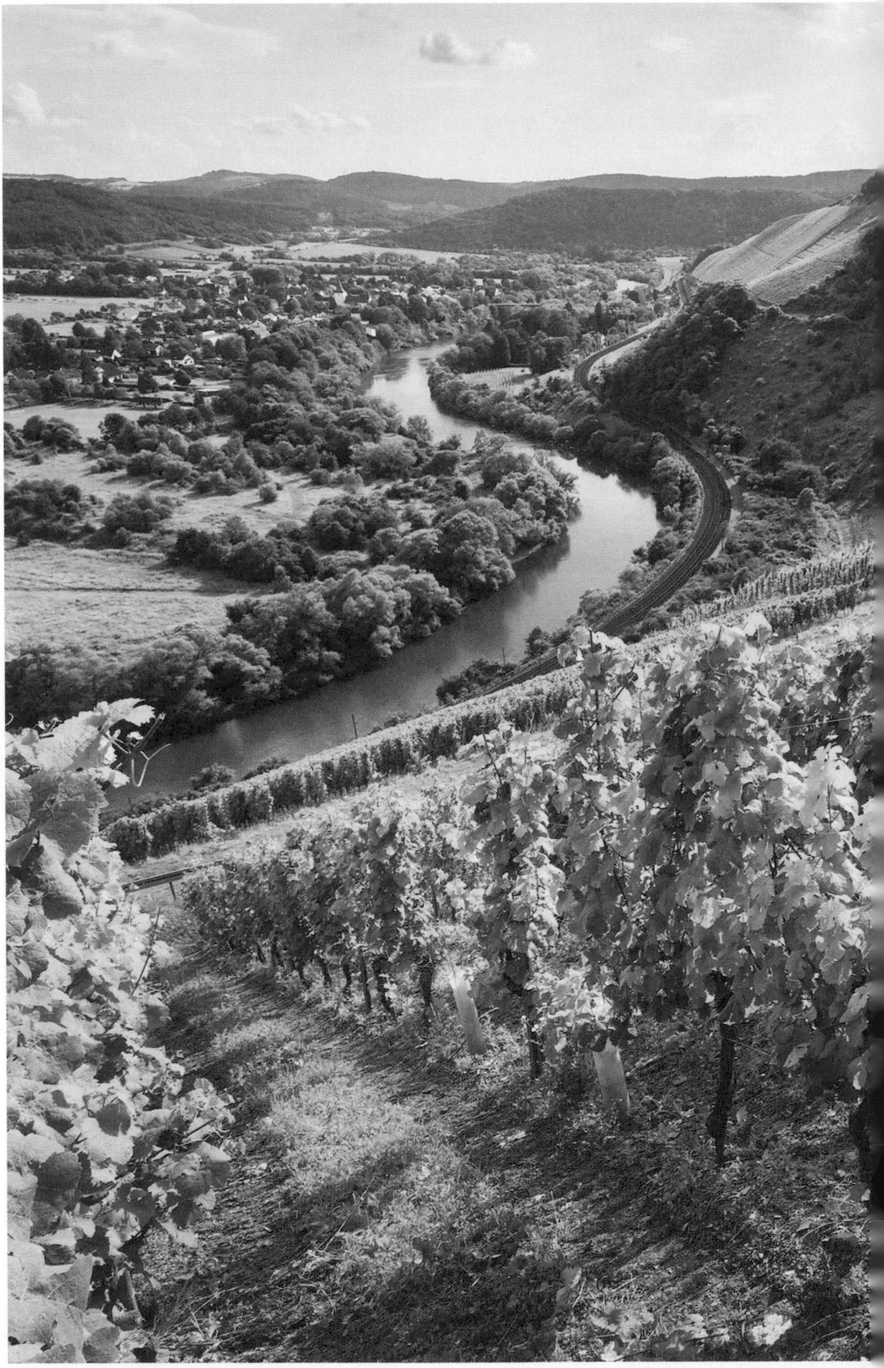

LUXY IMAGES / GETTY IMAGES ©

THE MOSELLE VALLEY

The Moselle Valley

Wending between vertiginous vine-covered slopes, the Moselle (in German, Mosel) is narrower than its neighbour, the Rhine, and has a more intimate charm. The German section of the river, which rises in France then traverses Luxembourg, flows for 195km from Trier to Koblenz on a slow, winding course, with entrancing scenery around every hairpin bend: brightly coloured, half-timbered medieval villages, crumbling hilltop castles, elegant Jugendstil (art nouveau) villas, and ancient wine warehouses.

Arriving in the Moselle Valley

Trier One of the gateways to the Moselle Valley at its southern end. Trier Hauptbahnhof handles many regional and national train services.

Koblenz At the northern end of the Moselle Valley with train connections to major cities in western Germany.

Cologne-Bonn Airport The most convenient airport for the Moselle Valley, though **Luxembourg Airport** is nearer to Trier and has many more international connections.

Sleeping

July through to October is the peak season in the Moselle. Almost all towns in the valley have a summertime camping ground, most right on the breeze-cooled riverbanks; book ahead. Christmas aside, from November to around Easter the majority of towns are very quiet, and some hotels close. You can book accommodation at www.mosellandtouristik.de.

Previous page: Vineyards near Trier (p255)
LUXY IMAGES/GETTY IMAGES ©

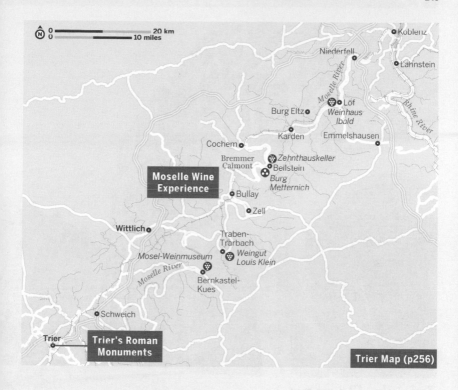

N
0 ——————— 20 km
0 ——————— 10 miles

Koblenz

Niederfell

Lahnstein

Moselle River

Rhine River

Burg Eltz

Löf
Weinhaus Ibald

Karden

Emmelshausen

Cochem

Bremmer Calmont

Zehnthauskeller

Moselle Wine Experience

Beilstein

Burg Metternich

Bullay

Zell

Wittlich

Traben-Trarbach

Mosel-Weinmuseum

Weingut Louis Klein

Moselle River

Bernkastel-Kues

Schweich

Trier

Trier's Roman Monuments

Trier Map (p256)

Trier (p255)

Porta Nigra

JOAQUIN OSSORIO CASTILLO/SHUTTERSTOCK ©

Trier's Roman Monuments

A Unesco-protected site, Germany's oldest city is home to its finest ensemble of Roman monuments, among them a mighty gate, amphitheatre, thermal baths, Imperial throne room, and the country's oldest bishop's church (which retains Roman sections).

Great For...

☑ Don't Miss

The Konstantin Basilika's new organ has 6500 pipes and generates a seven-fold echo.

Porta Nigra

This brooding 2nd-century **Roman city gate** (Map p256; adult/child €4/2.50; ⊗9am-6pm Apr-Sep, to 5pm Mar & Oct, to 4pm Nov-Feb) – blackened by time (hence the name, Latin for 'black gate') – is a marvel of engineering (pictured above). It's held together by nothing but gravity and iron clamps.

In the 11th century, the structure was turned into a church to honour Simeon, a Greek hermit who spent six years walled up in its east tower. After his death in 1134, he was buried inside the gate and later canonised as a saint.

Konstantin Basilika

Constructed around AD 310 as Constantine's throne room, the brick-built **basilica** (Map p256; ☑0651-9949 1200; www.konstantin -basilika.de; Konstantinplatz 10; ⊗10am-6pm

Kaiserthermen

MATABUN/GETTY IMAGES ©

Römerbrücke · Moselle River · Johanniterufer · Nikolausstr · Kaiserstr Südallee · Saarstr · Thermen am Viehmarkt · Konstantin Basilika · Kaiserthermen · Amphitheatre

❶ Need to Know

The three-day TrierCard (€9.90) gives 10% to 25% off museum and monument admissions and unlimited use of public transport,

✕ Take a Break

The Weinwirtschaft Friedrich-Wilhelm (p258) is the best place in town to refuel.

★ Top Tip

The Antiquities Card (two/four Roman sites & Rheinisches Landesmuseum €10/15) is a great deal.

Mon-Sat, 1-6pm Sun Apr-Oct, 10am-noon & 2-4pm Tue-Sat, 1-3pm Sun Nov-Mar) **FREE** is now an austere Protestant church. With built-to-impress dimensions (some 67m long, 27m wide and 33m high), it's the largest single-room Roman structure still in existence.

Amphitheatre

Trier's Roman **amphitheatre** (Map p256; Olewiger Strasse; adult/child €4/2.50; ⊘9am-6pm Apr-Sep, to 5pm Mar & Oct, to 4pm Nov-Feb) could accommodate 20,000 spectators for gladiator tournaments and animal fights. Beneath the arena are dungeons where prisoners sentenced to death waited next to starving beasts for the final showdown.

Kaiserthermen

Get a sense of the layout of this vast Roman **thermal bathing complex** (Imperial

Baths; Map p256; Weberbachstrasse 41; adult/child €4/2.50; ⊘9am-6pm Apr-Sep, to 5pm Mar & Oct, to 4pm Nov-Feb) with its striped brick-and-stone arches (pictured above) from the corner lookout tower, then descend into an underground labyrinth consisting of cavernous hot-and cold-water baths, boiler rooms and heating channels.

Römerbrücke

Spanning the Mosel, Germany's oldest **bridge** (Roman Bridge; Karl Marx Strasse) uses 2nd-century stone pilings (AD 144–152), built from black basalt from the Eifel mountains, which have been holding it up since legionnaires crossed on chariots.

Thermen am Viehmarkt

Found by accident in 1987 during the construction of a parking garage, and buried beneath WWII air-raid shelters, the remains of a 17th-century Capucinian monastery, one-time vineyards and cemeteries, these **thermal baths** (Map p256; Viehmarktplatz; adult/child €4/2.50; ⊘9am-5pm Tue-Sun) are sheltered by a dramatic glass cube.

Moselle Wine Experience

Disciples of the grape could do no worse in Germany than make a pilgrimage along the Moselle, sampling arguably the country's best whites as they go. Here we list some of the wine experiences on offer.

Visiting the Wineries

Exploring the wineries of the Moselle Valley is an ideal way to get to know German culture, interact with locals, and, of course, sample some truly exceptional wines.

Keep an eye out for signs reading 'Weinprobe', 'Wein Probieren', 'Weinverkauf' and 'Wein zu Verkaufen', which all mean that wine can either be bought or sampled. In spring, pale-purple wisteria flowers trailing from stone houses anticipate the bunches of grapes that will ripen in autumn.

From around April to mid-November, numerous wine festivals take place in towns and villages; for a complete list visit www.mosel-weinfeste.de.

Great For...

☑ Don't Miss

Try some of the less well-known grape types such as Elbling, Dornfelder and Kerner.

ALFOTOKUNST/SHUTTERSTOCK ©

Must-Sees for Wine Lovers

Mosel-Weinmuseum

Part of the St-Nikolaus-Hospital (p254) complex in Bernkastel-Kues, the small **Moselle Wine Museum** (☑06531-4141; www.moselweinmuseum.de; Cusanusstrasse 2, Kues; adult/child €5/2.50; ☺10am-6pm mid-Apr–Oct, 2-5pm Nov–mid-Apr) has interactive screens (best appreciated by German speakers) and features such as an Aromabar (you have to guess what you're smelling). The main event, though, is the cellar of the adjacent Vinothek, where you can indulge in an 'all you can drink' wine tasting (€18) with about 150 vintages to choose from. In winter the selection is more limited but tastings cost just €12.

Weingut Louis Klein

Along with whites like Riesling, Rivaner and Pinot Blanc, **Louis Klein** (☑06541-6246; www.klein-wein.de; Enkircher Strasse 20, Trarbach; 90-min cellar tour incl tastings €8; ☺10am-6pm Mon-Sat, to noon Sun, tours by reservation) is one of the few Moselle wine producers to specialise in reds, including Pinot Meunier, Pinot Noir, Cabernet Dorio, Cabernet Sauvignon, Merlot and Dornfelder. It occupies a monumental stone warehouse on the river; you can also arrange tastings in the vineyard amongst the vines.

Mosel Vinothek

In the cellar of the **Mosel Vinothek** (☑06531-4141; www.moselvinothek.de; Cusanusstrasse 2; wine tasting per person summer/winter €18/12; ☺10am-6pm Apr-Oct, 11am-5pm Feb, Mar, Nov & Dec) in Bernkastel-Kues, you can indulge in an 'all you can drink' wine tasting (€18) with about 150 vintages to choose from. In winter the selection is more limited but costs just €12.

It's adjacent to a small wine museum, with interactive screens (best appreciated by German speakers).

Weinhaus Ibald

Occupying a 1547 half-timbered building, wonderfully local **Weinhaus Ibald**

(📞02605-2043; www.weinhaus-ibald.de; Moselstrasse 34, Hatzenport; ⊙noon-10pm daily Easter-Oct, to 8pm Fri-Sun Nov-Mar; 🛜) specialises in Rieslings, sparkling Spätlese, Dornfelder reds, and Fruchsaft (fruit wine); the ultimate spot for a glass is on the vine-shaded terrace. Food ranges from homemade onion soup to sausage platters and gorgeous cakes, including rhubarb topped with meringue.

You can also stay in simple but comfortable **rooms** (doubles from €70).

Weinstube Spitzhäuschen

Wine bars don't come cuter than this crooked half-timbered **building** (📞06531-7476; www.spitzhaeuschen.de; Karlstrasse 13, Bernkastel; ⊙4-10pm Mon-Fri, from 3pm Sat & Sun Easter-Oct, 3-10pm Sat Nov-Dec, other times by appointment), Moselle's oldest, dating from 1416. It resembles a giant bird's house: its narrow base is topped by a much larger, precariously leaning upper floor which allowed carriages to pass through the narrow alley to the marketplace. Taste over 50 of the Schmitz family's local wines; small snacks are also available.

Zehnthauskeller

Starting in 1574, the **Zehnthauskeller** (📞02673-900 907; www.zehnthauskeller.de; Marktplatz 1; ⊙11am-10pm Tue-Sat, from noon Sun; 🛜) in Beilstein was used to store wine delivered as a tithe; it now houses a romantically dark, vaulted wine cellar where you can try six wines for €8.90, served by Dirndl-wearing staff. Live music plays on summer evenings.

Zehnthauskeller

Moselle Transport

Driving is the easiest way to see the Moselle, which, unlike the Romantic Rhine, is spanned by plenty of bridges.

Currently under construction, the *Hochmoselbrücke* (High Moselle Bridge) will link Ürzig and Zeltingen-Rachtig, with a carriageway stretching 158m above the river. It's part of a new highway connection, the 'Hochmoselübergang' (B50), providing a fast link to the Frankfurt area and beyond. Environmental concerns have seen it

★ Top Tip

Mosel Radweg, a hugely popular 275km-long cycling trail (www.mosel-radweg), heads from Trier down the Moselle all the way to Koblenz and upriver along the Luxembourg border and into the French region of Lorraine.

PALEIKIV/GETTY IMAGES ©

beset by delays, but it's expected to open in 2019. Check its progress via webcam at www.b50hochmoselbruecke.de.

The valley is also well served by public transport.

Train

The rail line linking Koblenz with Trier (€22.70, 1½ to two hours, at least hourly) follows the Moselle (and stops at its villages) only as far upriver as Bullay. (sample fares inKoblenz to Bullay €15.60, 45 minutes, hourly; Trier to Bullay €12.10, 45 minutes, two per hour).

From Bullay, small shuttle trains run along a spur line that terminates in Traben-Trarbach (€3.90, 20 minutes, up to four per hour).

Bus

The villages between Traben-Trarbach and Trier, including Bernkastel-Kues, are served year-round by bus 333 (www.moselbahn. de, day ticket €5.80, six daily Monday to Friday, three daily Saturday and Sunday).

From April to October the popular RegioRadler bus service has bicycle trailers (bicycle per trip €2.80; online reservations recommended).

Boat

Kolb (www.moselrundfahrten.de) is the Moselle's main boat operator, offering sightseeing cruises as well as one-way transport. Most services run from April to October.

☑ Don't Miss

If you are tackling the Moselle Valley on foot, be sure to stop off at Ediger-Eller, Bremm, Zell, Kröv, Ürzig and Zeltingen-Rachtig, all of which are worth an hour's break from the trail. Some of these have tiny wine cellars where some of the best-kept wine secrets of the Moselle are hidden by small-scale vintners.

Cochem

Cochem, with its bank of pastel-coloured, terrace-fronted restaurants lining the waterfront, tangle of narrow alleyways and dramatic castle precipitously perched on a rock, is one of the Moselle's most visited towns.

◎ SIGHTS

Reichsburg   Castle

(☑02671-255; www.reichsburg-cochem.de; Schlossstrasse 36; tours adult/child €6/3; ☺tours 9am-5pm mid-Mar–Oct, shorter hours Nov–mid-Mar) Like many others in the area, Cochem's original 11th-century castle fell victim to French troops in 1689, then stood ruined for centuries until wealthy Berliner Louis Ravene snapped it up for a pittance in 1868 and had it restored to its current – if not always architecturally faithful – glory. The 40-minute tours (some in English; leaflet/audioguide otherwise available) take in the decorative rooms that reflect 1000 years' worth of tastes and styles.

Bundesbank Bunker   Historic Site

(☑02671-915 3540; www.bundesbank-bunker. de; Am Wald 35; adult/child €10/5, shuttle bus one-way/return €2.50/4; ☺tours hourly 11am-3pm May-Oct, every two hours 11am-4pm Nov-Apr) Camouflaged as residential buildings and built to survive a nuclear war, this extraordinary Cold War secret bunker – owned by the German Federal Bank – was stocked with 15 billion Deutsche Marks to roll out in the event of war. One-hour guided tours descend 100 steps into the bunker, where the year-round temperature is 12 degrees Celsius (bring a jacket). From May to October, shuttle buses run from the **tourist office** (☑02671-600 40; www.ferienland-cochem.de; Endertplatz 1; ☺9am-5pm Mon-Sat, 10am-3pm Sun mid-Jun–Sep, shorter hours Oct–mid-Jun); otherwise it's a steep 1km walk or drive from the centre.

✪ EATING & DRINKING

Alt Thorschenke   German €€

(☑02671-7059; www.thorschenke.de; Brückenstrasse 3; mains €10.50-19; ☺11am-9pm; �) Wedged into the old medieval walls, away

Grevenburg

T W VAN URK/SHUTTERSTOCK ©

from the busy riverfront restaurants, Alt Thorschenke is a diamond find for regional specialities, such as herring with apple and onions, pork neck with mustard-cream sauce, and several different types of schnitzel – accompanied by wines from local producers. Upstairs are 27 small-but-charming rooms (doubles from €99), some with four-poster beds.

VinoForum
Wine

(🔊02671-917 1777; www.vinoforum-ernst.de; Moselstrasse 12-13, Ernst; ⏰10am-6pm Apr-Oct, 1-5pm Nov-Mar) Barrels are suspended from the ceiling at this ultra-contemporary *Vinothek*. Taste and buy exceptional wines made from grapes grown on the hillside behind and in the surrounding area, and look out for events, such as brunches, dinners and jazz concerts on the elevated terrace overlooking the Moselle. It's in the hamlet of Ernst, 4km east of Cochem.

ℹ️ GETTING THERE & AWAY

Cochem is a key Moselle Valley transport hub and has excellent connections.

Shuttle buses (€9.90, 1¼ hours, two daily) link Cochem with **Frankfurt-Hahn Airport** (HHN; www.hahn-airport.de; Lautzenhausen).

By train, destinations include Koblenz (€11.80, 40 minutes, two per hour), Trier (€14.90, 55 minutes, two per hour) and Bullay (€3.80, 10 minutes, two per hour), from where buses serve villages further upstream.

Kolb (www.moselrundfahrten.de) runs boats along the river from April to October.

Traben-Trarbach

Elegant Traben-Trarbach makes an excellent base for exploring the valley by bike or car. A major centre of the wine trade a century ago, the town's winemakers still welcome visitors for tastings and sales.

Traben, on the Moselle's left bank, is the commercial hub. It lost its medieval appearance to three major fires but was well compensated with beautiful *Jugendstil* villas, many of them designed by Berlin architect

Boat & Bike Combo

Superb cycling paths (www.mosel -radweg-etappen.com) traverse the countryside along and near the Moselle, including the 311km-long **Mosel-Radweg**, which runs from Bussan in France, skirting the Luxembourg border, to Koblenz. Tourist offices have maps. From April to October, boats run by Kolb (www.moselrundfahrten.de) link Bernkastel with Traben-Trarbach (one-way/ return €16/22, two hours, up to two daily). You can take along a bicycle for €2, making it easy to sail one way and ride the 24km back.

In Traben-Trarbach, **Zweirad Wagner** (🔊06541-1649; www.zweirad-wagner.de; Brückenstrasse 42, Trarbach; standard/elec-tric bike per day €10/25; ⏰8am-12.30pm & 2-6pm Mon-Fri, 9am-1pm Sat Apr-Oct, shorter hours Nov-May) rents bikes; in Bernkastel-Kues try Fun Bike Team (p255).

Bruno Möhring, whose works also include the ornate 1898 bridge gate, Brückentor, across the river in Trarbach. The two towns united in 1904.

Both banks of the Moselle have grassy riverfront promenades that are perfect for strolling.

◎ SIGHTS & ACTIVITIES

Grevenburg
Ruins

(Trarbach) The Grevenburg castle (pictured left), built in the mid-1300s, sits high in the

Kloster Machern
BILDAGENTUR ZOONAR GMBH/SHUTTERSTOCK ©

⟰ Divine Brews

The Moselle might be better known for its wine, but **Kloster Machern** (☏06532-951 50; www.brauhaus-kloster-machern.de; An der Zeltinger Brücke, Zeltingen-Rachtig; museum adult/child €3/1.50; ⊙museum 10am-6pm, bar 11am-1am, shop noon-5pm Easter-Oct, shorter hours Nov-Easter) is a former Cistercian monastery founded in the 13th century. It now houses this extraordinary brewery, with a bar made from a copper vat and strung with dry hops, a wicker-chair-filled terrace, and excellent local cuisine. Brews, including a Dunkel (dark), Hell (light) and Hefe-Weizen (wheat beer), are sold at its shop. Also here is a museum exhibiting religious iconography, plus puppets, toys and model railways. It's 7km northwest of Bernkastel-Kues.

craggy hills above Trarbach, with incredible valley views. Because of its strategic importance, it changed hands 13 times, was besieged six times, and destroyed seven times – no wonder that two walls are all that remain. It's reached via a steep 500m-long footpath, the **Sponheimer Weg**, that begins a block north of the bridge (there's no access by car). Its cafe serves wine, beer and pizza.

Mont Royal   Ruins

Above Traben are the remains of the vast Mont Royal fortress, constructed between 1687 and 1698 and designed by Vauban for Louis XIV as a base from which to extend French power. Ruinously expensive, it was dismantled before completion by the French themselves under the Treaty of Ryswick. The 1.5km-long footpath up to the site begins at the upper end of Römerstrasse.

Buddha Museum   Museum

(www.buddha-museum.de; Bruno-Möhring-Platz 1, Trarbach; adult/child €15/7.50; ⊙10am-6pm Tue-Sun) A magnificent 1906 *Jugendstil* former winery, designed by Bruno Möhring, is the unlikely home of the Buddha Museum, which has a beautifully presented collection of over 2000 wood, bronze and paper statues of the Buddha from all over Asia. Upstairs the peaceful rooftop garden has Moselle views. Tickets are valid all day.

Underground
Traben-Trarbach   Wine

(☏06541-839 80; www.traben-trarbach.de; tour €8; ⊙by appointment Fri, Sat & Mon Aug-Oct, Mon & Fri Apr-Jul, every 2nd Fri Nov-Mar) In the early 1900s, Traben-Trarbach was Europe's second-largest wine-trading centre (after Bordeaux) and consequently expanded its storage with cellars – some up to 100m long and several storeys deep – below the towns' streets. Fascinating 90-minute English- and German-language guided tours departing from the tourist office (p253) take you beneath the *Jugendstil* buildings into the cellar network, emerging in hidden gardens and vineyards.

✪ EATING

Alte Zunftscheune   German €€

(☏06541-9737; www.zunftscheune.de; Neue Rathausstrasse 15, Traben; mains €9-23; ⊙5-11pm Tue-Sat, 11.30am-3pm & 5-11pm Sun Easter-Oct, 6-11pm Fri, 5-11pm Sat & Sun Nov-Easter; ☏) Dine on delicious Moselle-style dishes – such as homemade black pudding and liver sausage, pork medallions with Riesling cream sauce, or grilled rump steak with asparagus and fried potatoes – in a series of wonderfully atmospheric rooms chock-full of rustic bric-a-brac, with beautiful timber staircases. Its cellar still has its original 1890s lighting. Reservations are recommended. Cash only.

ℹ️ INFORMATION

Tourist Office (☎06541-839 80; www.
traben-trarbach.de; Am Bahnhof 5, Traben;
⊙10am-5pm Mon-Fri, 11am-3pm Sat May-Aug,
10am-6pm Mon-Fri, 11am-3pm Sat Sep & Oct,
10am-4pm Mon-Fri Nov-Apr; 🛜) Adjacent to the
train station.

ℹ️ GETTING THERE & AWAY

Traben is home to the end-of-the-line train station, which is linked by small shuttle trains to the
railhead of Bullay (€3, 20 minutes, hourly), from
where there are connections to Koblenz and Trier.

Bernkastel-Kues

These charming twin towns are the hub of
the *Mittelmosel* (Middle Moselle) region.
Bernkastel, on the right (eastern) bank, is
a symphony in half-timber, stone and slate,
and teems with wine taverns. Kues, the
birthplace of theologian Nicolaus Cusanus
(1401–64), is less quaint but is home to
some key historical sights and has a lovely
riverfront promenade.

👁️ SIGHTS

Burg Landshut   Ruins
(☎06531-972 770; www.burglandshut.de;
Bernkastel; ⊙noon-9pm Thu-Tue) A rewarding
way to get your heart pumping is heading
from the Marktplatz up to this ruined 13th-
century castle (pictured below), framed
by vineyards and forests on a bluff above
Bernkastel. It's a very steep 750m walk
from town; allow 30 minutes. You'll be
rewarded with glorious valley views. The
spectacularly renovated restaurant (p254)
was unveiled in 2018; during restoration,
a 4th-century Roman tower's foundations
were also discovered. An hourly shuttle bus
from the riverfront costs €5 uphill, €3.50
downhill, or €7 return.

Marktplatz   Square
(Bernkastel) Bernkastel's pretty Marktplatz,
a block inland from the bridge, is enclosed
by a romantic ensemble of half-timbered
houses with beautifully decorated gables.
Look for the iron handcuffs, to which criminals were attached, on the facade of the
1608-built Rathaus.

Burg Landshut

SCIROCCO340/SHUTTERSTOCK ©

From left: Interior, Konstantin Basilika (p244); Vineyards beside the Moselle River; Old buildings enclosing the Marktplatz (p253), Bernkastel-Kues

St-Nikolaus-Hospital
Historic Building

(www.cusanus.de; Cusanusstrasse 2, Kues; guided tour €7; ⊙9am-6pm Sun-Fri, to 3pm Sat, guided tour 10.30am Tue & 3pm Fri Apr-Oct) **FREE** Most of Kues' sights, including the Mosel-Weinmuseum (p247) and Mosel Vinothek (p247), are conveniently grouped near the bridge in the late-Gothic St-Nikolaus-Hospital, an old-age home founded by Cusanus in 1458 for 33 men (one for every year of Jesus' life). You're free to explore the cloister and Gothic *Kapelle* (chapel) at leisure, but the treasure-filled library can only be seen on a guided tour.

🟢 ACTIVITIES

For a gentle bike ride, the **Mosel-Maare-Radweg** (www.maare-moselradweg.de), linking Bernkastel-Kues with Daun (in the Eifel Mountains), follows an old train line, so the gradients are reasonable. From April to October, you can take the RegioRadler bus (adult/bicycle €12.60/3, 1½ hours, every two hours) to the top and ride the 58km back down to Bernkastel-Kues.

⊗ EATING

Restaurant Burg Landshut
German €€

(🖉06531-972 770; www.burglandshut.de; Burg Landshut, Bernkastel; mains €14-25; ⊙noon-2pm & 6-9pm Thu-Tue Easter-Nov) Opened in 2018 in the ruined castle Burg Landshut (p253), this state-of-the-art restaurant is worth the steep climb (or shuttle-bus ride) for modern German cuisine such as sauerkraut and blood-sausage soup, and pike-perch with bacon and cabbage mash, topped off by desserts like Black Forest mousse with berry coulis. Panoramic views unfold over town.

Rotisserie Royale
European €€

(🖉06531-6572; www.rotisserie-royale.de; Burgstrasse 19, Bernkastel; mains €14.50-24.50, 5-course dinner menu €46.50; ⊙noon-2pm & 5-9pm Thu-Tue) Seriously good cooking inside this half-timbered house spans starters like pan-fried foie gras on a potato-and-apple rösti or sautéed calf's liver with black truffle foam, followed by mains such as catfish-stuffed cabbage, and desserts like chocolate ganache on eggnog foam with walnut sorbet to finish.

CHRISTIAN MUELLER/SHUTTERSTOCK ©

ⓘ INFORMATION

The **tourist office** (📞06531-500 190; www.bern kastel.de; Gestade 6, Bernkastel; audioguides 3 hr/1 day €6/8; ⊗9am-5pm Mon-Fri, from 10am Sat, to 1pm Sun May-Oct, 9.30am-4pm Mon-Fri Nov-Apr) reserves hotel rooms, sells hiking and cycling maps, and has an ATM. It also rents out audioguides to explore the two towns.

ⓘ GETTING THERE & AWAY

Buses run to Bullay (€12.60, 1¼ hours, three daily) and Trier (€11.55, 2¼ hours, three daily).

Boats operated by **Kolb** (📞06531-4719; www. moselrundfahrten.de; ⊗Apr-Oct) link Bernkastel with Traben-Trarbach (one-way/return €16/22, two hours, up to two daily). One-way bicycle transport costs €2.

ⓘ GETTING AROUND

In Bernkastel, **Fun Bike Team** (📞06531-940 24; www.funbiketeam.de; Schanzstrasse 22, Bern-kastel; standard/electric bike per day €12/25; ⊗9am-1pm & 2-6.30pm Mon-Fri, 9am-2pm Sat Apr-Oct, shorter hours Nov-Mar) rents out bikes.

Zeltingen-Rachtig–based **Fahrräder Wildmann** (📞06532-954 367; www.fahrraeder-wildmann.de; Uferallee 55, Zeltingen-Rachtig; standard/electric bike hire per day €10/22, bike transport from €80; ⊗9am-noon & 4-6pm Wed-Mon Apr-Oct, shorter hours Nov-Mar), 5km northwest of Bernkastel-Kues, hires out bikes, and has pickup, drop-off and luggage-transport services.

Trier

With an astounding nine Unesco World Heritage Sites, Germany's oldest city shelters the country's finest ensemble of Roman monuments (p244). Architectural treasures from later ages include Germany's oldest Gothic church, and Karl Marx' baroque birthplace.

Trier's proximity to both Luxembourg and France is apparent in its cuisine and the local esprit, enlivened by some 15,000 students from its renowned university. The mostly pedestrianised city centre is filled with cafes and restaurants, many inside gorgeous Gothic or baroque buildings, while wineries are scattered throughout the surrounding vineyards.

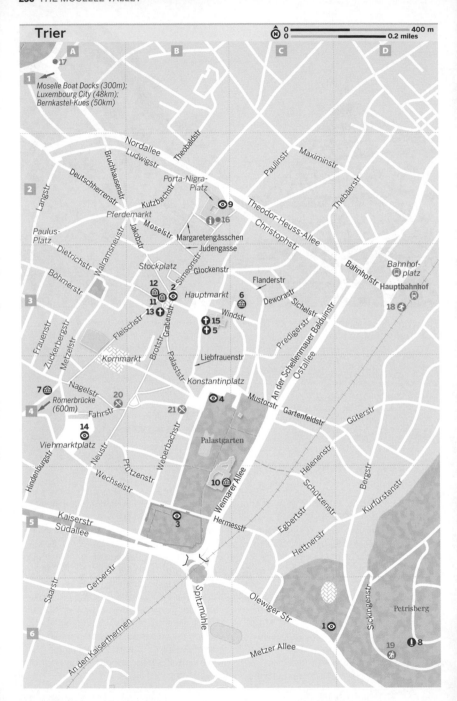

Trier

N 0 —————————— 400 m
   0 —————————— 0.2 miles

A   **B**   **C**   **D**

● 17

Moselle Boat Docks (300m);
Luxembourg City (48km);
Bernkastel-Kues (50km)

Nordallee
Ludwigstr
Theobaldstr
Paulinstr   Maximinstr

Bruchhausenstr
Deutschherrenstr
Langstr

Porta-Nigra-
Platz   ◉ 9

Theodor-Heuss-Allee
Thebäerstr

Kutzbachstr
Pferdemarkt   ❶ ● 16
Moselstr   Christophstr

Paulus-
Platz
Dietrichstr
Walramsneustr
Jakobstr
Margaretengässchen
Judengasse

Böhmerstr
Stockplatz   Simeonstr
Glockenstr

Bahnhofstr   Bahnhof-
platz
Hauptbahnhof

Flanderstr

12   ❷   ◉
11   Hauptmarkt   ❻   Dewoerstr   Sichelstr
13   Windstr
Frauenstr   Fleischstr   Brotstr   Grabenstr   ❶ 15   Predigerstr   An der Schellemmauer Balduinstr   Ostallee
Zuckerbergstr   Metzlstr   ❶ 5   18 ❸

Liebfrauenstr

Kornmarkt   Palaststr
Konstantinplatz

Nagelstr
7 ❶   20 ✕   ◉ 4   Mustorstr   Gartenfeldstr   Güterstr
Römerbrücke   Fahrstr   21 ✕
(600m)
14 ◉   Weberbachstr

Viehmarktplatz
Neustr   Palastgarten
Pützenstr
Hindenburgstr   Wechselstr
Helenenstr
Schützenstr
Bergstr
Kurfürstenstr

10 ❶
Weimarer Allee

Kaiserstr
Südallee
◉ 3   Hermesstr   Egbertstr   Hettnerstr

Gerberstr
Saarstr
Spitzmühle
Olewiger Str   Petrisberg

1 ◉
An den Kaiserthermen
Metzer Allee   19 ❶ 8

Trier

⊙ SIGHTS

Liebfrauenbasilika   Church

(Church of Our Lady; Map p256; www.trierer-dom.
de; Liebfrauenstrasse; ⊙10am-6pm Mon-Fri, to
4.30pm Sat, 12.30-6pm Sun Apr-Oct, 11am-5pm
Mon-Fri, to 4.30pm Sat, 12.30-5pm Sun Nov-Mar)
Germany's oldest Gothic church was built
in the 13th century. It has a cruciform structure supported by a dozen pillars symbolising the 12 Apostles (look for the black stone
from where all 12 articles of the Apostle's
Creed painted on the columns are visible)
and some colourful post-war stained glass.

Trierer Dom   Cathedral

(Map p256; ☑0651-979 0790; www.trierer-dom.
de; Liebfrauenstrasse 12; ⊙6.30am-6pm Apr-Oct,
to 5.30pm Nov-Mar) Looming above the Roman
palace of Helena (Emperor Constantine's
mother), this cathedral (pictured p259) is
Germany's oldest bishop's church and still
retains Roman sections. Today's edifice
is a study in nearly 1700 years of church
architecture with Romanesque, Gothic and
baroque elements. Intriguingly, its floorplan
is of a 12-petalled flower, symbolising the
Virgin Mary.

To see some dazzling ecclesiastical
equipment and peer into early Christian
history, head upstairs to the **Domschatz**
(Cathedral Treasury; Map p256; ☑0651-710 5378;
www.trierer-dom.de/bauwerk/domschatz; adult/
child €1.50/0.50; ⊙10am-5pm Mon-Sat, from
12.30pm Sun Apr-Oct & Dec, 11am-4pm Tue-Sat,

from 12.30pm Sun Nov & Jan-Mar) or around the
corner to the **Museum am Dom Trier** (Map
p256; ☑0651-710 5255; www.bistum-trier.de/mu-
seum; Bischof-Stein-Platz 1; adult/child €3.50/2;
⊙9am-5pm Tue-Sat, from 1pm Sun).

Rheinisches
Landesmuseum   Museum

(Roman Archaeological Museum; Map p256; www.
landesmuseum-trier.de; Weimarer Allee 1; adult/
child incl audioguide €8/4; ⊙10am-5pm Tue-Sun)
A scale model of 4th-century Trier and
rooms filled with tombstones, mosaics, rare
gold coins (including the Trier Gold Hoard
found in 1993, the largest preserved Roman
gold hoard in the world, with over 2600
gold coins) and some fantastic glass are
highlights of this museum, which affords an
extraordinary look at local Roman life.

Hauptmarkt   Square

(Map p256) Anchored by a 1595 fountain dedicated to St Peter and the Four
Virtues, Trier's central market square is
surrounded by medieval and Renaissance
architectural treasures such as the **Rotes
Haus** (Red House; Dietrichstrasse 53; ⊙closed
to the public), and the Steipe, which now
houses the **Spielzeugmuseum** (Toy Museum; ☑651-758 50; www.spielzeugmuseum-trier.
de; Dietrichstrasse 50/51; adult/child €5/2.50;
⊙11am-5pm Tue-Sun; 👪), as well as the
Gothic **St-Gangolf-Kirche** (⊙7am-6pm).
Small market stalls (flowers, sausages etc)
set up most days, except Sunday.

Fairy-tale Burg Eltz

At the head of the beautiful Moselle side-valley the Eltz, **Burg Eltz** (02672-950 500; www.burg-eltz.de; Burg-Eltz-Strasse 1, Wierschem; tour adult/child €9/6.50; ⊙9.30am-5.30pm Apr-Oct) is one of Germany's most romantic medieval castles. Never destroyed, this fairy-tale vision of turrets, towers, oriels, gables and half-timber has jutted forth from a rock framed by thick forest for nearly 900 years and is still owned by the original family. The decorations, furnishings, tapestries, fireplaces, paintings and armour you see during the 40-minute tour (English brochures provided; English-language tours by appointment) are also centuries old.

Museum Karl-Marx-Haus   Museum
(Map p256; www.fes.de/museum-karl-marx -haus; Brückenstrasse 10; adult/child €5/3.50; ⊙9am-6pm Apr-Oct, 1-5pm Mon, 10am-5pm Tue-Sun Nov-Mar) Revamped in 2018 on the 200th anniversary of Marx' birth, the early-18th-century baroque town house is where the author of *The Communist Manifesto* and *Das Kapital* was born in 1818. It now houses exhibits covering his life, work, allies and enemies, social democracy, his decades of exile in London (where he died in 1883), and his intellectual and political legacy.

TOURS & ACTIVITIES
City Walking Tour   Walking
(Map p256; adult/child €7.90/4.50; ⊙1pm May-Oct) Guided 75-minute walking tours in English begin at the tourist office.

Kolb   Cruise
(Map p256; 0651-26 666; www.moselrund fahrten.de; Georg-Schmitt-Platz 2; ⊙May-Oct) Choose from a range of river tours such as a 4¼-hour trip to Bernkastel (one-way/

return €25/35). Trips leave from the **boat docks** (Zurlaubener Ufer).

Weinkulturpfad   Hiking
(Wine Culture Path; Map p256) Panoramic views unfold from **Petrisberg**, the vine-covered hill just east of the Roman amphitheatre. Halfway up, the Weinkulturpfad leads through the grapes to Olewig (1.6km). Next to the Petrisberg/Aussicht stop for buses 4 and 85, a **multilingual panel** (Map p256; Sickingenstrasse) traces local history from the first-known human habitation (30,000 years ago) through the last ice age to the Romans.

EATING
Kartoffel Kiste   German €
(Map p256; www.kistetrier.de; Fahrstrasse 13-14; mains €7-17; ⊙11.30am-10pm;) Fronted by a bronze fountain, local favourite Kartoffel Kiste specialises, as its name suggests, in baked, breaded, gratinéed, soupified and sauce-doused potatoes. If you're after something heartier (albeit pricier), it also does great schnitzel and steaks. There are 220 seats inside and, in warmer weather, another 120 on the terrace.

Weinwirtschaft Friedrich-Wilhelm   German €€
(Map p256; 0651-994 7480; www.weinwirt schaft-fw.de; Weberbach 75; mains €12.50-27.50; ⊙11.30am-2.30pm & 5.30-10pm Mon-Fri, 11.30am-10pm Sat & Sun) A historic former wine warehouse with exposed brick and joists now houses this superb restaurant. Creative dishes incorporate local wines, such as trout poached in sparkling white wine with mustard sauce and white asparagus, or local sausage with Riesling sauerkraut and fried potatoes. Vines adorn the trellis-covered garden; the attached wine shop is a great place to stock up.

Weinhaus Becker   International €€€
(0651-938 080; www.beckers-trier.de; Olewiger Strasse 206; 1-/3-course lunch menu €18/28, 3-/4-course dinner menu €45/58, mains €21-34; ⊙noon-2pm & 6-10pm Tue-Sun) Within the

Trierer Dom (p257)

Becker's hotel complex, 3km southeast of the centre, this supremely elegant wine house serves sublime internationally influenced dishes like cod with pumpkin, banana and macadamia nuts, or quail with parsnip foam and roasted mushrooms, accompanied by (very) local wines made from grapes grown on the hillside opposite. Also here is the ultragourmet, twin-Michelin starred **Becker's Restaurant** (5-/8-course dinner menu €125/158; ☺7-9pm Tue-Sat).

ⓘ INFORMATION

Tourist Office (Map p256; ☑0651-978 080; www.trier-info.de; An der Porta Nigra; ☺9am-6pm Mon-Sat, 10am-5pm Sun Mar-Dec, 10am-5pm Mon-Sat Jan & Feb)

ⓘ GETTING THERE & AWAY

Trier has frequent train connections to Saarbrücken (€20.90, one to 1½ hours, two per hour) and Koblenz (€24, 1½ to two hours, two per hour).

There are also regular trains to Luxembourg City (€19.40, 50 minutes, at least hourly), with onward connections to Paris (€80, 3½ to 4½ hours, at least hourly).

ⓘ GETTING AROUND

The city centre is easily explored on foot. Buses (www.vrt-info.de) cost €2; a public transport day pass costs €5.90. The Olewig wine district is served by buses 6, 16 and 81. There are **bus stops** (Map p256) on Bahnhofsplatz.

Bikes in tip-top condition can be rented at the Hauptbahnhof's **Radstation** (Fahrradservicestation; Map p256; ☑0651-148 856; www.bues-trier. de; Bahnhofsplatz; adult/child/electric bike per day from €12/6/30; ☺9am-6pm May-Sep, 10am-6pm Mon-Fri, to 2pm Sat Oct-Apr), next to track 11, and from the tourist office, as well as many hotels.

Cologne (p211)

In Focus

Mauerpark (p68), Berlin

DI GREGORIO GIULIO/SHUTTERSTOCK ©

Germany Today

Today, Europe's most populous nation is its biggest economic power and consequently has – albeit reluctantly – taken on a more active role in global politics, especially in the Greek debt and Syrian refugee crises. A founding member of the European Union, Germany is solidly committed to preserving the alliance, ensuring it is poised to deal with the political, social and military challenges of this increasingly complex world.

Land of Immigration

Immigration remains at the centre of public debate and seriously threatened the stability of the German government in mid-2018. By the end of 2017, Germany's foreign population had reached a record high at 10.6 million, an increase of 5.8% compared to the previous year. While Germany has seen a drop in the arrival of refugees and asylum seekers from war-torn countries such as Syria, Afghanistan and Iraq, immigration from EU countries including Poland, Bulgaria and Romania has risen sharply.

In response to the migrant crisis in 2015, Germany set a precedent with its open border policy, opening the doors to around one million refugees, with Chancellor Angela Merkel encouraging other EU nations to show solidarity and follow suit. The influx has been startling:

belief systems
(% of population)

58 Christian

37 Unaffiliated or other

5 Muslim

if Germany were 100 people

81 would be German
4 would be Polish
3 would be Turkish
2 would be Russian
1 would be Romanian
1 would be Italian
8 would be other

population per sq km

👤 ≈ 30 people

Germany   UK   USA

Hamburg, for instance, accepted 40,000 refugees in 2016, more than the UK government committed to over a five-year period.

Despite Merkel's admirable intentions and 'Wir schaffen das' ('We can do it') attitude, there have been many hurdles to overcome. Immigration has been largely to areas where housing is plentiful but unemployment is higher, making integration more difficult. There has been a spike in violence, as well as a spate of terrorist attacks, ostensibly stoking far-right, anti-immigration sentiment. Of the latter, the lorry that drove into crowds at a Berlin Christmas market in 2016, and the Munich shopping mall massacre, stand out.

Federal Elections 2017

Though admitting that responding to the refugee crisis had been challenging, Merkel stood her ground in the run-up to the 2017 federal elections, defending her decisions as 'humane' and saying that faced with a similar crisis she would do the same again. Not all Germans agreed. Though Merkel emerged triumphant – being re-elected for her fourth term in a grand coalition between the country's two largest parties, the centre-left SPD and the centre-right CDU/CSU – her conservative party received its worst result since 1949, clinching 33% of the vote (down from 41.5% in 2013).

The SDP suffered a major blow in the elections, securing just 20% of the vote. It lost ground largely in areas with high unemployment, as support shifted to smaller parties such as the right-wing nationalist Alternative for Germany (AfD), which latched onto the growing undercurrent of discontent on issues such as immigration, asylum, 'Islamification' and national security. The AfD gained 13% of the vote, enough to secure access to the Bundestag; it's the first far-right nationalist party to enter German parliament in more than half a century. A major AfD stronghold is the eastern state of Saxony-Anhalt, one of Germany's poorest states.

Rise of the Right

The growing popularity of the AfD sent shock waves throughout Germany, with many Germans expressing deep concern about its place in parliament (as of 2017 it's the third-largest party in the Bundestag). In many towns and cities, locals have clashed with migrants, resulting in spates of xenophobic attacks and violence. In 2018, members of the far-right group Freital were found guilty of terror crimes and attempted murder, after propagating a 'climate of fear' with explosives attacks on refugee homes. In 2015, 18,000 supporters of the anti-Islam group PEGIDA marched in Dresden, the biggest protest of its kind. Some 30,000 counter-demonstrators protested in other German cities. Cologne expressed its outrage at the anti-Muslim march by turning off its cathedral lights.

Even Berlin's hip, multicultural Neukölln neighbourhood has seen a rise in hate crimes and arson attacks targeting migrants and political activists.

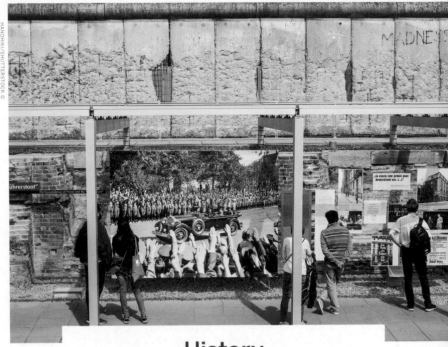

HANDHIKI/SHUTTERSTOCK ©

History

Until becoming a nation-state in 1871, Germany was a patchwork of principalities and city-states. Movements and events associated with its territory have shaped European history since the early Middle Ages. The impact of figures such as Charlemagne, Martin Luther, Otto von Bismarck and Adolf Hitler resonates today, when Germany is a leading proponent of European unity.

100 BC–AD 9

The Romans clash with Germanic tribes until defeat at the Battle of the Teutoburg Forest halts Rome's expansion eastwards.

4th Century

The arrival of Hun horsemen triggers the Great Migration. Germanic tribes are displaced and flee to parts of the Western Roman Empire.

732

The king of the Franks wins the Battle of Tours and stops the progress of Muslims into Western Europe, preserving Christianity in the Reich.

Gedenkstätte Berliner Mauer (Outdoor Memorial; p43), Berlin

Tribes and the Romans

The early inhabitants of present-day Germany were Celts and later nomadic German tribes. Under Emperor Augustus, the Romans began conquering the German lands from around 12 BC, pushing as far as the Rhine and the Danube. Attempts to expand their territory further east were thwarted in AD 9, when Roman general Varus lost three legions – about 20,000 men – in the bloody Battle of the Teutoburg Forest. By AD 300, four main groups of tribes had formed: Alemanni, Franks, Saxons and Goths.

Frankish Reich

Based on the Rhine's western bank, the Frankish Reich (Empire) existed from the 5th to the 9th centuries and was the successor state of the Western Roman Empire, which had crumbled in 476. Under the leadership of the Merovingian and later the Carolingian

919–1125	1241	1348–50
Saxon and Salian emperors rule Germany, creating the Holy Roman Empire in 962, reaffirming the precedent established by Charlemagne.	Hamburg and Lübeck sign an agreement to protect each other's trading routes, creating the basis for the powerful Hanseatic League.	The plague wipes out 25% of Europe's population and pogroms are launched against Jews.

dynasties, it became Europe's most important political power in those early medieval times. In its heyday, the Reich included present-day France, Germany, the Low Countries (Netherlands, Belgium and Luxembourg) and half the Italian peninsula.

Its most powerful ruler was Charlemagne (r 768–814), a Carolingian. From his grandiose residence in Aachen, he conquered Lombardy, won territory in Bavaria, waged a 30-year war against the Saxons in the north and was crowned kaiser by the pope in 800, an act that was regarded as a revival of the Roman empire. Charlemagne's burial in Aachen Dom (Aachen Cathedral) turned the court chapel into a major pilgrimage site.

After Charlemagne's death, fighting between his son and three grandsons ultimately led to the dissolution of the Frankish Reich in 843. The Treaty of Verdun split the territory into three kingdoms: the Westfrankenreich (West Francia), which evolved into today's France; the Ostfrankenreich (East Francia), the origin of today's Germany; and the Mittlere Frankenreich (Middle Francia), which encompassed the Low Countries and areas in present-day France and northern Italy.

Middle Ages

Strong regionalism in Germany today has its roots in the early Middle Ages, when the symbolic heart of power was the cathedral in Aachen and dynasties squabbled and intrigued over territorial spoils. Aachen hosted the coronation of 31 German kings from 936 until 1531, starting with Otto I (aka Otto the Great). Otto proved himself on the battlefield, first by defeating Hungarian troops and then by conquering the Kingdom of Italy. In 962, he renewed Charlemagne's pledge to protect the papacy, and the pope reciprocated by crowning him emperor and marking the birth of the Holy Roman Empire. For the next 800 years the Kaiser and the pope were strange, and often uneasy, bedfellows.

Power struggles between popes and emperors, the latter of which also had to contend with local princes and prince-bishops, were behind many of the upheavals in the early Middle Ages. In 1254, after the death of the last Hohenstaufen emperor, Friedrich II, the Reich plunged into an era called the Great Interregnum, when no potential successor could gain sufficient support, leaving the Reich rudderless until the election of Rudolf I in 1273. Rudolf was the first of 19 emperors of the Habsburg dynasty that mastered the art of politically expedient marriage and dominated Continental affairs until the early 20th century.

In the 14th century, the basic structure of the Holy Roman Empire solidified. A key document was the Golden Bull of 1356 (so named for its golden seal), a decree issued by Emperor Charles IV that was essentially an early form of an imperial constitution. Most importantly, it set out precise rules for elections by specifying the seven Kurfürsten (prince-electors) entitled to choose the next king to be crowned Holy Roman Emperor by the pope. The privilege fell to the rulers of Bohemia, Brandenburg, Saxony and the Palatinate, as well as to the archbishops of Trier, Mainz and Cologne. A simple majority was sufficient in electing the next king.

1356	1517	1618–48
The Golden Bull formalises the election of the kaiser. Archbishops, regional rulers and the count of Palatinate become prince-electors.	Martin Luther's ideas challenge the selling of indulgences, capturing a mood of disillusionment within the Church.	The Thirty Years' War leaves the population depleted and regions reduced to wasteland. The Reich disintegrates into more than 300 states.

For ordinary Germans, times were difficult. They battled with panic lynchings, pogroms against Jews and labour shortages – all sparked by the plague (1348–50) that wiped out at least 25% of Europe's population. While death gripped ordinary Germans, universities were being established all over the country around this time, with Heidelberg's the first, in 1386.

Luther & the Reformation

In the 16th century, the Renaissance and humanist ideas generated criticism of rampant church abuses, most famously the practice of selling indulgences to exonerate sins. In the university town of Wittenberg in 1517, German monk and theology professor Martin Luther (1483–1546) made public his *Ninety-Five Theses*, which criticised not only indulgences but also questioned papal infallibility, clerical celibacy and other elements of Catholic doctrine. This was the spark that lit the Reformation. Threatened with excommunication, Luther broke from the Catholic Church and went into hiding in Wartburg castle, in Eisenach, where he translated the New Testament into German.

In 1555, Emperor Karl V's Peace of Augsburg decree allowed princes to decide the religion of their principality. Lutheran doctrine prospered in the secular north, while the clerical lords in the south, southwest and Austria stuck with Catholicism. In 1618 religious disparity degenerated into the bloody Thirty Years' War, ending with the Peace of Westphalia treaty of 1648 that rendered the Reich a nominal, impotent state.

Age of Englightenment

In Bavaria, meanwhile, revolutionary rumblings brought out King Ludwig I's reactionary streak. An arch Catholic, he restored the monasteries, introduced press censorship and authorised the arrest of students, journalists and university professors whom he judged to be subversive. Bavaria was becoming restrictive even as French and American democratic ideals flourished elsewhere in Germany.

On 22 March 1848 Ludwig I abdicated in favour of his son, Maximilian II (r 1848–64), who finally put into place many of the constitutional reforms his father had ignored, such as abolishing censorship and introducing freedom of assembly. His son Ludwig II (r 1864–86) introduced further progressive measures (welfare for the poor, liberalised marriage

Hanseatic League

The origins of the Hanseatic League go back to various guilds and associations, established from about the mid-12th century by out-of-town merchants to protect their interests. After Hamburg and Lübeck signed an agreement in 1241 to protect their ships and trading routes, they were joined in their league by Lüneburg, Kiel and a string of Baltic Sea cities stretching east to Greifswald. By 1356 this had grown into the Hanseatic League, encompassing half a dozen other large alliances of cities, with Lübeck playing the lead role.

1740–86
Berlin becomes 'Athens on the Spree', as Absolutism in Europe gives way to the Enlightenment, heralding a cultural explosion.

1789–1815
The French Revolution and, the Napoleonic Wars sweep away the last remnants of the Middle Ages. Napoleon takes Berlin in 1806.

1806–13
The Holy Roman Empire collapses and Napoleon creates the 16-member Confederation of the Rhine.

Jüdisches Museum

WORLDWIDE/SHUTTERSTOCK ©

laws and free trade) early in his reign but ultimately became caught up in a world inspired by mythology, focussing on building grand palaces such as Schloss Neuschwanstein instead of running a kingdom. His death by drowning in shallow water in Lake Starnberg continues to spur conspiracy theories to this day.

Napoleon & Revolutions

In the aftermath of the 1789 French Revolution, a Frenchman named Napoleon Bonaparte (Napoleon I) took control of Europe and significantly altered its fate through a series of wars. The defeat of Austrian and Russian troops in the Battle of Austerlitz in 1805 led to the 1806 collapse of the Holy Roman Empire, the abdication of Kaiser Franz II and a variety of administrative and judicial reforms.

In 1815, at the Congress of Vienna, Germany was reorganised into the Deutscher Bund, a confederation of 39 states with a central legislative assembly, the Reichstag, established in Frankfurt. Austria and Prussia dominated this alliance, until a series of bourgeois democratic revolutions swept through German cities in 1848, resulting in Germany's first-ever freely elected parliamentary delegation convening in Frankfurt's Paulskirche. Austria, meanwhile, broke away from Germany, came up with its own constitution and promptly relapsed into monarchism. As revolution fizzled in 1850, the confederation resumed, with Prussia and Austria again as dominant members.

Bismarck & the Birth of an Empire

The creation of a unified Germany with Prussia at the helm was the glorious ambition of Otto von Bismarck (1815–98), who had been appointed as Prussian prime minister by King Wilhelm I in 1862. An old-guard militarist, he used intricate diplomacy and a series of wars with neighbouring Denmark and France to achieve his aims. By 1871 Berlin stood as the proud capital of the Deutsches Reich (German Empire), a bicameral, constitutional

1814–15	1848	1870–71
The post-Napoleon Congress of Vienna redraws the map of Europe, creating in the former Reich the German Alliance, with 35 states.	*The Communist Manifesto* by Karl Marx and Friedrich Engels, is published in London by a group of Germans living in exile in Britain.	Bismarck creates a unified Germany, with Prussia at its helm and Berlin as its capital. Wilhelm I, King of Prussia, becomes Kaiser Wilhelm I.

monarchy. On 18 January the Prussian king was crowned kaiser at Versailles, with Bismarck as his 'Iron Chancellor'.

The early years of the German empire – a period called Gründerzeit (foundation years) – were marked by major economic growth, fuelled in part by a steady flow of French reparation payments. Hundreds of thousands of people poured into the cities in search of work in factories. New political parties gave a voice to the proletariat, especially the Socialist Workers' Party (SAP), the forerunner of the Sozialdemokratische Partei Deutschlands (Social Democratic Party of Germany; SPD).

Bismarck tried to make the party illegal but, when pressed, made concessions to the growing and increasingly antagonistic socialist movement, enacting Germany's first modern social reforms, though it was contrary to his true nature. When Wilhelm II (r 1888–1918) came to power, he wanted to extend social reform, while Bismarck envisioned stricter antisocialist laws. By March 1890, the kaiser had had enough and excised his renegade chancellor from the political scene. Bismarck's legacy as a brilliant diplomat unravelled as a wealthy, unified and industrially powerful Germany embarked upon a new century.

World War I

The assassination on 28 June 1914 of Archduke Franz Ferdinand, heir to the Austro-Hungarian throne, triggered a series of diplomatic decisions that led to WWI, the bloodiest European conflict since the Thirty Years' War. Initial euphoria and faith in a quick victory soon gave way to despair, as casualties piled up in the battlefield trenches and stomachs grumbled on the home front. When defeat came in 1918, it ushered in a period of turmoil and violence. On 9 November 1918, Kaiser Wilhelm II abdicated, bringing an inglorious end to the monarchy.

The seeds of acrimony and humiliation that later led to WWII were sown in the peace conditions of WWI. Germany, militarily broken, teetering on the verge of revolution and caught in a no man's land between monarchy and modern democracy, signed the Treaty of Versailles (1919), which made it responsible for all losses inflicted upon its enemies. Its borders were trimmed and it was forced to pay high reparations.

The Weimar Republic

In July 1919 the federalist constitution of the fledgling republic was adopted in the town of Weimar, where the constituent assembly had sought refuge from the chaos of Berlin. Germany's first serious experiment with democracy gave women the vote and established basic human rights, but it also gave the chancellor the right to rule by decree – a concession that would later prove critical in Hitler's rise to power.

The Weimar Republic (1919–33) was governed by a coalition of left and centre parties, but pleased neither communists nor monarchists. In fact, the 1920s began as anything

1890–91	1914–18	1918–19
Influenced by Marx's writing, the Sozialdemokratische Partei Deutschlands (SPD) adopts its present name.	WWI: Germany, Austria-Hungary and Turkey go to war against Britain, France, Italy and Russia. Germany is defeated.	Kaiser Wilhelm II abdicates, and a democratic Weimar Republic is founded. Women receive suffrage and human rights are enshrined in law.

but 'golden', marked, as they were, by the humiliation of a lost war, hyperinflation, mass unemployment, hunger and disease.

Economic stability gradually returned after a new currency, the Rentenmark, was introduced in 1923 and with the Dawes Plan in 1924, which limited the crippling reparation payments imposed on Germany after WWI. But the tide turned again when the US stock market crashed in 1929, plunging the world into economic depression. Within weeks, millions of German were jobless, and riots and demonstrations again filled the streets.

Hitler's Rise to Power

The volatile, increasingly polarised political climate led to clashes between communists and members of a party that had been patiently waiting in the wings – the National-sozialistische Deutsche Arbeiterpartei (National Socialist German Workers' Party, NSDAP, or Nazi Party), led by an Austrian failed artist and WWI corporal named Adolf Hitler. Soon jackboots, brown shirts, oppression and fear would dominate daily life in Germany. Hitler's NSDAP gained 18% of the national vote in the 1930 elections. In the 1932 presidential election, Hitler challenged incumbent Reichspräsident (President of the Reich) Paul von Hindenburg, but only managed to win 37% of the second-round vote. However, a year later, on 30 January 1933, faced with failed economic reforms and persuasive right-wing advisors, Hindenburg appointed Hitler chancellor.

Hitler moved quickly to consolidate absolute power and to turn the nation's democracy into a one-party dictatorship. He used Berlin's Reichstag fire as a pretext to push through the Enabling Act, allowing him to decree laws and change the constitution without consulting parliament. When Hindenburg died a year later, Hitler merged the offices of president and chancellor to become Führer of the Third Reich and so began the darkest period in German history.

Jewish Persecution

Jewish people were specifically targeted in what would be a long-term campaign of genocide. In April 1933 Joseph Goebbels, *Gauleiter* (district leader) of Berlin and head of the well-oiled Ministry of Propaganda, announced a boycott of Jewish businesses. Soon after, Jewish people were expelled from public service and banned from many professions, trades and industries. The Nuremberg Laws of 1935 deprived 'non-Aryans' of German citizenship and many other rights.

The international community, meanwhile, turned a blind eye to the situation in Germany, perhaps because many leaders were keen to see some order restored to the country after decades of political upheaval. Hitler's success at stabilising the shaky economy – largely by pumping public money into employment programs – was widely admired. The 1936 Olympic summer games in Berlin were a PR triumph, as Hitler launched a charm offensive. Terror and persecution resumed soon after the closing ceremony.

1933	**1935**	**1938**
Hitler becomes chancellor of Germany. The federal states become powerless, and opposition parties and free-trade unions are banned.	The Nuremberg Laws are enacted. A new law deprives Jews and other 'non-Aryans' of German citizenship.	The Munich Agreement allows Hitler to annex the Sudetenland, an ethnic-German region of Czechoslovakia.

The targeting of Jewish people escalated on 9 November 1938, with the Reichspogromnacht (often called Kristallnacht, or Night of Broken Glass). Using the assassination of a German consular official by a Polish Jew in Paris as a pretext, Nazi thugs desecrated, burned and demolished synagogues and Jewish cemeteries, property and businesses across the country. Jews had begun to emigrate after 1933, but this event set off a stampede.

The fate of those Jewish people who stayed behind deteriorated after the outbreak of WWII in 1939. At Hitler's request, a conference in January 1942 in Berlin's Wannsee came up with the *Endlösung* (Final Solution): the systematic, bureaucratic and meticulously documented annihilation of European Jews. Sinti and Roma, political opponents, priests, homosexuals and habitual criminals were targeted as well. Of the roughly seven million people who were sent to concentration camps, only 500,000 survived.

World War II

WWII began on 1 September 1939 with the Nazi attack on Poland. France and Britain declared war on Germany two days later, but even this could not prevent the quick defeat of Poland, Belgium, the Netherlands and France. Other countries, including Denmark and Norway, were also soon brought into the Nazi fold.

In June 1941 Germany broke its nonaggression pact with Stalin by attacking the USSR. Though successful at first, Operation Barbarossa quickly ran into problems, culminating in the defeat at Stalingrad (today Volgograd) the following winter, forcing the Germans to retreat. With the Normandy invasion of June 1944, Allied troops arrived in formidable force on the European mainland, supported by unrelenting air raids that reduced Germany's cities to rubble and the country's population by 10%. The final Battle of Berlin began in mid-April 1945. More than 1.5 million Soviet soldiers barrelled towards the capital from the east, reaching Berlin on 21 April and encircling it on 25 April. Two days later they were

Night of the Long Knives

The Sturmabteilung (SA) was a Nazi organisation charged with policing Nazi party meetings and disrupting those convened by political opponents. It played an important role in Hitler's ascent to power, and by 1934 had become powerful in its own right thanks to its leader Ernst Röhm. The SA numbered two million members, thus easily outnumbering the German army. On 30 June 1934, Hitler, feeling threatened, ordered the black-shirted Schutzstaffel (SS) to round up and kill the SA leadership (including Röhm and at least 75 others) to bring the organisation to heel.

Hitler hushed up the 'Night of the Long Knives' until 13 July, when he announced to the Reichstag that the SA would now serve under the command of the army, which would swear an oath of allegiance to Hitler. Justice would be executed by the SS under the leadership of former chicken farmer Heinrich Himmler, giving the SS unchallenged power and making it Nazi Germany's most powerful and feared force.

1939	1939–45	1945
WWII: Hitler invades Poland on 1 September. Two days later France and Britain declare war on Germany.	Millions of Jews are murdered during the Holocaust and 62 million civilians and soldiers die – 27 million in the Soviet Union alone.	Hitler commits suicide in a Berlin bunker as a defeated Germany surrenders. Germany is split into Allied and Soviet-occupied zones.

Dachau Memorial Site

SMAL0050/SHUTTERSTOCK ©

in the city centre, fighting running street battles with the remaining troops, many of them boys and elderly men.

On 30 April the fighting reached the government quarter where Hitler was holed up in his bunker with his long-time mistress Eva Braun, whom he'd married just a day earlier. Finally accepting the inevitability of defeat, the couple killed themselves. As their bodies were burning in the chancellery courtyard, Red Army soldiers raised the Soviet flag above the Reichstag.

On 7 May 1945, Germany surrendered unconditionally. Peace was signed at the US military headquarters in Reims (France) and at the Soviet military headquarters in Berlin. On 8 May 1945, WWII in Europe officially came to an end.

East & West

In 1949 the division of Germany – and Berlin – was formalised. The western zones evolved into the Bundesrepublik Deutschland (BRD, Federal Republic of Germany or FRG) with Konrad Adenauer as its first chancellor and Bonn, on the Rhine, as its capital. An economic aid package, dubbed the Marshall Plan, created the basis for West Germany's Wirtschafts-wunder (economic miracle), which saw the economy grow at an average 8% per year between 1951 and 1961. The recovery was largely engineered by economics minister Ludwig Erhard, who dealt with an acute labour shortage by inviting about 2.3 million foreign workers, mainly from Turkey, Yugoslavia and Italy, to Germany, thereby laying the foundation for today's multicultural society.

The Soviet zone, meanwhile, grew into the Deutsche Demokratische Republik (DDR, German Democratic Republic or GDR) with East Berlin as its capital and Wilhelm Pieck as its first president. A single party, the Sozialistische Einheitspartei Deutschlands (SED, Socialist Unity Party of Germany), led by party boss Walter Ulbricht, dominated economic, judicial and security policy. In order to suppress any opposition, the Ministry for State Security, or Stasi, was established in 1950.

1949	1951–61	1961
A separate East Germany (German Democratic Republic, GDR) is established in the Soviet-occupied zone; Berlin is its capital.	Ludwig Erhard unleashes West Germany's *Wirtschafts-wunder* (economic miracle). The economy averages an annual growth rate of 8%.	On the night of 13 August, the GDR government begins building the Berlin Wall, a 155km-long barrier surrounding West Berlin.

Economically, East Germany stagnated, in large part because of the Soviets' continued policy of asset stripping and reparation payments. Stalin's death in 1953 raised hopes for reform but only spurred the GDR government to raise production goals even higher.

The Wall: What Goes Up...

Through the 1950s the economic gulf between the two Germanys widened, prompting hundreds of thousands of East Berliners to seek a future in the West. Eventually, the exodus of mostly young and well-educated East Germans strained the troubled GDR economy so much that – with Soviet consent – its government built a wall to keep them in. Construction of the Berlin Wall, the Cold War's most potent symbol, began on the night of 13 August 1961, leaving Berliners stunned. Ensuing protests and demonstrations were ignored. In October 1961, US and Soviet tanks faced off at Checkpoint Charlie, reaching the brink of war, but the wall stayed.

...Must Come Down

German reunification came as a surprise to the world and ushered in a new and exciting era. The so-called Wende (turning point, ie the fall of communism) came about as a gradual development that ended in a big bang – the collapse of the Berlin Wall on 9 November 1989.

The Germany of today, with 16 unified federal states, was hammered out through a volatile political debate and a series of treaties. A common currency and economic union became realities in July 1990. On 31 August 1990, the Unification Treaty, in which both East and West pledged to create a unified Germany, was signed. In September this was followed by the Two-Plus-Four Treaty, which was signed in Moscow by representatives of East and West Germany, the USSR, France, the UK and the US. This ended postwar occupation zones and fully transferred sovereignty to a unified Germany. Formal unification became effective on 3 October 1990 (now Germany's national holiday) and Germany's first unified elections were held in December. In 1991, the Bundestag (German parliament) voted in favour of moving the government to Berlin. The city was also reinstated as the German capital, and on 8 September 1994, the last Allied troops stationed in Berlin left the city.

Since Reunification

The single most dominant figure throughout the 1990s was Helmut Kohl. Under his leadership, East German assets were privatised and infrastructure modernised, creating a boom that saw massive growth in the former GDR for the first half of the decade. This was followed by a dramatic slump, creating an eastern Germany that consisted of unification winners and losers. In 1998, a coalition of the SPD and Bündnis 90/Die Grünen (Alliance 90/The Greens) parties defeated the CDU/CSU and FDP coalition.

1972	**1989**	**2005**
Terrorists murder two competitors and take nine hostage at the Munich Olympics. A botched rescue operation kills all nine.	The Berlin Wall comes down and the reunified city becomes the capital. Communist regimes across Eastern Europe start to fall.	Angela Merkel becomes Germany's first female chancellor.

Germany's National Day

The Berlin Wall fell on 9 November 1989, so when it came time to pick a date for a public holiday to mark German reunification it seemed only natural that that would be it. Unfortunately, the same date also played key roles in German history on two prior, less joyful, occasions. On this day in 1923 Hitler launched his ill-fated Munich coup, which landed him in jail where he penned *Mein Kampf*. And in 1938 Nazi thugs vandalised Jewish businesses and synagogues during the infamous Kristallnacht. On a positive note, 9 November was also the day in 1918 when Kaiser Wilhelm II abdicated, ending German monarchical rule and establishing the first German republic. Still, in the end, Germany's national holiday was set on the less evocative, but much more tactful, date of 3 October – the anniversary of administrative reunification in 1990.

The New Millennium

The formation of a coalition government of SPD and Alliance 90/The Greens in 1998 marked the first time an environmentalist party had governed nationally anywhere in the world. The rise of the Greens and recently, the democratic socialist Die Linke (The Left), has changed the political landscape of Germany, making absolute majorities difficult to achieve. The 2005 election brought a grand coalition of CDU/CSU and SPD with Angela Merkel at the helm. Born in the GDR in 1954, the Russian-speaking quantum chemist was the first woman on the job.

The election of 2009 confirmed the trend towards smaller parties with the grand coalition losing considerable votes, allowing the Left to establish itself at the federal level. The trend reversed slightly in 2013 with the big parties regaining some votes and heralding the meteoric rise of a new conservative party, the Euro-skeptic Alternative für Deutschland (AfD, Alternative for Germany). Founded in April 2013, the party advocates for a return to the Deutschmark, radical tax changes and restricted immigration. Although missing the 5% Bundestag threshold, the AfD party gained representation in the European Parliament and in the state parliaments of Brandenburg, Saxony, Thuringia, Hamburg and Bremen.

In July 2015 Frauke Petry, a conservative nationalist was elected party leader. Her strict Islamophobic stance and popularity among sympathisers of the anti-Islam, anti-immigrant PEGIDA ('Patriotic Europeans against the Islamisation of the West') movement, prompted flocks of more-moderate members to leave the party.

In 2017, Germany handled more asylum applications than the rest of the EU combined. Immigration policy and processing and its draining of government resources is key to the rise of the AfD and PEGIDA. Support for them reached a highpoint in the 2017 elections with the party winning 13.3% of the vote and entering national parliament.

2008
The global economic crisis bites into export industries. Banks are propped up by state funds as unemployment and state debt rise.

2015
Germany welcomes around one million refugees. Numbers of asylum seekers continue to climb in subsequent years.

2017
The country marks the 500th anniversary of the Reformation with festivals, concerts and special exhibitions across the country.

Reichstag (p38), Berlin

NIKADA/GETTY IMAGES ©

Arts & Architecture

Germany's creative population has made major contributions to International culture, particularly during the 18th century when the courts at Weimar and Dresden attracted some of the greatest minds in Europe. With such rich traditions to fall back on, inspiration has seldom been in short supply for the new generations of German artists, despite the upheavals of the country's recent history.

Literary Legacies

German literature in the Middle Ages was written in umpteen dialects, based on the oral tradition and typified by lyrical poetry, ballads and secular epics such as the famous *Nibelungen* saga (from the 12th century). Martin Luther's translation of the Bible from Greek to German in 521–22 created a common German language and thus paved the way for modern literature. But this didn't hit its stride until the Enlightenment, two centuries later.

The undisputed literary colossus of the period was Johann Wolfgang von Goethe, most famous for his two-part drama *Faust* about the archetypal human quest for

Oberbaum bridge features prominently in *Run Lola Run*

★ **Celluloid Classics**

The Legend of Paul and Paula (1973)
GDR cult classic

Wings of Desire (1997) An angel in
love with a mortal

Run Lola Run (1998) High-energy
Berlin drama

The Lives of Others (2006)
The Stasi unmasked

meaning and knowledge. Goethe and his friend Friedrich Schiller were key figures in a celebrated period known as *Weimarer Klassik* (Weimar Classicism).

In the mid-19th century, realist novels captured the imagination of the newly emerging middle class. Main exponents include Theodor Fontane who's best known for his 1894 society novel *Effi Briest*, and Gerhard Hauptmann whose plays and novels focused on social injustice and the harsh life of the working class.

During the time of the Weimar Republic, Berlin's underworld served as the focus for the novel *Berlin Alexanderplatz* (1929) by Alfred Döblin. Among post-WWII generation writers, Günter Grass became the most celebrated after bursting into the limelight with *Die Blechtrommel* (*The Tin Drum*; 1959). In East Germany, Christa Wolf won high esteem for her 1963 story *Der geteilte Himmel* (*Divided Heaven*) about a young woman whose fiancé abandons her for life in the West.

After reunification literary achievement stagnated at first, as writers from the East and West began a process of self-examination, but it picked up steam in the late 1990s. Thomas Brussig's tongue-in-cheek *Helden wie Wir* (*Heroes Like Us*; 1998) was one of the first post-reunification novels and offers an insightful look at East German society. And Russian-born Wladimir Kaminer's amusing, stranger-than-fiction hit *Russendisko* (*Russian Disco*; 2000) firmly established the author in Germany's light-hearted literary scene.

Caught on Film

Since the foundation of the UFA studios in Potsdam in 1917, Germany has had an active and successful film industry. Marlene Dietrich (1901–92) became the country's first international superstar, starting out in silent films and later moving to Hollywood. Director Fritz Lang made a name for himself with seminal films *Metropolis* (1927) and *M* (1931).

The best-known director of the Nazi era was Leni Riefenstahl (1902–2003), whose *Triumph of the Will* (1934), depicting the Nuremberg rallies, won great acclaim but later rendered her unemployable.

The 1960s and 1970s saw a great revival of German cinema, spearheaded by energetic, politically aware young directors such as Rainer Werner Fassbinder, Wim Wenders, Volker Schlöndorff and Margarethe von Trotta.

A smash hit after reunification was Tom Tykwer's *Run Lola Run* (1998), which established his reputation as one of Germany's best new directors. Wolfgang Becker's GDR comedy *Good Bye, Lenin!* (2003) was another international hit as was Florian Henckel von Donnersmarck's Academy Award-winning *The Lives of Others* (2006) about the operations of the Stasi in the 1980s.

Classical to Electronic Sounds

Forget brass bands and oompah music – few countries can claim the impressive musical heritage of Germany, which generated the likes of Johann Sebastian Bach, Georg Friedrich Händel, Ludwig van Beethoven, Richard Strauss, Robert Schumann, Johannes Brahms and Richard Wagner, to name a few.

Germany has also made significant contributions to the contemporary music scene. Internationally renowned artists include punk icon Nina Hagen, '80s balloon girl Nena, and rock bands from the Scorpions to Die Toten Hosen and Rammstein.

Kraftwerk pioneered the original electronic sounds, which morphed into techno and became the seminal club music from the 1990s onwards, especially in Berlin and Frankfurt. Today, Germany has the largest electronic music scene in the world, and DJs such as Ellen Allien, Paul Kalkbrenner, Paul van Dyk and Sven Väth have become household names on the global party circuit.

Architecture through the Ages

The first great wave of significant buildings came with the Romanesque period (1000–1200), outstanding examples of which include the cathedrals at Worms, Speyer and Mainz. Gothic architecture brought such traits as ribbed vaults, pointed arches and flying buttresses nicely exemplified in Cologne's cathedral, Trier's Liebfrauenkirche, Freiburg's Münster, Lübeck's Marienkirche, and the Münster in Ulm.

For classic baroque, Balthasar Neumann's Residenz in Würzburg, the Passau Cathedral and the Frauenkirche and Zwinger palace in Dresden are must-sees. The neoclassical period of the 19th century was dominated by Karl Friedrich Schinkel, who was especially prolific in Berlin and northern Germany. His Neue Wache and the Altes Museum in Berlin are considered masterpieces of the style.

No modern movement has had greater influence on design than the Bauhaus, founded in 1919 by Walter Gropius. You can still visit the seminal school and private homes of Gropius and his fellow professors in Dresden-Rosslau. For an overview, drop by the Bauhaus Archive in Berlin. The Nazis shut down the school in 1932 and reverted to the pompous and monumental. Berlin's Olympic Stadium and the party rally grounds in Nuremberg are among the few surviving buildings from that dark period.

Frankfurt shows Germany's take on the modern high-rise and for the boldest new architecture head to Berlin where international 'starchitects' including Daniel Libeskind, David Chipperfield and Lord Norman Foster have put their stamp on the city's post-reunification look. Stuttgart, meanwhile, added the stunning Porsche Museum to its cityscape in 2009, while in Hamburg an old docklands area has been turned into a futuristic new city quarter called HafenCity.

Artistic Achievement

German arts first heyday was during the Renaissance period, which came late to Germany but flourished quickly. The heavyweight of the period is Albrecht Dürer (1471–1528), who was the first to seriously compete with the Italian masters. Dürer influenced court painter Lucas Cranach the Elder (1472–1553) who worked in Wittenberg for more than 45 years.

Two centuries later, the baroque period brought great sculpture, including works by Andreas Schlüter in Berlin. This was followed by neoclassicism in the 19th century, which

Konstantin Basilika (p244), Trier

★ **Unesco World Heritage Sites**

Roman monuments (p244), Trier

Kölner Dom (p215), Cologne

Schloss Sanssouci (p88), Potsdam

Museumsinsel (p50), Berlin

ushered back interest in the human figure and an emphasis on Roman and Greek mythology. This segued into Romanticism, which drew heavily on emotion and dreamy idealism, nicely captured in the paintings of Caspar David Friedrich and Otto Runge.

In 1905 Ernst Ludwig Kirchner, along with Erich Heckel and Karl Schmidt-Rottluff, founded the artist group Die Brücke (The Bridge) in Dresden. This turned the art world on its head with ground-breaking visions that paved the way for German expressionism. By the 1920s art had become more radical and political, with artists such as George Grosz, Otto Dix and Max Ernst exploring the new concepts of Dada and surrealism. Käthe Kollwitz is one of the era's few major female artists, known for her social-realist drawings and prints.

After 1945 abstract art became a mainstay of the German scene, with key figures such as Joseph Beuys, Monica Bonvicini and Anselm Kiefer enjoying worldwide reputations. After reunification, the New Leipzig School achieved success at home and abroad with figurative painters such as Neo Rauch generating much acclaim.

Hitting the Stage

Germany's theatre history began during the Enlightenment in the late 18th century, an epoch dominated by humanistic ideals and authors such as Gotthold Ephraim Lessing, Friedrich Schiller and Johann Wolfgang von Goethe.

Starting in the late 19th century, Berlin emerged as the capital of the German theatre scene. At the Deutsches Theater, Max Reinhardt became the most influential expressionist director, collaborating briefly with dramatist Bertolt Brecht whose *Threepenny Opera* premiered in 1928. Like so many others, both men went into exile under the Nazis. Returning in 1949, Brecht founded the Berliner Ensemble and became East Germany's most important director. In the 1950s Heiner Müller – a Marxist critical of GDR-style socialism – became unpalatable in both Germanys.

In West Germany, directors such as Peter Stein earned contemporary German theatre its reputation for producing classic plays in an innovative and provocative manner. Frank Castorf, meanwhile, is arguably Germany's most dynamic contemporary director, heading up Berlin's Volksbühne since 1992. He regularly tears down the confines of the proscenium stage with Zeitgeist-critical productions that are somehow populist and elitist all at once. Contemporary playwrights to watch out for include Rene Pollesch, Moritz Rinke, Botho Strauss, Rainald Goetz and Roland Schimmelpfennig.

Cross-country skiing

ROBERT NIEDRING/GETTY IMAGES ©

Germany Outdoors

No matter what kind of activity gets you off the couch, you'll be able to pursue it in this land of lakes, rivers, mountains and forests. Each season offers its own special delights, be it hiking among spring wild-flowers, swimming in a lake warmed by the summer sun, biking among kaleidoscopic autumn foliage or schussing through winter snow. And wherever you go, you'll find local outfitters eager to gear you up.

Hiking & Mountaineering

Wanderlust? Germany coined the word. Ramble through romantic river valleys, hike among fragrant pines, bag Alpine peaks or simply go for a walk by the lake or through the dunes. Many of the nicest trails traverse national and nature parks or biosphere reserves. Trails are usually well signposted, sometimes with symbols quaintly painted on tree trunks. To find a route matching your fitness level and time frame, pick the brains of local tourist-office staff, who can also supply you with maps and tips.

The Bavarian Alps are Germany's mountaineering heartland, whether for day treks or multiday hut-to-hut clambers. Keep in mind that hiking in the Alps is no walk in the park. You need to be in reasonable condition and come equipped with the right shoes, gear and topographic maps or GPS. Before heading out, seek local advice and instruction on

Long-Distance Cycling Routes

Altmühltal Radweg (160km) Easy to moderate; Rothenburg ob der Tauber to Beilngries, following the Altmühl River through the Altmühltal Nature Park.

Bodensee-Königssee Radweg (418km) Moderate; Lindau to Berchtesgaden along the foot of the Alps with magnificent views of the mountains, lakes and forests.

Donauradweg (434km) Easy to moderate; Neu-Ulm to Passau – a delightful riverside trip along one of Europe's great streams.

Romantische Strasse (359km) Easy to moderate; Würzburg to Füssen – one of the nicest ways to explore Germany's most famous holiday route; busy during summer.

routes, equipment and weather as trails can be narrow, steep and have icy patches, even in summer.

The Deutscher Alpenverein (DAV; www.alpenverein.de) is a goldmine of information and maintains hundreds of Alpine mountain huts, many of them open to the public, where you can spend the night and get a meal. Local DAV chapters also organise various courses (climbing, mountaineering etc) and guided treks.

For another excellent resource, see www.wanderbares-deutschland.de for information about dozens of walking trails and a handy interactive map. It's mostly in German, but some routes are also detailed in English.

Cycling

Strap on your helmet! Germany is superb cycling territory, whether you're off on a leisurely spin along the beach, an adrenalin-fuelled downhill ride or a multiday bike-touring adventure. Practically every town and region has a network of signposted bike routes; most towns have at least one bike-hire station (often at or near the train station).

Germany is also criss-crossed by more than 200 long-distance trails covering 70,000km, making it ideal for *Radwandern* (bike touring). Routes combine lightly travelled back roads, forestry tracks and paved highways with dedicated bike lanes. Many traverse nature reserves, meander along rivers or venture into steep mountain terrain.

For inspiration and route planning, check out www.germany.travel/cycling, which provides (in English) an overview of routes and free downloads of route maps and descriptions.

For on-the-road navigation, the best maps are those published by the national cycling organsation Allgemeiner Deutscher Fahrrad Club (ADFC; www.adfc.de). These indicate inclines, track conditions, repair shops and UTM grid coordinates for GPS users. ADFC also offers a useful directory called Bett & Bike (www.bettundbike.de), available online or in bookshops, that lists bicycle-friendly hotels, inns and hostels.

Water Sports & Riverboats

Germany's lakes, rivers, canals and coasts offer plenty of water-based action, even if the swimming season is relatively short (June to September) since water temperatures rarely climb above 21°C. Slip into a canoe or kayak to absorb the natural rhythm of the waterways threading through Bavaria's lush Altmühltal Nature Park. Or drift across Lake Constance to Switzerland and Austria with the Alps on the horizon. The season runs from around April to October and a one-/two-person canoe or kayak will set you back around €20-30 per day. Stiff breezes and big waves draw sailors, surfers, windsurfers and kite surfers north. Sylt on the North Sea and Rügen on the Baltic have some of the top conditions and schools in the country for water-based activities.

If you'd rather let someone else do the hard work, put your feet up and watch the great outdoors drift past on a riverboat cruise along some of Germany's grandest rivers (from Easter to October).

High on the list is the Romantic Rhine (p238), where boats drift past vine-covered hills, cliffs crowned with robber-knight castles and picturesque villages. Or combine wine-tasting with a mini-cruise along the Moselle between Koblenz and Trier, each bend in the river revealing vine-draped loveliness.

In Berlin you can mix sightseeing with a meander along the Spree, in Hamburg the Elbe, in Passau the Danube, and in Stuttgart the Neckar. For a taste of history, hop aboard a paddle-wheel steam boat in Dresden (p181).

Winter Sports

Modern lifts, primed ski slopes from 'Sesame Street' to 'Death Wish', cross-country trails through untouched nature, cosy mountain huts, steaming mulled wine, hearty dinners by crackling fires: these are all hallmarks of a German skiing holiday.

The Bavarian Alps, only an hour's drive south of Munich, offer the best downhill slopes and most reliable snow conditions. The most famous resort is Garmisch-Partenkirchen, which regularly hosts international competitions and is but a snowball's toss from the Zugspitze, Germany's highest mountain. It has 60km of slopes, mostly geared towards intermediates.

Picture-book pretty Oberstdorf in the Allgäu Alps has 125km of slopes. It's good for boarders with snow parks and a half-pipe to play on, 75km for cross-country skiers to glide along and 55km of skating tracks. For low-key skiing and stunning scenery there is Berchtesgaden, presided over by the jagged Karwendel range.

Can't or won't ski? All resorts offer snowy fun from tobogganing to ice-skating, snow-shoeing and winter walking.

Berlin (p35)

The Germans

There's much fascination with the German state of mind. The nation and its people have seen two 20th-century wars, carry the memory of the Jewish Holocaust, were on the chilling edge of Cold War division, and now live in a juggernaut-like economy that draws half of Europe in its wake and is the world's third-highest global exporter.

When a 2017 BBC Worldwide poll found that Germany was considered the most positively viewed nation in the world, it surprised many people, most of all the Germans themselves – having long been called arrogant, aggressive and humourless, they were hardly used to such positive feedback. But the poll shows that times are a-changing, proving that modern leadership, a belief in the power of diplomacy and, let's not forget, a pretty good national soccer team can ultimately make a difference.

The National Psyche

It pays to ignore the stereotypes, jingoism and headlines describing Germany in military terms and instead see the country through its regional nuances. Germany was very slow to become a nation, so look closely to notice the many different local cultures within the one set of borders. You will also find that it's one of Europe's most multi-cultural countries, with Turkish, Greek, Italian, Russian and Balkan influences.

Germans like to pack what they mean into the words they use, and get straight to the point rather than hint or suggest; facing each other squarely in conversation, firm handshakes, and a hug or a kiss on the cheek among friends are par for the course.

Smoking

Germany was one of the last countries in Europe to legislate against smoking and most visitors will notice almost immediately how much more second-hand cigarette smoke is in the air. Almost 29% of German men and 20% of women smoke. Smoking bans are different in each state.

Many Germans are very much fans of their own folk culture. Even a young Bavarian from, say, the finance department of a large company, might don the Dirndl (traditional Bavarian skirt and blouse) around Oktoberfest time and swill like a hearty, rollicking peasant. On Monday she'll be back at the desk, soberly crunching numbers.

The Former East

Today around 15 million people live in former East Germany, where until 1989 travel was restricted, the state was almighty and life was secure (but also strongly regulated) from the cradle to the grave. Not surprisingly many former East Germans, who lived well in the former socialist state, had a difficult time coming to terms with a more competitive, unified Germany.

Many 'easterners' still maintain that the GDR had its good qualities, and some elderly former East German citizens say they were happier or lived better at that time. More than a quarter-century after reunification, the eastern states continue to lose brains and skills to the west.

Green Germany

Germans are the original Greens. While they can't claim to have invented environmentalism, they were there at its political birth and coined the word to describe the movement.The Greens' concern for the health of the planet and strong opposition to nuclear power strikes a chord with the local populace; Germans are vigilant recyclers, often prefer to ride bicycles than drive, and carry their groceries in reusable cloth shopping bags or wicker baskets. These practices are simply second nature in Germany.

Football

Football ignites the passion of Germans everywhere and has contributed much to building the confidence of the nation. The national team has won the World Cup four times – in 1954, 1974, 1990 and again in 2014. Germany has also hosted the World Cup twice, in 1974 and 2006. Domestically, Germany's Bundesliga has fallen behind other European leagues such as England's Premier League but still throws up some exciting duels. On the European stage, Germany's most successful domestic club is the FC Bayern Munich, which has been Deutscher Meister (national champion) 25 times and won the UEFA Champions League five times, the last time in 2012/13.

Dresdner Stollen (p287)

German Cuisine

Germany might not have the culinary kudos of some of its neighbours, but its robust, fresh flavours have made it a rising star in Europe's kitchen. You'll never forget your first forkful of black forest gateau, the crisp Rieslings sipped in Rhineland taverns, or the roast pork served with foamy Weizen (wheat beer) at a Bavarian beer fest. Bring an appetite, a taste for adventure and get stuck in.

The State of German Cuisine

As in Britain, Germany has redeemed itself gastronomically in the past decade. Of course, if you crave traditional comfort food, you'll certainly find plenty of places to indulge in pork, potatoes and cabbage. These days though, 'typical' local fare is lighter, healthier, creative and more likely to come from organic eateries, ethnic restaurants and gourmet kitchens. In fact in 2015 Germany's Michelin skies twinkled brighter than ever before with 233 one-star, 38 two-star and 11 three-star restaurants.

Top chefs are putting creative spins on tried-and-trusted specialties in a wave that's referred to as the *Neue Deutsche Küche* (New German Cuisine). Many have jumped on the locavore bandwagon, letting the trifecta of 'seasonal-regional-organic' ingredients steer their menus. Many travel to the countryside to source free-range meats, wild-caught fish, farm-fresh fruit and vegetables, handmade cheeses and other delectables, preferably sustainably grown. Menus increasingly champion traditional (and long underrated) ingredients such as root vegetables, old-fashioned grains and game and other meat products like goat liver or cheeks.

Price Ranges

For one main course (including 19% tax):

€ Less than €12

€€ €12 to €22

€€€ More than €22

Traditional Staples

Bread

As German expats living around the world will tell you: the food they miss the most from their homeland is the bread. Indeed, German bread is a world-beater. Its 300 varieties are tasty and textured, often mixing wheat and rye flour.

Schwarzbrot (or 'black' rye bread) is actually brown, but a much darker shade than the slightly sour *Bauernbrot* – divine with a slab of butter. Pumpernickel bread is steam-cooked instead of baked, making it extra moist, and actually is black. *Vollkorn* means wholemeal, and bread coated in sunflower seeds is *Sonnenblumenbrot*. If you insist on *Weissbrot* (white bread), the Germans have that, too.

Fresh bread rolls (*Brötchen* in the north, *Semmel* in Bavaria, *Wecken* in the rest of southern Germany) can be covered in *Mohnbrötchen* (poppy seeds), cooked with *Rosinenbrötchen* (sweet raisins), *Salzstangel* (sprinkled with salt) or treated in dozens of other, different ways. *Brezeln* are traditional pretzels covered in rock salt.

Potatoes

Chipped, boiled, baked, mashed, fried: Germans love their potatoes. The *Kartoffel* is not only Vegetable *Nummer Eins* in any meat-and-three veg dish, it can also be incorporated into any course of a meal, from *Kartoffelsuppe* (potato soup) as a starter, to *Kartoffelsalat* (potato salad) and *Reibekuchen* (potato pancakes).

In between, you can try *Himmel und Erde* (Heaven and Earth), a dish of mashed potatoes and stewed apples served with black pudding; or potato-based *Klösse* (dumplings). *Pellkartoffeln* or *Ofenkartoffeln* are jacket potatoes, usually topped with a dollop of *Quark* (a yoghurtlike curd cheese).

Cabbage

Sauerkraut is a quintessential German side dish that many outside the country find impossible to fathom. Before the 2006 FIFA World Cup, one football magazine suggested: 'It's pickled cabbage; don't try to make it sound interesting.' Okay, we won't. It's shredded cabbage, doused in white-wine vinegar and slowly simmered. But if you haven't at least tried *Rotkohl* (the red-cabbage version), you don't know what you're missing. Braising the cabbage with sliced apples and wine turns it into *Bayrischkraut* or *Weinkraut*.

Sausage

In the Middle Ages German peasants found a way to package and disguise animals' less-appetising bits – creating the wurst. Today it's a noble and highly respected element of German cuisine, with strict rules determining the authenticity of wurst varieties. In some cases, as with the finger-sized Nuremberg sausage, regulations even ensure offal no longer enters the equation.

Dining Tips

Restaurants are often formal places with full menus, crisp white linen and high prices. Some restaurants are open for lunch and dinner only but more casual places tend to be open all day. Same goes for cafes, which usually serve both coffee and alcohol, as well as light meals, although ordering food is not obligatory. Many cafes and restaurants offer inexpensive weekday 'business lunches' that usually include a starter, main course and drink for under €10.

English menus are not a given, even in big cities, though the wait staff will almost invariably be able to translate for you. The more rural and remote you travel, the less likely it is that the restaurant will have an English menu, or multilingual staff for that matter. It helps to learn a smattering of German.

Handy speed-feed shops, called *Imbiss*, serve all sorts of savoury fodder, from sausage-in-a-bun to doner kebab and pizza. Many bakeries serve sandwiches alongside pastries.

While there are more than 1500 sausage species, all are commonly served with bread and a *süss* (sweet) or *scharf* (spicy) *Senf* (mustard).

Bratwurst, served countrywide, is made from minced pork, veal and spices, and is cooked in different ways (boiled in beer, baked with apples and cabbage, stewed in a casserole or simply grilled or barbecued).

The availability of other sausages differs regionally. A *Thüringer* is long and spiced, while a *Wiener* is what hot-dog fiends call a frankfurter. Saxony is all about the *Bregenwurst* (brain sausage), Bavaria sells the white, veal-and-pork-based *Weisswurst*, and Berliners swear by their *Currywurst* (slices of sausage topped with curry powder and ketchup).

Seasonal Specialities

While you shall be forgiven for laughing at the unmistakably phallic shape of the chlorophyll-deprived *weisser Spargel* (white asparagus), between late April and late June Germans go nuts for the erotic stalks, which are best enjoyed steamed alongside ham, hollandaise sauce or butter, and boiled potatoes. The stalks also show up as asparagus soup, in quiches and salads and even as ice cream.

Spargelzeit (asparagus season) is a highlight of the culinary calendar, which actually kicks off a bit earlier with *Bärlauch* (wild garlic), showing up in salads and as pesto in early spring. Fresh fruit, especially all sorts of berries (strawberries, blueberries, raspberries, gooseberries), red currants and cherries brighten up the market stalls in summer.

In late summer and early autumn, hand-picked mushrooms such as *Steinpilze* (porcini) and earthy *Pfifferlinge* (chanterelles) show up on menus everywhere. A typical winter meal is cooked *Grünkohl* (kale) with smoked sausage, which is often served at Christmas markets. *Gans* (stuffed goose) is a Martinmas tradition (11 November) and also popular at Christmas time.

Fast-Food Faves

International fast-food chains are ubiquitous, of course, but there's plenty of home-grown fast food as well. In fact, some of your best German food experiences are likely to be the snack-on-the-hoof kind. Street food is a tasty way to get versed in wurst and chomp your way around the globe, often with change from a €5 note. In the bigger cities, stalls sizzle up Greek, Italian, Mexican, Middle Eastern and Chinese bites.

The *Imbiss* fast-food stall is a ubiquitous phenomenon, allowing you to eat on the run. Germany's Turkish population invented the modern *Döner Kebab* (doner kebab), adding salad and garlic-yoghurt sauce to spit-roasted lamb, veal or chicken in pita bread. Most kebab joints also do veggie versions. In the briny north, snack on fish (usually herring) sandwiches.

Vegetarians & Vegans

Germany was slow in coming, but is now embracing meat-free fare with the fervour of a religious convert. Health-conscious cafes and restaurants have been sprouting faster than alfafa and serve up inspired menus that leave the classic veggie or tofu burger in the dust. With dishes like sweet-potato saltimbocca, tandoori seitan, pearl-barley strudel with chanterelles, or parmesan dumplings, chefs strive to push the creative envelope.

Even veganism has made significant inroads: Germany's first all-vegan supermarket opened in Berlin in 2011, followed by the city's first vegan gourmet restaurant the same year. Even many nonvegetarian restaurants now offer more than the token vegetable lasagne. For a comprehensive list of vegan and vegetarian restaurants in Germany, see www.happycow.net/europe/germany.

Sweet Temptations

Lebkuchen Soft gingerbread made with nuts, fruit peel, honey and spices; popular at Christmas

Black forest gateau A multilayered chocolate sponge, cream and kirsch confection, topped with morello cherries and chocolate shavings

Aachener Printen Aachen's crunchy spiced cookie, similar to gingerbread

Lübecker Marzipan A creamy blend of almonds and sugar – from Lübeck

Stollen Christmas-time spiced cake Loaded with sultanas, marzipan and candied peel; the best is from Dresden

Kaffee und Kuchen

Anyone who has spent any length of time in Germany knows the reverence bestowed on the 3pm ritual of *Kaffee und Kuchen* (coffee and cake). More than just a chance to devour delectable cakes and tortes, Germans see it as a social event. You'll find *Cafe-Konditoreien* (cafe-cake shops) pretty much everywhere – in castles, in the middle of the forest, even on top of mountains. Track down the best by asking sweet-toothed locals where the cake is *hausgebacken* (home-baked).

While coffee in Germany is not as strong as that served in France or Italy, you can expect a decent cup. All the usual varieties are on offer, including cappuccinos and lattes, although you still frequently see French-style bowls of *Milchkaffee* (milky coffee). Order a *Kanne* (pot) or *Tasse* (cup) of *Kaffee* (coffee) and what you will get is filter coffee, usually with a portion of *Kaffeesahne* (coffee cream).

Cycling through vineyards

NNATTALLI/SHUTTERSTOCK ©

Germany's Beer & Wine

Few things are as deeply ingrained in the German psyche as the love of beer. 'Hopfen und Malz – Gott erhalt's!' (Hops and malt are in God's hands) goes the saying, which is fitting given the almost religious intensity with which beer is brewed, consumed and celebrated – not least at Oktoberfest. Brewing here goes back to Germanic tribes, and later to monks, so it follows a hallowed tradition.

Beer

The 'secret' of the country's golden nectar dates back to the *Reinheitsgebot* (purity law), demanding breweries use just four ingredients – malt, yeast, hops and water. Passed in Bavaria in 1516, the *Reinheitsgebot* stopped being a legal requirement in 1987, when the EU struck it down as uncompetitive. However, many German brewers still conform to it anyway, seeing it as a good marketing tool against mass-market, chemical-happy competitors. Nevertheless, the craft-beer movement, which does not adhere to the Reinheitsgebot, has been making inroads in Germany in recent years, most notably in Berlin and Hamburg.

Beer Varieties

Despite giving themselves just four ingredients to play with, German brewers turn out 5000 distinctively different beers. They achieve this via subtle variations in the basic production process. At the simplest level, a brewer can choose a particular yeast for top or bottom fermenting (the terms indicating where the yeast lives while working – at the top or bottom of the brewing vessel).

The most popular form of brewing is bottom fermentation, which accounts for about 85% of German beers, notably the *Pils* (pilsner), most Bock beers and the *Helles* (pale lager) type found in Bavaria. Top fermentation is used for the *Weizenbier/Weissbier* (wheat/white beer) popular in Berlin and Bavaria, Cologne's Kölsch and the very few stouts brewed in the country. Many beers are regional, meaning that, for example, a Saxon Rechenberger cannot be found in Düsseldorf, where the locally brewed *Altbier* is the taste of choice.

Pils (pilsner) This bottom-fermented full beer, with pronounced hop flavour and creamy head, has an alcohol content of around 4.8%.

Weizenbier/Weissbier (wheat beer) Predominant in the south, especially in Bavaria, this has 5.4% alcohol content. A *Hefeweizen* has a stronger shot of yeast, whereas *Kristallweizen* is clearer with more fizz. These beers are fruity and spicy, often recalling bananas and cloves. Decline offers of lemon as it ruins the head and – beer purists say – the flavour.

Dunkles (dark lager) Brewed throughout Germany, but especially in Bavaria. With a light use of hops, it's full-bodied with strong malty aromas.

★ Beer Gardens

Chinesischer Turm beer garden

Helles (pale lager) Helles (pale or light) refers to the colour, not the alcohol content, which is still 4.6% to 5%. Brewing strongholds are Bavaria, Baden-Württemberg and the Ruhr region. It has strong malt aromas and is slightly sweet.

Altbier A dark, full beer with malted barley from the Düsseldorf area.

Berliner Weisse Berlin's top-fermented beer, which comes *rot* (red) or *grün* (green), with a *Schuss* (dash) of raspberry or woodruff syrup respectively. A cool, fruity summer choice.

Bockbier Strong beers with 7% alcohol. There's a *Bock* for every occasion, such as *Maibock* (for May/spring) and *Weihnachtsbock* (for Christmas). *Eisbock* is dark and aromatic.

Kölsch By law, this top-fermented beer can only be brewed in or around Cologne. It's alcohol content is about 4.8%, it has a solid hop flavour and pale colour, and is served in small glasses (0.2L) called *Stangen* ('sticks').

Schwarzbier (black beer) Slightly stronger, this dark, full beer has an alcohol content of 4.8% to 5%. It's fermented using roasted malt.

Where to Drink

Up and down this hop-crazy country you will find buzzing microbreweries and brewpubs, cavernous beer halls and chestnut-shaded beer gardens that invite you to linger, quaff a cold one and raise a toast – *Prost!*

Munich offers a taste of Oktoberfest year-round in historic beer halls, where you can hoist a mass litre of Weizen and sway to oompah bands, and leafy beer gardens for imbibing and chomping on warm pretzels *(Brez'n)* and *Weisswurst* (herb-veal-pork sausage). This festive spirit spills into other Bavarian cities, such as Regensburg and Bamberg, and into villages where monks brew potent dark beers as they have for eons. Breweries offering a peek behind the scenes include Beck's in Bremen.

Wine

For decades the name of German wine was sullied by the cloyingly sweet taste of Liebfraumilch and the naff image of Blue Nun. What a difference a decade can make. Thanks to rebranding campaigns, a new generation of wine growers and an overall rise in quality, German wine is staging a comeback in the 21st century. This triumph was marked in 2014, when 63 medals were awarded to German wines, including Horst Sauer, which received two Gold Outstandings for Escherndorfer Lump Riesling Trockenbeerenauslese and Escherndorfer Lump Silvaner.

Even discerning wine critics have been pouring praise on German winemakers of late. According to Master of Wine Tim Atkin (www.timatkin.com), 'Germany makes the best Rieslings of all', and, waxing lyrical on the country's Pinot Noirs, he muses, 'if only the Germans didn't keep most of them to themselves'.

For a comprehensive rundown of all German wine-growing regions, grape varieties, news of the hottest winemakers, and information on tours or courses, visit www.winesofgermany.co.uk and www.german wines.de.

Grape Varieties

Having produced wines since Roman times, Germany now has more than 1000 sq km of vineyards, mostly on the Rhine and Moselle riverbanks. Despite the common association with Riesling grapes (particularly in its best wine regions) the less acidic Müller-Thurgau (Rivaner) grape is more widespread.

What Germans call *Grauburgunder* is known to the rest of the world as Pinot gris or Pinot grigio. German reds are light and lesser known. *Spätburgunder* (Pinot Noir), is the best of the bunch and goes into some velvety, full-bodied reds with an occasional almond taste.

Wine Regions

There are 13 official wine-growing areas, the best being the Mosel-Saar-Ruwer region. It boasts some of the world's steepest vineyards, where the predominantly Riesling grapes are still hand-picked. Slate soil on the hillsides gives the wines a flinty taste. Chalkier riverside soils are planted with the Elbling grape, an ancient Roman variety.

East of the Moselle, the Nahe region produces fragrant, fruity and full-bodied wines using Müller-Thurgau and Silvaner grapes, as well as Riesling.

Riesling grapes are also the mainstay in Rheingau and Mittelrhein (Middle Rhine), two other highly respected wine-growing pockets. Rheinhessen, south of Rheingau, is responsible for Liebfraumilch, but also some top Rieslings.

Other wine regions include the Pfalz (Rheinland-Palatinate), Hessische Bergstrasse (Hesse), Baden (Baden-Württemberg), Würzburg (Bavaria) and Elbtal (Saxony).

The Württemberg region around Stuttgart produces some of the country's best reds, while Saxony-Anhalt's Saale-Unstrut region is home to Rotkäppchen (Little Red Riding Hood) sparkling wine, a former GDR brand that's been a big hit in reunited Germany.

Better than Glühwein

Served in winter and designed to inure you to the sudden drop in temperatures, hot spiced *Glühwein* is a common commodity at Germany's popular Christmas markets. However, a far more spectacular and intoxicating mulled wine is *Feuerzangenbowle* (literally 'fire-tongs-punch'), where a flaming rum-soaked sugar cube falls into the spiced red wine, producing a delicious, heady drink. It's become a cult tipple, thanks to a movie of the same name.

Survival Guide

Directory A–Z

Accessible Travel

Download Lonely Planet's free Accessible Travel guides from http://lptravel.to/AccessibleTravel.

○ Germany is fairly progressive when it comes to barrier-free travel. Access ramps and/or lifts are available in many public buildings, including train stations, museums, concert halls and cinemas. In historical towns, though, cobblestone streets make getting around difficult.

○ Trains, trams, underground trains and buses are increasingly accessible. Some stations also have grooved platform borders to assist blind passengers in navigating. Seeing-eye dogs are allowed on all forms of public transport. For the hearing impaired, upcoming station names are often displayed electronically on public transport.

○ Newer hotels have lifts and rooms with extra-wide doors and spacious bathrooms.

○ Some car rental agencies offer hand-controlled vehicles and vans with wheelchair lifts at no charge, but you must reserve them well in advance. In parking lots and garages, look for designated spots marked with a wheelchair symbol.

○ Many local and regional tourist offices have special brochures (usually in German) for people with disabilities.

Accommodation

Except in high season, around holidays and during major trade shows it's generally not necessary to book accommodation in advance.

Hotels Range from mum-and-dad joints to restored castles and international chains.

Hostels Both indie hostels and those belonging to Hostelling International are plentiful

Ferienwohnungen Furnished flats and holiday homes, particularly prevalent in rural areas. Inexpensive option for families and groups.

Gasthäuser/Gasthöfe Country inns, often in lovely locations, offer cultural immersion and a restaurant.

Pensionen The German version of B&Bs is prevalent in rural areas and offers good value.

Costs

Accommodation costs vary wildly between regions, and between cities and rural areas. What gets

you a romantic suite in a countryside inn in the Bavarian Forest may only be worth a two-star room in Munich. City hotels geared to the suit brigade often lure leisure travellers with lower rates on weekends. Seasonal variations are common in holiday regions, less so in the cities.

Reservations

Most tourist offices and properties now have an online booking function with a best-price guarantee. If you've arrived in town and don't have reservations or online access, swing by the tourist office, where staff can assist you in finding last-minute lodgings. After hours, vacancies with contact details and addresses may be posted in the window or in a display case.

Hotels

You'll find a hotel to suit every mood, moment and budget in Germany, including small family-run

Which Floor?

In Germany, as elsewhere in Europe, 'ground floor' refers to the floor at street level. The 1st floor (what would be called the 2nd floor in the US) is the floor above that. Lonely Planet follows German usage.

places; good old-fashioned *Gasthöfe* (inns) in the countryside, full of history and creaking charm; five-star spa hotels; and boutique city sleeps geared towards lifestyle-savvy travellers.

Cheaper rooms may have shared facilities (*WC und Dusche auf der Etage*). Increasingly, city hotels are not including breakfast in their room rates, so always check for the price of *Früh-stück* first.

Chain Hotels

Hotel chains stretch from cookie-cutter anonymity to central five-star properties with historical flair and top-notch facilities (air-con, wi-fi, 24-hour check-in etc.). Most offer last-minute and/or weekend deals. Rivalling the big international chains are home-grown contenders such as **Dorint** (www.dorint.com), the luxury **Kempinski** (www.kempiski.com) group, city hotel chain **Leonardo** (www.leonardo-hotels.com) and **Steigenberger** (www.

steigenberger.com), offering five-star luxury often in historic buildings.

Pensions, Inns & Private Rooms

The German equivalent of B&Bs, *Pensionen* are small and informal and an excellent low-cost alternative to hotels. *Gasthöfe/Gasthäuser* (inns) are similar, but usually have restaurants serving regional and German food to a local clientele. *Privatzimmer*

are guest rooms in private homes, though privacy seekers may find these places a bit too intimate.

Amenities, room size and decor vary. The cheapest rooms may have shared facilities. What they lack in amenities, though, they often make up for in charm and authenticity, with friendly hosts who take a personal interest in ensuring that you enjoy your stay.

Climate

Berlin

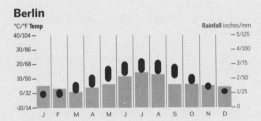

Frankfurt Am Main

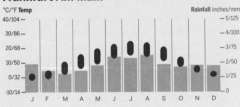

Munich

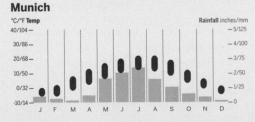

Some tourist offices keep lists of available rooms; you can also look around for *'Zimmer Frei'* (rooms available) signs in house or shop windows. They're usually quite cheap, with per-person rates generally topping out at €30, including breakfast.

Agritourism

Family-friendly farm holidays are a terrific (and inexpensive) back-to-nature choice. Kids get to run free and interact with barnyard animals. Accommodation ranges from bare-bones digs with shared facilities to fully furnished holiday apartments. Minimum stays are common, as is an *Endreinigungsgebühr* (final cleaning fee). Properties swing from organic, dairy and equestrian farms to wine estates. Note that places advertising *Landurlaub* (country holiday) no longer actively work their farms.

Customs Regulations

Goods brought in and out of countries within the EU incur no additional taxes, provided duty has been paid somewhere within the EU and the goods are for personal use. Duty-free shopping is only available if you're leaving the EU.

Duty-free allowances (for anyone over 17) arriving from non-EU countries:

My Home is My Castle

If you're the romantic type, consider a fairy-tale getaway in a castle, palace or country manor dripping with character and history. They're typically in the countryside, strategically perched atop a crag, perhaps overlooking a river or rolling hills. And it doesn't take a king's ransom to stay in one; even wallet-watchers can fancy themselves knight or damsel when staying in a castle converted into a youth hostel. More typically, though, properties are luxury affairs, blending mod cons with baronial ambience and old-fashioned trappings such as four-poster beds, antique armoires and heavy drapes. Sometimes your hosts are even descendants of the original castle builders – often some local baron, count or prince.

- 200 cigarettes or 100 cigarillos or 50 cigars or 250g of loose tobacco or a proportional combination of these goods.

- 1L of strong liquor or 2L of less than 22% alcohol by volume, plus 4L of wine, plus 16L of beer.

- other goods up to the value of €300 if arriving by land, or €430 if arriving by sea or air (€175 for under 15 years).

Discount Cards

Concession discounts are widely available for seniors, children and students. In some cases, you may be asked to show ID. Tourist offices in many cities sell Welcome Cards, which entitle visitors to discounts on museums, sights and tours, plus unlimited trips on local public transport. They can be good value if you plan on taking advantage of most of the benefits and don't qualify for any of the standard discounts.

If you qualify for one of the following discount cards, you can reap additional benefits on travel, shopping, attractions or entertainment:

Camping Card International (www.campingcardinternational.com) Up to 25% savings in camping fees; cardholders have third-party liability insurance while on the campground.

International Student Identity Card (www.isic.org) The most popular discount card, but only for full-time students. Available at ISIC points (see website) and online. Cost vary by country and range from US$15 to US$30.

International Youth Travel Card (www.isic.org) Similar to ISIC but for non students under 30 years of age. Available at ISIC points.

Electricity

Type C
220V/50Hz

Type F
230V/50Hz

Food

For details on German cuisine and drink, see p248.

Health

Health care in Germany is of a high standard; your main risks are likely to be sunburn, foot blisters, insect bites, mild stomach problems and hangovers. Tap water is drinkable.

Before You Go

o A signed and dated letter from your doctor describing your medical conditions and medications (including generic names) is a good idea. It is illegal to import codeine-based medication without a doctor's certificate.

o No vaccinations are required for travel to Germany, but the World Health Organization (WHO) recommends that all travellers be covered for diphtheria, tetanus, measles, mumps, rubella and polio.

Availability and Cost of Healthcare

o Excellent health care is widely available from *Rettungsstellen* (emergency rooms) at *Krankenhäuser* (hospitals) and at *Ärzte* (doctors' offices).

o For minor illnesses or injuries (headache, bruises, diarrhoea), trained staff in pharmacies can provide advice, sell prescription-free medications and make doctors' referrals if further help is needed.

o Condoms are widely available in drugstores, pharmacies and supermarkets. Birth control pills require a doctor's prescription.

Pharmacies

o German *Drogerien* (chemists, drugstores) do not sell any kind of medication, not even aspirin. Even *rezeptfrei* (over-the-counter) medications for minor health concerns, such as a cold or upset stomach, are only available at an *Apotheke* (pharmacy).

o For more serious conditions, you will need to produce a *Rezept* (prescription) from a licensed physician. If you take regular medication, be sure to bring a supply for your entire trip, as the same brand may not be available in Germany.

o The names and addresses of pharmacies open after hours (these rotate) are posted in every pharmacy window, or call 01141.

Insurance

o Comprehensive travel insurance to cover theft, loss and medical problems is highly recommended.

o Some policies specifically exclude dangerous activities, such as motorcycling, scuba diving and even trekking; read the fine print.

- Check that the policy covers ambulance or an emergency flight home.

- Before you leave, find out if your insurance plan makes payments directly to providers or reimburses you for health expenditures.

- Paying for your airline ticket with a credit card sometimes provides limited travel accident insurance – ask your credit card company what it is prepared to cover.

- If you have to make a claim, be sure to keep all necessary documents and bills.

- Consider coverage for luggage theft or loss. If you already have a homeowner's or renter's policy, check what it will cover and only get supplemental insurance to protect against the rest.

- If you have prepaid a large portion of your holiday, trip cancellation insurance is worthwhile.

- Worldwide travel insurance is available at www.lonelyplanet.com/travel -insurance. You can buy, extend and claim online any time – even if you're already on the road.

Internet Access

- Some cafes and bars have wi-fi hot spots that let customers hook up for free, although you usually need to ask for a password.

European Health Insurance Card

Citizens of the EU, Switzerland, Iceland, Norway and Liechtenstein receive free or reduced-cost, state-provided (not private) health-care coverage with the European Health Insurance Card (EHIC) for medical treatment that becomes necessary while in Germany. It does not cover emergency repatriation home. Each family member needs a separate card. UK residents can find information on how to obtain the card at www.ehic.org.uk.

You will need to pay directly and fill in a treatment form; keep the form to claim any refunds. In general you can claim back around 70% of the standard treatment cost.

Citizens of other countries need to check whether there is a reciprocal arrangement for free medical care between their country and Germany.

- Almost without exception, free wi-fi access (W-LAN in Germany; pronounced vay-lan) is available at hotels, hostels and guesthouses.

- In some accommodation wi-fi may be limited to some areas; if you need in-room access, be sure to specify at the time of booking.

- Wi-fi is available for a fee on select ICE train routes, including Berlin to Cologne and Frankfurt to Munich and in DB Lounges (free in 1st class). Around 135 stations, including those in Berlin, Munich, Hamburg and Frankfurt, offer 30 minutes of free wi-fi with registration via DeutscheTelekom.

- Locate wi-fi hot spots at www.hotspot-locations.com.

- In Berlin, free public wi-fi is available at 650 access points throughout the city. See www.berlin.de/stadt plan/w-lan-hotspots for a map of locations.

Legal Matters

- The permissible blood alcohol content is 0.05%; drivers caught exceeding this are subject to stiff fines, a confiscated licence and even jail time. Drinking in public is not illegal, but be discreet.

- Cannabis *consumption* is not illegal, but the possession, acquisition, sale and cultivation of it is considered a criminal offence. There is usually no prosecution for possessing 'small quantities', although the definition of 'small' varies by state, ranging from 6 to 20 grams. Dealers face far stiffer penalties, as do people caught with any other recreational drugs.

- If arrested, you have the right to make a phone call

and are presumed innocent until proven guilty, although you may be held in custody until trial. If you don't know a lawyer, contact your embassy.

LGBTIQ+ Travellers

Germany is a magnet for *schwule* (gay) and *lesbische* (lesbian) travellers, with the rainbow flag flying especially proudly in Berlin and Cologne. There are also sizeable communities in Hamburg, Frankfurt and Munich.

● Legal stuff: Homosexuality has been legal since the late 1960s. Same-sex marriage is legal.

● Attitudes tend to be more conservative in the countryside, among older

people and in the eastern states.

● As elsewhere, Germany's lesbian scene is less public than its male counterpart and is centred mainly on women's cafes and bars.

● Gay pride marches are held throughout Germany in springtime; the largest, in Cologne and Berlin, draw hundreds of thousands of rainbow revellers and friends.

Publications

Blu (www.blu.fm) Free print and online magazine with searchable, up-to-the-minute location and event listings.

L-Mag (www.l-mag.de) Bimonthly magazine for lesbians. Available at newsagents.

Spartacus International Gay Guide (https://spartacus.gayguide.travel) Annual English-language travel guide

for men. Available online, in bookstores and as an app.

Websites & Apps

German National Tourist Office (www.germany.travel/en/ms/lgbt/home/home.html) Dedicated LGBTIQ+ pages.

Spartacus World (www.spartacusworld.com) Hip hotel, style and event guide.

Patroc Gay Travel Guide (www.patroc.com) Travel information to 25 European destinations.

Maps

Most tourist offices distribute free (but often very basic) maps. For driving around Germany, however, you'll need a detailed road map or atlas such as those published by Falk, RV Verlag or the General German Automobile Club (ADAC; p308). Look for them at bookshops, tourist offices, newsagents and petrol stations. Find downloadable maps and driving directions at www.google.de/maps, www.stadtplandienst.de or www.viamichelin.de.

Money

The unit of currency in Germany is the euro (€). Euros come in seven notes (€5, €10, €20, €50, €100, €200 and €500) and eight coins (€0.01, €0.02, €0.05, €0.10, €0.20, €0.50, €1 and €2).

Smoking Regulations

● Germany was one of the last countries in Europe to legislate against smoking. However, there is no nationwide law, with regulations left to each of the 16 states, creating a rather confusing set of anti smoking laws.

● Generally, smoking is a no-no in schools, hospitals, airports, train stations and other public facilities. But when it comes to bars, pubs, cafes and restaurants, every state does it just a little differently.

● Since 2011, Bavaria bans smoking practically everywhere, even in Oktoberfest tents. However, in most other states, lighting up is allowed in designated smoking rooms in restaurants and clubs.

● One-room establishments smaller than 75 sq m may allow smoking, provided they serve no food and only admit patrons over 18. The venue must be clearly designated as a *Raucherbar* (smokers' bar).

ATMs & Debit Cards

○ The easiest and quickest way to obtain cash is by using your debit (bank) card at a *Geldautomat* (ATM) linked to international networks such as Cirrus, Plus, Star and Maestro.

○ ATMs are plentiful in towns and cities and usually accessible 24/7.

○ ATM cards often double as debit cards, and many shops, hotels, restaurants and other businesses accept them for payment. Most cards use the 'chip and PIN' system; instead of signing, you enter your PIN. If your card isn't chip-and-PIN enabled, you may be able to sign the receipt, but ask first.

○ Deutsche Bahn ticket vending machines at train stations and local public transport may not accept non-chip-and-PIN cards.

Cash

Cash is king in Germany. Always carry some with you, and plan to pay cash almost everywhere. It's also a good idea to set aside a small amount of euros as an emergency stash.

Credit Cards

○ Credit cards are becoming more widely accepted, but it's best not to assume you'll be able to use one – ask first. Sometimes a minimum purchase amount applies. Even so, a piece of plastic is vital

---

Practicalities

Newspapers Major national newspapers include daily broadsheet *Frankfurter Allgemeine Zeitung* (www.faz.net), the *Süddeutsche Zeitung* (www.sueddeutsche.de) and weekly *Die Zeit* (www.zeit.de).

Magazines Popular news weeklies include *Der Spiegel* (www.spiegel.de) and *Focus* (www.focus.de).

Radio National radio stations include Deutsche Welle (www.dw.com). Regional stations feature a mixed format of news, talk and music.

---

in emergencies and also useful for phone or internet bookings. Visa and Mastercard are more commonly accepted than American Express or Diners Club.

○ Avoid getting cash advances on your credit card via ATMs, as fees are steep and you'll be charged interest immediately (in other words, there's no grace period as with purchases).

○ Report lost or stolen cards to the central number 116 116 or the following:

American Express ☏069-9797 1000

Mastercard ☏0800-819 1040

Visa ☏0800-811 8440

Moneychanging

○ Commercial banks usually charge a stiff fee (€5 to €10) per foreign-currency transaction, no matter the amount, if they offer exchange services at all.

○ *Wechselstuben* (currency exchange offices) at airports, train stations

and in bigger towns usually charge lower fees. Traveller-geared Reisebank (www.reisebank.de) branches are ubiquitous in Germany and are usually found at train stations. They keep longer hours than banks and are usually open on weekends.

○ Exchange facilities in rural areas are rare.

Tipping

Hotels €1 per bag is standard. It's nice to leave a little cash for the room cleaners (€1 or €2 per day).

Restaurants Bills always include *Bedienung* (service charge); most people add 5% or 10% unless service was truly abhorrent.

Bars About 5%, rounded to nearest euro. For drinks brought to your table, tip as for restaurants.

Taxis Tip about 10%, rounded to the nearest euro.

Toilet attendants Loose change.

Opening Hours

The following are typical opening hours; these may vary seasonally and between cities and villages. We've provided those applicable in high season. For specifics, see individual listings.

Banks 9am–4pm Monday to Friday, extended hours usually Tuesday and Thursday, some open Saturday

Bars 6pm–1am or later

Boutiques 11am–7pm Monday–Friday, to 6pm Saturday

Cafes 8am–8pm

Clubs 11pm to early morning

Post offices 9am–6pm Monday to Friday, to 1pm Saturday

Restaurants 11am–11pm (food service often stops at 9pm in rural areas)

Shops 10am–8pm Monday–Saturday

Supermarkets 8am–8pm or later; some 24 hours)

○ Although Germany has strict privacy laws, in practice no one seems to mind being photographed in the context of an overall scene, but if you want a close-up shot, you should ask first.

○ Many museums, palaces and some churches charge a separate 'photography fee' (usually €2 or €3) if you want to take (noncommercial) pictures.

Public Holidays

Germany observes three secular and eight religious public holidays. Banks, shops, post offices and public services close on these days. States with predominantly Catholic populations, such as Bavaria and Baden-Württemberg, also celebrate Epiphany (6 January), Corpus Christi (10 days after Pentecost), Assumption Day (15 August) and All Saints' Day (1 November). Reformation Day (31 October) is only observed in eastern Germany (but not in Berlin).

The following are *gesetzliche Feiertage* (public holidays):

Neujahrstag (New Year's Day) 1 January

Ostern (Easter) March/April; Good Friday, Easter Sunday and Easter Monday

Christi Himmelfahrt (Ascension Day) Forty days after Easter

Maifeiertag/Tag der Arbeit (Labour Day) 1 May

Pfingsten (Whit/Pentecost Sunday & Monday) Fifty days after Easter

Tag der Deutschen Einheit (Day of German Unity) 3 October

Weihnachtstag (Christmas Day) 25 December

Zweiter Weihnachtstag (Boxing Day) 26 December

Photography

Germany is a photographer's dream. A good general reference guide is *Lonely Planet's Guide to Travel Photography*.

○ Germans tend to be deferential around photographers and will make a point of not walking in front of your camera, even if you want them to.

School Holidays

Each state sets its own school holidays but, in general, German children have six weeks off in summer and two weeks each around Christmas, Easter and October. Traffic is worse at the beginning of school holidays in population-rich states such as North Rhine–Westphalia and can become a nightmare if several states let out their schools at the same time.

Germans are big fans of miniholidays around public holidays, which are especially common in spring, when many holidays fall on a Thursday or Monday. On those 'long weekends' you can expect heavy crowds on the roads, in the towns and everywhere else. Lodging is at a premium at these times.

Safe Travel

Germany is a very safe country in which to live and travel, with crime rates that are quite low by international standards. Though theft and other crimes against travellers occur rarely, you should still take all the usual precautions:

o Lock hotel rooms and cars, not leaving valuables unattended.

o Keep an eye out for pickpockets in crowded places; don't take midnight strolls in city parks.

o Many hostels provide lockers, but you need your own padlock.

o Train stations tend to be magnets for people who might harass you or make you feel otherwise uncomfortable, especially at night.

Telephone

German phone numbers consist of an area code, starting with ✆0, and the local number. Area codes are between three and six digits long; local numbers are between three and nine digits. If dialling from a landline within the same city, you don't need to dial the area code. You must dial it if using a mobile.

Calling Germany from abroad Dial your country's international access code, then ✆49 (Germany's country code), then the area code (dropping the initial 0) and the local number.

Calling internationally from Germany Dial ✆00 (the international access code), then the country code, the area code (without the zero if there is one) and the local number.

Important Numbers

Germany country code	✆49
International access code	✆00
Ambulance, fire brigade	✆112
Police	✆110

Mobile Phones

If you have a European or Australian phone, save money by slipping in a German SIM card. These are sold at supermarkets, pharmacies, convenience stores and electronics shops and can be topped up as needed.

o German mobile numbers begin with a four-digit prefix, such as ✆0151, ✆0157, ✆0170 or ✆0178.

o Mobile (cell) phones are called 'Handys' and work on GSM 900/1800. If your home country uses a different standard, you'll need a multiband GSM phone while in Germany.

o Data roaming charges were scrapped in the EU as of 2017, but callers from other countries should

check costs with their provider.

o If you have an unlocked phone that works in Germany, you may be able to save money by buying a prepaid, rechargeable local SIM card for €10 (including calling time).

o The cheapest and least complicated of these are sold at discount supermarkets, such as Aldi, Netto and Lidl. Telecommunications stores (eg Deutsche Telekom, O₂ and Vodafone) also sell SIMs. Top-up cards are widely available in kiosks and supermarkets.

o If you want to purchase an inexpensive unlocked phone, try the electronics chains Media Markt and Saturn. Prices start at €20.

o Calls made to a mobile phone are more expensive than those to a landline, but incoming calls are free

o The use of mobile phones while driving is *verboten* (forbidden), unless you're using a headset.

Time

Clocks in Germany are set to Central European Time (GMT/UTC plus one hour). Daylight saving time kicks in at 2am on the last Sunday in March and ends on the last Sunday in October. Use of the 24-hour clock (eg 6.30pm is 18.30) is the norm. As daylight saving times vary across regions, the following time differences are indicative only.

City	Noon in Berlin
Auckland	11pm
Cape Town	1pm
London	11am
New York	6am
San Francisco	3am
Sydney	9pm
Tokyo	8pm

Toilets

○ German toilets are sit-down affairs. Men are expected to sit down when peeing.

○ Free-standing 24-hour self-cleaning toilet pods have become quite common. The cost is €0.50 and you have 15 minutes. Most are wheelchair-accessible.

○ Toilets in malls, clubs, beer gardens etc often have an attendant who expects a tip of between €0.20 and €0.50.

○ Toilets in airports are usually free, but in main train stations they are often maintained by private companies like McClean, which charge as much as €1.50 for the privilege.

○ Along autobahns, facilities are spaced about 20km to 30km apart.

Tourist Information

○ The German National Tourist Office (www.germany.travel) should be your first port of call for travel in Germany.

○ **Visit Berlin** (☎030-25 00 23 33; www.visitberlin.de; ☺9am-6pm Mon-Fri), the Berlin tourist board, has branches at the airports, the main train station, the Brandenburg Gate, Alexanderplatz, the Central Bus Station (ZOB) and on Kurfürstendamm, plus a call centre for information and bookings.

Visas

Visas are generally not required for tourist stays up to 90 days (or at all for EU nationals); some nationalities need a Schengen Visa .

○ EU nationals only need their passport or national identity card to enter, stay and work in Germany for three months. If you plan to stay longer, you must register with the authorities at the *Bürgeramt* (Citizens' Registration Office) within two weeks of your arrival.

○ Citizens of Australia, Canada, Israel, Japan, New Zealand, Poland, Switzerland and the US only need a valid passport (no visa) if entering Germany as tourists for up to three months within a six-month period. Passports must be valid for another four months beyond the intended departure date. For stays exceeding 90 days, contact your nearest German embassy or consulate, and begin your visa application well in advance.

○ Nationals from other countries need a Schengen Visa, named for the 1995 Schengen Agreement that abolished international border controls between many European countries. Applications for a Schengen Visa must be filed with the embassy or consulate of the country that is your primary destination. It is valid for stays of up to 90 days. Legal residency in any Schengen country makes a visa unnecessary, regardless of your nationality.

○ For full details, see www.auswaertiges-amt.de and check with a German consulate in your country.

Transport

Getting There & Away

Entering the Country

Entering Germany is usually a very straightforward procedure. If you're arriving from any of the 25 other Schengen countries, such as the Netherlands, Poland, Austria or the Czech Republic, you no longer have to show your passport or go through customs in Germany, no matter which nationality you are. If you're coming in from non-Schengen countries, full border procedures apply.

Air

Most travellers arrive in Germany by air, or by rail and road connections from neighbouring countries. Flights and tours can be booked online at lonelyplanet.com/bookings.

Airports & Airlines

Frankfurt Airport is the main gateway for transcontinental flights, although Düsseldorf and Munich also receive their share of overseas air traffic. Until the opening of the new Berlin Brandenburg Airport, scheduled for 2020, flights to Berlin

will arrive at its two smaller international airports, Tegel and Schönefeld. There are also sizeable airports in Hamburg, Cologne/Bonn and Stuttgart, and smaller ones in such cities as Bremen, Dresden, Hanover, Leipzig-Halle, Münster-Osnabrück, Baden-Baden and Nuremberg.

Lufthansa (www.lufthansa.com), Germany's national flagship carrier and a Star Alliance member, operates a vast network of domestic and international flights and has one of the world's best safety records. Practically every other national carrier from around the world serves Germany, along with budget airlines easyJet (www.easyjet.com), Flybe (www.flybe.com), airBaltic (www.airbaltic.com), Ryanair (www.ryanair.com) and Eurowings (www.eurowings.com)

Boat

Germany's main ferry ports are Kiel and Travemünde (near Lübeck) in Schleswig-Holstein, and Rostock and Sassnitz (on Rügen Island) in Mecklenburg–Western Pomerania. All have services to Scandinavia. From Kiel, there are also services to Klaipėda in Lithuania, and from Travemünde you can reach Liepāja and Ventspils in Latvia (saving much time on the roads in eastern Poland). Timetables change from season to season.

Return tickets are often cheaper than two

one-way tickets. Some ferry companies now set fares the way budget airlines do: the earlier you book, the less you pay. Seasonal demand is a crucial factor (school holidays and July and August are especially busy), as is the time of day (an early-evening ferry can cost much more than one at 4am). For overnight ferries, cabin size, location and amenities affect the price. Book well in advance if you're bringing a car.

People under 25 and over 60 may qualify for discounts. To get the best fares, check out the booking service offered by Ferry Savers (www.ferrysavers.com).

Bus

Long-distance coach travel to Germany from such cities as Milan, Vienna, Amsterdam and Copenhagen has become a viable option thanks to a new crop of companies offering good-value connections aboard comfortable buses with snack bars and free wi-fi. Major operators include:

MeinFernbus (☏030-300 137 300; www.meinfernbus.de)

Flixbus (☏030-300 137 300; https://global.flixbus.com)

Departure Tax

Departure tax in Germany costs between €7 and €40 (depending on the distance flown). The tax is usually included in the price of a ticket.

Megabus (☎in the UK 0900 1600 900; www.megabus.com)
Eurolines (☎in the UK 08717-818177; www.eurolines.com).

For routes, times and prices, check www.busliniensuche.de (also in English).

A backpacker-geared hop-on, hop-off service, **Busabout** (☎in the UK 0808 281 1114; www.busabout.com) runs coaches along three interlocking European loops between May and October. Passes are sold online and through travel agents.

Germany is part of the north loop. Within Germany, the service stops in Berlin, Dresden, Munich and Stuttgart.

You can opt for a Stop Pass, offering the best value for short trips, which lets you select three to 15 cities to visit (ticket prices begin at £299), or the Unlimited Pass (£949), giving access to all routes and 46 cities over a six-month period.

Car & Motorcycle

When bringing your own vehicle to Germany, you need a valid driving licence, car registration and proof of third-party insurance. Foreign cars must display a nationality sticker unless they have official European plates. You also need to carry a warning (hazard) triangle and a first-aid kit.

There are no special requirements for crossing the border into Germany by car. Under the Schengen Agreement there are no passport controls if entering the country from the Netherlands, Belgium, Luxembourg, Denmark, Austria, Switzerland, the Czech Republic and Poland.

From the Eurotunnel

Coming from the UK, the fastest way to the Continent is via the **Eurotunnel** (☎in Germany 01805-000 248, in the UK 08443 35 35 35; www.eurotunnel.com). These shuttle trains whisk cars, motorbikes, bicycles and coaches from Folkestone in England through the Channel Tunnel to Coquelles (near Calais, France) in about 35 minutes. From there, you can be in Germany in about three hours. Loading and unloading takes about one hour.

Shuttles run daily round the clock, with up to four departures hourly during peak periods. Fares are calculated per vehicle, including up to nine passengers, and depend on such factors as time of day, season and length of stay. Standard one-way tickets start at £30. The website and travel agents have full details.

Train

Rail services link Germany with virtually every country in Europe. In Germany ticketing is handled by **Deutsche Bahn** (☎0180-699 66 33; www.bahn.de). Long-distance trains connecting major German cities with those in other countries are called Euro-City (EC) trains. Seat reservations are essential during the peak summer season and around major holidays, and are recommended at other times.

Deutsche Bahn work in cooperation with ÖBB (www.oebb.at) to provide a night rail service to major European cities, such as Basel, Zürich, Vienna, Milan, Venice, Zagreb and Budapest. There are three different levels of comfort:

Schlafwagen (sleeping car) Private, air-conditioned compartment for up to three passengers; the deluxe version (*1. Klasse*) has a shower and toilet.
Liegewagen (couchette) Sleeps up to six people; when you book an individual berth, you must share the compartment with others; women may ask for a single-sex couchette at the time of booking but are advised to book early.
Sitzwagen (seat carriage) Roomy reclining seat.

Resources

www.raileurope.com Detailed train information and ticket and train-pass sales from Rail Europe.

www.railteam.eu Journey planner provided by an alliance of seven European railways, including Eurostar, Deutsche Bahn and France's SNCF. No booking function yet.

www.seat61.com Comprehensive trip-planning information, including ferry details from the UK.

Eurostar

Thanks to the Channel Tunnel, travelling by train between the UK and Germany is a fast and enjoyable option. High-speed **Eurostar** (⌁from outside the UK +44 1233 617 575, in the UK 03432 186 186; www.eurostar.com) passenger trains hurtle at least 10 times daily between London and Paris (the journey takes 2¼ hours) or Brussels (1¾ hours). In either city you can change to regular or other high-speed trains to destinations in Germany.

Eurostar fares depend on carriage class, time of day, season and destination. Children, rail-pass holders and those aged between 12 and 25 and over 60 qualify for discounts. For the latest fare information, including promotions and special packages, check the website.

Rail Passes

If you want to cover lots of territory in and around Germany within a specific time, a rail pass is a convenient and good value option. Passes cover unlimited travel during their period of validity on national railways as well as on some private lines, ferries and riverboat services.

There are two types: the Eurail Pass, for people living outside Europe, and the InterRail Pass, for residents of Europe, including residents of Russia and Turkey.

Eurail

Eurail Passes (www.eurail. com) are valid for travel in up to 28 countries and need to be purchased – on the website, through a travel

Climate Change & Travel

Every form of transport that relies on carbon-based fuel generates CO_2, the main cause of human-induced climate change. Modern travel is dependent on aeroplanes, which might use less fuel per kilometre per person than most cars but travel much greater distances. The altitude at which aircraft emit gases (including CO_2) and particles also contributes to their climate change impact. Many websites offer 'carbon calculators' that allow people to estimate the carbon emissions generated by their journey and, for those who wish to do so, to offset the impact of the greenhouse gases emitted with contributions to portfolios of climate-friendly initiatives throughout the world. Lonely Planet offsets the carbon footprint of all staff and author travel.

agent or at www.raileurope. com – before you leave your home country. Various passes are available (prices quoted are for 2nd class):

Global Pass Unlimited travel for 15 or 22 consecutive days, or one, two or three months. There are also versions that give you five days of travel within a 10-day period or 10 or 15 days of travel within a two-month period. The 15-day continuous version costs €480.

Select Pass Five, six, eight or 10 days of travel within two months in up to four bordering countries in 1st or 2nd class; a 2nd-class five-day pass in four countries costs €344.

Regional Pass Gets you around two neighbouring countries on four, five, six, eight or 10 days within two months. The Germany–Austria Pass for five days costs €247 in 2nd class.

Groups of two to five people travelling together save 15% off the regular adult fares. If you're under 26, prices drop 35%, but you must travel in 2nd class.

Children aged between four and 11 get a 50% discount on the adult fare. Children under four travel free.

The website has details, as well as a ticket-purchasing function allowing you to pay in several currencies.

InterRail

InterRail Passes (www. interrail.eu) are valid for unlimited travel in 30 countries. As with the Eurail Pass, you can choose from several schemes.

Global Pass Unlimited travel in 30 countries, available for 15 days (€472), 22 days (€493) or one month (€637) of continuous travel; for five travel days within a 15-day period (€269) or for 10 travel days within a one-month period (€381).

Germany Pass Buys three/four/six/eight days of travel within a one-month period for €192/218/262/297. This pass is not available if you are a resident of Germany.

Prices quoted are for one adult travelling in 2nd

Low Emissions Stickers

To decrease air pollution caused by fine particles, most German cities now have low-emissions environmental zones that may only be entered by cars displaying an *Umweltplakette* (emissions sticker, sometimes also called *Feinstaubplakette*). And yes, this includes foreign vehicles. No stickers are needed for motorcycles.

The easiest way to obtain the sticker is by ordering it online from www.umwelt-plakette.de, a handy website in many languages. The cost is €31.90. You can cut this amount in half if you order from the TÜV (Technical Inspection Authority) at www.tuev-sued.de or www.tuev-nord.de, both of which provide easy instructions in English. Once in Germany, stickers are also available from designated repair centres, car dealers and vehicle-licensing offices. Drivers caught without one will be fined €80.

class. Different prices apply to 1st-class tickets and for travellers under 26 or over 60. Children under four travel for free and do not need a pass. Up to two children under 11 travel free with a child pass if accompanied by at least one person with an adult pass.

Getting Around

Air

Most large and many smaller German cities have their own airports, and numerous carriers operate domestic flights within Germany. Unless you're flying from one end of the country to the other, say Berlin to Munich or Hamburg to Munich, planes are only marginally quicker than trains once you factor in the time it takes to get to and from airports.

Lufthansa (www.lufthansa.com) has the densest route network. The other main airline offering domestic flights is Eurowings. Destination airports are Berlin-Tegel, Cologne-Bonn, Dortmund, Dresden, Düsseldorf, Hamburg, Hanover, Karlsruhe-Baden-Baden, Leipzig-Halle, Nuremberg, Sylt, Stuttgart, Usedom.

Bicycle

Cycling is allowed on all roads and highways but not on the autobahns (motorways). Cyclists must follow the same rules of the road as cars and motorcycles. Helmets are not compulsory (not even for children), but wearing one is common sense. Dedicated bike lanes are common in bigger cities.

Bicycles may be taken on most trains but require a separate ticket (*Fahrradkarte*), costing €9 per trip on long-distance trains (IC, EC and night trains), or €10 on international routes. You need to reserve a space at least one day ahead and leave your bike in the bike compartment, which is usually at the beginning or end of the train. Bicycles are not allowed on high-speed ICE trains.

The fee on local and regional trains (IRE, RB, RE, S-Bahn) is €5.50 per day. There is no charge at all on some local trains. For full details, enquire at a local station or call 01805-99 66 33.

Many regional bus companies have vehicles with special bike racks. Bicycles are also allowed on practically all boat and ferry services.

Boat

Considering that Germany abuts two seas and has a lake- and river-filled interior, don't be surprised to find yourself in a boat at some point. For basic transport, ferry boats are primarily used when travelling to or between the East Frisian Islands in Lower Saxony; the North Frisian Islands in Schleswig-Holstein; Helgoland, which also belongs to Schleswig-Holstein; and the islands of Poel, Rügen and Hiddensee in Mecklenburg–Western Pomerania.

Scheduled boat services operate along sections of the Rhine, the Elbe and the Danube. There are also ferry services in river sections with no or only a few bridges, as well as on major lakes such as the Chiemsee and Lake Starnberg in Bavaria and Lake Constance in Baden-Württemberg.

From around April to October, local operators run scenic river or lake cruises lasting from one hour to a full day.

Bus

Local & Regional

Buses are generally slower, less dependable and more polluting than trains, but in some rural areas they may be your only option for getting around without your own vehicle. This is especially true of the Harz Mountains, sections of the Bavarian Forest and the Alpine foothills. Separate bus companies, each with their own tariffs and schedules, operate in the different regions.

The frequency of services varies from 'rarely' to 'constantly'. Commuter-geared routes offer limited or no service in the evenings and at weekends, so keep this in mind or risk finding yourself stuck in a remote place on a Saturday night. Make it a habit to ask about special fare deals, such as daily or weekly passes or tourist tickets.

In cities, buses generally converge at the Busbahnhof (bus terminal) or Zentraler Omnibus Bahnhof (ZOB; central bus station), which is often near the Hauptbahnhof (central train station).

Long Distance

The route network has grown enormously in recent years, making exploring Germany by coach easy, inexpensive and popular. Buses are modern, clean, comfortable and air-conditioned. Most companies offer snacks and beverages as well as free on-board wi-fi.

Fierce competition has kept prices extremely low. A trip from Berlin to Hamburg costs as little as €8, while the fare from Frankfurt to Munich averages €15.

MeinFernbus, Flixbus, Postbus (www.postbus.de), and Eurolines are the biggest operators, but there are dozens of smaller, regional options as well. A handy site for finding out which operator goes where, when and for how much is www.busliniensuche.de.

From April to October, special tourist-geared service the **Romantic Road Coach** (☏09851-551 387; www.romantic-road.com) runs one coach daily in each direction between Frankfurt and Füssen (for Schloss Neuschwanstein) via Munich; the entire trip takes around 12 hours. There's no charge for breaking the journey and continuing the next day. Note that buses get incredibly crowded in summer. Tickets are available for the entire route or for short segments. Buy them online or from travel agents, **EurAide** (www.euraide.de; Desk 1, Reisezentrum, Hauptbahnhof; ☉10am-7pm

Mon-Fri Mar-Apr & Aug-Dec, 9.30am-8pm May-Jul) in Munich or *Reisezentrum* (travel centre) offices in larger train stations.

Car & Motorcycle

German roads are excellent and motoring around the country can be a lot of fun. The country's pride and joy is its 11,000km network of autobahns (motorways, freeways). Every 40km to 60km, you'll find elaborate service areas with petrol stations, toilet facilities and restaurants; many are open 24 hours. In between are *Rastplatz* (rest stops), which usually have picnic tables and toilet facilities. Orange emergency call boxes are spaced about 2km apart.

Autobahns are supplemented by an extensive network of *Bundesstrassen* (secondary 'B' roads, highways) and smaller *Landstrassen* (country roads). No tolls are charged on any public roads.

If your car is not equipped with a navigational system, having a good map or road atlas is essential, especially when negotiating the tangle of country roads. Navigating in Germany is not done by the points of the compass. That is to say that you'll find no signs saying 'north' or 'west'. Rather, you'll see signs pointing you in the direction of a city, so you'd best make sure you have a map. Maps cost a few euros and are sold at bookstores, train stations, airports and petrol stations. The best are published by Freytag & Berndt, ADAC, Falk and Euromap.

Driving in the cities can be stressful thanks to congestion and the expense and scarcity of parking. In city centres, parking is usually limited to parking lots and garages charging between €0.50 and €2.50 per hour. Note that some *Parkplatz* (parking lots) and *Parkhaus* (garages) close at night and charge an overnight fee. Many have special parking slots for women that are especially well lit and close to exits.

Many cities have electronic parking-guidance systems directing you to the nearest garage and indicating the number of available spaces. Street parking usually works on the pay-and-display system and tends to be short term (one or two hours) only. For low-cost or free long-term and overnight parking, consider leaving your car outside the centre in a Park & Ride (P+R) lot.

Automobile Associations

Germany's main motoring organisation, the **ADAC** (General German Automobile Club; ☑for information 0800 510 1112, for roadside assistance from mobile 222 2222; www.adac.de), has offices in all major cities and many smaller ones. Its roadside-assistance program is also available to members of its affiliates, including British (AA), American (AAA)

and Canadian (CAA) associations.

Driving Licence

Drivers need a valid driving licence. International Driving Permits (IDP) are not compulsory, but having one may help German police make sense of your home licence (always carry that, too) and may simplify the car- or motorcycle-hire process.

Car Hire

As anywhere, rates for car hire vary considerably, but you should be able to get an economy-size vehicle from about €40 to €60 per day, plus insurance and taxes. Expect surcharges for rentals originating at airports and train stations, additional drivers and one-way hire. Child or infant safety seats may be hired for about €5 per day and should be reserved at the time of booking.

Rental cars with automatic transmission are rare in Germany and will usually need to be ordered well in advance.

To hire your own wheels, you'll need to be at least 25 years old and possess a valid driving licence and a major credit card. Some companies lease to drivers between the ages of 21 and 24 for an additional charge (about €12 to €20 per day). Younger people or those without a credit card are usually out of luck. For insurance reasons, driving into an Eastern European country, such as the Czech

Republic or Poland, is often a no-no.

All the main international companies maintain branches at airports, major train stations and towns. These include the following:

Alamo (☑0800-723 9253; www.alamo.de)

Avis (☑069-500 700 20; www.avis.de)

Europcar (☑040-520 188 000; www.europcar.de)

Hertz (☑01806-333 535; www.hertz.de)

National (☑0800-121 8303; www.nationalcar.de)

Sixt (☑01806-25 25 25; www.sixt.de)

Pre booked and prepaid packages arranged in your home country usually work out much cheaper than on-the-spot rentals. The same is true of fly/drive packages. Deals can be found on the internet and through companies including:

Auto Europe (☑in Germany 0800-560 0333; www.autoeurope.com)

Holiday Autos (☑in the UK 020 3740 9859; www.holidayautos.co.uk)

DriveAway Holidays (☑in Australia 1300 363 500; www.driveaway.com.au).

Peer-to-peer Rentals

Peer-to-peer car rental is still in its infancy in Germany. The main service is Drivy (www.drivy.de). You need to sign up on its website, find a car you'd like to rent, contact the owner and sign the rental agreement at the time you're handed the keys. Renters need to be at least 21 and to have had a driving licence for at least two years. If your licence was not issued in an EU member country, Norway, Iceland or Liechtenstein, you need to have an International Drivers' Permit. Payment is by credit card or PayPal. Rentals include full insurance and roadside assistance. For full details, see the website.

Insurance

German law requires that all registered vehicles, including those brought in from abroad, carry third-party-liability insurance. You could face huge costs by driving uninsured or underinsured. Germans are very fussy about their cars; even nudging someone's bumper when jostling out of a tight parking space may well result in your having to pay for an entirely new one.

Normally, private cars registered and insured in another European country do not require additional insurance, but do check this with your insurance provider before leaving home. Also keep a record of who to contact in case of a breakdown or accident.

When hiring a vehicle, make sure your contract includes adequate liability insurance at the very minimum. Rental agencies almost never include insurance that covers damage to the vehicle itself, called Collision Damage Waiver (CDW) or Loss Damage Waiver (LDW). It's optional, but driving without it is not recommended. Some credit card companies cover CDW/LDW for a certain period if you charge the entire rental to your card; always confirm with your card issuer what it covers in Germany. Note that some local agencies may refuse to accept your credit card coverage as proof of insurance.

Road Rules

Driving is on the right-hand side of the road and standard international signs are in use. If you're unfamiliar with these, pick up a pamphlet at your local motoring organisation or visit the ADAC website (search for 'traffic signs'). Obey the road rules and speed limits carefully.

Speed- and red-light cameras as well as radar traps are common, and notices are sent to the car's registration address, wherever that may be. If you're renting a car, the police will obtain your home address from the rental agency. There's a long list of fineable actions, including some perhaps surprising ones such as using abusive language or gestures, and running out of petrol on the autobahn.

The usual speed limits are 50km/h on main city streets and 100km/h outside built-up areas, unless otherwise marked. Limits drop to 30km/h in residential streets. And yes, it's true: there really are no speed limits on autobahns... in theory. In fact, there are many stretches where slower speeds must be observed (near towns, road construction), so be sure to keep an eye out for those signs or risk getting ticketed. And, obviously, the higher the speed, the higher the fuel consumption and emissions.

Other important driving rules:

o The highest permissible blood alcohol level for drivers is 0.05%, which for most people equates to one glass of wine or two small beers.

o Seat belts are mandatory for all passengers, including those in the back seat, and there's a €30 fine if you get caught not wearing one. If you're in an accident, not wearing a seat belt may invalidate your insurance. Children need a child seat if under four years and a seat cushion if under 12; they may not ride in the front until age 12.

o Motorcyclists must wear a helmet.

o Mobile phones may be used only if they are equipped with a hands-free kit or speakerphone.

o Pedestrians at crossings have absolute right of way over all motor vehicles.

o Always watch out for cyclists when turning right; they have the right of way.

o Right turns at a red light are only legal if there's a green arrow pointing to the right.

o Winter tyres are mandatory for snow- and

ice-covered roads during the winter months (generally November to March, but check the specific regional legislation).

Local Transport

Germany's cities and larger towns have efficient public-transport systems. Bigger cities, such as Berlin and Munich, integrate buses, trams, U-Bahn (underground, subway) trains and S-Bahn (suburban) trains into a single network.

Fares are determined by zones or time travelled, sometimes by both. A multi-ticket strip (Streifenkarte or 4-Fahrtenkarte) or Tageskarte (day pass) generally offers better value than a single-ride ticket. Normally, tickets must be stamped upon boarding in order to be valid. Fines are levied if you're caught without a valid ticket.

Bicycle

Germans love to cycle, be it for errands, commuting, fitness or pleasure. Many cities have dedicated bicycle lanes, which must be used unless obstructed. There's no helmet law, not even for children, although using one is recommended, for obvious reasons. Bicycles must be equipped with a white light at the front, a red one at the back and yellow reflectors on the wheels and pedals.

Bus & Tram

Buses are a ubiquitous form of public transport, and practically all towns have their own comprehensive network. Buses run at regular intervals, with restricted services in the evenings and at weekends. Some cities operate night buses along popular routes to get night owls safely home.

Occasionally, buses are supplemented by Strassenbahnen (trams), which are usually faster because they travel on their own tracks, largely independent of other traffic. In city centres they sometimes run underground. Bus and tram drivers generally sell single tickets and day passes only.

S-Bahn

Metropolitan areas, such as Berlin and Munich, have a system of suburban trains called the S-Bahn. They are faster and cover a wider area than buses or trams but tend to be less frequent. S-Bahn lines are often linked to the national rail network and sometimes connect urban centres. Rail passes are generally valid on these services. Specific S-Bahn lines are abbreviated with 'S' followed by the number (eg S1, S7).

Taxi

Taxis are expensive and, given the excellent public transport systems, not recommended unless you're in a real hurry. (They can be slower than trains or trams.) Cabs are metered and charged at a base rate (flag-fall) plus a per-kilometre fee. These charges are fixed but vary from city to city. Some drivers charge extra for bulky luggage or night-time rides. It's rarely possible to flag down a taxi; more typical is to order one by phone (look up Taxiruf in the phone book) or board at a taxi rank. If you're at a hotel or restaurant, ask staff to call one for you. Taxis also often wait outside theatres or performance venues. Smartphone owners can order a taxi via the Mytaxi app (downloadable for free via iTunes or Google Play) in more than 30 German cities.

Uber (www.uber.com), an app that allows private drivers to connect with potential passengers, is not widely used in Germany after a court ruled in 2015 that the services UberPop and UberBlack violate German transportation laws. Uber reacted by creating UberX, which uses only professionally licensed drivers and is available in Berlin, Düsseldorf and Munich. Trip costs tend to be between 3% and 12% less than regular taxi fares. Exclusive to Berlin at the time of writing is UberTaxi, which hooks passengers up with regular taxis. Normal rates apply.

U-Bahn

Underground (subway) trains are known as U-Bahn in Germany and are the fastest form of travel in big cities. Route maps are posted in all stations, and at many you'll be able to pick up a printed copy from the stationmaster or ticket office. The frequency of trains usually fluctuates with demand, meaning there are more trains during commuter rush hours than in the middle of the day. Tickets bought from vending machines must usually be validated before the start of your journey. Specific U-Bahn lines are abbreviated with 'U' followed by the number (eg U1, U7).

Train

Germany's rail system is operated almost entirely by Deutsche Bahn (DB), with a variety of train types serving just about every corner of the country. The DB website has detailed information (in English and other languages), as well as a ticket-purchasing function with detailed instructions.

There is a growing number of routes operated by private companies – such as Ostdeutsche Eisenbahn in Saxony and Bayerische Oberlandbahn in Bavaria – but integrated into the DB network.

Tickets may be bought using a credit card up to 10 minutes before departure at no surcharge. You will need to present a printout of your ticket, as well as the credit card used to buy it, to the conductor. Smartphone users can register with Deutsche Bahn and download the ticket via the free DB Navigator app.

Tickets are also available from vending machines and agents at the *Reisezentrum* (travel centre) in train stations. The latter charge a service fee but are useful

A Primer on Train Types

Here's the low-down on the alphabet soup of trains operated by Deutsche Bahn:

InterCity Express (ICE) Long-distance, high-speed trains that stop at major cities only and run at one- or two-hour intervals.

InterCity (IC), EuroCity (EC) Long-distance trains that are fast, but slower than the ICE; also run at one- and two-hour intervals and stop in major cities. EC trains run to major cities in neighbouring countries.

InterRegio-Express (IRE) Regional trains connecting cities with few intermediary stops.

City Night Line (CNL) Night trains with sleeper cars and couchettes.

RegionalBahn (RB) Local trains, mostly in rural areas, with frequent stops; the slowest in the system.

Regional Express (RE) Local trains with limited stops that link rural areas with metropolitan centres and the S-Bahn.

S-Bahn Local trains operating within a city and its suburban area.

if you need assistance with planning your itinerary (if necessary, ask for an English-speaking clerk).

Children under 15 travel for free if accompanied by at least one parent or grandparent. The only proviso is that the names of children aged between six and 14 must be registered on your ticket at the time of purchase. Children under six always travel free and without a ticket.

Smaller stations have only a few ticket windows, and the smallest ones are equipped with vending machines only. English instructions are usually provided.

Tickets sold on board incur a surcharge and are not available on regional

trains (RE, RB, IRE) or the S-Bahn. Agents, conductors and machines usually accept debit cards and major credit cards. With few exceptions (station unstaffed, vending machine broken), you will be fined if caught without a ticket.

Most train stations have *Schliessfach* (coin-operated lockers) costing from €1 to €4 per 24-hour period. Larger stations have staffed *Gepäckaufbewahrung* (left-luggage offices), which are a bit more expensive than lockers. If you leave your suitcase overnight, you'll be charged for two full days.

Reservations

● Seat reservations for long-distance travel are

highly recommended, especially if you're travelling any time on Friday, on a Sunday afternoon, during holiday periods or in summer. Choose from window or aisle seats, row or facing seats, or seats with a fixed table.

○ Reservations are €4.50 (free if travelling 1st class) and can be made online and at ticket counters until 10 minutes before departure. You need to claim your seat within 15 minutes of boarding the train.

Classes

German trains have 1st- and 2nd-class cars, both of them modern and comfortable. If you're not too fussy, paying extra for 1st class is usually not worth it, except perhaps on busy travel days, when 2nd-class cars can get very crowded. Seating is either in compartments of up to six people or in open-plan carriages with panoramic windows. On ICE trains you'll also enjoy reclining seats, tables and audio systems in your armrest. Newer-generation ICE trains also have individual laptop outlets, mobile-phone reception in 1st class and, on some routes, wi-fi access.

Trains and stations are nonsmoking. ICE, IC and EC trains are air-conditioned

and have a restaurant or self-service bistro.

Tickets

Standard, nondiscounted train tickets tend to be quite expensive. On specific trains, a limited number of tickets are available at the discounted *Sparpreis* (saver fare). You need to book early or be lucky to snag one of these tickets, though. There's a €5 service charge if tickets are purchased by phone, from a travel agent or in the station ticket office. Other promotions, discounted tickets and special offers become available all the time. Check www.bahn.com for the latest deals.

Deutsche Bahn offers a trio of fabulous permanent rail deals: the *Schönes-Wochenende-Ticket* (Nice Weekend Ticket), the *Quer-durchs-Land-Ticket* (Around Germany Ticket) and the *Länder-Tickets* (Regional Tickets). As with regular tickets, children under 15 travel for free if accompanied by at least one parent or grandparent. Tickets can be purchased online, from vending machines or, for a €2 surcharge, from station ticket offices.

German Rail Pass

If your permanent residence is outside Europe (which for this purpose includes Turkey and Russia), you

qualify for the German Rail Pass (GRP). Tickets are sold online through www.germanrailpasses.com and www.raileurope.com, and by agents in your home country.

○ The **GRP Flexi** allows for three, four, five, seven, 10 or 15 days of travel within one month.

○ The **GRP Consecutive** is available for five, 10 or 15 consecutive days.

○ Passes are valid on all trains within Germany, including ICE trains, and IC buses to Strasbourg, Prague, Krakow, Antwerp, Brussels, London, Zagreb and Copenhagen; and on EuroCity trains to Kufstein, Innsbruck, Bolzano, Trento, Verona, Bologna, Liège and Brussels.

○ Sample fares with GRP Flexi in 2nd class: three-day pass €207, seven-day pass €290. Children between six and 11 pay half fare. Children under six travel free.

○ Those aged 12 to 25 qualify for the **German Rail Youth Pass**, starting at €166 in 2nd class for three days of travel within one month.

○ Two adults travelling together can use the **German Rail Twin Pass**, starting at €311 in 2nd class for three days of travel within one month.

Language

German pronunciation is very similar to that of English, and if you read our pronunciation guides below as if they were English, you'll be understood just fine. Note that in our guides 'ew' is pronounced like 'ee' with rounded lips, and that 'kh' and 'r' are both throaty sounds. Stressed syllables are in italics.

To enhance your trip with a phrasebook, visit **lonelyplanet.com**. Lonely Planet iPhone phrasebooks are available through the Apple App store.

Basics

Hello.
Guten Tag.   goo·ten taak
How are you?
Wie geht es Ihnen? vee geyt es ee·nen
I'm fine, thanks.
Gut , danke .   goot dang·ke
Excuse me./Sorry.
Entschuldigung.   ent·shul·di·gung
Yes./No.
Ja./Nein.   yaa/nain
Please./You're welcome./That's fine.
Bitte.   bi·te
Thank you.
Danke.   dang·ke
Goodbye.
Auf Wiedersehen.   owf vee·der·zey·en
Do you speak English?
Sprechen Sie   shpre·khen zee
Englisch?   eng·lish
I don't understand.
Ich verstehe nicht. ikh fer·shtey·e nikht
How much is this?
Was kostet das?   vas kos·tet das
Can you reduce the price a little?
Können Sie mit dem ker·nen zee mit dem
Preis heruntergehen? prais he·run·ter·gey·en

Accommodation

I'd like to book a room.
Ich möchte bitte ein ikh merkh·te bi·te ain
Zimmer reservieren. tsi·mer re·zer·vee·ren

How much is it per night?
Wie viel kostet es   vee feel kos·tet es
pro Nacht?   praw nakht

Eating & Drinking

I'd like ..., please.
Ich hätte gern..., bitte. ikh he·te gern... bi·te
That was delicious!
Das hat hervorragend das hat her·fawr·
geschmeckt!   rah·gent ge·shmekt
Bring the bill/check, please.
Die Rechnung, bitte. dee rekh·nung bi·te
I don't eat ...
Ich esse kein ...   ikh e·se kain ...

I'm allergic to ...
Ich bin allergisch   ikh bin a·lair·gish
gegen ...   gey·gen ...
  fish   *Fisch*   fish
  poultry *Geflügelfleisch* ge·flew·gel·flaish
  red meat *Rind-und* rint·unt
            Lammfleisch lam·flaish

Emergencies

Help!
Hilfe!   hil·fe
I'm ill.
Ich bin krank.   ikh bin krangk
Call a doctor!
Rufen Sie einen Arzt! roo·fen zee ai·nen artst
Call the police!
Rufen Sie die Polizei! roo·fen zee dee po·li·tsai

Directions

Where's a/the ...?
Wo ist ...?   vaw ist ...
  ATM
  der Geldautomat dair gelt·ow·to·maat
  bank
  eine Bank   ai·ne bangk
  market
  der Markt   dair markt
  museum
  das Museum   das mu·zey·um
  restaurant
  ein Restaurant ain res·to·rahng
  toilet
  die Toilette dee to·a·le·te
  tourist office
  das Fremden- das frem·den·
  verkehrsbüro fer·kairs·bew·raw

Behind the Scenes

Acknowledgements

Climate map data adapted from Peel MC, Finlayson BL & McMahon TA (2007) 'Updated World Map of the Köppen-Geiger Climate Classification', Hydrology and Earth System Sciences, 11, 1633-44.

This Book

This 2nd edition of Lonely Planet's *Best of Germany* guidebook was curated by Benedict Walker, and researched and written by Kerry Christiani, Marc Di Duca, Catherine Le Nevez, Leonid Ragozin and Andrea Schulte-Peevers. The previous edition was curated by Marc Di Duca, and written by Marc, Kerry Christiani, Catherine Le Nevez, Tom Masters, Andrea Schulte-Peevers, Ryan Ver Berkmoes and Benedict Walker. This guidebook was produced by the following:

Destination Editor Niamh O'Brien

Senior Product Editor Genna Patterson

Product Editor Rachel Rawling

Regional Senior Cartographer Mark Griffiths

Book Designer Lauren Egan

Assisting Editors Bruce Evans, Victoria Harrison, Jodie Martire

Assisting Cartographers Hunor Csutoros, Valentina Kremenchutskaya

Cover Researcher Naomi Parker

Thanks to Hannah Cartmel, Shona Gray, Vicky Smith

Send Us Your Feedback

We love to hear from travellers – your comments keep us on our toes and help make our books better. Our well-travelled team reads every word on what you loved or loathed about this book. Although we cannot reply individually to postal submissions, we always guarantee that your feedback goes straight to the appropriate authors, in time for the next edition. Each person who sends us information is thanked in the next edition, the most useful submissions are rewarded with a selection of digital PDF chapters.

Visit lonelyplanet.com/contact to submit your updates and suggestions or to ask for help. Our award-winning website also features inspirational travel stories, news and discussions.

Note: We may edit, reproduce and incorporate your comments in Lonely Planet products such as guidebooks, websites and digital products, so let us know if you don't want your comments reproduced or your name acknowledged. For a copy of our privacy policy visit lonelyplanet.com/privacy.

Index

A

accessible travel 293
accommodation 293-5, *see also individual locations*
language 313
activities 19, 20, 22-4, 279-81
air travel 303, 306
Altstadt (Freiburg) 154-5
Altstadt (Heidelberg) 142-3
Altstadt (Nuremberg) 190-1
archaeological sites, see Cold War sites, Roman sites, WWII sites
architecture 277
area codes 301
art galleries, *see* museums & galleries
arts 275-8
ATMs 299
Augsburg 205

B

Bacharach 232-3
Baden-Baden 156-7, 165-8, **166**
food 167
information 167
sights 166-7
travel to/from 168
travel within 167
bathrooms 302
beer 100-1, 123, 222, 252, 288-90
beer halls & gardens 123
Berlin 4, 36-83, **36**, **60-1**, **64-5**, **70**, **74**, **78**, **80**
accommodation 37, 83
activities 71
drinking & nightlife 78-81
entertainment 81
food 74-8

information 81
itineraries 36, 60-1, **60-1**
LGBTIQ+ travellers 68
shopping 73-4
sights 62-71
tours 71-3
travel to/from 37, 81-2
travel within 82
Berliner Dom 49
Berlin Film Festival 22
Berlin Wall 42-5, 272-3, **44-5**
Bernkastel-Kues 253-4
bicycle travel, *see* cycling
Bingen 231-2
Black Forest 10, 152-71, **153**
accommodation 153
itineraries 152
travel to/from 153
walks 158-61
BMW Welt 113
boat travel 303, 306-7
books 25, 275-6
Boppard 234-7
Brandenburger Tor 40-1
Braubach 238
budget 17
Burg Eltz 258
bus travel
local 307, 310
long-distance 303-4, 307

C

car travel 304, 307-10
driving licences 308
hire 308-9
insurance 309
organisations 308
road rules 309-10
castles & palaces 18
Belvedere auf dem Pfingstberg 93
Burg Eltz 258
Burg Landshut 253

Burg Maus 233
Grevenburg 251-2
Hohes Schloss 136
Kaiserburg 191
Marmorpalais 92
Pfalzgrafstein 232
Reichsburg 250
Residenz 102-5
Residenzschloss 178-9
Schloss Cecilienhof 92
Schloss Charlottenburg 52-5
Schloss Heidelberg 144-5
Schloss Hohenschwangau 134
Schloss Neuschwanstein 132-5
Schloss Nymphenburg 112
Schloss Sanssouci 88-91
Schloss Stolzenfels 238
Zwinger 180
cathedrals, *see* churches & cathedrals
cell phones 16, 301
Charlemagne 266
Checkpoint Charlie 44, 62
children, travel with 32-3
Cologne 220
Munich 115
Nuremburg 193
Christmas markets 24
Christkindlesmarkt 195
churches & cathedrals 19
Asamkirche 106
Berliner Dom 49
Frauenkirche (Munich) 107
Frauenkirche (Dresden) 176
Freiburger Münster 154
Heiliggeistkirche 142
Jesuitenkirche 146
Kaiser-Wilhelm-Gedächtniskirche 71
Kloster Lichtenthal 167
Kölner Dom 214-15
Liebfrauenbasilika 257
Michaelskirche 110
Peterskirche 232

000 Map pages

Symbols & Map Key

Look for these symbols to quickly identify listings:

- ◉ Sights
- ✦ Activities
- ⊜ Courses
- ☞ Tours
- ✦ Festivals & Events
- ✪ Eating
- ☻ Drinking
- ✿ Entertainment
- 🔒 Shopping
- ❶ Information & Transport

These symbols and abbreviations give vital information for each listing:

- 🌿 Sustainable or green recommendation
- **FREE** No payment required

- ☎ Telephone number
- ⊕ Opening hours
- P Parking
- ⊖ Nonsmoking
- ❄ Air-conditioning
- @ Internet access
- 📶 Wi-fi access
- 🏊 Swimming pool
- 🚌 Bus
- ⛴ Ferry
- 🚊 Tram
- 🚆 Train
- 📖 English-language menu
- 🥗 Vegetarian selection
- 👪 Family-friendly

Find your best experiences with these Great For... icons.

 Art & Culture

 Beaches

 Budget

Cafe/Coffee

🚲 Cycling

 Detour

 Drinking

 Entertainment

 Events

Family Travel

 Food & Drink

 History

Local Life

 Nature & Wildlife

 Photo Op

 Scenery

 Shopping

 Short Trip

Sport

 Walking

❄ Winter Travel

Sights

- Beach
- Bird Sanctuary
- Buddhist
- Castle/Palace
- Christian
- Confucian
- Hindu
- Islamic
- Jain
- Jewish
- Monument
- Museum/Gallery/ Historic Building
- Ruin
- Shinto
- Sikh
- Taoist
- Winery/Vineyard
- Zoo/Wildlife Sanctuary
- Other Sight

Points of Interest

- Bodysurfing
- Camping
- Cafe
- Canoeing/Kayaking
- Course/Tour
- Diving
- Drinking & Nightlife
- Eating
- Entertainment
- Sento Hot Baths/ Onsen
- Shopping
- Skiing
- Sleeping
- Snorkelling
- Surfing
- Swimming/Pool
- Walking
- Windsurfing
- Other Activity

Information

- Bank
- Embassy/Consulate
- Hospital/Medical
- Internet
- Police
- Post Office
- Telephone
- Toilet
- Tourist Information
- Other Information

Geographic

- Beach
- Gate
- Hut/Shelter
- Lighthouse
- Lookout
- Mountain/Volcano
- Oasis
- Park
- Pass
- Picnic Area
- Waterfall

Transport

- Airport
- BART station
- Border crossing
- Boston T station
- Bus
- Cable car/Funicular
- Cycling
- Ferry
- Metro/MRT station
- Monorail
- Parking
- Petrol station
- Subway/S-Bahn/ Skytrain station
- Taxi
- Train station/Railway
- Tram
- Tube Station
- Underground/ U-Bahn station
- Other Transport

Catherine Le Nevez

Catherine's wanderlust kicked in when she roadtripped across Europe from her Parisian base aged four, and she's been hitting the road at every opportunity since, travelling to around 60 countries and completing her Doctorate of Creative Arts in Writing, Masters in Professional Writing, and postgrad qualifications in Editing and Publishing along the way. Over the past dozen-plus years she's written scores of Lonely Planet guides and articles covering Paris, France, Europe and far beyond.

Leonid Ragozin

Leonid Ragozin studied beach dynamics at the Moscow State University, but for want of decent beaches in Russia, he switched to journalism and spent 12 years voyaging through different parts of the BBC, with a break for a four-year stint as a foreign correspondent for the Russian Newsweek.

Leonid is currently a freelance journalist focusing largely on the conflict between Russia and Ukraine (both his Lonely Planet destinations), which prompted him to leave Moscow and find a new home in Rīga. He tweets @leonidragozin.

Andrea Schulte-Peevers

Born and raised in Germany and educated in London and at UCLA, Andrea has travelled the distance to the moon and back in her visits to some 75 countries. She has earned her living as a professional travel writer for more than two decades and authored or contributed to nearly 100 Lonely Planet titles as well as to newspapers, magazines and websites around the world. She also works as a travel consultant, translator and editor. Andrea's destination expertise is especially strong when it comes to Germany, Dubai and the UAE, Crete and the Caribbean Islands. She makes her home in Berlin and tweets @ASchultePeevers.

Our Story

A beat-up old car, a few dollars in the pocket and a sense of adventure. In 1972 that's all Tony and Maureen Wheeler needed for the trip of a lifetime – across Europe and Asia overland to Australia. It took several months, and at the end – broke but inspired – they sat at their kitchen table writing and stapling together their first travel guide, *Across Asia on the Cheap*. Within a week they'd sold 1500 copies. Lonely Planet was born.

Today, Lonely Planet has offices in Franklin, London, Melbourne, Oakland, Dublin, Beijing, and Delhi, with more than 600 staff and writers. We share Tony's belief that 'a great guidebook should do three things: inform, educate and amuse'.

Our Writers

Benedict Walker

A beach baby from Newcastle, Australia, Benedict turned 40 in 2017 and decided to start a new life in Leipzig, Germany. Writing for Lonely Planet was a childhood dream come true, and Benedict grew up to cover big chunks of Australia, Canada, Germany, Japan, USA, Switzerland, Sweden and Japan. Benedict is on instagram @wordsandjourneys.

Kerry Christiani

Kerry is an award-winning travel writer, photographer and Lonely Planet author, specialising in Central and Southern Europe. Based in Wales, she has authored/co-authored more than a dozen Lonely Planet titles. An adventure addict, she loves mountains, cold places and true wilderness. She features her latest work at https://its-a-small-world.com and tweets @kerrychristiani. Kerry also researched the Plan Your Trip, In Focus and Survival Guide sections.

Marc Di Duca

A travel author for more than a decade, Marc has worked for Lonely Planet in Siberia, Slovakia, Bavaria, England, Ukraine, Austria, Poland, Croatia, Portugal, Madeira and on the Trans-Siberian Railway, as well as writing and updating tens of other guides for other publishers. When not on the road, Marc lives near Mariánské Lázně in the Czech Republic with his wife and two sons.

More Writers

STAY IN TOUCH LONELYPLANET.COM/CONTACT

AUSTRALIA The Malt Store, Level 3, 551 Swanston St, Carlton, Victoria 3053 ☏03 8379 8000, fax 03 8379 8111

IRELAND Digital Depot, Roe Lane (off Thomas St), Digital Hub, Dublin 8, D08 TCV4

USA 124 Linden Street, Oakland, CA 94607 ☏510 250 6400, toll free 800 275 8555, fax 510 893 8572

UK 240 Blackfriars Road, London SE1 8NW ☏020 3771 5100, fax 020 3771 5101

 twitter.com/ lonelyplanet

 facebook.com/ lonelyplanet

 instagram.com/ lonelyplanet

 youtube.com/ lonelyplanet

 lonelyplanet.com/ newsletter